SANSKRIT MANUAL

SANSKRIT MANUAL

A Quick-reference Guide to the Phonology and Grammar of Classical Sanskrit

Compiled by
RODERICK S. BUCKNELL

MOTILAL BANARSIDASS
SINCE 1903 IN INDOLOGY

MOTILAL BANARSIDASS PUBLISHERS
PRIVATE LIMITED • DELHI

6th Reprint : Delhi, 2016
First Edition : Delhi, 1994

ISBN : 978-81-208-1188-1 (Cloth)
ISBN : 978-81-208-1189-8 (Paper)

MOTILAL BANARSIDASS
41 U.A., Bungalow Road, Jawahar Nagar, Delhi 110 007
8 Mahalaxmi Chamber, 22 Bhulabhai Desai Road, Mumbai 400 026
203 Royapettah High Road, Mylapore, Chennai 600 004
236, 9th Main III Block, Jayanagar, Bangalore 560 011
8 Camac Street, Kolkata 700 017
Ashok Rajpath, Patna 800 004
Chowk, Varanasi 221 001

Publisher's Cataloging-in-Publication:
Sanskrit Mannual
Compiled by Roderick S. Bucknell
ISBN : 978-81-208-1188-1 (Cloth)
ISBN : 978-81-208-1189-8 (Paper)
I. Sanskrit Grammar II. Phonology
III. Linguistics IV. Bucknell, Roderick S.

Printed in India
by RP Jain at NAB Printing Unit,
A-44, Naraina Industrial Area, Phase I, New Delhi–110028
and published by JP Jain for Motilal Banarsidass Publishers (P) Ltd,
41 U.A. Bungalow Road, Jawahar Nagar, Delhi-110007

CONTENTS

List of tables vii

Preface ix

PART I: PHONOLOGY

1. The speech-sounds 1
2. External sandhi 1
3. Internal sandhi 5
4. Vocalic gradation 7
5. Alphabetic sequence 9

PART II: GRAMMAR

A. Nominals 11

1. Nouns 11
2. Adjectives 14
3. Numerals 29
4. Demonstratives 32
5. Pronouns 32

B. Verbs 34

1. Present and Imperfect 41
2. Perfect 47
3. Aorist 50
4. Precative 53
5. Periphrastic future 54
6. Simple future and conditional 54
7. Passive voice 55
8. Secondary conjugations 56
9. Participles 59
10. Non-finite verb-forms 63
11. Verbal roots and the ten verb classes 64
12. Using the verb tables 65
13. Using the indexes 68

Tables 1 to 30 71

Abbreviations 253

Bibliography 255

LIST OF TABLES

1. The speech-sounds classified on articulatory criteria .. 73
2. Rules of external sandhi 74
3. Ambiguous sandhis 76
4. Rules of internal sandhi for retroflexion 77
5. Vocalic gradation series 79
6. Declensional paradigms for nouns/adjectives
   (i) Masculine 80
   (ii) Neuter 84
   (iii) Feminine 87
7. Irregular declensions of nouns/adjectives
   (i) Masculine 90
   (ii) Neuter 95
   (iii) Feminine 96
8. Adjective types in the three genders 99
9. Comparison of adjectives by method 1 100
10. Comparison of adjectives by method 2 101
11. The numerals 102
12. Declension of the numerals 1 to 10 106
13. Declension of the demonstratives 108
14. Declension of the pronouns 110
15. Conjugation of the verb nayati 114
16. Conjugational paradigms for the present and imperfect 116
17. Irregular conjugations in the present and imperfect . 126
18. Conjugational paradigms for the reduplicating perfect 138
19. Irregular conjugations in the reduplicating perfect .. 141
20. Key to conjugation types in the reduplicating perfect (active) 142
21. Conjugational paradigm for the periphrastic perfect . 144
22. Conjugational paradigms for the aorist 145
23. Irregular conjugations in the aorist 147
24. Conjugational paradigm for the precative 148
25. Conjugational paradigm for the periphrastic future . 148
26. Guide to Table 27 and the paradigms 149
27. Principal parts of verbs 152
28. Index to verb stems 207
29. Index to verb endings 232
30. Index to noun/adjective endings 242

PREFACE

This book is designed to serve as a convenient quick-reference guide to the grammar of Classical Sanskrit, for the use of university students and others. It is not intended to be a complete grammar of the language. Rather, its purpose is to present, mainly in the form of easily read tables, essential reference information such as the rules of sandhi, the declensional and conjugational paradigms, and the principal parts of major verbs.

About two-thirds of the book consists of tables. The remainder is text, with advice on how to use the tables and explanations of the grammatical principles underlying them. Most of the grammatical information has been abstracted, with substantial modification of the presentation, from existing Sanskrit grammars, especially those of Whitney, MacDonell, and Kale. An exception is the set of three indexes: 'Index to verb stems', 'Index to verb endings', and 'Index to noun endings' (Tables 28-30). These probably have no counterpart elsewhere.

The manual originated as a set of photocopied notes which was supplied, as a supplement to existing textbooks, to first and second year students of Sanskrit in the Department of Studies in Religion at The University of Queensland. Over a period of seven years those notes were progressively modified and expanded until they became the present fairly comprehensive reference work. While still primarily intended for beginning and intermediate students, the manual should also be found useful by scholars working with Sanskrit at any level.

Much of the difficulty encountered by students of Sanskrit is due, it can be argued, to unsatisfactory presentation. This derives largely from a tendency, on the part of those who compile Sanskrit textbooks, to accept uncritically the traditional grammarians' concepts and modes of description. In this manual that tendency has been resisted. Certain concepts and modes of description that are very firmly established in the tradition of Sanskrit grammar are set aside in favour of ones that are self-evidently simpler and more appropriate. To this extent the present work is innovative — and no doubt also controversial. The nature of the innovative features will become apparent in the section on 'Principles of presentation'.

Scope

The range of grammatical categories covered in the manual is maximally wide. I recognize that some of the categories dealt with (e.g. the precative, and the causative aorist) are rare, and that the information given on them is of correspondingly limited use. I maintain, however, that their inclusion serves an important function: gaining a panoramic view of the total grammatical landscape makes one better able to appreciate those sections of it that one is already familiar with. For example, Table 15, which purports to set out all the conjugational forms of a representative verb (nayati), no doubt contains a number of forms that are unlikely to be encountered in practice; yet their inclusion serves the important function of completing the conjugational picture. Daunting as that total picture may be, it enables the student to see how known conjugational patterns fit within the overall framework.

As regards the scope of the two tables dealing with specific verbs, 'Principal parts of verbs' (Table 27) and 'Index to verb stems' (Table 28), the choice of verbs to be included was determined ultimately by the content of Lanman's *Reader*. The two tables cover every verb (apart from exclusively Vedic ones) contained in Lanman, to a total of 432. This ensures that the manual meshes in well with students' continuing studies, since Lanman seems likely to remain a major text in university Sanskrit courses for many years to come.

Principles of presentation

The main medium of presentation is carefully designed tables. These, by setting out the information in visual, picture-like form, facilitate comprehension and eventual mastery of the patterns, as well as being the most convenient format for reference purposes. For example, the rules of external sandhi, which most grammars and primers present in the form of numerous verbal statements, are here presented as a single table. This reveals at a glance not only the individual rules but also the broad phonetic principles underlying them. (Probably the only previous textbook to make use of such a table is Coulson's.)

Roman transcription is used rather than devanāgari. Certain characteristics of the devanāgari script, particularly the frequent departures from a simple left-to-right sequence of consonant and vowel letters, make it rather unsuitable as a medium for presenting grammatical information (by obscuring regularities and patterns of correspondence). The roman transcription, besides being free of these defects, has certain positive pedagogical advantages. For example, its use of subscribed dots, though typographically troublesome, draws attention to the internal sandhi rules relating to retroflexion — as in instances like viṣeṇa.

The grammatical terminology is in English rather than Sanskrit. For example, the terms 'active' and 'middle' are used instead of the traditional 'parasmaipada' and 'ātmanepada'. The English terminology, while possibly lacking the precision and specificity of the Sanskrit, has certain overriding advantages. Apart from being self-evidently easier for the English-speaking student to understand and work with, it is in many instances considerably more informative; for example, 'dative case' conveys information that 'caturthī vibhakti' does not.

In the case of the ten verb classes, the traditional names are abandoned entirely, as being mnemonically not very helpful. For example, for the ninth class the term 'kryādigaṇa', derived from the type representative verb krīṇāti, is replaced by '-nāti verbs' or 'the -nāti class', derived from the characteristic conjugational ending.

But the revision goes further than a mere change of the nomenclature. The traditional tenfold classification itself is virtually abandoned. That classification is based principally on the manner in which the verb stem is derived from the root, a criterion that is both linguistically and pedagogically unsatisfactory. Sanskrit textbooks implicitly recognize this. Invariably they begin their account of the verb classes by introducing classes 1, 4, 6, and 10 together as constituting a single major category, and providing a single paradigm representing them all. This practice amounts to an acknowledgement that the principal classificatory criterion ought to be the pattern of conjugational endings attached to the stem. The manner in which the stem itself is derived from the root is rightly treated as a secondary consideration. The classification adopted here recognizes this: the verbs traditionally classed as 1, 4, 6, and 10 are treated as a single class, termed 'the -ati class' after their characteristic ending (i.e. the ending in the most important conjugational form, the third person singular of the present indicative active).

On the other hand, the traditional class 2 is here recognized (as is often implicitly done in existing grammars) as comprising four distinct classes, each with its characteristic set of endings and pattern of vowel gradation. Thus each verb in this revised classification is identified with, and in fact defined by, a particular conjugational paradigm. The different ways in which the verbal stem is derived from the root are treated as largely devoid of classificatory significance. Indeed, roots receive little attention in the treatment of verbs presented here. This is a major departure from standard practice. The justification for it becomes evident when one examines critically the implications of following the traditional approach.

Let us consider how the traditional verb class 1 (bhvādigaṇa) is introduced to students in most Sanskrit primers. The rules for obtaining the verb stem from the root are described more or less as follows: (1) strengthen the vowel to guṇa grade (unless it is long and followed by a consonant, or short and followed by two consonants); (2) add the linking vowel -a-; (3) apply the relevant internal sandhi rule. For example, for the root ji the three steps yield ji → je- → je-a- → jaya-, from which one can then produce the actually occurring forms jayati etc. In addition to knowing this set of rules, one has to know that ji belongs to class 1, and that it is predominantly conjugated in the active (rather than the middle) voice. Dictionaries and the vocabulary lists in primers supply that information with entries of the form √ji 1 P (where P stands for 'parasmaipada' (active)). They also usually supply the principal form jayati, no doubt in recognition of the hazards involved in applying the rules and of the existence of exceptions. Thus the typical vocabulary entry appears as √ji 1 P (jayati) 'conquer'.

But clearly the information regarding the root (ji), the verb class (1), and the voice (P) tells the student little of value, for the single item jayati already says it all. Thus at this stage in the student's career the concept of roots, together with the rules which that concept makes necessary, is an unwarranted complication. Introducing beginning students to the concept of roots does nothing to facilitate presentation of the linguistic facts, or ease the task of mastering the present and imperfect tenses. It has the very opposite effect. Students' interests would be better served if verbs were cited in their most commonly occurring form; for example, the above verb might as well be introduced simply as jayati 'conquer'.

Such considerations underlie the treatment of verbs presented here. The discussion proceeds not from hypothetical roots but from actually occurring verb forms, conventionally cited in the third singular of the present indicative active (or middle), thus: jayati 'conquer', labhate 'obtain', jānāti 'know', sunoti 'press'.

It is not only in the early stages of a student's career that the concept of roots causes unnecessary difficulty. Consider, for example, traditionally formulated accounts of the aorist. They pay much attention to how the aorist verb stem may be derived from the root. The 'rules' whereby one can identify which roots follow which mode of derivation are so involved and so unreliable as to be of little real use. The practical reality is that, except in a few very distinctive root types, one cannot infer the form of the aorist with any confidence; one simply has to look it up. Any realistic presentation of the aorist must therefore proceed not from roots but from actual aorist forms, in particular from the form cited in dictionaries, the third singular active or middle.

This reality is recognized in this manual. In the section on the aorist nothing is said about how one may, for example, get from the root ji to the aorist ajaiṣīt. It is taken for granted that the form ajaiṣīt can be known only by referring to a dictionary or a list of verb forms (such as Table 27). Accordingly the discussion focuses on how to conjugate once this basic form is known. The identifiable aorist paradigms (or classes of aorist) are set out and described, and information is given on how one may identify which class any particular verb belongs to. Here again the terminology is simple and mnemonic; e.g. ajaiṣīt belongs to the -sīt class of aorists.

The traditional practice of presenting verbs in terms of derivation from roots has another major disadvantage: it depends on, and thus reinforces, the very unsatisfactory traditional account of vowel gradation. According to that account, the root (e.g. ji) is in the fundamental grade, and it yields the present stem (ji → je-, jay-) by being raised or strengthened to the guṇa grade. Now, according to the findings of historical linguistics, the mechanism of vowel gradation is actually the reverse of that just described: in reality the guṇa grade (as in the present indicative jayati, infinitive jetum, etc.) is the source, while the fundamental grade (as in the perfect passive participle jita- and the root ji) is derived from it by reduction or weakening (cf. Mayrhofer, p. 37). The traditional account has it back to front.

The fact that the traditional account reverses the mechanism of vowel gradation as between fundamental and guṇa grades does not matter greatly in the case of ji and many other roots; however, there are also many roots for which it creates problems. Consider, for example, the root vad 'speak'. According to the traditional account, the root vad yields the present indicative stem vad- by the usual process of strengthening to guṇa grade; and the fact that this strengthening does not result in any vowel change is covered by stating that the guṇa-grade counterpart of the vowel 'a' is also 'a'. This artificial device does not, however, resolve a second problem: the perfect passive participle of vad is udita-, an exception to the general rule that the stem of the perfect passive participle is identical with the root. This is dealt with by further stating that roots in va, ya, and ra usually replace these by u, i, and ṛ respectively (the process termed samprasāraṇa) in the perfect passive participle. Such ad hoc adjustments seem unavoidable, given the basic premises. For example, one could not discard vad as the root and set up a root ud instead, because strengthening that to guṇa grade would yield od- rather than vad-.

The problems illustrated in vad commonly occur wherever a root has va, ya, or ra; e.g., vas → vasati, uṣita-; yaj → yajati, iṣṭa-; grah → gṛhṇāti (exception!), gṛhīta-. As noted, the traditional attempts at solving them are ad hoc and generally unsatisfactory. Clearly the real solution is to recognize that the mechanism of gradation between the guṇa and fundamental grades actually proceeds in the reverse direction: vad-, as in the present indicative stem, is guṇa grade; and its corresponding fundamental-grade form (obtained from the guṇa by weakening) is ud-, as in the perfect passive participle udita-. Once this is allowed, the problems vanish; ad hoc qualifications become unnecessary.

This solution is adopted here. It is recognized that the guṇa grade is basic to the gradation series, yielding the fundamental grade by weakening (and the vṛddhi grade by strengthening). It is also recognized that the phenomenon of gradation is much more widely applicable than the traditional account allows; for example, where the traditional account has u → o/av → au/āv, the present account has u ← o/av → au/āv *and* u ← va → vā. In addition, the artificial a → a → ā of the traditional account is replaced by the natural and obvious ø ← a → ā (as in ca*khn*uḥ, *khan*ati, *khān*ayati).

These revisions of the presentation of vowel gradation go hand in hand with the de-emphasizing of the notion of derivation from roots. Once the primacy of 'fundamental grade' is rejected, the primacy of the verbal root goes out with it. But in spite of this, and in spite of all the shortcomings in the concept of roots noted earlier, roots clearly cannot be ignored entirely in a work of this nature. Roots are invariably emphasized in existing grammars and primers, and are widely applied in the design of dictionaries etc.; and they do after all have a certain mnemonic usefulness. Familiarity with the concept of roots is therefore indispensable, and can be taken for granted in a student of Sanskrit. In recognition of this, roots *are* discussed in this manual. However, they are introduced at a relatively late stage and are presented for what they are: handy labels artificially derived from the actually occurring verb (and noun) forms. Also, in keeping with common practice the 432 verbs in Table 27, 'Principal parts of verbs', are identified by their roots (used as headings) and arranged alphabetically according to those roots. For similar reasons the ten verb classes are also discussed briefly in the text and included in Table 27. Thus this manual strikes a balance between the demonstrable desirability of innovation and the practical indispensability of certain established traditions.

Acknowledgment and Request

I wish to record my indebtedness and gratitude to David Dargie for his care, patience, and ingenuity in preparing the three indexes. I would like also to ask readers to offer suggestions on how this manual might be improved, and to point out any errors, which can so easily occur in a work of this nature.

RODERICK S. BUCKNELL

The University of Queensland
Brisbane, Australia
December 1992

PART I. PHONOLOGY

1. The Speech-sounds

The sounds of Sanskrit, when classified on articulatory criteria, fall naturally into the two-dimensional array shown in Table 1 (page 73). On the vertical axis of this array are shown the six *places* of articulation; on the horizontal are shown the *manners* of articulation, specified in terms of a number of overlapping features. It will be found that familiarity with these features, and with the total array, facilitates understanding of the rules of sandhi and other phenomena to be described below.

The collocation of the speech-sounds in words is subject to numerous constraints. For present purposes it suffices to list the following most noteworthy constraints applying in any individual word cited in isolation:

A word may begin with any consonant or vowel other than ḥ ṃ ṅ ñ ṇ ṝ ḷ. A word may end with one of the eight consonants k ṭ t p ṅ n m ḥ, or with any vowel other than ṝ and ḷ. At the beginning of a word, and within it, complex clusters of consonants are possible, e.g. *kramyante*, *strībhyā*m, d*ṛṣṭvā*, la*kṣmyā*; however, at the end of a word consonant clusters almost never occur.

2. External Sandhi

When individual words are put together in sentences, the boundaries between them are often blurred by phonetic interactions between the abutting sounds: the final sound of each word modifies, and/or is modified by, the initial sound of the word following it. This phenomenon is called 'external sandhi' — 'external' because it occurs between each word and the next rather than within individual words.

Because of external sandhi the process of translating into or out of Sanskrit entails a step in which the appropriate phonetic changes are allowed for. For example, the translating of the sentence 'There was a king' into Sanskrit proceeds through the following two steps. First one puts together the required component words: āsīt, 'was' or 'there was'; and rājā, 'a king'. Then one applies to these isolated forms of the words the appropriate sandhi rule: a word-final -t, when followed by a word-initial r-, changes to -d, while the r- remains unchanged. This yields the actual sentence āsīd rājā. (Though d is not permitted as a word-final consonant in the isolated forms of words, it *is* possible in their sandhi-derived forms.) The steps are, therefore, as follows:

1) 'There was a king.'
2) āsīt rājā (isolated forms)
3) āsīd rājā (sandhi forms)

When translating *out of* Sanskrit the above procedure is reversed. First the appropriate rule is applied in reverse to obtain the isolated forms of the words: āsīd rājā is identified as derived by sandhi from āsīt rājā. Then the individual words āsīt and rājā are translated, if necessary using a dictionary and the appropriate tables of noun and verb paradigms.

(a) *Rules of external sandhi*

The complete set of rules for external sandhi is summarized in Table 2. Section (i) of that table covers those cases where the first of the two words involved in sandhi ends in a consonant; Section (ii) covers those cases where the first word ends in a vowel.

Along the upper margin of Section (i) in Table 2 are shown the eight possible word-final consonants (-k, -ṭ, etc.). One of the eight, -ḥ, is divided into four types to cover four slightly different situations that prevail according as the vowel preceding the ḥ is (1) a, (2) ā, (3) any short vowel other than a, or (4) any long vowel other than ā. Types (3) and (4) are represented in the table by -iḥ and -īḥ respectively.

Along the right-hand margin of Section (i) are shown the consonants and vowels which may serve as initial for the second of the two words involved in sandhi. Consonant-initials having identical sandhi behaviour are grouped into sets (e.g. k-, kh-,...s-); and all of the vowel initials other than a- are grouped into a single set, represented by V-.

To apply sandhi rules when translating *into* Sanskrit, one moves from the upper and right-hand margins *into* the rectangle. The form assumed by a given word-final consonant when followed by a given word-initial is indicated by the letter shown at the intersection of the corresponding axes within the rectangle. Suppose, for example, that one is translating into Sanskrit, and has put together the component words āsīt and rājā. One then goes to -t on the upper margin and moves down the -t column to the level of r- on the right margin. At the intersection is -d, indicating that -t must change to -d, whence āsīd rājā.

Some letters within the rectangle are labelled with an asterisk, and the corresponding initial at the right margin is followed by a notation in square brackets. This indicates that the sandhi involves a change in the initial as well as in the final. For example, in the case of -t ś- the table shows -c*, while the notation to the right of ś- reads *ś- → ch-. This signifies that the -t changes to -c while the ś- changes to ch-. Hence, the total change is from -t ś- to -c ch-. As an example, consider the translating into Sanskrit of the sentence 'There was an enemy'. The steps are:

1) 'There was an enemy.'
2) āsīt śatruḥ (isolated forms)
3) āsīc chatruḥ (sandhi forms)

When translating *out of* Sanskrit, one first seeks the given form of the word-final within the rectangle, on a level with the given word-initial on the right margin; then one moves *out* to the isolated word-final on the upper margin. For example,

1) āsīc chatruḥ
2) āsīt śatruḥ (or āsīt chatruḥ, but a word chatruḥ is not to be found)
3) 'There was an enemy.'

Section (ii) of Table 2 summarizes the rules of external sandhi in cases where the first of the two words involved ends in a vowel. The possible word-final vowels are shown along the upper margin, and as in Section (i) all possible word-initials are shown along the right margin. The groupings are different, however, and all the consonants are represented by C-. Because sandhi between two vowels often entails a change in the second (i.e. word-initial) vowel, such changes are shown within the rectangle (rather than at the right under * as in Section (i)). For example, when translating *into* Sanskrit, -ā u- becomes -o-:

1) 'The maiden said.'
2) kanyā uvāca
3) kanyovāca

and when translating *out of* Sanskrit, -e '- is resolved into -e a-:

1) svarge 'pi
2) svarge api
3) 'even in heaven.'

(b) *Ambiguities in resolving sandhi*

As seen above in the case of āsīc chatruḥ, the resolving of sandhi when translating out of Sanskrit may introduce ambiguity: āsīc chatruḥ could be from either āsīt śatruḥ or āsīt chatruḥ. This ambiguity can be resolved only by recognizing the familiar word śatruḥ and, if necessary, confirming that there does not exist a word chatruḥ.

All such cases of ambiguous sandhi are summarized in Table 3. For example, the case of āsīc chatruḥ is covered by the entry -c ch- with its two possible resolutions, -t ch- and -t ś-.

(c) *Exceptions to the rules of external sandhi*

In general the rules embodied in Table 2 apply indiscriminately to all words within a sentence regardless of grammatical categories and functions. There are, however, the following exceptions.

(i) The ending of a word in the vocative case, or of an associated expletive, usually does not enter into sandhi; for example:

rāma ihi	'O Rama, go!'	(*not* rāmehi)
he indra	'Hey, Indra!'	(*not* ha indra)

(ii) The dual-number endings -ī, ū, and -e, whether of nouns/adjectives or of verbs, do not enter into sandhi; nor does the -ī of the masculine nominative plural demonstrative amī 'those'; for example:

munī avadatām	'The two sages said.'
labhete aśvān	'They two obtain horses.'

(iii) The word saḥ 'he' departs from the rules for -aḥ in that it becomes sa before all consonants; e.g. sa gacchati, sa tiṣṭhati. Otherwise it is regular; e.g. sa uvāca, so 'vadat (from saḥ avadat), gacchati saḥ. Eṣaḥ 'this', a derivative of saḥ, behaves similarly.

(iv) The ending -aḥ of the words punaḥ 'again', prātaḥ 'early', and antaḥ 'between' behaves in a manner analogous to -iḥ. It thus diverges from the rules for -aḥ when it is followed by any voiced sound; e.g. punar gacchati, punar uvāca. Otherwise it is regular; e.g. punaḥ paśyati, punaś calati, punar rakṣati. The -āḥ of the word dvāḥ 'door' (nominative singular) behaves similarly.

(d) *Regularities in the sandhi rules*

Table 2 will be found easier to understand — and, eventually, to memorize — if considered in conjunction with Table 1. For example, the obvious division of Section (i) of Table 2 into upper and lower parts (marked by the horizontal broken line) corresponds to the division of the speech sounds into voiceless and voiced; all word-initials above the broken line are voiceless, all those below it are voiced. Another example is provided by the seven sandhi derivatives of word-final -aḥ. One observes a simple regularity in the sandhi-derived fricative endings: palatal -aś before palatal c-, ch-; etc. Also the fundamental importance of the division of word-initials into voiceless and voiced is again apparent.

3. INTERNAL SANDHI

Whereas external sandhi operates *between adjacent words*, internal sandhi operates *within individual words*. External sandhi causes the endings and/or beginnings of words to assume different phonetic forms in different phonetic environments and has to be taken into account by the writer or reader every time a sentence is composed or analysed; in contrast to this, internal sandhi serves to explain certain facts about the internal phonetic structure of words as they are found in the dictionary or as they are built up from their stems and inflexional endings using the tables of noun and verb paradigms.

Many of the rules of internal sandhi are identical with those of external sandhi; for example, the plural instrumental of the noun marut 'wind-god' is marudbhiḥ, with -t changed to -d before the voiced consonant bh of the inflexional ending -bhiḥ. (See Table 2, Section (i) -t bh-, and Table 6, paradigm [6] (page 81).) Other rules of internal sandhi differ from those of external sandhi. For example, the genitive plural of marut is marutām, with the voiceless -t retained despite the following vowel. (Contrast Table 2, Section (i), -t V-.) Only the two most important rules of internal sandhi are stated here, namely those concerning the retroflexion of s and n; other rules will be noted in later sections as they become relevant.

Rule (i)
Within a word, s changes to ṣ if it is *followed* by any sound other than r, ṛ, or ṝ, and is *preceded* — either immediately or with *intervening* ḥ or ṃ — by k or r or any vowel other than a or ā.

This involved rule becomes much easier to comprehend when considered in terms of Table 1, as is done in Table 4, Section (i). The following examples illustrate the application (or non-application) of Rule (i) in various situations: saḥ, eṣaḥ, kathāsu, deveṣu, bhikṣuṣu, haviṣī, havīṃṣi, haviḥṣu, bhaviṣyati, puṣpam, tisraḥ, tisṛbhiḥ. The retroflexion is transmitted to an immediately following t, th, or n; e.g. dṛṣṭvā, tiṣṭhati, viṣṇuḥ. Exceptions to Rule (i) are found in certain individual words, such as pustakam and kusumam, and in many desideratives beginning with s, e.g. siseviṣate.

Rule (ii)
Within a word, n changes to ṇ if it is immediately *followed* by a vowel, n, m, y, or v, and is *preceded* at whatever distance by r, ṛ, ṝ, or ṣ, provided there is no *intervening* consonantal dental, retroflex, or palatal other than y.

This rule is depicted in Table 4, Section (ii). The following are examples of its application (or non-application), most based on the instrumental suffix -ena: devena, varṇena, nagareṇa, dharmeṇa, rathena, dhātṛṇā, mṛgeṇa, mṛtena, pitṝn, pitṝṇām, kṛṣṇena, viṣeṇa, puṣpeṇa, kāṣṭhena.

Rule (ii) may apply to the output of Rule (i); e.g. lakṣmaṇaḥ, puṣpeṇa, niṣaṇṇaḥ. Here the ṣ is conditioned by the sound preceding it (Rule (i)), and in its turn conditions the following ṇ (Rule (ii)).

Rules (i) and (ii) usually do not apply across the boundaries between the components of a compound noun or adjective. For example, in naranārīṇām 'of men and women', the second n is not influenced by the preceding r because these two sounds belong to different components of the compound, its structure being nara+nārīṇām. On the other hand, the rules do usually apply between a prefix and the verbal stem to which it is attached; e.g. ni-sīdati → niṣīdati, pra-namati → praṇamati.

4. Vocalic Gradation

The vocalic alternations observable in the stems of different verb forms (and of some nominal forms also) can to a large extent be accounted for in terms of the phenomenon of vocalic gradation. This phenomenon is illustrated in the following example, based on various forms of the verb 'die'.

The infinitive, 'to die', is martum, where mar- is the stem and -tum the characteristic sign of the infinitive. The same component mar- is found in maraṇam 'death', mariṣyati 'he will die', etc. However, we find a rather different component in mārayati 'he causes to die, he kills', mārī 'dying', etc., and a different one again in mṛta- 'dead', amṛta 'he died', mṛtvā 'having died', and mamruḥ 'they died' (the r in mamruḥ being an internal sandhi variant of ṛ).

The three elements, ar ār and ṛ/r, are recognized as constituting a *gradation series*:

Zero grade	1st grade	2nd grade
ṛ/r	ar	ār
*mṛ*ta-	*mar*tum	*mār*ayati
ma*mr*uḥ	*mar*aṇam	*mār*ī

The first (so-called guṇa) grade, ar, is fundamental to the series. From it the second (vṛddhi) grade, ār, is obtained by 'strengthening', i.e. lengthening the a to ā; and the zero grade is obtained by 'weakening', i.e. diminishing the a to nothing, with the result that the remaining semivowel, r, if not followed by another vowel, takes on the role of a vowel, ṛ. The relationship among the three grades is, therefore, as shown:

Zero ←	1st →	2nd
ṛ/r	ar	ār

A similar series, but with the positions of vowel and semivowel reversed, is found in the verb 'grab':

Zero ←	1st →	2nd
ṛ	ra	rā
*gṛh*īta-	*grah*itum	*grāh*ayati

Similar series again are found with the remaining three semivowels: y, l, and v; and a necessarily incomplete series without semivowel also exists. The total set of gradation series, with examples, is shown in Table 5. (Compare the Vocalic section of Table 1.)

From Table 5 it can be seen that for each series in which the a and ā *precede* the semivowel (e.g. ay āy) there exists a corresponding series in which a and ā *follow* the semivowel (e.g. ya yā) — except for the extremely rare dental series. The open series (ø a ā), in which there is no semivowel, naturally lacks this distinction.

The series y ay āy has a variant form i/ī e ai. The difference between these two is determined entirely by a rule of internal sandhi: y ay āy are found before a following vowel, i/ī e ai before a following consonant. A similar sandhi-determined pair of variants exists in the labials: v av āv before vowels, u/ū o au before consonants. In the retroflexes there is the beginning of such a pairing, but it is incomplete because of the non-existence of 'retroflex diphthongs'. No such sandhi-determined pairing is found in those series in which a and ā follow the semivowel, because in such series the group in question is necessarily always followed by a consonant.

The length of the vowel in zero grade is unpredictable; e.g., in the palatal series it is sometimes i, sometimes ī. Usually there is consistency within any particular verb, but one finds many exceptions; e.g., alongside śruta-, śrutvā, etc. with short u one finds śrūyate with long ū.

The pairing of series depending on whether a and ā precede or follow the semivowel does not extend to zero grade. Consequently two different 1st-grade forms may have identical zero-grade counterparts; e.g., o and va both have u as their zero-grade counterpart. This phenomenon is most strikingly illustrated in instances such as the following (from the verbs 'burn' and 'dwell'), where the perfect passive participles in two different series happen to be identical:

	Zero ←	1st →	2nd
'burn':	*uṣ*ita-	*oṣ*aṇam	
'dwell':	*uṣ*ita-	*vas*anam	*vās*ayati

In the open series in Table 5 (ø a ā), zero grade is represented by absence of any vowel. But because this would often lead to unpronounceable groupings of consonants, in practice some vowel, usually a or ā, is provided, either by insertion or by substitution for a consonant. In the example given in Table 5, the zero-grade derivative of *khan*, namely *khn*, is represented in the form ca*khn*uḥ, a combination which presents no phonetic difficulty. However, where one might expect, by analogy with nīta-, mṛta-, etc., that the perfect passive participle would be khnta-, one finds instead khāta-; the n has been replaced by ā. Another example is provided by the following set of forms: *tap*ta- *tap*anam *tāp*ayati. Here the phonetically unacceptable *tp*ta-has been avoided by insertion of *a*.

In spite of these and other departures from the pattern presented in Table 5, recognition of vocalic gradation makes possible many useful grammatical generalizations, particularly regarding verb-forms.

5. Alphabetic Sequence

The conventional alphabetic sequence, used in ordering entries in dictionaries etc., is based on Table 1, but departs from its logical arrangement in some respects. The sequence is:

a ā i ī u ū ṛ ṝ ḷ e ai o au ṃ ḥ k kh g gh ṅ c ch j jh ñ
ṭ ṭh ḍ ḍh ṇ t th d dh n p ph b bh m y r l v ś ṣ s h

In an optional orthographic variant, any nasal preceding a stop is written as ṃ; e.g., aṅgam may be written aṃgam, and antara may be written aṃtara. Words written in this second way are nevertheless ordered in dictionaries as if written in the first way. For example, saṃgaḥ (= saṅgaḥ) comes after sagotra- and before saciḥ; but saṃsāraḥ (in which ṃ does *not* precede a stop and therefore cannot be alternatively written with some other nasal) comes before sakala.

PART II. GRAMMAR

A. NOMINALS

The Sanskrit noun, adjective, numeral, demonstrative, and pronoun have sufficient in common to be regarded as constituting a single large word-class, here called the Nominals. The noun and adjective are particularly closely related, being represented in a single set of paradigms (Table 6); the numeral, demonstrative, and pronoun are more distinctive, each having its own set of paradigms (Tables 12-14). These five sub-classes of nominals will now be described in turn.

1. Nouns

In general, each Sanskrit noun belongs inherently to one or another of three grammatical *genders*: masculine, neuter, or feminine. For example,

Masculine: devaḥ 'god', muniḥ 'sage', paśuḥ 'beast'
Neuter: phalam 'fruit', vāri 'water', madhu 'honey'
Feminine: kathā 'story', nadī 'river', vadhūḥ 'wife'

(How to recognize the gender of any given noun is discussed below.)

Nouns are declined for *number* and *case*. There are three grammatical numbers: singular, dual, and plural. For example,

Sing.	Dual	Plural
devaḥ 'a god'	devau 'two gods'	devāḥ 'gods (more than two)'
muniḥ 'a sage'	munī 'two sages'	munayaḥ 'sages (more than two)'

There are eight cases; their general significance is as follows.

Case	*Syntactic/logical relationship*
Nominative:	Indicates the grammatical subject.
Accusative:	Indicates the grammatical object.
Instrumental:	Indicates the means, manner, or accompanying factor/person; = 'by', 'with', '-ly'.
Dative:	Indicates the recipient, purpose, or destination; = 'to', 'for'.
Ablative:	Indicates the starting-point, source, reason, or standard of comparison; = 'from', 'out of', 'because', 'than'.
Genitive:	Indicates the possessor or subordinator; = 'of'.
Locative:	Indicates the location in space or time; = 'at', 'in', 'when'.
Vocative:	Indicates the individual addressed in direct speech; = 'O!'.

The intersection of the two 'dimensions' of number and case yields, for each noun, a set of 3 × 8 = 24 forms. (Some of the forms happen to be outwardly identical, thus reducing the count of outwardly distinct forms to 19 or fewer.) For example, the masculine noun devaḥ 'god' has the following set of forms.

	Sing.	Dual	Plural
Nom:	devaḥ	devau	devāḥ
Acc:	devam	devau	devān
Ins:	devena	devābhyām	devaiḥ
Dat:	devāya	devābhyām	devebhyaḥ
Abl:	devāt	devābhyām	devebhyaḥ
Gen:	devasya	devayoḥ	devānām
Loc:	deve	devayoḥ	deveṣu
Voc:	deva	devau	devāḥ

For example,

devāya	=	'to a/the god' (dat. sing.)
deva	=	'O god!' (voc. sing.)
devaiḥ	=	'by the gods' (inst. plur.)
devayoḥ	=	'of the two gods' (gen. dual) or 'in the two gods' (loc. dual)

All masculine nouns whose nominative singular ends in -aḥ (e.g., gajaḥ, putraḥ, aśvaḥ, rāmaḥ) are declined like devaḥ. For example, gajaḥ 'elephant' has the following forms:

gajaḥ	gajau	gajāḥ
gajam	gajau	gajān
gajena	gajābhyām	etc.

The 3 × 8 pattern given above for devaḥ is, therefore, a model or *paradigm;* it is followed by all masculine nouns in -aḥ. Such nouns constitute by far the most numerous group. (In memorizing paradigms such as that of devaḥ, one should read horizontally, not vertically, i.e.: 'devaḥ devau devāḥ; devam devau devān; ...'.)

The devaḥ paradigm is one of sixteen paradigms that can be recognized for 'regular' masculine nouns (and adjectives; see below). These sixteen are set out in Table 6, Section (i) (pages 80 ff). For example, muniḥ 'sage', along with almost all other masculine nouns in -iḥ, is declined as shown in paradigm [2] (page 80). A further fifteen paradigms of regular neuter nouns are given in Table 6 (ii), and nine for regular feminines in Table 6 (iii). A limited number of nouns/adjectives fail to conform to these paradigms. They are therefore regarded as 'irregular'; their declensional patterns are set out in Table 7.

In dictionaries, nouns are usually cited in either of two forms: (i) in the nominative singular, or (ii) in a hypothetical underlying stem-form. Examples of these two methods of citation can be found in popular dictionaries such as those of V.S. Apte and M. Monier-Williams.

In Apte's dictionaries, method (i) is used as far as possible, but method (ii) is resorted to when necessary for clarity. For example, the words for 'elephant', 'city', and 'creeper' are given as gajaḥ, nagaram, and latā respectively, i.e. in the nominative singular. No indication of gender is given, it being expected that the student will recognize the endings -aḥ, -am, and -ā as characteristic of the masculine, neuter, and feminine genders respectively — and therefore as indicating, in addition, that the three nouns in question follow paradigms [1], [17], and [32] respectively of Table 6. On the other hand, the words for 'merchant', 'mind', and 'mother' are *not* given in their nominative singular forms vaṇik, manaḥ, and mātā (see paradigms [7], [23], [40]). Instead they are given as 'vaṇij *m*', 'manas *n*', and 'mātṛ *f*'. These are hypothetical stem-forms which may be thought of as underlying the actually occurring forms; the gender (*m*, *n*, *f*) is stated because there is no way it could be inferred with certainty. The rationale behind this citing of some nouns in hypothetical stem-forms will become clear in the descriptions given below for the various paradigms. Suffice it here to note that this practice has the advantage of making the most common endings, -aḥ, -am, -ā, and others, unambiguous as indicators of gender and paradigm; for example, because members of paradigm [23] are cited in the -as form (manas rather than manaḥ), one knows that *every* word whose citation or dictionary forms ends in -aḥ is masculine and follows paradigm [1].

In the dictionaries of Monier-Williams, hypothetical stem-forms are more widely used, being adopted even for members of the very common paradigms [1] and [17]. For example, 'elephant' and 'city' are given as 'gaja *m*' and 'nagara *n*' respectively. (However, 'creeper' (paradigm [32]) is given in the nominative singular as 'latā *f*'.)

From the practical point of view the method adopted by Apte has the advantage of presenting the majority of nouns in forms which actually occur, and which bear their own in-built gender labels. For example, the student wishing to learn the gender of 'city', will find it easier and more realistic to memorize the word as 'nagaram' rather than as 'nagara (neuter)'. On the other hand, the method adopted by Monier-Williams has the advantage of drawing attention to correspondences across the genders; for example, it identifies the masculine, neuter, and feminine endings -aḥ, -am, -ā as constituting a related set, a point whose significance becomes apparent in the next section, on adjectives.

The characteristics of the various noun/adjective paradigms will be described after the adjectives have been dealt with.

2. Adjectives

(a) *Gender Agreement*

Unlike the noun, the adjective does not belong inherently to one of the three genders. Instead, it acquires the gender of the noun it qualifies or refers to. For example, the adjective 'dear', cited in dictionaries in the hypothetical stem form priya-, acquires, in the singular nominative, the following three gender forms:

Masc:	priyaḥ	e.g.	priyaḥ putraḥ	'a dear son'
			priyaḥ pitā	'a dear father'
Neut:	priyam	e.g.	priyaṃ mitram	'a dear friend'
			priyaṃ nāma	'a dear name'
Fem:	priyā	e.g.	priyā kanyā	'a dear daughter'
			priyā patnī	'a dear wife'

The three forms, priyaḥ, priyam, priyā, correspond to the noun types devaḥ, phalam, kathā (paradigms [1], [17], [32]) respectively. Most adjectives whose stem-form has, like priya-, a final -a-, form their masculine, neuter, and feminine in this way with -aḥ, -am, and -ā respectively. (For exceptions see next page.)

The agreement between an adjective and its noun extends also to case and number. For example, priya- assumes forms such as the following:

priyāṇāṃ putrāṇām	'of the dear sons'
priya pitaḥ	'O dear father!'
priye nāmni	'in a dear name'
priyayā patnyā	'with a dear wife'

These forms of priya- are drawn from the appropriate paradigms, [1], [17], or [32], according as the gender required is masculine, neuter, or feminine.

The various adjective types that exist represent almost all of the paradigms [1] to [40]. For example, the adjective 'powerful' given in the dictionary as balin-, forms masculine balī, neuter bali, and feminine balinī, which then follow paradigms [11], [28], and [33] respectively. Table 8 sets out the necessary information on the different existing types of stem-forms of adjectives, with their corresponding masculine, neuter, and feminine forms (all in the nominative singular), and the paradigm which each of these follows. Each type is represented in the table by a common example, and the paradigms followed are indicated by their numbers in square brackets. (Some important irregular adjectives not covered by Table 8 are noted on pages 26-28 under 'Irregular noun/adjective declensions'.) It will be found that Table 8, in addition to its primary function, provides a handy overview of the total set of noun/adjective paradigms.

As Table 8 shows, stem-forms in -a- or -ant- are ambiguous as indicators of the pattern followed. Adjectives with stem-forms in -ant- are present or future active participles. Whether they follow nayaṇt- (with feminine in -antī), or yuñjant- (with feminine in -atī-), depends on various factors discussed in the section on participles. (See pages 59-63. Further ambiguity may arise from the fact that the nayant- and yuñjant- types are often cited as nayat- and yuñjat-, thus confusing them with the dadhat- type.)

Adjectives with stem-form in -a- in moṣt cases follow priya-; however, a limited number follow sundara- in forming their feminine in -ī. The principal examples of the latter type are:

(i) The ordinal caturtha- '4th', which has feminine caturthī, and similarly all higher ordinals (see Table 11); for example,

pañcama-	pañcamī	'5th'
aṣṭādaśa-	aṣṭādaśī	'18th'

(ii) Adjectives that are, in origin, derived from nouns by strengthening of the first vowel to 2nd grade; e.g.

śaiva-	śaivī (a derivative of the noun Śivaḥ)
gāndharva-	gāndharvī

(iii) Derivative adjectives in -maya and -tana; e.g.

cinmaya-	cinmayī
adyatana-	adyatanī

(iv) A few miscellaneous adjectives, including

codana-	codanī
taruṇa-	taruṇī
purāṇa-	purāṇī (also -ṇā)
sadṛśa-	sadṛśī
sundara-	sundarī

(b) *Comparison of adjectives*

There exist two distinct methods whereby the comparative and superlative degrees of adjectives may be formed. Method 1 is applicable to all adjectives; method 2 is applicable only to a relatively small, closed set of adjectives.

(i) Method 1

This method consists in attaching the suffixes -tara- (comparative) and -tama- (superlative) to the stem form of the simple adjective (e.g. priya- priyatara- priyatama-) or to a slightly modified version of it (e.g. balin- balitara- balitama-). Table 9 shows how this applies to different types of stem-forms. The set of types covered by Table 9 is essentially the same as that covered by Table 8, with this exception that the śreyas type is lacking in Table 9 because, being itself a comparative form (according to method 2, below), it has no place here.

The comparative and superlative forms shown in Table 9 are themselves stem-forms; they make the three gender forms in -aḥ, -am, -ā, and so are declined according to paradigms [1], [17], and [32], regardless of the class of the original adjective in its positive form. Thus, the masculine, neuter, and feminine of the positive, comparative, and superlative forms of priya- and balin-, with their corresponding declensional paradigms (indicated by numbers), are as follows:

	Positive	Comparative	Superlative
Masc:	priyaḥ [1]	priyataraḥ [1]	priyatamaḥ [1]
Neut:	priyam [17]	priyataram [17]	priyatamam [17]
Fem:	priyā [32]	priyatarā [32]	priyatamā [32]
Masc:	balī [11]	balitaraḥ [1]	balitamaḥ [1]
Neut:	bali [28]	balitaram [17]	balitamam [17]
Fem:	balinī [33]	balitarā [32]	balitamā [32]

For example,

priyataraṃ mitram	'a dearer friend'
priyatamā kanyā	'the dearest daughter'
priyatamāyai kanyāyai	'to the dearest daughter'
balinyā senayā	'by a powerful army'
balitamābhyāṃ senābhyām	'by the two most powerful armies'

(ii) Method 2

The restricted number of adjectives to which method 2 applies are already covered by method 1; they are, therefore, capable of forming their comparative and superlative in two different ways. Method 2 consists in adding -īyas- (comparative) and -iṣṭha- (superlative), or sometimes simply -yas- and -ṣṭha-, to a modified version of the stem form. This modification of the stem entails abbreviation to a single syllable, sometimes accompanied by vowel strengthening and/or other more drastic changes. For example, priya- 'dear' forms preyas- and preṣṭha-; and laghu- 'light' forms laghīyas- and laghiṣṭha-.

The comparative stem form thus produced makes the three gender forms as shown in Table 8 opposite śreyas-, i.e. by replacing -as with -ān, -aḥ, and -asī; and these three forms then follow paradigms [14], [23], and [33] respectively. (Paradigm [14] is exclusively for masculine comparatives of this type.) The superlative makes its gender-forms with -aḥ, -am, and -ā, and these then follow paradigms [1], [17], and [32] respectively. For example, the adjectives priya- and laghu- form their comparative and superlative in the three genders as follows:

	Positive	Comparative	Superlative
Masc:	priyaḥ [1]	preyān [14]	preṣṭhaḥ [1]
Neut:	priyam [17]	preyaḥ [23]	preṣṭham [17]
Fem:	priyā [32]	preyasī [33]	preṣṭhā [32]
Masc:	laghuḥ [3]	laghīyān [14]	laghiṣṭhaḥ [1]
Neut:	laghu [19]	laghīyaḥ [23]	laghiṣṭham [17]
Fem:	laghuḥ [38] or laghvī [33]	laghīyasī [33]	laghiṣṭhā [32]

In addition to the fairly regular formation illustrated in priya- and laghu-, there are many formations so irregular that the derivational connexion between the positive and its comparative and superlative counterparts is often remote, or even (as in English sets such as 'good, better, best') no more than semantic. Because of these varying degrees of irregularity, adjectives compared by method 2 are best listed individually. Table 10 sets out the most important instances.

(c) *Noun/adjective declensional paradigms (Table 6)*

The characterizing features of the forty declensional paradigms for nominals will now be summarized. (The gender headings are not exclusive; e.g. a few feminine nouns are included under the Masculine heading because they have identical declension.)

(i) Masculine

[1] **devaḥ** 'god': Paradigm [1] in Table 6 is followed by those nouns whose citation form is given in dictionaries as '---aḥ' or as '---a (masc.)'; e.g. gajaḥ 'elephant', putraḥ 'son'. It is also followed by the masculine of adjectives whose stem-form ends in -a-, of comparatives and superlatives in -a-, and of ordinals; e.g., nīcaḥ 'low' (masc. of nīca-), śucitaraḥ 'purer', śreṣṭhaḥ 'best', tṛtīyaḥ '3rd'.

[2] **muniḥ** 'sage': Masc. nouns cited as '---iḥ' or as '---i (masc.)'; e.g. agniḥ 'fire', nṛpatiḥ 'king'. Also, the masc. of adjectives in -i- such as śuciḥ 'pure' (masc. of śuci-). Patiḥ, when it means 'husband', is irregular; see [46].

[3] **paśuḥ** 'beast': Masc. nouns cited as '---uḥ' or as '---u (masc.)'; e.g. śatruḥ 'enemy', guruḥ 'teacher'. Also, masc. of adjectives in -u-; e.g. laghuḥ 'light'.

[4] **netā** 'leader': Masc. agent nouns whose citation form has final -ṛ; e.g. dātā 'donor', rakṣitā 'protector'. Also, the kinship term naptā 'nephew'. (This paradigm exhibits all three grades of the retroflex gradation series, ṛ/r ar ār; e.g. net*ṛ*ṣu/net*r*ā net*ar*i net*ār*aḥ.)

[5] **pitā** 'father': Masc. kinship terms whose citation form has final -ṛ; e.g. bhrātā 'brother', jāmātā 'son-in-law'. However, naptā 'nephew' follows [4].

[6] **marut** 'wind-god': Masc. and feminine nouns and adjectives whose citation form has final -k, -t, or -p; also, masc. of present active participles in -at- — but not of those in -ant- (which follow [12]), nor of the possessive adjectives in -mat- or -vat- (which follow [13]). For example, sarvaśak 'omnipotent', sarit 'stream', bibhrat 'carrying', dharmagup 'guardian of the law'. The stem-final -k, -t, or -p is preserved throughout the paradigm, except that before the six case-endings that begin with bh it becomes voiced to -g, -d, -b; e.g. marut has instrumental dual marudbhyām.

[7] **vaṇik** 'merchant': Masc. and fem. nouns and adjectives whose citation form ends in a consonant other than -k, -t, -p, -ḥ, -n, or -as; e.g. the words cited as vaṇi*j*, priyavā*c*, triṣṭu*bh*, di*ś*, upāna*h*. The final consonant of the citation form is preserved in those caseforms in which it is followed by a vowel; e.g., vaṇi*j*, tristu*bh*, di*ś*, and vi*ś* have nominative plural vaṇi*j*aḥ, triṣṭu*bh*aḥ, di*ś*aḥ, and vi*ś*aḥ respectively. However, in the nominative singular where no sound follows, this consonant is replaced by some more or less closely related consonant from among the set of five permitted non-nasal word-finals, -k, -ṭ, -t, -p, -ḥ (see page 1); e.g., vaṇi*j*, triṣṭu*bh*, di*ś*, and vi*ś* have singular nominative vaṇi*k*, triṣṭu*p*, di*k* and vi*ṭ* respectively.

As the instance of diś and viś shows, it is not always possible to predict which of the four permitted word-final stops will replace the stem-final of the citation-form. The reverse is also true; e.g., vaṇik and dik are from vaṇi*j* and di*ś* respectively. For this reason dictionaries usually indicate the nominative singular alongside the citation form.

For practical purposes the best way of specifying the two consonants involved in the alternation is to name the nominative singular and plural; e.g. vaṇik—vaṇijaḥ. Once these two forms are known, the entire paradigm is known. The first of the two consonants named (k in our example) occurs where no sound follows (i.e. in the nominative and vocative singular) and before the -su or -ṣu of the locative plural; and it becomes voiced (to g) before the six -bh- case-endings. (For the purposes of this rule, the voiced counterpart of ḥ is r.) The second of the two consonants named (j in our example) occurs before all vowel case-endings. It is therefore advisable to think of words of this type in terms of their nominative singular and plural (which, in any case, are the most commonly occurring forms); i.e. one should learn the words as 'vaṇi*k*—vaṇi*j*aḥ', 'di*k*—di*ś*aḥ', etc. Examples of the most frequent such pairs of consonants are set out in the following list. For completeness the three consonant-finals covered by [6] are included, since they are really only special cases of the present type.

k—k:	sarvaśa*k*—sarvaśa*k*aḥ	'omnipotent'
k—c:	vā*k*—vā*c*aḥ	'voice'
k—j:	vaṇi*k*—vaṇi*j*aḥ	'merchant'
k—ś:	di*k*—di*ś*aḥ	'compass-point'
k—ṣ:	dadhṛ*k*—dadhṛ*ṣ*aḥ	'bold'

k—h:	kāmadhu*k*—kāmadu*h*aḥ	'wish-granting'
ṭ—j:	samrā*ṭ*—samrā*j*aḥ	'ruler'
ṭ—ś:	vi*ṭ*—vi*ś*aḥ	'resident'
ṭ—ṣ:	dvi*ṭ*—dvi*ṣ*aḥ	'enemy'
ṭ—h:	madhuli*ṭ*—madhuli*h*aḥ	'bee'
t—t:	maru*t*—maru*t*aḥ	'wind-god'
t—d:	āpa*t*—āpa*d*aḥ	'calamity'
t—dh:	sami*t*—sami*dh*aḥ	'faggot'
t—h:	upāna*t*—upāna*h*aḥ	'sandal'
p—p:	dharmagu*p*—dharmagu*p*aḥ	'guardian of law'
p—bh:	triṣṭu*p*—triṣṭu*bh*aḥ	'a Vedic metre'
ḥ—r:	dvā*ḥ*—dvā*r*aḥ	'door'
ḥ—ṣ:	do*ḥ*—do*ṣ*aḥ	'arm'

Slight departures from the pattern described above occur in the last two types listed. As mentioned above, the voiced counterpart of ḥ is here to be regarded as r; in addition, dvāḥ has r in the locative plural: dvārṣu. Thoroughly irregular nouns whose citation forms would seem to qualify them for membership of this class, include the word cited as pad and its derivatives — see [47], [48]; prāñc and others in -ñc — see [50] to [54]; ap [71]; gir [72]; and pur [73].

[8] **vedhāḥ** 'wise man': Masc. and fem. nouns and adjectives whose citation form ends in -as (but excluding the masculine of comparatives in -yas- [14], and of perfect participles in -ivas- [15] and -vas- [16]); e.g. candramāḥ 'moon', apsarāḥ 'nymph', sumanāḥ 'good natured'.

[9] **ātmā** 'self': Masc. and fem. nouns and adjectives whose citation form has final -an preceded by *two* consonants; e.g. brahmā 'the creator-god', yajvā 'worshipper', suparvā 'well-jointed'.

[10] **rājā** 'king': Masc. and fem. nouns and adjectives whose citation form has final -an preceded by *one* consonant; e.g. garimā 'heaviness', sīmā 'boundary', sunāmā 'well-named'. (This paradigm exhibits all three grades of the open gradation

series, ø a ā; e.g. rā*jñā* rā*jani* rā*jāna*ḥ. In the case of zero grade the nasal assimilates to the adjacent stop: n → ñ.)

[11] **hastī** 'elephant': Masc. nouns and possessive adjectives whose citation form has final -in; e.g. svāmī 'master', yogī 'acetic practitioner', dhanī 'rich'.

[12] **nayan** 'leading': Masc. of future active participles, and of present active participles having stem-forms in -ant- or -ānt- (though often cited in -at- or -āt-, see pages 16, 60-61); e.g. rakṣan 'protecting', sunvan 'pressing', bhān 'shining', neṣyan 'about to lead'.

[13] **dhīmān** 'wise': Masc. of possessive adjectives whose citation form ends in -mat- or -vat-; e.g. murtimān 'having form', bhagavān 'blessed'. Also kiyān and iyān, masc. of kiyat- 'how much?' and iyat- 'so much'.

[14] **śreyān** 'better': Masc. of comparative adjectives formed according to method 2 (pages 17-18; all with citation forms in -yas- or -īyas-); e.g. preyān 'dearer', laghīyān 'lighter'.

[15] **tenivān** 'having stretched': Masc. of perfect active participles whose citation form ends in -ivas- (see pages 61-62); e.g. rarakṣivān 'having protected', tutudivān 'having hit'.

[16] **cakṛvān** 'having done': Masc. of perfect active participles whose citation form has final -vas- without a preceding short i (see pages 61-62); e.g. vidvān 'having known', śuśruvān 'having heard', ninīvān 'having led'. Before -uṣ- endings (e.g. sing. instrumental -uṣā) ṛ → r, u → uv, ī → y (or → iy if two consonants precede); e.g. cakṛvān—cakruṣā, śuśruvān—śuśruvuṣā, ninīvān—ninyuṣā.

(ii) Neuter

[17] **phalam** 'fruit': Nouns whose citation form is given as '---am' or as '---a (neut.)', and the neuter of adjectives whose citation form ends in -a-; e.g. vanam 'forest', yugam 'yoke', nīcam 'low'.

[18] **vāri** 'water': Neuter nouns/adjectives with citation form in -i; e.g. śuci 'pure' — but not akṣi, asthi, dadhi, or sakthi, all of which are irregular (see [64]). Adjectives in this class may optionally follow [2] (muniḥ) in the singular dative, ablative, genitive, and locative, and in the dual genitive and locative; e.g., śuci has in the singular dative either śucine (following [18]) or śucaye (following [2]).

[19] **madhu** 'honey': Neuter nouns/adjectives with citation form in -u; e.g. aśru 'tear', vastu 'property', guru 'heavy', laghu 'light'. Adjectives in this class may optionally follow [3] in the cases specified above for [18].

[20] **dhātṛ** 'that which creates': Neuter agent nouns/adjectives with citation form in -ṛ; e.g. dātṛ 'that which gives', rakṣitṛ 'that which protects', sumātṛ 'having a good mother'.

[21] **jagat** 'world': Followed by three classes of words: (a) Neuter nouns/adjectives with citation form in -k, -t, or -p; e.g. sarvaśak 'omnipotent', trivṛt 'threefold'. (b) The neuter of possessive adjectives in -mat- or -vat-; e.g. dhīmat 'wise', bhagavat 'blessed'. (c) The neuter of present active participles other than those with stem-form in -ant- or -ānt-, for which see [29]; e.g. bibhrat 'carrying', jānat 'knowing', tudat 'hitting', bhāt 'shining'; also the neuter of all future active participles (which, however, may optionally also follow [29]), e.g. neṣyat, dāsyat. Present active participles of verbs of the -Vti class (e.g. bibhrat, juhvat, dadhat) optionally have -ati in place of -anti in the nominative, accusative, and vocative plural.

[22] **asṛk** 'blood': Neuter nouns/adjectives with citation-form endings as for [7]. There is consonant alternation as for [7], which again is best specified by naming the nominative singular and plural; e.g. as*ṛk*—as*ṛñji* 'blood', priyav*āk*—priyavāñci 'kindly-spoken'. The nasal, if followed by a stop, assimilates to that stop; otherwise it becomes ṃ.

[23] **manaḥ** 'mind': Neuter nouns/adjectives with citation form in -(y)as; e.g. yaśaḥ 'glory', sumanaḥ 'good-natured', śreyaḥ 'better'.

[24] **haviḥ** 'oblation': Neuter nouns/adjectives with citation form in -is; e.g. jyotiḥ 'light', rociḥ 'lustre', udarciḥ 'radiant'.

[25] **āyuḥ** 'age': Neuter nouns/adjectives with citation form in -us; e.g. cakṣuḥ 'eye', dhanuḥ 'bow', dīrghāyuḥ 'long-lived'.

[26] **karma** 'deed': Neuter nouns/adjectives whose citation form has final -an preceded by *two* consonants; e.g. carma 'leather', janma 'birth', suparva 'well-jointed'.

[27] **nāma** 'name': Neuter nouns/adjectives whose citation form has final -an preceded by *one* consonant; e.g. sāma 'Vedic song', hema 'gold', sunāma 'well-named'.

[28] **bali** 'powerful': Neuter of possessive adjectives whose citation form has final -in; e.g. dhani 'rich', manasvi 'wise'.

[29] **nayat** 'leading': Neuter of present active participles with stem-form in -ant- or -ānt- (i.e. those whose masc. is covered by [12]); e.g. rakṣat, tudat, bhāt, nāyayat, ninīṣat, (see pages 60-61). Also neuter of all future active participles (which, however, may optionally also follow [21]); e.g. neṣyat, dāsyat.

[30] **tenivat** 'having stretched': Neuter of perfect active participles whose citation form ends in -ivas- (see pages 61-62); e.g. rarakṣivat 'having protected', tutudivat 'having hit'.

[31] **cakṛvat** 'having done': Neuter of perfect active participles whose citation form has final -vas- without a preceding short i (see pages 61-62); e.g. vidvat 'having known', śuśruvat 'having heard', ninīvat 'having led'. Before -uṣ- endings the stem is modified as in [16].

(iii) Feminine

[32] **kathā** 'story': Nouns whose citation form ends in -ā (all are feminine); also, fem. adjectives in -ā, i.e. the majority of feminines from adjectives whose citation form ends in -a-; e.g. kanyā 'daughter, maiden', senā 'army', priyā 'dear', preṣṭhā 'dearest'.

[33] **nadī** 'river': Polysyllabic nouns whose citation form ends in -ī (all are fem.); also, fem. adjectives formed with -ī, (see

Table 8); e.g. devī 'goddess', nārī 'woman', sundarī 'beautiful'. However, fem. adjectives in -ī that are covered by [34] are excluded; and the words cited as lakṣmī, tarī, and tantrī are irregular — see [68].

[34] **dhīḥ** 'intelligence': Monosyllabic nouns whose citation form is given as ending in -ī or -īḥ (all are fem.); also fem. of adjectives having such monosyllables as their final member; e.g. śrīḥ 'fortune', hrīḥ 'modesty', sudhīḥ 'intelligent'. The corresponding masc. adjectives (see Table 8) differ in that where alternative case-forms are offered, only the second is permitted; e.g., sudhīḥ (masc.) has in the dative singular only sudhiye — cf. [42]. Some masc. adjectives of this type also reduce -iy- to -y- throughout — cf. [43].

[35] **matiḥ** 'mind': Fem. nouns whose citation form is given as ending in -i or -iḥ; also fem. of adjectives with citation form in -i; e.g. jātiḥ 'birth', rātriḥ 'night', śuciḥ 'pure'.

[36] **vadhūḥ** 'wife': Polysyllabic nouns whose citation form is given as ending in -ū or -ūḥ (all are fem.); also fem. of polysyllabic adjectives in -ū, except those covered by [37]; e.g. śvaśrūḥ 'mother-in-law', juhūḥ 'sacrificial ladle', aticamūḥ 'victorious'. The corresponding masc. adjectives (see Table 8) differ in substituting -ūn for -ūḥ in the accusative plural.

[37] **bhūḥ** 'earth': Monosyllabic nouns whose citation form is given as ending in -ū or -ūḥ (all are fem.); also, fem. of adjectives having such monosyllables as their final member; e.g. bhrūḥ 'eyebrow', svabhūḥ 'self-existent'. The corresponding masc. adjectives differ as described under [34].

[38] **dhenuḥ** 'cow': Fem. nouns whose citation form is given as ending in -u or -uḥ; also, fem. of adjectives with citation form in -u, when made in -uḥ rather than in -vī (Table 8); e.g. hanuḥ 'jaw', rajjuḥ 'rope', tanuḥ 'thin'.

[39] **nauḥ** 'ship': Fem. or masc. monosyllabic nouns cited as ending in -au or -auḥ; e.g. glauḥ 'moon'. Dyauḥ 'sky' and gauḥ 'cow, bull' are cited as dyo and go respectively and are irregular; see [69], [70].

[40] **mātā** 'mother': Fem. kinship terms having citation form in -ṛ; e.g. duhitā 'daughter'. However, svasā 'sister' exceptionally has ār instead of ar in six case-forms:

	Sing.	Dual	Plural
Nom:	svasā	svas*ā*rau	svas*ā*raḥ
Acc:	svas*ā*ram	svas*ā*rau	svasṝḥ
Voc:	svasaḥ	svas*ā*rau	svas*ā*raḥ

(d) *Irregular noun/adjective declensions* (Table 7)

The distinction recognized here between 'regular' and 'irregular' is based to some extent on mere practical convenience: often a declensional pattern has been classified as 'irregular' simply because it is of relatively rare occurrence. In some instances an irregular pattern of declension is followed by just one noun or adjective; in others it is followed by a small class of nouns or adjectives, and so constitutes a minor paradigm. Information relating to such matters is now presented in brief.

(i) Masculine

[41] **viśvapāḥ** 'all-protector': Cited as viśvapā. Masc. agent nouns whose final component is a verbal root in -ā; e.g. śaṅkhadhmāḥ 'conch-blower', somapāḥ 'soma-drinker'.

[42] **yavakrīḥ** 'corn-buyer': Cited as yavakrī. Masc. agent nouns whose final component is a verbal root in -ī preceded by *two* consonants; also, the masc. of some adjectives as described under [34]; e.g. sudhīḥ 'intelligent' — see Table 8.

[43] **senānīḥ** 'army commander': Cited as senānī. Masc. agent nouns whose final component is the suffix -nī or a verbal root in -ī or -ū preceded by *one* consonant; e.g. grāmaṇīḥ 'village chief', khalapūḥ 'sweeper'. Also, the masc. of some adjectives as described under [34]; e.g. pradhīḥ 'intelligent' — cf. Table 8.

[44] **rāḥ** 'wealth': Cited as rai.

[45] **sakhā** 'friend': Cited as sakhi.

[46] **patiḥ** 'husband': Cited as patiḥ or pati. However, compounds from -patiḥ, such as nṛpatiḥ 'king', follow [2] muniḥ, as does patiḥ itself when it has the meaning 'lord'.

[47] **pāt** 'foot': Cited as pad. Can also be declined as pādaḥ, following [1].

[48] **dvipāt** 'biped': Cited as dvipād. Masc. compounds from -pāt; e.g. catuṣpāt 'quadruped', supāt 'having good feet'.

[49] **anaḍvān** 'ox': Cited as anaḍuh.

[50] **prāṅ** 'forward, eastward': Cited as prāñc. Similarly avāṅ 'downward'. Neuter nom. and acc.: prāk prācī prāñci; other cases as for masc. prāṅ. Fem. prācī follows [33].

[51] **pratyaṅ** 'backward, westward': Cited as pratyañc. Similarly nyaṅ 'downward', samyaṅ 'going together'. Neut. pratyak pratīcī pratyañci. Fem. pratīcī.

[52] **udaṅ** 'northward': Cited as udañc. Neut. udak udīcī udañci. Fem. udīcī.

[53] **anvaṅ** 'following': Cited as anvañc. Similarly viśvaṅ 'going apart'. Neut. anvak anūcī anvañci. Fem. anūcī.

[54] **tiryaṅ** 'going horizontally, animal': Cited as tiryañc. Neut. tiryak tiraścī tiryañci. Fem. tiraścī.

[55] **pumān** 'man': Cited as puṃs.

[56] **panthāḥ** 'path': Cited as pathin. Similarly manthāḥ 'churning-rod', ṛbhukhāḥ 'Indra'.

[57] **pūṣā** 'sun': Cited as pūṣan. Similarly aryamā 'sun'.

[58] **gohā** 'cow-killer': Cited as gohan. Compounds from -hā 'killer', e.g. brahmahā 'priest-killer'.

[59] **śvā** 'dog': Cited as śvan. Fem. śunī [33].

[60] **yuvā** 'young man': Cited as yuvan. Fem. yuvatiḥ [35].

[61] **maghavā** 'generous, Indra': Cited as maghavan. May follow [13].

[62] **mahān** 'great': Cited as mahat. Neut. mahat [63]. Fem. mahatī [33].

(ii) Neuter

[63] **mahat** 'great': Cf. [62].

[64] **dadhi** 'yoghurt': Similarly akṣi 'eye', asthi 'bone', sakthi 'thigh'.

[65] **ahaḥ** 'day': Cited as ahan.

(iii) Feminine

[66] **jarā** 'old age': Alternatively may follow [32].

[67] **strī** 'woman'.

[68] **lakṣmīḥ** 'fortune': Cited as lakṣmī. Similarly tarīḥ 'boat', tantrīḥ 'string'.

[69] **dyauḥ** 'sky': Cited as dyo.

[70] **gauḥ** 'cow, speech': Cited as go. Also treated as masc., = 'bull'.

[71] **āpaḥ** 'water': Declined only in plural. Cited in singular ap.

[72] **gīḥ** 'speech': Cited as gir. Similarly āśīḥ—āśiṣaḥ 'blessing', but forms āśīrbhyām etc. and āśīḥṣu.

[73] **pūḥ** 'city': Cited as pur. Similarly dhūḥ 'yoke'.

3. NUMERALS

(a) *Cardinals*

The cardinal numbers, in their nominative case-forms, are set out in Table 11. The four forms shown there for 19 are equivalent and freely interchangeable. They represent two basic formation types: one type (navadaśa) is analogous in formation to the preceding number (aṣṭādaśa 18); the other type (ūnaviṃśatiḥ/ekonaviṃśatiḥ/ekānnaviṃśatiḥ) amounts to subtraction of 1 from the following number (viṃśatiḥ 20). Parallel sets of four equivalent forms, not shown in Table 11, exist for 29, 39, ... 99. Similarly the pairs of forms shown for 42, 43, 52, 53, 62, 63, 72, 73, 92, 93 are equivalent and interchangeable; this pairing of forms is not paralleled in the teens, 20s, 30s or 80s.

Of the two or three equivalent forms for numbers above 100, the first form shown is avoided wherever it would lead to ambiguity. For example, for 103 tryadhikaṃ śatam or tryadhikaśatam is preferred, and for 300 trīṇi śatāni is preferred; the simpler alternative is in both instances triśatam, which is therefore ambiguous. (In the older Vedic language, a distinction in accent prevented ambiguity: tríśatam 103 *versus* triśatám 300.) However, where no possibility of ambiguity exists, the shorter form may be used. For example, 123 = trayoviṃśatiśatam. As a further option, the element -adhika may always be replaced by -uttara; e.g. 103 = tryuttaraṃ śatam or tryuttaraśatam. The three forms shown for 1, 2, 3, and 4 are not alternatives but gender-forms, as explained below.

As regards their declensional behaviour, the cardinal numbers fall into two broad sub-sets: (i) 1 to 19 (navadaśa), and (ii) 19 (ūnaviṃśatiḥ/ekonaviṃśatiḥ/ekānnaviṃśatiḥ) and upwards.

The cardinal numbers as far as 19 (navadaśa) behave in much the same way as the adjectives, but with some limitations and simplifications. Agreement in gender with the associated noun is found only in 1, 2, 3, and 4. The masculine, neuter, and feminine forms of these four numerals (in the nominative case) are shown in Table 11.

Agreement in grammatical number is limited by the fact that 1 and 2 are necessarily singular and dual respectively, while 3 to 19 (navadaśa) are plural. (The word eka- 'one' does exist in the plural, but the meaning is then 'some, a few'.)

Case agreement with the associated noun is complete, except that the vocative is rare. The case-forms are broadly similar to those of the relevant noun-types, but with a few unique features. Table 12 sets out the forms as far as 10, again with gender distinction extending only as far as 4. The numbers from ekādaśa (11) to navadaśa (19) are declined like daśa (10). For example,

ekasmai putrāya	'to one son'
catvāro devāḥ	'4 gods' (nominative)
pañcānāṃ bhrātṝṇām	'of the 5 brothers'
aṣṭādaśabhiḥ kanyābhiḥ	'by 18 maidens'.

The cardinal numbers from 19 (ūnaviṃśatiḥ/ekonaviṃśatiḥ/ekānnaviṃśatiḥ) upwards are nouns. From 19 to 99 they are feminine and declined in the singular: those that end in -iḥ follow matiḥ [35]; those in -śat follow marut [6]. For example,

caturviṃśatir devāḥ	'24 gods' (nom.)
caturviṃśatyā devaiḥ	'by 24 gods'
trayastriṃśad devāḥ	'33 gods' (nom.)
trayastriṃśato devānām	'of 33 gods'.

The numbers 100, 1000, 10000, 100000 etc. are used in the singular, dual, or plural as required by their multiplier; e.g. 200 = dve śate, 3000 = trīṇi sahasrāṇi. They acquire the case expected in the associated noun, while the noun itself either retains its expected case or is put into the genitive plural. For example,

śataṃ devāḥ	'100 gods' (nom.)
śataṃ devānām	" "
aṣṭādhikaśatena devaiḥ	'by 108 gods'
aṣṭādhikaśatena devānām	" "
aṣṭādhikena śatena devaiḥ	" "
aṣṭottaraśatena devaiḥ	" "
etc.	
dvābhyāṃ śatābhyāṃ devaiḥ	'by 200 gods'
etc.	

(b) *Ordinals*

The citation forms of the ordinals are set out in Table 11, to the right of the corresponding cardinals. The word for 'first' bears no resemblance to the word for 'one'; '2nd', '3rd', '4th', and '6th' are derived irregularly from their corresponding cardinals; and all the remaining ordinals are derived from their cardinals in regular and obvious ways. Suffixes shown in parentheses are optional; for example, the entry 'viṃśa(titama)-' for '20th' is to be read as 'viṃśa- or viṃśatitama-'.

The ordinals are adjectives; each agrees in gender, number, and case with the noun it qualifies. The words for '1st', '2nd', and '3rd', as well as tur(ī)ya- (one of the two words for '4th'), form their feminine in -ā and follow kathā [32]; caturtha- (the other word for '4th') and all higher ordinals form their feminine in -ī and follow nadī [33]. The masculine and neuter forms follow devaḥ [1] and phalam [17] respectively; for example,

	Masc.	Neut.	Fem.
'1st':	prathamaḥ [1]	prathamam [17]	prathamā [32]
'5th':	pañcamaḥ [1]	pañcamam [17]	pañcamī [33]

However, '1st', '2nd', and '3rd' may, in the singular dative, ablative, genitive, and locative of all genders, optionally take the endings shown for 'one' in Table 12. For example,

prathamāyai kanyāyai	'to the 1st daughter'
prathamasyai kanyāyai	" "
dvitīyāt putrāt	'from the 2nd son'
dvitīyasmāt putrāt	" "
tṛtīye gṛhe	'in the 3rd house'
tṛtīyasmin gṛhe	" "

When ordinals above 100 are expressed (optionally) with two discrete words (the first of which ends in -adhika or -uttara), both words are declined. For example,

aṣṭādhikaśatatame gṛhe	'in the 108th house'
aṣṭādhike śatatame gṛhe	" "

4. DEMONSTRATIVES

This limited subclass has only two members: 'this', cited as idam-; and 'that', cited as adas-. Each agrees in gender, number, and case with the noun it qualifies. The declensional patterns for these two words in the three genders are set out in Table 13. (The form amī (masculine nominative plural) has unusual sandhi behaviour; see page 4. For etad- 'this', see next section.)

5. PRONOUNS

The personal pronouns exhibit a 'dimension' that is not found in the other nominals but is shared with the verbs, namely *person*. The three persons of Sanskrit are traditionally listed (for several good reasons) in the reverse of the European order:

	Sing.	Dual	Plural
3rd person:	he/she/it	they two	they (more than two)
2nd person:	thou	you two	you " "
1st person:	I	we two	we " "

Gender is recognized throughout the 3rd person: 'they two' and 'they (more than two)' each have three forms for the genders, paralleling the singular 'he', 'she', and 'it'. The 3rd person pronoun agrees in gender with the noun to which it refers. Agreement in number and case applies throughout; however, the vocative is lacking. The full pattern for the personal pronouns is given in Table 14. (Saḥ 'he' has unusual sandhi behaviour; see page 5.) The hypothetical stem-forms traditionally adopted for citing the pronouns in the three persons are: 3rd: tad-; 2nd: yuṣmad-; 1st: asmad-.

In the 2nd and 1st persons there exists an incomplete set of 'enclitic' forms, also shown in Table 14. These enclitic forms are semantically equivalent to the longer common forms — for example, te = tava, naḥ = asmān; however, they may be substituted for them only in enclitic position, i.e. not at the beginning of a sentence or a metrical foot, and not before ca, vā, or eva.

Whereas the patterns for the 2nd and 1st person pronouns are unique, those for the 3rd person pronoun (tad-) in the three genders constitute a paradigm followed by a sizable group of words. Examples include etad- 'this', yad- 'which' (the relative pronoun), anya- 'other', itara- 'different', katara- 'which (of two)?', katama- 'which (of many)?', etc. Etad- 'this' is a derivative of tad-, and is the only member of this group that follows tad- in having the exceptional s (necessarily changed to ṣ) in the masculine and feminine nominative singular. It is semantically close to idam- (see previous page).

Corresponding to the set of forms for etad- 'this' there exists an incomplete set of 'substitute' forms, enam enau etc., also given in Table 14. These substitute forms may replace the corresponding forms of etad- itself whenever some form of etad- has already been used with similar reference earlier in the same sentence. In addition, these substitute forms may replace the corresponding forms of idam- under similar circumstances.

There is a further group of words which, while closely resembling tad-, differ from it in (a) substituting -am for -at in the neuter nominative/accusative singular, and (b) having vocative forms. This group is represented in Table 14 by sarva- 'all'. Other important members of the group include eka- 'one', ekatara- 'either', viśva- 'all', and ubhaya- 'both'. In addition, there exist several other words (most having directional meanings) which, while capable of being declined like devaḥ [1], phalam [17], and kathā [32], are also optionally declined like sarva- in the three genders. Examples are: adhara- 'lower', antara- 'inner', apara- 'other', avara- 'western', dakṣiṇa- 'southern', uttara- 'northern', para- 'later', pūrva- 'earlier', sva- 'own'. For example, 'in the southern forest' is either dakṣiṇe vane (following phalam [17]), or dakṣiṇasmin vane (following sarvam).

Another variety again is represented in the interrogative kim 'which?'. This important word follows tad- except in the neuter nominative/accusative singular where it has kim. No other examples of this particular pattern exist (except in the obvious derivatives kiṃ-cit, kiṃ-cana, etc.).

There are, then, under the heading of pronouns, three subtypes distinguished by their neuter nominative/accusative singular:

		Masc.	Neut.	Fem.
(a)	anya-:	anyaḥ	any*at*	anyā
(b)	sarva-:	sarvaḥ	sarv*am*	sarvā
(c)	kim-:	kaḥ	k*im*	kā

B. VERBS

The numerous conjugational forms assumed by the Sanskrit verb require the recognition of five 'dimensions': number, person, voice, mood, and tense. The variables on these dimensions are as follows:

(a) 3 numbers:	singular, dual, plural
(b) 3 persons:	third, second, first
(c) 3 voices:	active, middle, passive
(d) 3 moods:	indicative, optative, imperative
(e) 7 tenses:	present, imperfect, perfect, aorist, periphrastic future, simple future, conditional.

Of these five, number is found also in all the nominals, and person is found also in the pronouns. The remainder are unique to the verbs.

(a) *The three numbers*

A verb 'agrees' in number with its grammatical subject: there exists a set of singular, dual, and plural forms of the verb corresponding to, but formally distinct from, the three numbers seen in the nominals. For example,

Singular	Dual	Plural
śiṣyaḥ paṭh*ati* 'A student reads'	śiṣyau paṭh*ataḥ* 'Two students read'	śiṣyāḥ paṭh*anti* 'Students read'
sa nay*ati* 'He leads'	tau nay*ataḥ* 'They two lead'	te nay*anti* 'They lead'

The endings -ati, -ataḥ, and -anti are the characteristic endings for the singular, dual and plural numbers respectively, in the third person present indicative active of the most numerous class of verbs. Comparable sets of endings exist in the other persons, voices, moods, and tenses, as indicated below.

(b) *The three persons*

A verb agrees with its subject in person as well as in number. The intersection of the dimensions of number and person yields for each voice, mood, and tense of a verb a 3 × 3 pattern of forms; for example,

	Sing.	Dual	Plural
3rd:	nayati	nayataḥ	nayanti
2nd:	nayasi	nayathaḥ	nayatha
1st:	nayāmi	nayāvaḥ	nayāmaḥ

'He/she/it leads'	'They two lead'	'They lead'
'Thou leadest'	'You two lead'	'You (plur.) lead'
'I lead'	'We two lead'	'We lead'

(In memorizing, read horizontally: nayati nayataḥ nayanti; nayasi nayathaḥ nayatha; etc.) This pattern corresponds to the 3 × 3 pattern into which the nominative forms of the personal pronouns naturally fall (cf. pages 32 and 110-111):

	Sing.	Dual	Plural
3rd:	saḥ	tau	te
2nd:	tvam	yuvām	yūyam
1st:	aham	āvām	vayam

(Since the verb endings indicate person as well as number, the personal pronoun subject is often omitted; e.g., nayasi is understood as tvaṃ nayasi.)

(c) *The three voices*

Of the three voices, the active and passive have clearly distinct functions, resembling those of their counterparts in English. For example,

Active	Passive
devo nayati	devo nīyate
'The god leads'	'The god is led'

The middle voice is less clearly definable. Theoretically it is applicable when the action is performed for the benefit of the subject him- or herself rather than for the benefit of another. However, in practice this distinction is rarely discernible; in the classical language the middle form devo nayate means much the same as the active devo nayati. The choice between active and middle has come to be more a matter of conventional usage, so much so that in some verbs the middle form is rarely or never used, while in others it is the active that has fallen into disuse. Nevertheless, many verbs do retain the formal distinction between active and middle, thus exhibiting the full set of three voices.

The set of nine forms shown in (b) for the active voice has counterparts in the middle and passive voices, as shown:

Active:	nayati	nayataḥ	nayanti
	nayasi	nayathaḥ	nayatha
	nayāmi	nayāvaḥ	nayāmaḥ
Middle:	nayate	nayete	nayante
	nayase	nayethe	nayadhve
	naye	nayāvahe	nayāmahe
Passive:	nīyate	nīyete	nīyante
	nīyase	nīyethe	nīyadhve
	nīye	nīyāvahe	nīyāmahe

For example,

nayathaḥ	'You two lead'
nīyāmahe	'We are led'

It will be noted that the stem is identical in the active and middle, while the endings are identical in the middle and passive. That is, the middle voice forms can be thought of as combining the active stem (nay-) with the passive endings (-ate, -ete, -ante, etc.).

(d) *The three moods*

The moods serve to identify an utterance as

(i) a statement: *indicative mood;*
(ii) a mild exhortation or a hypothetical possibility: *optative mood;* or
(iii) a command, direct or indirect: *imperative mood.*

(The examples considered under (a), (b), and (c) above were all in the indicative mood.) For example,

(i)	Indicative:	nayati	'He leads'
		nayasi	'Thou leadest'
(ii)	Optative:	nayet	'He should lead'
		nayeḥ	'Thou shouldst lead'
(iii)	Imperative:	nayatu	'Let him lead!'
		naya	'Lead!'

The mood dimension intersects with the dimensions already considered, raising the number of forms from 27 to 81:

ACTIVE:

Indicative:	nayati	nayataḥ	nayanti
	nayasi	nayathaḥ	nayatha
	nayāmi	nayāvaḥ	nayāmaḥ
Optative:	nayet	nayetām	nayeyuḥ
	nayeḥ	nayetam	nayeta
	nayeyam	nayeva	nayema
Imperative:	nayatu	nayatām	nayantu
	naya	nayatam	nayata
	nayāni	nayāva	nayāma

MIDDLE:

Indicative:	nayate	nayete	nayante
	nayase	nayethe	nayadhve
	naye	nayāvahe	nayāmahe
Optative:	nayeta	nayeyātām	nayeran
	nayethāḥ	nayeyāthām	nayedhvam
	nayeya	nayevahi	nayemahi
Imperative:	nayatām	nayetām	nayantām
	nayasva	nayethām	nayadhvam
	nayai	nayāvahai	nayāmahai

PASSIVE:

Indicative:	nīyate	nīyete	nīyante
	nīyase	nīyethe	nīyadhve
	nīye	nīyāvahe	nīyāmahe
Optative:	nīyeta	nīyeyātām	nīyeran
	nīyethāḥ	nīyeyāthām	nīyedhvam
	nīyeya	nīyevahi	nīyemahi
Imperative:	nīyatām	nīyetām	nīyantām
	nīyasva	nīyethām	nīyadhvam
	nīyai	nīyāvahai	nīyāmahai

(e) *The seven tenses*

The tenses serve principally to indicate the time of the action or state relative to the time of speaking. Only three elementary time situations are in question, namely present, past, and future; a fourth, represented by the 'conditional' tense, may be regarded as a combination of future with past:

present	future
past	future-in-the-past
'He leads'	'He will lead'
'He led'	'He would lead'

These four correspond with the seven tenses as follows:

Time situation	*Tense*
present:	present
past:	imperfect perfect aorist
future:	periphrastic future simple future
future-in-the-past:	conditional

Subtle semantic distinctions among the different past tenses early became blurred, so that in the classical language the three are for most purposes interchangeable. The same is true of the two future tenses.

The examples considered above under (a) to (d) were all in the present tense: the pattern of 81 forms shown under (d) represents only the first of the seven tenses. However, it is not the case that each of the other six tenses has a comparable set of 81 forms. This is because each of the non-present tenses, with one partial exception, exists in only one of the three moods, namely the indicative. Each non-present tense is therefore represented by a set of just 27 forms — with the exception of the aorist, which in effect exists in the optative mood as well as the indicative. The intersection of tense with the other five dimensions therefore yields 270 forms in all. The complete pattern of 270 forms for the verb nayati is set out in Table 15.

The expression 'the verb nayati' used in the preceding sentence illustrates a convention that will be adopted henceforth when referring to different verbs: the third singular present indicative active (which, generally speaking, is the most commonly occurring of the 270 forms) will be adopted as the citation form — unless a verb does not exist in the active voice, in which case the corresponding middle-voice form will be adopted instead. Thus, to speak of 'the verb paṭhati' or 'the verb labhate' is equivalent to speaking of 'the verb *read*' or 'the verb *obtain*'. Verbs whose citation form ends in -ati (or -ate) will be referred to as '-ati verbs' or 'the -ati class'. Another terminological convention to be adopted henceforth is to refer (as most grammars do) to the aorist optative as 'the precative'. The aorist indicative can then simply be called 'the aorist'; indeed the word 'indicative' can be taken as understood in all references to the non-present tenses other than the precative.

When patterns comparable to that for nayati are drawn up for other verbs, it is found that the nayati pattern is not, in its totality, a paradigm. Rather, it is a composite of several smaller patterns, certain of which are paradigms with widespread applicability. Five such component paradigms can be recognized. They are obtained by dividing up the total pattern as in the following diagram.

	Active	*Middle*	*Passive*
Present Indicative:			
Present Optative:	1. Present/		
Present Imperative:	Imperfect		
Imperfect:			
Perfect:	2. Perfect		
Aorist:	3. Aorist		
Precative:	4. Precative		
Periphrastic future:	5. Periph. Future		
Simple future:			
Conditional:			

The entire passive section, as well as the simple future and conditional tenses are excluded from this subdivision into paradigms for reasons that will be evident from Table 15: the endings in the passive are, with a single exception (namely the 3rd singular aorist), identical with those of the corresponding forms in the middle voice; and similarly the endings in the simple future and conditional are identical with those of the corresponding forms in the present indicative and imperfect respectively. Consequently, all the forms of the passive and of the simple future and conditional are readily derivable provided one knows the appropriate stems. (Details on how to obtain this information and apply it are given later. For verbs outside the -ati class, the endings in the present/imperfect passive and in the simple future and conditional are as for the -ati class, i.e. they are invariably as shown in Table 15.)

The total verb pattern can thus be reduced to five component sections. These will now be considered in turn.

1. PRESENT AND IMPERFECT

[1] The -ati class (exemplified in the verb nayati 'lead')

The first section, covering the present and imperfect tenses, is reproduced as a discrete paradigm in Table 16 [1]. In it an unchanging stem is associated with a set of 72 different endings, and in the imperfect with a prefixed a- as well. This paradigm is followed by every -ati verb, with only the following exceptions:

(a) Verbs which do not exist in one or other of the two voices: for such verbs naturally only half of the paradigm is relevant.

(b) Verbs whose citation form begins with a vowel: in such verbs the initial vowel goes to the 2nd grade in the imperfect; e.g. icchati has, in the imperfect, aicchat etc. (not, as might have been expected, ecchat etc.).

If one knows the citation form of any -ati verb one can apply it to the nayati paradigm to obtain any other required form. For example, wishing to translate 'Let us protect!' into Sanskrit, and knowing that the citation form ('he protects') is rakṣati, one finds from the nayati paradigm the relevant ending -āma, and thus sets up the required form rakṣāma. Conversely, wishing to translate alabhe out of Sanskrit, one finds from the paradigm that a---e is for the imperfect middle, 1st person; then, on establishing the meaning of the citation form labhate, one arrives at the translation 'I attained'.

The citation forms of verbs may be sought in a dictionary or in Table 27. (For convenience, references to verbs listed in Table 27 will henceforth generally be accompanied by the serial numbers they bear in that table; e.g. 'nayati (189)'.) In Table 27 the citation form is the first form listed below the English gloss (opposite the heading 'Cit:'). The presence of an M following it (e.g. 'nayati M') indicates that the verb in question exists in the middle voice as well as in the active. The presence of an A (e.g. 'kampate A' (38)) indicates that the verb is normally used only in the middle voice, but does occasionally appear in the active also. Absence of M or A indicates that the verb lacks the middle or active voice respectively.

Of the verbs listed in Table 27, about 70 per cent are -ati verbs, a proportion which probably reflects accurately the situation in the language as a whole. However, there do exist seven other smaller classes of verbs, here referred to, after their citation forms, as -āti, -iti, -auti, -nāti, -noti, -Vti, and -Cti.

(V denotes here the vocalics e, ar, o and ā; C denotes any consonant.) Each of these classes has its own present/imperfect paradigm, distinct from the others yet sharing with them certain general features. The full set of eight present/imperfect paradigms is presented in Table 16.

Which of these eight paradigms any particular verb follows is usually self-evident from its citation form. For example, rauti ((293) in Table 27) is clearly an -auti verb, i.e. it follows paradigm [4] in Table 16. The few uncertain cases are clarified in Table 27 by including the paradigm number after the citation form; e.g. 'jāgarti [7]' (109 in Table 27). They are also pointed out in the following account, which summarizes the principal features of the seven remaining classes.

[2] The -āti class (exemplified in bhāti 'shine')

Members of this class all have just two syllables in their citation form; for example, pāti, yāti, khyāti, snāti. (Thus jānāti and jahāti are excluded; they belong to the -nāti and -Vti classes respectively.) All -āti verbs lack middle-voice forms. The endings in the -āti paradigm closely parallel those of the active section of the -ati paradigm; major differences do occur, however, in the imperative 2nd singular, and in the alternative form of the imperfect 3rd plural.

[3] The -iti class (e.g. svapiti 'sleep')

This very small class includes only svapiti, aniti, jakṣiti, and śvasiti. Another verb roditi 'cry' appears from its ending as if it would belong to this class; however, it in fact departs from the paradigm in several respects, so is treated as 'irregular' and conjugated in full in Table 17 [12]. All -iti verbs lack middle-voice forms.

[4] The -auti class (e.g. stauti 'praise')

This is another small class; it has only about a dozen members. Four of these, namely stauti, kauti, tauti, and rauti, can take the alternative endings (stavīti etc.) indicated in the footnote to the paradigm. Unlike the -ati, -āti, and -iti paradigms, in each of which one can identify an unchanging stem to which the different endings are attached, the -auti paradigm contains two different types of stem:

(a) 'strong' stems, formed with the 1st grade av before a following vowel, or with the 2nd grade au before a consonant (in one instance āv before a vowel); and

(b) 'weak' stems, formed with the zero-grade u before a consonant, or uv before a vowel.

For example, stauti has strong stems in **stauti**, **stavāni**, etc. and weak stems in **stutaḥ**, **stuvanti**, etc. This distinction of strong stems versus weak stems has been made clear in the paradigm by printing the 13 strong stems in *italics*.

The verb bravīti 'say' closely resembles the alternative version of the stauti paradigm (stavīti etc.), differing from it only in substituting ū for u before endings beginning in consonants. This verb may therefore be regarded as an irregular member of this class; it is given in full in Table 17 [13].

Two important features of the -auti class are shared also by the four remaining classes (the -nāti, -noti, -Vti, and -Cti classes), namely:

(a) the above-noted distinction of strong versus weak stems, with a fixed distribution of the two types (13 strong, 59 weak) within the total paradigm; and

(b) a nearly invariable set of 'standard endings'.

These two features are summarized in the following layout. (*Italics* indicate that the associated stem is in the strong form).

	Active:			Middle:		
Pres.	*-ti*	-taḥ	-anti	-te	-āte	-ate
Indic.	*-si*	-thaḥ	-tha	-se	-āthe	-dhve
	-mi	-vaḥ	-maḥ	-e	-vahe	-mahe
Opta-	-yāt	-yātām	-yuḥ	-īta	-īyātām	-īran
tive	-yāḥ	-yātam	-yāta	-īthāḥ	-īyāthām	-īdhvam
	-yām	-yāva	-yāma	-īya	-īvahi	-īmahi
Imper-	*-tu*	-tām	-antu	-tām	-ātām	-atām
ative	-hi	-tam	-ta	-sva	-āthām	-dhvam
	-āni	*-āva*	*-āma*	*-ai*	*-āvahai*	*-āmahai*
Imper-	*-t*	-tām	-an	-ta	-ātām	-ata
fect	*-ḥ*	-tam	-ta	-thāḥ	-āthām	-dhvam
	-am	-va	-ma	-i	-vahi	-mahi

It will be noted that, as regards the endings, the -āti and -iti paradigms also follow this pattern (in the active), but that the -ati paradigm departs from it at many points.

[5] The -nāti class (e.g. jānāti 'know')

Members of this class all have three syllables in their citation form. (Thus snāti is excluded; it belongs to the -āti class.) Two sub-classes must be recognized depending on whether the sound preceding the n in the citation form is

(a) a vowel, e.g. jānāti, krīṇāti; or

(b) a consonant, e.g. aśnāti, grathnāti.

In sub-class (a) the imperative active 2nd singular is formed with -nīhi, as shown in the paradigm; in sub-class (b) it is formed instead with -āna. For example,

(a) jānāti — jānīhi

(b) grathnāti — grathāna.

A distinction between strong and weak stems exists, exactly as in the -auti class. In the 13 strong stems the n is followed by ā; in the 59 weak stems it is followed by ī, except that where the ending (as shown in the above set of 'standard endings') begins with a vowel, the ī is dropped (e.g. jānanti).

[6] The -noti class (e.g. sunoti 'press')

Here again there are two sub-classes, depending on whether the sound preceding the n of the citation form is

(a) a vowel, e.g. sunoti, tanoti; or

(b) a consonant, e.g. āpnoti, rādhnoti.

Verbs in sub-class (b) exhibit the following slight departures from the given paradigm:

(i) The u shown in the paradigm as being optional (it is shown in parentheses) becomes obligatory; e.g. āpnuvaḥ versus sun(u)vaḥ.

(ii) The consonant cluster nv must be broken by insertion of u to give nuv; e.g. āpnuvanti versus sunvanti.

(iii) The imperative active 2nd singular takes -hi, as in the set of 'standard endings'; e.g. āpnuhi versus sunu.

The standard arrangement of strong and weak stem-forms is maintained. The strong stems have 1st-grade o/av, the weak have zero-grade u/(u)v.

[7] The -Vti class (e.g. juhoti 'sacrifice')

Here the letter V stands for any of following four vocalics: e, ar, o (all 1st-grade), and ā (2nd-grade); e.g. bibh*e*ti, pip*ar*ti, juh*o*ti, daridr*ā*ti.

The members of this class are so idiosyncratic that no one of them can be cited that is in every respect representative. The pattern for juhoti may be taken as the paradigm, provided one excepts its peculiarity of taking -dhi rather than -hi in the imperative 2nd singular. The principal characterizing features of this class are:

(i) the endings -ati, -atu, and -uḥ (rather than the usual -anti, -antu, and -an) in the active 3rd plural of the present indicative, present imperative, and imperfect respectively; and

(ii) the additional strong stem before -uḥ in the imperfect active 3rd plural: ajuhavuḥ. These two features apart, the pattern for juhoti parallels perfectly that for -noti verbs of sub-class (b), such as āpnoti.

The idiosyncracies of individual members of this class will now be summarized. As noted above, juhoti has -dhi rather than -hi in the imperative active 2nd singular: juhudhi. Verbs in -arti, e.g. piparti, bibharti, jāgarti, simplify the endings in the 3rd and 2nd singular of the imperfect to avoid word-final consonant clusters; e.g. the expected apipart and apiparḥ both become apipaḥ. Jihreti has ī/iy rather than i/y in the weak stems; e.g. jihreti jihrītaḥ jihriyati. Bibheti optionally has ī/iy rather than i/y in the weak stems; e.g. bibheti bibhĭ̄taḥ bibh(i)yati. (ĭ̄ denotes i or ī; similarly ă̄ and ŭ̄.)

There are several irregular members of this class, whose patterns are given in full in Table 17, namely: [14] eti 'go' (eti lacks middle-voice forms except when it bears the prefix adhi-) and [15] karoti 'do', both of which lack the features (i) and (ii) described above, and have other peculiarities as well; [16] dadhāti 'put' (followed also by dadāti 'give'); [17] jahāti 'abandon'; [18] mimīte 'measure' (followed also by jihīte 'go forth'); and [19] śete 'sleep', which has 1st-grade e/ay throughout the middle voice, and an inserted r in some forms.

[8-11] The -Cti class (e.g. yunakti 'join', dveṣṭi 'hate', vaṣṭi 'wish', ruṇaddhi 'obstruct').

This is probably the numerically largest class after the -ati class. The C denotes any consonant (though in practice only about a dozen different consonants occur in this position); and the combination -Cti is to be understood as including also -Cṭi and -Cdhi. The verbs piparti, bibharti, and jāgarti belong not to this class but to the -Vti class, ar being a first-grade vocalic.

The typical representative of this class is the verb yunakti [8]. As can be seen from its paradigm, the class departs from the standard set of endings in the following two respects:

(a) In the imperative active 2nd singular it has -dhi rather than -hi;

(b) In the imperfect 3rd and 2nd singular, the characteristic -t and -ḥ are dropped to avoid word-final consonant clusters. (However, some verbs instead preserve the ḥ of the imperfect 2nd singular while dropping the stem-final consonant.) The standard arrangement of strong and weak stems is preserved, with first-grade/zero-grade pairs such as bhinad-/bhind-, as-/s-, dveṣ-/dviṣ-, vaś-/uś-, and doh-/duh-.

Verbs in -Cti have much in common with nouns ending in consonants other than -ḥ or -n, such as marut [6] and vaṇik [7] (pages 20-21). For example, in the verb yunakti, just as in the noun vaṇik, the stem-final consonant appears in three variants:

(i) k before zero and voiceless consonants: ayuna*k*, yuna*k*ṣi, yuṅ*k*tha.
(ii) g before voiced stops: yuṅ*g*dhi, yuṅ*g*dhve.
(iii) j before vowels, semivowels, and nasals: yuna*j*āma, yuñ*j*anti, yuñ*j*mahe.

The difference between k and g is a matter of internal sandhi; that between these and j is a matter of consonant alternation. Just as consonant-ending nouns are best cited by stating their singular and plural forms in the nominative, for example, vaṇik—vaṇijaḥ, so -Cti verbs are best cited by stating their singular and plural forms in the 3rd person of the present indicative active, e.g. yunakti—yuñjanti, vetti—vidanti. This mode of citation has the advantage of simultaneously making clear three things:

(i) the consonant alternation: k—j, t—d, etc.;
(ii) the distinction of strong stem versus weak stem; and
(iii) the assimilation of any associated nasal: n → ñ etc.

In Table 27 the singular citation form of each -Cti verb (e.g. yunakti (277)) is given in the table proper, while its plural counterpart (e.g. yuñjanti) is given in a footnote.

The verb yunakti—yuñjanti illustrates the most common pair of alternating consonants found in regular -Cti verbs, namely k—j. There exist five other such pairs; the full list is as follows:

k—c:	rinakti—riñcanti	'leave'
k—j:	yunakti—yuñjanti	'join'
ṭ—ḍ:	iṭṭe—īḍate	'praise'
t—d:	vetti—vidanti	'know'
ṣ—j:	mārṣṭi—mṛjanti	'rub'
ṣ—ś:	vaṣṭi—uśanti	'wish'

Many -Cti verbs do not display such alternation, any changes in the stem-final consonant being purely a matter of internal sandhi; for example,

dveṣṭi—dviṣanti	'hate'
asti—santi	'be'
īrte—īrate	'move'

The situation is sometimes complicated by internal sandhi phenomena other than the simple voicing before voiced stops seen in yunakti. The most important cases are illustrated in the additional paradigms based on dveṣṭi—dviṣanti 'hate', vaṣṭi—uśanti 'wish', and ruṇaddhi—rundhanti 'obstruct'. The dveṣṭi paradigm [9] demonstrates that a stem-final ṣ changes to ṭ, ḍ, and k before zero, dh, and s respectively, and that it induces retroflexion in a following t, th, or dh. The vaṣṭi paradigm [10] (middle forms are lacking) resembles that for dveṣṭi, but with the further complication that ṣ alternates with ś. (This yields a total of four different values for C: ṣ, ś, ṭ, and ḍ.) The ruṇaddhi paradigm [11] shows how the aspiration and voicing that basically belong with the stem-final consonant, as seen in rundhanti, are transferred to the t or th of all endings that begin with those sounds. The citation form ruṇaddhi may, therefore, be thought of as derived by internal sandhi from ruṇadhti.

Irregular verbs of this class are numerous. The most important are given in Table 17, namely: [20] asti 'be', [21] āste 'sit', [22] śāsti 'instruct' (with the endings characteristic of the -Vti class), [23] hanti 'kill', [24] dogdhi 'milk' (cf. [11]), and [25] leḍhi 'lick'.

2. Perfect

The perfect tense is said to be strictly applicable only where the action referred to occurred in the remote past or was not personally witnessed by the speaker; however, in practice it is fairly freely interchanged with the other past tenses (the imperfect and the aorist).

There are two types of formation of the perfect. One type is characterized by a more or less obvious partial reduplication of the initial syllable; e.g. perfect jijīva 'lived' corresponding to present jīvati (112), ninãya 'led' (present nayati (189)), and āsa 'was' (present asti (11)). The other type involves a periphrastic construction comparable in form to English 'was saying' etc.; e.g. perfect kathayām āsa 'told' (present kathayati (37)), and arthayāṃ cakre 'asked for' (present arthayate (6)). With a few exceptions, any particular verb makes only one of these two types of perfect. The reduplicating perfect, numerically the more important of the two, will be described first.

(a) *Reduplicating perfect*

For the reduplicating perfect it is expedient to recognize eleven paradigms; see Table 18 [1] to [11]. These have much more in common with one another than do the various present/imperfect paradigms, being characterized by a single, nearly invariable set of endings, namely:

	Active			Middle		
3rd:	-a	-atuḥ	-uḥ	-e	-āte	-ire
2nd:	-(i)tha	-athuḥ	-a	-iṣe	-āthe	-idhve
1st:	-a	-iva	-ima	-e	-ivahe	-imahe

Departures from this pattern are found only in paradigms [8] and [9], both of which omit the vowel i from all endings except -ire; and in [11], where the active singular endings -a, -(i)tha, -a are replaced by -au, -ātha, -au respectively. The i of the active 2nd singular ending -(i)tha is obligatorily absent in [8] and [9], and is optional in [11]. In the remaining eight paradigms it is very inconsistent: in most verbs it is optional, but in a significant number it is obligatorily present. Under these circumstances no useful rules regarding its occurrence can be formulated.

The principal differences among the eleven paradigms have to do with the choice of vocalic grade in the vowel or vocalic group of the syllable immediately preceding the ending; e.g. jijīva (zero grade), viv*e*śa (1st grade), nin*ā*ya (2nd grade), nin*ā̆*ya (optionally either 1st or 2nd grade). In most of the paradigms there is a clear-cut contrast between 1st or 2nd grade in the three active singular forms and zero grade in the remaining fifteen forms. This distribution resembles that found in the indicative present and imperfect (p. 43). It is indicated in Table 18 by combined use of *italics* and asterisk, as in the following example.

Zero grade:	ninyuḥ
1st grade:	*ninayitha*
2nd grade:	*nināya**
1st or 2nd grade:	*ninăya*(*)

Departures from the above-noted pattern of distribution occur in [1], where all eighteen forms are in the same grade (all zero, all 1st, or all 2nd), and in [10] and [11], where the situation is obscured by exceptional treatment of the stem and/or the active singular endings.

In Table 27, opposite the heading 'Per:', the perfect of each verb is cited in the active 3rd singular, or, if no active form exists, in the middle 3rd singular. In the latter case, one conjugates on any paradigm except [8] (only for dadre and papre (158, 211)) and [9] (only for cucyuve and pupluve (104, 217)). In the former case, that of verbs having perfect active forms and therefore cited in the active in Table 27, one has to be able to identify which of the eleven paradigms any particular verb follows. This is sometimes very straightforward; for example, the perfect counterpart of gāyati 'sing' (84), given in Table 27 as jagau, clearly follows [11], since only that paradigm has the -au ending. More often, however, one has to examine the phonetic structure of the cited form in more detail.

To facilitate this process a 'key' is provided (Table 20). In the key the terms 'initial' and 'final' denote the first and last sound respectively of the cited form; and the term 'stem vocalic' denotes the vowel or vocalic group in the syllable preceding the ending, that is, the italicised segment in the following examples: nin*i*nda, bub*o*dha, cask*a*nda, sas*ar*ja, vav*ā*ra, tuṣṭ*āv*a, śiśr*āy*a, suṣ*vā*pa, viv*yā*dha, jagr*ā*ha. The key is so designed that possibly ambiguous instances such as taty*ā*ja pose no problem.

Regarding the distribution of verbs among the different paradigms there is, generally speaking, no correlation between the situation in the perfect and that in the present/imperfect. The only significant exception to this is that all verbs which follow the present/imperfect -āti paradigm, follow the perfect paradigm [11]; e.g. present khyāti, perfect cakhyau (69); present bhāti, perfect babhau (228).

There exist two major instances of irregular conjugation in the perfect, namely āha 'said' (13) and veda 'know' (338). The patterns for these two verbs are given as [12] and [13] in Table 19. (Āha is defective as well as irregular; and veda, though perfect in form, has present reference, i.e. 'know' rather than 'knew'.)

(b) *Periphrastic perfect*

This type of perfect is made by combining a nominal derivative of the verb with the appropriate perfect form of either asti 'be' (11) or karoti 'do' (45), i.e. either āsa or cakāra. (Rarely babhūva, perfect of bhavati 'become' (236) may be used instead.) In the active voice either āsa or (less often) cakāra is used; in the middle voice only cakre (the middle voice form of cakāra) is used. For example, the perfect counterpart of kṣālayati 'wash' ((60), active voice only) is kṣālayām āsa or kṣālayāṃ cakāra, while the perfect counterpart of īkṣate 'see' ((20), middle only) is īkṣāṃ cakre. (For the conjugation of cakāra, see Table 18 [8].) The example in Table 21, based on kalayati 'count' ((40), active and middle) may serve as the paradigm.

In Table 27 the convention is adopted of citing active-voice periphrastic perfects always with āsa, often abbreviated to ā, and middle-voice ones with cakre, always abbreviated to c. Thus the perfects of kathayati (active), edhate (middle), and kalayati (active and middle) appear as 'kathayām ā', 'edhāṃ c', and 'kalayām āsa/c' respectively (see page 156).

The periphrastic perfect is the type made by most verbs whose citation form ends in -ayati, by most whose citation form begins with a long vowel other than ā, and by a few others as well. Some verbs can take either the periphrastic or the reduplicating perfect. In the case of verbs whose citation form ends in -ayati, the nominal component of the periphrastic perfect is invariably formed by replacing -ati with -ām; e.g. corayati → corayām (101).

3. AORIST

The aorist tense is said to be strictly appropriate only for events which have occurred in the very recent past and/or which have present relevance; however, in practice it is fairly freely interchanged with the other past tenses (the imperfect and perfect).

Seven aorist paradigms may be recognized; see Table 22. With a few exceptions the endings are constant throughout:

	Active			Middle		
3rd:	-t	-tām	-an/-uḥ	-ta	-ātām	-a(n)ta
2nd:	-ḥ	-tam	-ta	-thāḥ	-āthām	-dhvam
1st:	-am	-va	-ma	-i	-vahi	-mahi

These endings are virtually identical with those of the imperfect as set out on page 43. The aorist further resembles the imperfect in having a prefixed a-. In a few verbs aorist and imperfect are actually identical in form; usually, however, the two tenses are formally distinct; for example:

			Imperf.	Aorist
sarati	'flow'	(392):	asarat	asarsit
siñcati	'sprinkle'	(386):	asiñcat	asicat
nayati	'lead'	(189):	anayat	anaiṣīt

Differences among the seven aorist paradigms relate mainly to: (a) the vowel and/or consonant(s) intervening between stem and ending; and (b) the distribution of the vocalic grades. The first of these two differences provides a simple means for recognizing, from the forms cited in Table 27, which aorist paradigm any particular verb follows. In Table 27, opposite the heading 'Aor:' the aorist is cited in the active 3rd singular, or if the verb does not exist in the active, in the middle 3rd singular. The key to recognizing the seven paradigms is as follows:

	Active	Middle
[1]	-at	-ata
[2]	-sat	-sata
[3]	-sīt	-sta
[4]	-Csīt	-Cta
[5]	-āsīt	
[6]	-īt	-iṣṭa
[7]	-āt	-ita

Here s includes its retroflex counterpart ṣ, C denotes any consonant other than s or ṣ, and the t in -Cta includes dh, ṭ, and ḍh. Thus, for example, the aorists given in Table 27 as 'arucat M' (294), 'alambiṣṭa' (305), and 'alabdha' (304) may be recognized as following paradigms [1] (active and middle), [6] (middle), and [4] (middle) respectively. The only exceptions are aorists in -aṃsīt (e.g. anaṃsīt (184)). These follow paradigm [5] in the active (but with aṃ instead of ā) and [3] in the middle; for example, active: anaṃsīt anaṃsiṣṭām etc.; middle: anaṃsta anaṃsātām etc. Ambiguity occasionally arises from the fact that some stems end in s or ṣ; e.g. amarṣīt 'forgot' (267) belongs to class [6] rather than class [3], its structure being a-marṣ-īt rather than a-mar-ṣīt. Such doubtful cases can usually be resolved by examining the corresponding present form (mṛṣyati) or, if this is not known, by taking into account the vocalic gradation. (Since ar is 1st grade, amarṣīt must be class [6]; see next paragraph.) The characteristic endings listed above can also serve as mnemonic labels for the seven classes: one can speak of the 'the -at class of aorists', 'the -sat class', and so on.

The distribution of the vocalic grades in each class follows the active/middle division. (It is shown in Table 22, using the same code as for the perfect; see page 49.) In the -at and -sat classes ([1] and [2]) there is no distinction of grade. In the -sīt class [3], the active forms are in 2nd grade and the middle in 1st grade. In the -Csīt class [4], the active forms are in 2nd grade and the middle forms are usually in zero grade; however, where the active has simple ā, the middle has *a* rather than the expected ø; e.g. active apākṣīt, middle ap*a*kta (cf. page 9). In the -īt class [6], it is usually the case that the active forms are in 1st grade for some verbs and in 2nd grade for others, while the middle forms are always in 1st grade; e.g. abodhīt abodhiṣṭa ((222), both 1st grade), alāvīt alaviṣṭa ((317), active 2nd grade, middle 1st grade). However, a few verbs have zero grade throughout, e.g. avijīt avijiṣṭa (337); and a very small number have 2nd grade throughout, e.g. ayācīt, ayāciṣṭa (276). In the case of verbs of this last type there could be doubt about how to conjugate; this problem is overcome in Table 27 by stating the middle 3rd singular forms of such verbs in footnotes. In the -āt class [7] the active always has ā, and the middle i; however, only three aorists of this class is fact have middle forms, namely adāt (146), adhāt (168), and asthāt (400).

In the aorist -Csīt class [4], internal sandhi effects may produce consonant alternation similar to that found in the present/imperfect -Cti class. Some vowel changes are also encountered; for example:

			Active	Middle
sṛjati	'emit'	(393):	asrākṣīt	asṛṣṭa
vasati	'dwell'	(329):	avātsīt	avāsta
ruṇaddhi	'hinder'	(297):	arautsīt	aruddha
dahati	'burn'	(145):	adhākṣīt	adagdha
vahati	'carry'	(332):	avākṣīt	avoḍha

Instances of this relatively rare phenomenon are indicated in Table 27 by citing the middle 3rd singular in footnotes.

The aorists of the verbs karoti 'do' (45) and bhavati 'become' (236) depart widely from the paradigms; they are therefore regarded as irregular and given in Table 23.

4. PRECATIVE

The precative (or benedictive) is recognized as 'a kind of aorist optative', though in fact it usually has present reference and therefore signifies much the same as the present optative. It is in any case very rare in Classical Sanskrit and is included here more for completeness than for practical usefulness.

The paired precative paradigms given in Table 24 serve for all verbs, since the endings are invariable. For most verbs the stem for the precative *active* forms is identical with that for the present indicative passive. The precative active 3rd singular can therefore be readily obtained by substituting -āt for -ate in the form shown opposite the heading 'Pas:' in Table 27. For example, for the verb vahati 'carry' (332) the passive is given as uhyate; the precative active 3rd singular is therefore uhyāt, from which one can then set up all nine active forms. A small number of verbs are exceptional in forming their precative active; these are indicated in the footnotes to the passives in Table 27; e.g. gāyati 'sing' (84) has passive gīyate, but forms precative active geyāt (with e rather than ī).

The precative *middle* 3rd singular is, with a few exceptions, obtained by substituting -īṣṭa for the ending -yati or -yate of the simple future (Table 27, 'Fut:'). For example, the verb vạhati (332) is shown as having simple future vakṣyati; its precative middle 3rd singular is therefore vakṣīṣṭa. The few exceptions to this principle are indicated in the footnotes to the simple future in Table 27.

5. Periphrastic Future

The periphrastic future is semantically indistinguishable from the simple future (Section 6, below), but is much less commonly used. Its middle-voice forms are particularly rare.

The conjugation of the periphrastic future is covered by the single paradigm set out in Table 25. The active (or middle) 3rd singular form, on which the paradigm is based, is not given directly in Table 27, but can be obtained from the infinitive (listed opposite 'Inf:') by replacing -um with -ā. For example, for nayati 'lead' (189) the infinitive is given as netum, whence the 3rd singular of the periphrastic future is netā; and rakṣati 'protect' (281), with infinitive rakṣitum, has periphrastic future rakṣitā. Occasionally the periphrastic future is not so simply related to the infinitive; e.g. kṣodum → kṣottā (63). Such instances are indicated in footnotes.

The -tā form that underlies the paradigm is in origin the agent noun corresponding to the verb, e.g., netā is literally 'leader'. The 3rd person forms in the paradigm are then actually the nominative singular, dual, and plural of the agent noun, as shown in noun paradigm [4] of Table 6 (netā). The 2nd and 1st person forms are based on the singular of the agent noun, this time followed by the present indicative forms of the verb asti 'be' (Table 17 [20]). For example, netāsmi, 'I will lead' is from netā asmi, literally 'I am a leader'.

This completes the account of the five sets of paradigms identified (on page 40) as the essential kernel of a description of the total declensional pattern for verbs (Table 15). It now remains to account for the rest of that pattern: first the simple future and conditional tenses in the active and middle voices, and then the passive voice in all tenses and moods.

6. Simple Future and Conditional

The declensional endings for the simple future and the conditional are identical with those for the present indicative and the imperfect respectively of -ati verbs. One is, therefore, able to set up the entire pattern for the simple future and conditional if one knows any one of the 36 declensional forms in those two tenses. In Table 27, opposite the heading 'Fut:' the 3rd singular active (or middle, but middle forms are rare) of the simple future is given. For example, for the verb tanoti 'stretch' (121) the entry is 'taniṣyati'; hence the patterns are:

Simple Future:	taniṣyati	taniṣyataḥ	taniṣyanti
	taniṣyasi	etc.	
Conditional:	ataniṣyat	ataniṣyatām	ataniṣyan
	ataniṣyaḥ	etc.	

(Compare the corresponding forms for nayati in Table 15.) The characteristic mark of the future tense is -sy- immediately before the declensional ending.

7. PASSIVE VOICE

In the present and imperfect the passive-voice endings are identical with the middle-voice endings of -ati class verbs, regardless of which class the verb follows in the active and middle voices. In Table 27, opposite the heading 'Pas:', is given the 3rd person singular of the present indicative passive for each verb listed. For example, for tanoti 'stretch' (121) the passive is given as tanyate; hence the present/imperfect passive section of the conjugational pattern for that verb is:

Present indicative:	tanyate	tanyete	etc.
Present optative:	tanyeta	tanyeyātām	etc.
Present imperative:	tanyatām	tanyetām	etc.
Imperfect:	atanyata	atanyetām	etc.

(Compare the corresponding forms for nayati, Table 15.)

In the perfect tense, the passive is identical in form with the middle; or (to put in another way) the middle forms may also be used with passive sense.

In the aorist, it is always possible, as in the perfect, to use middle forms with passive sense. However, many verbs have, in addition, a set of exclusively passive forms. Where this is the case, the first of the nine forms, i.e. the 3rd singular of the aorist passive, is given in Table 27 in a footnote to the aorist entry. For example, for pacati 'cook' (193) the aorist entry apākṣīt has the footnote 'Pas apāci'. Knowing this form, one can set up the entire aorist passive pattern because the endings of the remaining eight forms are always identical with those of the aorist middle of the -īt class (Table 22 [6]). For example, pacati, with aorist passive 3rd singular apāci, has the following set of forms:

apāci	apāciṣātām	apāciṣata
apāciṣṭhāḥ	apāciṣāthām	apāciḍhvam
apāciṣi	apāciṣvahi	apāciṣmahi

However, since it is always possible for aorist middle forms to be used with passive meaning, the above pattern may be replaced by apakta apakṣātām etc. (Table 22 [4]).

In the precative, periphrastic future, simple future, and conditional, it is again the case that middle voice forms may be used with passive sense, but that in many verbs there exist also sets of exclusively passive forms. The verbs for which there exist exclusively passive forms in these four tenses are those which have such forms in the aorist. The stem is identical with the 3rd singular of the aorist passive as cited in the footnotes to the aorist in Table 27, but (except in the conditional) without the initial a-; and the endings are identical with those of the corresponding middle voice forms. For example, for pacati (193), with aorist passive apāci, the stem for the passive in the precative, the two futures, and the conditional is pāci-; and hence the passive forms themselves are:

Precative:	pāciṣīṣṭa	pāciṣīyāstām	etc.
Periph. future:	pācitā	pācitārau	etc.
Simple future:	pāciṣyate	pāciṣyete	etc.
Conditional:	apāciṣyata	apāciṣyetām	etc.

(Compare the corresponding forms for nayati, Table 15.)

8. Secondary Conjugations

Three 'secondary conjugations' can be formed from most verbs: the causative, desiderative, and intensive. These will now be discussed, beginning with the most important, the causative.

(a) *Causative*

Usually it is the case that if the primary or original verb is intransitive, its causative derivative is transitive, and if the primary verb is transitive its causative is doubly transitive, i.e.

capable of taking two objects. This is illustrated in the following examples, based on rohati 'grow' (299), mriyate 'die' (262), and pacati 'cook' (193).

Primary verb	Causative derivative
vṛkṣo *rohati* 'The tree grows.'	rāmo vṛkṣaṃ *ropayati* 'Rāma causes the tree to grow.'
mṛgo *mriyate* 'The deer dies.'	rāmo mṛgaṃ *mārayati* 'Rāma kills the deer.'
dāsaḥ phalāni *pacati* 'The servant cooks the fruits.'	rāmo dāsaṃ phalāni *pācayati* 'Rāma gets the servant to cook the fruits.'

In Table 27, opposite the heading 'Cau:', the causative of each verb is given in the 3rd singular present indicative active (or middle, but middle-voice forms are rare). Causatives are all of the -ati class in the present/imperfect. In addition they are all characterized by the presence of -ay- before the ending; i.e. they appear in Table 27 with final -ayati. (Note, however, that some primary verbs already have final -ayati in their citation form, e.g. kathayati (37).)

Each causative is, like the primary verb from which it derives, capable, in principle at least, of conjugation in all tenses, moods, and voices. Thus, if the verb nayati 'lead' has the set of 270 forms shown in Table 15, its causative derivative nāyayati 'cause to lead' has a comparable set of 270 forms. It is not, however, necessary to list in Table 27 the passive, simple future, perfect, etc. of each causative, because most of those forms are predictable, there being considerable regularity in their structure vis-à-vis that of the cited causative form. This is illustrated in the following sample list, based on the verbs bodhati 'waken' (222), bhavati 'become'(236), and karoti 'do' (45).

Causative:	bodhayati	bhāvayati	kārayati
Caus. Passive:	bodhyate	bhāvyate .	kāryate
Caus. Future:	bodhayiṣyati	bhāvayiṣyati	kārayiṣyati
Caus. Perfect:	bodhayām āsa	bhāvayām āsa	kārayām āsa
Caus. Infinitive:	bodhayitum	bhāvayitum	kārayitum
Caus. Aorist:	abūbudhat	abībhavat	acīkərat

In this set only the aorist is exceptional. The passive, future, perfect, and infinitive of the causative are formed by substituting for -ayati the endings -yate, -ayiṣyati, -ayām āsa, and -ayitum respectively. (The causative precative active and middle are formed from the causative passive and causative simple future respectively as described earlier; and the causative periphrastic future is formed from the causative infinitive. The causative passive in tenses other than the present and imperfect is identical with the causative middle.)

The causative aorist is always of the -at type (Table 22 [1]). Its stem is formed with partial reduplication of the root syllable, and usually also some modification of the vowel. However, the rules governing this process are not readily generalizable; for this reason the most important causative aorists are given in Table 27, opposite the heading 'CAo:'

(b) *Desiderative*

This, the second of the three secondary conjugations, signifies a desire for the action or state expressed by the primary verb; for example, pipāsati 'he desires to drink' and pipaṭhiṣati 'he desires to read', as against simple pibati 'he drinks' (201) and paṭhati 'he reads' (195).

In Table 27 the desiderative is shown, opposite 'Des:', in the 3rd singular active or middle. All desideratives are of the -ati type in the present/imperfect; they are characterized by the presence of -s- or -iṣ- before the conjugational ending, and by partial reduplication of the root syllable.

Like the causative, the desiderative can yield a complete set of forms paralleling those of the primary verb. There is, however, even more regularity in the structure of the derivative forms; the following list, based on bodhati 'waken' (222), may therefore be taken as the model for all desideratives.

Desiderative:	bubodhiṣati M
Desid. Passive:	bubodhiṣyate
Desid. Future:	bubodhiṣiṣyati M
Desid. Perfect:	bubodhiṣām āsa/cakre
Desid. Infinitive:	bubodhiṣitum
Desid. Aorist:	abubodhiṣīt M

Here the only difference from the situation in the causative series is that the aorist stem is predictable and is conjugated according to the -īt type (middle in -iṣṭa, Table 22 [6]). However, apart from the first one, the various desiderative forms exemplified in the above list are rarely encountered in practice.

(c) *Intensive*

The intensive (or frequentative) signifies intensity or frequency of the action or state denoted by the primary verb; for example, rorudyate 'he weeps long and bitterly', as against simple roditi 'he weeps' (296).

There are two types of intensive, one having active and middle voice forms, the other having only middle forms. For example, nayati 'lead' (189) has intensives nenayīti (active/middle type) and nenīyate (exclusively middle type). The active/middle type is of extremely rare occurrence in the classical language; consequently no examples of it are given in Table 27, nor is its conjugation discussed here. The exclusively middle type is of rather more frequent occurrence. In Table 27 attested examples of it are given in footnotes to the desiderative.

In conjugation the middle voice intensive follows the middle voice section of the paradigm for -ati verbs in the present/imperfect; e.g. nenīyate nenīyete etc. Theoretically it can be conjugated in the other tenses as well, though actual occurrences are rare. The expected set of derivative forms is as in the following list, based on the verb bodhati:

Intensive:	bobudhyate
Int. Passive:	bobudhyate
Int. Future:	bobudhiṣyate
Int. Perfect:	bobudhāṃ cakre
Int. Infinitive:	bobudhitum
Int. Aorist:	abobudhiṣṭa

9. PARTICIPLES

Participles in Sanskrit exist in the three voices — active, middle, and passive, and in three of the tenses — present, perfect, and future. The intersection of these two dimensions would be expected to yield 3 × 3 = 9 forms. However, the actual number may be higher because there are, potentially at least, three different future passive participles and two perfect active participles; or it may be lower, because a verb which (according to Table 27) lacks active or middle forms in one or other of the three tenses in question will normally lack the corresponding participles.

The following two patterns display the sets of participles for two representative verbs, nayati 'lead' ((189) and Table 16 [1]) and dadhāti 'put' ((168) and Table 17 [16]).

	Active	*Middle*	*Passive*
Present:	nayant-	nayamāna-	nīyamāna-
Perfect:	ninīvas- nītavat-	ninyāna-	nīta-
Future:	neṣyant-	neṣyamāṇa-	netavya- ---- neya-
Present:	dadhat-	dadhāna-	dhīyamāna-
Perfect:	dadhivas- hitavat-	dadhāna-	hita-
Future:	dhāsyant-	dhāsyamāna-	dhātavya- dhānīya- dheya-

The participles are adjectives. In their manner of assuming gender forms and declining them, they behave as shown in Table 8. All of the middle and passive participles follow the pattern of priya- (Table 8, first line). Of the active forms, the present follows nayant-/yuñjant- or dadhat-, according as it ends in -ant- or -at-; the first of the two perfects follows either tenivas- or vidvas- according as it ends in -ivas- or -vas-, while the second follows dhīmat-; and the future follows nayant-.

A summary is now given of the manner whereby the stem-form of each participle can be obtained from the information contained in Tables 16-19 and 27.

(a) *Present active participle*

The stem-form of the present active participle is most simply obtained by deleting the final -i from the 3rd plural of the present indicative active. For example, rakṣati 'protect' (281), being an -ati verb, has present indicative active 3rd plural rakṣanti (Table 16 [1]), whence its present active participle is rakṣant-; and juhoti 'sacrifice' (424) has 3rd plural juhvati (Table 16 [7]), whence juhvat-.

As shown in Table 8 (yuñjant- and nayant-), present active participles in -ant- form their feminine either in -atī or in -antī. The -atī formation is followed by all verbs whose citation form does not end in -ati; e.g. sunvant- (from sunoti) → sunvatī. The -antī formation is followed by all verbs whose citation form ends in -ati or -āti; e.g. rakṣant- (from rakṣati) → rakṣantī. However, certain -ati verbs optionally (but rarely) also follow the -atī formation. These are identified in Table 27 by the presence of '6' at the right of the heading; e.g. '340 viś-6'. (The 6 indicates the traditional verb-class; see pages 64-65.) Thus viśant- → viśantī or viśatī. Verbs of the -āti class also may follow either formation; e.g. bhānt- → bhāntī or bhātī.

(b) *Present middle participle*

This is obtained from the 3rd plural of the present indicative middle as follows: The ending -ante is replaced by -amāna-; and the ending -ate is replaced by -āna-. For example, pacati 'çook' (193) has 3rd plural present indicative middle pacante, whence its present middle participle is pacamāna-; jihīte 'go forth' ((421, Table 17 [18], and page 45) has jihate, whence the participle is jihāna-; and bhinatti 'split' ((232) and Table 16 [8]) has bhindate, whence bhindāna-. However, āste (15) irregularly has āsīna-.

(c) *Present passive participle*

Here the -ate ending of the passive form given in Table 27 is replaced by -amāna-. For example, for the three verbs cited in (b) above, the passives are given as pacyate, hāyate, and bhidyate; so the present passive participles are pacyamāna-, hāyamāna-, and bhidyamāna- respectively.

(d) *Perfect active participle*

(i) The first of the two perfect active participles is most simply obtained by suffixing -s- to the 1st person dual of the perfect active (Table 18); however, if that form has -yiva (but not -iyiva), this is first changed to -īva. For example, tanoti stretch' (121) has perfect active 1st dual teniva (Table 18 [10]), whence its perfect active participle is tenivas-; jayati 'conquer' (110) has jigyiva (Table 18 [4]), whence jigīvas-; and karoti 'do' (45), has cakṛva (Table 18 [8]), whence cakṛvas-.

As a consequence of this, those verbs whose perfects follow [8] or [9] in Table 18, and those which fuse yi to give ī, form perfect active participles of the -vas type rather than of the -ivas type (-īvas is reckoned as of the former type), and therefore follow the vidvas- pattern (Table 8). All other verbs form present active participles of the -ivas type, and therefore follow tenivas- (Table 8).

(ii) The second of the two perfect active participles is formed by suffixing -vat- to the perfect passive participle, for which see (f) below. For example, nayati 'lead' (189), having perfect passive participle nīta-, makes, for its second perfect active participle, nītavat-. The gender forms follow dhīmat- (Table 8).

(e) *Perfect middle participle*

This is obtained from the 3rd singular of the perfect middle by replacing -e with -āna-. For example,
nayati: ninye → ninyāna-; karoti: cakre → cakrāṇa-.

(f) *Perfect passive participle*

This, the most widely used of all the participles, is given for each verb in Table 27, opposite the heading 'PPP:'. For example, nayati 'lead' (189) has perfect passive participle nīta-; and nahati 'bind' (186), has naddha-. The perfect passive participle of a causative is formed by substituting -ita- for -ayati; e.g. mārayati → mārita-. The PPP of a desiderative is formed by substituting -ita- for -ati or -ate; e.g. īpsati → īpsita-.

(g) *Future active participle*

This is formed from the simple future active, as given in Table 27, by replacing -ati with -ant-. For example, nayati (189) has future neṣyati, so makes its future active participle neṣyant-. The feminine is formed in -antī or (rarely) -atī.

(h) *Future middle participle*

This is formed from the simple future middle, as given in Table 27, by replacing -ate with -amāna-; e.g. labhate 'obtain' (304), which has future lapsyate or labhiṣyate, makes lapsyamāna- or labhiṣyamāṇa-.

(i) *Future passive participle*

There are three types of future passive participle, characterized by the endings -avya-, -nīya-, and -ya-. In principle all three types may be formed for any particular verb; however, in practice it is often the case that one or more of them are not actually attested.

The -avya- type is obtained by substituting -avya- for the ending -um of the infinitive as given in Table 27; however, since not all verbs customarily form this type of future passive participle, this method may be applied with confidence only where the infinitive entry in the table is followed by the letter F (for 'Future'). For example, nayati has for the infinitive 'netum F', indicating that it may form netavya-; but nindati 'blame' (188) has 'ninditum' with no F, indicating that the expected ninditavya- is not attested or rare, and hence that the -nīya- or -ya- form is to be preferred.

The remaining two types of future passive participle are given directly in Table 27 opposite the two headings 'FPP:'; e.g. for nindati both nindanīya- and nindya-; and for nayati only neya-.

10. NON-FINITE VERB-FORMS

Table 27 includes certain important verb-forms that are neither conjugated nor declined, namely the infinitive and the absolutive.

(a) *Infinitive*

The infinitive (listed opposite 'Inf:') has been mentioned already as a convenient source of the form of the periphrastic future and of the future passive participle in -avya-. The infinitive as given in Table 27 corresponds semantically to the simple primary form of the verb; for example, netum icchāmi 'I wish to lead' (189), gantuṃ śaknoti 'He is able to go' (72). There are also infinitives corresponding to the secondary conjugations. They are formed by substituting -itum for -ati in the causative and desiderative, and for -yate in the intensive (cf. pages 56-59). For example, mārayati → mārayitum 'to kill' (262).

(b) *Absolutive*

There are two forms of the absolutive. One, the form given in Table 27 opposite the heading 'Abs:', is used when no prefix is attached; for example, for nayati the form nītvā, meaning 'having led' (189). The other form, used when a prefix is attached, is not given in Table 27 because it can be obtained by deleting the final -te from the passive; e.g. for nayati, with passive nīyate, the form is -nīya, as in pariṇīya 'having led around, having married'. Occasionally, however, this second absolutive is not so simply related to the passive; such instances are indicated in footnotes to the passive.

11. Verbal Roots and the Ten Verb Classes

The Indian grammarians have long considered that the various existing forms of any particular verb are to be seen as derived from an underlying entity termed the root. For example, nayati, nīyate, neṣyati, anaiṣīt, etc., which are different voice and tense forms of the one verb 'lead' (189), as well as nominal derivatives like netā 'leader', are regarded as derived from 'the root nī'. Similarly, nauti, nūyate, noṣyati, anāvīt, etc. ('praise' (190)) are assigned to a root nu.

These roots, while having no real existence, do have a certain usefulness, particularly as mnemonic labels. In particular, they are used in dictionaries as headings under which all the associated verb forms are grouped. In recognition of this practice, and of the convenience of such a labelling device, the verb-forms in Table 27 are grouped under their roots as headings, which in their turn are ordered alphabetically. For example, the alphabetical sequence of the roots nind, nī, nu (188-190) has precedence over that of the verbs themselves, nindati, nayati, nauti.

As a very general rule, the root of a given verb may be obtained from the perfect passive participle by deleting the ending -ta, -ita, or -na, while making due allowance for internal sandhi effects. For example, nīta- → nī (189), rakṣita- → rakṣ (281), lagna- → lag (300), labdha- → labh (304). However, many unpredictable factors make this rule far from infallible: sometimes the vocalic is weakened: tolita- → tul; sometimes it is strengthened: gṛhīta- → grah; and sometimes there is disagreement among scholars as to what the root should be: the root of gāyati 'sing' (84) is variously given as gā and gai.

Knowing the root of a verb, one is in no position to set up the actually occurring verb forms. For example, the seemingly very similar roots tap, tam, taḍ, and tan correspond to the very diverse actual present indicative forms tapati, tāmyati, tāḍayati and tanoti respectively. The grammarians have dealt with this problem by recognizing a set of ten verb classes, reflecting the different ways in which the present indicative is related to the root. For example, class 8 is characterized by the ending -oti; the root of tanoti can then be given in the dictionary as 'tan-8'. Similarly, the root said to underlie nayati is given as 'nī-1', where class 1 is characterized by the -ati ending and strengthening of the root vocalic to 1st grade. The student is expected to get from nī to nayati by strengthening the vocalic (→ ne), adding the conjugational ending (→ ne-ati), and applying the appropriate internal sandhi rule (→ nayati).

In recognition of the above practice, each root heading in Table 27 is followed by a numeral denoting the verb class to which it is traditionally assigned. The correspondences between these and the eight present/imperfect classes recognized in Table 16 are as follows:

1, 4, 6, 10	=	-ati
2	=	-āti, -iti, -auti, -Cti
3	=	-Vti
5, 8	=	-oti
7	=	-Cti
9	=	-nāti

Regarding these, the only point to note here is that verbs labelled as belonging to class 6 are the ones which can form their present active participle feminine in either -antī or -atī (cf. page 61).

12. Using the Verb Tables

The tabulated information on verbs is presented in two very different forms: (a) declensional patterns, both paradigmatic and irregular (Tables 16-25); and (b) lists of the principal parts of a range of verbs (Table 27). These two are complementary: from Table 27 one obtains, for any particular verb, certain key forms, which one then 'feeds into' the appropriate conjugational paradigms to obtain the specific forms required; or one does the reverse of this. Table 27 also gives some key adjectival derivatives of verbs (the participles), which are to be fed into the appropriate declensional paradigms (Tables 6, 7). How this process operates has been indicated piecemeal in preceding sections; it will now be reviewed systematically. Attention is directed first to Table 27.

The heading to each list in Table 27 contains, from left to right, (a) the serial number (1 to 432) of the entry; (b) the verbal root as usually cited in Indian dictionaries and grammars; and (c) the number (1 to 10) of the verb class to which the verb is traditionally assigned on the basis of its conjugational pattern in the present/imperfect. Next below these is an English gloss, included principally for mnemonic purposes, it being often only a very incomplete guide to the meaning of the verb.

Then follow thirteen entries in a fixed sequence, to which an abbreviated key is provided in the three-letter headings (Cit, Pas, etc.) at the left-hand end of each row. Of these thirteen entries, the first eight (Cit to CAo) are finite verbal forms subject to conjugation for voice, mood, tense, etc.; the next two (Inf, Abs) are non-finite (i.e. uninflected) forms; and the last three (PPP and two FPPs) are adjectival derivatives capable of assuming gender-forms which are then subject to declension for number and case.

Some important forms not given in the lists are more or less readily derivable from the given forms; e.g., the periphrastic future can be obtained directly from the infinitive (-um → -ā). Others cannot be so derived and are therefore given in footnotes. The footnotes provide principally the following:

(1) Forms that cannot be inferred because (a) they are exceptions to the rules given earlier (and summarized in Table 27, see below), or (b) the needed source form is lacking. For example, for verb 110, footnote 7 states that the absolutive with prefix is -jitya (an exception to the rule: the passive jīyate would lead one to expect -jīya). And for verb 26, footnote 1 states that the absolutive with prefix is -uñchya, a fact not otherwise knowable since the passive is lacking.

(2) Unpredictable forms, in particular plural counterparts of citation forms of -Cti verbs. For example, for verb 27, footnote 2 indicates that the plural of unatti is undanti: knowing the pair unatti—undanti, one can then set up any form in the present/imperfect.

(3) Alternatives to forms given in the body of the table. For example, for verb 28, footnote 7 states that for the PPP, besides ubdha-, the forms ubhita- and umbhita- are also permitted. However, alternatives are not given for the rare desiderative and causative aorist.

(4) Middle-voice forms when these are not as expected given the cited active form. For example, for verb 163, footnote 2

states that the aorist active adyutat has as its middle-voice counterpart adyotiṣṭa (where one would otherwise have expected adyutata).

(5) The middle-voice intensive and the aorist passive in -i, which are footnoted to the desiderative and the aorist respectively.

The information derivable from Table 27 is summarized in Table 26. There each of the three-letter headings is followed by a specification of the form cited — but without redundant details such as '3rd singular' which is applicable to all the finite verb forms cited, 'indicative' which is applicable to all non-present forms, and 'active/middle' which is to be understood in all forms other than passives.

The sign ' ⇒ ' denotes 'may be fed into' and is followed by the relevant table and paradigm numbers; for example:

Fut: Simple future ⇒ Table 16 [1] Present Indicative

This signifies that the form cited in Table 27 opposite the heading 'Fut:' is the simple future (understood to be in the 3rd singular indicative active/middle), and that this form is to be fed into the Present Indicative section of Paradigm [1] of Table 16. (The first form in that paradigm is nayati; a simple future such as gamiṣyati is 'fed into' that paradigm by substituting gamiṣy- for nay- throughout.)

The sign ' → ' denotes 'may be transformed into', and is followed by a specification of the form that may be derived from the head form, together with (in parentheses) a formulaic statement of the mechanism of this transformation, or a reference to the page where that mechanism is described. For example, under 'Fut:' appears

→ Precative middle (-syati/-syate → -sīṣṭa)

This signifies that the form cited in Table 27 for the simple future yields the precative middle if one replaces -syati (or -syate) with -sīṣṭa.

The sign 'fn.:' signifies that the information mentioned to its right may (where relevant) be found in Table 27 in a footnote to the head entry. For example, 'fn.: Aorist passive in -i' appearing under 'Aor:' signifies that the aorist passive in -i is given (for those verbs which have such a form) in a footnote to the aorist entry in Table 27. Below such a 'fn.:' entry indented lines beginning with ' → ' are statements of how the form given in the footnote may be transformed to yield further forms. For example, the one immediately below 'fn.: Aorist passive in -i' states how the aorist passive may be transformed to yield the precative passive.

Where several different paradigms are given (to the right of ⇒), it will be necessary, in practice, to decide which is the appropriate one. In the present/imperfect this will usually be evident from the ending; for example, any verb whose citation form ends in -nāti must be fed into the -nāti paradigm, i.e. Table 16 [5]. In possibly confusing cases the appropriate paradigm number is added (in Table 27) after the cited form. In the reduplicating perfect, difficult cases can usually be resolved by using the key (Table 20). In the aorist the ending again provides a clear guide; see the list on p. 51. In the case of adjectival derivatives (i.e. participles) there are usually three paradigms listed, corresponding to the three genders. Where alternatives are offered (e.g. [15]/[16]), the criteria for making the choice will be found in the appropriate part of the section on participles (pages 59-63).

Translation out of Sanskrit involves a general reversal of the above process. For example, faced with a form namāmaḥ, one identifies the stem nam- with verb 184, 'bow' (Table 27), and the ending -āmaḥ with the 1st plural of the present indicative active (Table 16 [1]), yielding the translation 'we bow'. However, this process is often beset by various problems, and in recognition of this a set of three indexes (Tables 28-30) is provided. The use of these indexes will now be described.

13. Using the Indexes

One common problem in translating out of Sanskrit is difficulty in recognizing verb stems. For example, it is not immediately evident that pece is a form of the verb cited as pacati ('cook', 193 in Table 27), or that jihremi is considered to be derived from the root hrī ('blush', 429). To facilitate resolution of this problem is the main purpose of Table 28, 'Index to verb stems'. Table 28 lists alphabetically all the verb stems occurring in the present/imperfect, passive, future, causative, reduplicating perfect, and aorist of all the verbs covered in Table 27. Each listed stem is identified by the number (1 to 432) of the verb in

Table 27, together with the relevant heading: Cit, Pas, Fut, Cau, Per, or Aor. This enables ready identification of difficult forms.

For example, in the case of pece one looks up the stem pec- in Table 28, and finds it identified as '193 Per'. Then one turns to Table 27 to locate verb 193 (pac 'cook') and the row headed 'Per:' (papāca M). If further help is needed, one may also consult Tables 20 and 18 (on the reduplicating perfect) to complete the identification: pece is perfect middle, 3rd or 1st singular = 'he cooked' or 'I cooked'. In the case of jihremi, one looks up jihre- in Table 28, and finds '429 Cit'. Then one goes to Table 27 for verb 429 and 'Cit:' — and if necessary to Table 16 [7] (present/imperfect, verbs in -Vti) for the complete answer: jihremi is present indicative active, 1st singular = 'I blush, I am ashamed'.

Any doubt about what counts as the stem, e.g. whether one should be looking for jihre- or jihr-, poses no problem: both possibilities are often included, and in any case scanning the relevant section of Table 28 will quickly locate the required entry. Table 28 does not include the prefixed a- of the imperfect or conditional, a fact that has to be allowed for when looking up a given form. For example, given the form abibhet and finding no abibhe- in the table, one should try bibhe-. The identification '233 Cit', in which 'Cit' covers the entire present/imperfect paradigm, makes it clear that the given form (abibhet) is imperfect. On the other hand, Table 28 does include the prefixed a- of the aorist. For example, given the form abhaiṣīt, one does find abhai-, identified as '233 Aor'. As far as possible, all the existing stems in each tense are given. For example, in addition to pec- the table includes papāc-, papac-, and papak-, all identified as '193 Per'.

If identifying the conjugational form in question proves difficult, one can consult Table 29, 'Index to verb endings'. This table lists alphabetically all the regular conjugational endings occurring in the major tenses and moods: the present indicative, optative, and imperative, the imperfect, the reduplicating perfect, and the aorist. Each entry heading is followed by a five-part notation indicating:

(a) the table and section in which the given ending is exemplified — e.g. '16 [6]', signifing 'Table 16 paradigm [6]' (i.e. -noti verbs);

(b) the tense/mood: Ind, Opt, Imv, Imf, Per, Aor, signifying Present Indicative, Present Optative, Present Imperative, Imperfect, Reduplicating Perfect, or Aorist;

(c) the voice: Act, Mid, signifying Active or Middle;

(d) the person: 3, 2, 1, signifying third, second, or first;

(e) the grammatical number: sg, du, pl, indicating singular, dual, or plural.

For example, given the form nametam, one looks up the ending -etam and finds it notated as '16 [1] Opt Act 2 du', i.e. optative active 2nd dual, exemplified in Table 16 [1] (i.e. -ati verbs). It is often the case that a single ending occurs in the table more than once, each time with a different notation; for example, given the form namatām, and looking up the ending -atām, one finds eight possibilities listed. Of these, the ones indicating imperfect and aorist can be eliminated immediately, since namatām lacks the prefixed a-. Consideration of the stem nam- (identified, if necessary, using Tables 28 and 27) indicates an -ati verb (i.e. Table 16 [1]), whence the possibilities are further narrowed to those notated 16 [1]. That is, there are just two possible interpretations: imperative active 3rd dual, and imperative middle 3rd singular. Ready recognition of such ambiguities is a major benefit of using Table 29.

In fact, however, there is a further dimension to the ambiguity: namatām could also be a form of the present active participle. That possibility is covered in Table 30, 'Index to noun/adjective endings'. That table lists alphabetically all the declensional endings contained in Table 6, indicating for each of them the case and number in question, and the particular paradigm, [1] to [40], in which the ending is exemplified. For example, the ending -atām is identified as genitive plural and referred to Table 6, paradigms [12], [13], and [29]. In fact only [12] and [29] are found to be relevant: namatām could be the genitive plural of the present active participle, masculine or neuter.

Noun/adjective endings display no less ambiguity than verb endings. For example, the one adjectival form priye (ending -e) could represent any of the following nine possibilities: feminine vocative singular, masculine/neuter locative singular, and neuter/feminine nominative/accusative/vocative dual. Looking up the ending in Table 30 draws one's attention to all these possibilities, and helps in deciding which will yield the appropriate translation.

TABLES

Table 1. The speech-sounds classified on articulatory criteria

	voiceless			voiced							
open:	ḥ				h[1]	ṃ		a	ā		
velar:		k	kh	g	gh	ṅ					
palatal:	ś	c	ch	j	jh	ñ	y	i	ī	e	ai
retroflex:	ṣ	ṭ	ṭh	ḍ	ḍh	ṇ	r	ṛ	ṝ		
dental:	s	t	th	d	dh	n	l	ḷ			
labial:		p	ph	b	bh	m	v	u	ū	o	au

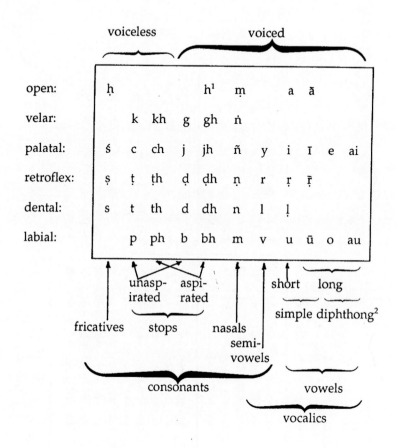

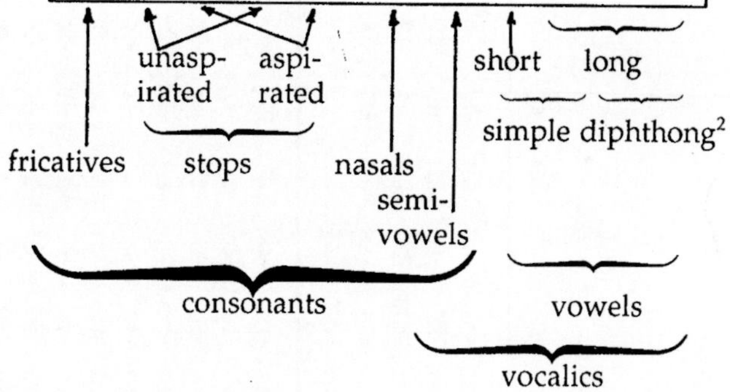

[1]Locating h (the voiced counterpart of ḥ) in the same column as gh, jh, etc. is a little artificial but proves expedient for purposes of description.

[2]Although e and o are both pure vowels (resembling the long vowels in English 'd*ai*ry' and 'st*o*ry' respectively), they are traditionally classified as diphthongs in recognition of their historical origins and their sandhi behaviour.

Table 2. Rules of external sandhi.

(i) Word-final consonants

-k	-ṭ	-t	-p	-ṅ	-m	-n	-aḥ	-āḥ	-iḥ[1]	-īḥ[2]	ø
-k	-ṭ	-t	-p	-ṅ	-ṃ	-n	-aḥ[3]	-āḥ[3]	-iḥ[3]	-īḥ[3]	k-, kh-, p-, ph-, ṣ-, s-
-k	-ṭ	-c*	-p	-ṅ	-ṃ	-ñ*	-aḥ[3]	-āḥ[3]	-iḥ[3]	-īḥ[3]	ś- [*ś- → ch-][4]
-k	-ṭ	-c	-p	-ṅ	-ṃ	-ṃś	-aś	-āś	-iś	-īś	c-, ch-
-k	-ṭ	-ṭ	-p	-ṅ	-ṃ	-ṃṣ	-aṣ	-āṣ	-iṣ	-īṣ	ṭ-, ṭh-
-k	-ṭ	-t	-p	-ṅ	-ṃ	-ṃs	-as	-ās	-is	-īs	t-, th-
-g	-ḍ	-d	-b	-ṅ	-ṃ	-n	-o	-ā	-ī	-ī	r-
-g	-ḍ	-d	-b	-ṅ	-ṃ	-n	-o	-ā	-ir	-īr	g-, gh-, d-, dh-, b-, bh-, y-, v-
-g	-ḍ	-j	-b	-ṅ	-ṃ	-ñ	-o	-ā	-ir	-īr	j-, jh-
-g	-ḍ	-ḍ	-b	-ṅ	-ṃ	-ṇ	-o	-ā	-ir	-īr	ḍ-, ḍh-
-g	-ḍ	-l̐	-b	-ṅ	-ṃ	-ṃ[5]	-o	-ā	-ir	-īr	l-
-g*	-ḍ*	-d*	-b*	-ṅ	-ṃ	-n	-o	-ā	-ir	-īr	h- [*h- → gh-, ḍh-, dh-, bh-]
-ṅ	-ṇ	-n	-m	-ṅ	-ṃ	-n	-o	-ā	-ir	-īr	n-, m-
-g	-ḍ	-d	-b	-ṅ[6]	-m	-n[6]	-o*	-ā	-ir	-īr	a- [*a- → ’-]
-g	-ḍ	-d	-b	-ṅ[6]	-m	-n[6]	-a	-ā	-ir	-īr	V-[7]

(ii) Word-final vowels

-a/-ā	-i/-ī	-u/-ū	-ṛ	-au	-ai	-e	-o	C-[8]
-ā-	-ya-	-va-	-ra-	-āva-	-ā a-	-e '-	-o '-	a-
-ā-	-yā-	-vā-	-rā-	-āvā-	-ā ā-	-a ā-	-a ā-	ā-
-e-	-ī-	-vi-	-ri-	-āvi-	-ā i-	-a i-	-a i-	i-
-e-	-ī-	-vī-	-rī-	-āvī-	-ā ī-	-a ī-	-a ī-	ī-
-o-	-yu-	-ū-	-ru-	-āvu-	-ā u-	-a u-	-a u-	u-
-o-	-yū-	-ū-	-rū-	-āvū-	-ā ū-	-a ū-	-a ū-	u-
-ar-	-yṛ-	-vṛ-	-ṝ-	-āvṛ-	-ā ṛ-	-a ṛ-	-a ṛ-	ṛ-
-ai-	-ye-	-ve-	-re-	-āve-	-ā e-	-a e-	-a e-	e-
-ai-	-yai-	-vai-	-rai-	-āvai-	-ā ai-	-a ai-	-a ai-	ai-
-au-	-yo-	-vo-	-ro-	-āvo-	-ā o-	-a o-	-a o-	o-
-au-	-yau-	-vau-	-rau-	-āvau-	-ā au-	-a au-	-a au-	au-

[1]Similarly -uḥ. [2]Similarly -ūḥ, -eḥ, -oḥ, -aiḥ, & -auḥ.

[3]-ḥ may optionally assimilate before ś-, ṣ-, or s-; e.g. -ḥ ś- → -ḥ ś- or → -ś ś-.

[4]After -n, ś- may remain unchanged; i.e. -n ś- → -ñ ch- or → -ñ ś-.

[5]Alternatively -n may change to -l̃ (a nasalized l) when followed by l-; i.e -n l- → -ṃ l- or → -l̃ l-.

[6]Word-final -n or -ṅ, if preceded by a short vowel, is doubled before a following vowel; e.g. -in e- → -inn e-.

[7]Here V denotes any vowel other than a.

[8]C denotes any consonant. When the preceding word ends in a short vowel, ch- → cch-.

Table 3. Ambiguous external sandhis.

Sandhi	→	Possible resolutions			
-g gh-	→	-k gh-	-k h-		
-ṅ n-	→	-ṅ n-	-k n-		
-ṅ m-	→	-ṅ m-	-k m-		
-c ch-	→	-t ch-	-t ś-		
-ṭ ṭ-	→	-ṭ ṭ-	-t ṭ-		
-ṭ ṭh-	→	-ṭ ṭh-	-t ṭh-		
-ḍ ḍ-	→	-ṭ ḍ-	-t ḍ-		
-ḍ ḍh	→	-ṭ ḍh-	-ṭ h-	-t ḍh-	
-d dh-	→	-t dh-	-t h-		
-n n-	→	-n n-	-t n-		
-n m-	→	-n m-	-t m-		
-b bh-	→	-p bh-	-p h-		
-m n-	→	-m n-	-p n-		
-m m-	→	-m m-	-p m-		
-a V-[1]	→	-aḥ V-	-e V-	-o V-	
-ā V-	→	-āḥ V-	-ai V-		
-ā C-[2]	→	-ā C-	-āḥ C-		
-ī r-	→	-ī r-	-īḥ r-	-iḥ r-	
-ū r-	→	-ū r-	-ūḥ r-	-uḥ r-	
-e[3] r-	→	-e r-	-eḥ r-		
-o C-[2]	→	-o C-	-aḥ C-		
-o ʼ-	→	-o a-	-aḥ a-		
-ar-	→	-a ṛ-	-ā ṛ-		
-ā-	→	-a a-	-a ā-	-ā a-	-ā ā-
-ī-	→	-i i-	-i ī-	-ī i-	-ī ī-
-ū-	→	-u u-	-u ū-	-ū u-	-ū ū-
-e-	→	-a i-	-a ī-	-ā i-	-ā ī-
-o-	→	-a u-	-a ū-	-ā u-	-ā ū-
-ai-	→	-a e-	-a ai-	-ā e-	-ā ai-
-au-	→	-a o-	-a au-	-ā o-	-ā au-

[1]Here V denotes any vowel.
[2]Here C denotes any *voiced* consonant.
[3]Similarly for o, ai, au.

Table 4. Rules of internal sandhi for retroflexion.

(i) Retroflexion of s:

> Within a word, s changes to ṣ if it is *followed* by any sound other than r, ṛ, or ṝ, and is *preceded* — either immediately or with *intervening* ḥ or ṃ — by k or r or any vowel other than a or ā.

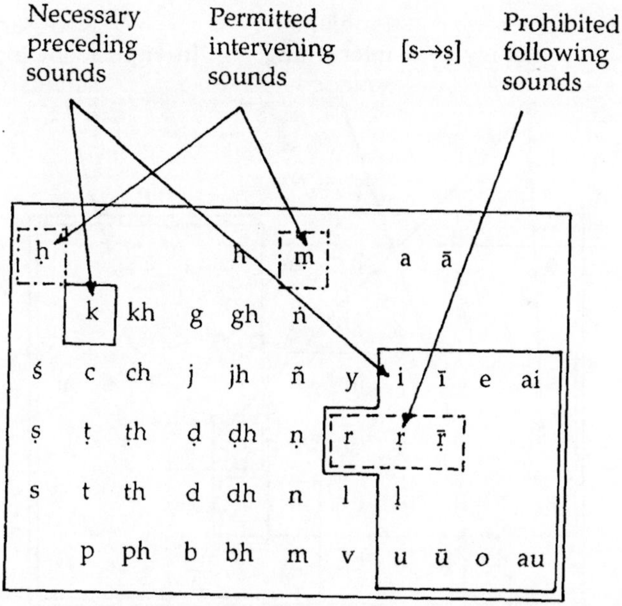

(ii) Retroflexion of n:

Within a word, n changes to ṇ if it is immediately *followed* by a vowel, n, m, y, or v, and is *preceded* at whatever distance by r, ṛ, ṝ, or ṣ, provided there is no *intervening* consonantal dental, retroflex, or palatal other than y.

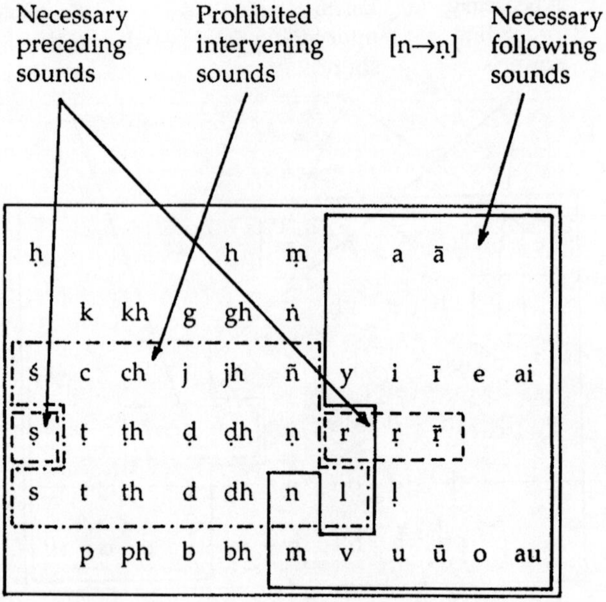

Table 5. Vocalic gradation series.

	Rules			*Examples*		
	0 ←	1 →	2	zero ←	1st →	2nd
open:	ø	a	ā	cakhnuḥ	kh*a*nanam	kh*ā*nayati
palatal:	i/ī	e	ai	n*ī*ta-	n*e*tum	an*ai*ṣīt
	y	ay	āy	nin*y*uḥ	n*ay*anam	n*āy*ayati
	i/ī	ya	yā	*i*ṣṭa-	*ya*janam	*yā*jayati
retroflex:	ṛ	--	--	m*ṛ*ta-	--	--
	r	ar	ār	mam*r*uḥ	m*ar*aṇam	m*ār*ayati
	ṛ	ra	rā	g*ṛ*hīta-	g*ra*haṇam	g*rā*hayati
dental:	ḷ	al	āl	k*ḷ*pta-	k*al*panam	k*āl*pa-
labial:	u/ū	o	au	śr*u*ta-	śr*o*tum	aśr*au*ṣīt
	v[1]	av	āv	śuśr*uv*uḥ	śr*av*aṇam	śr*āv*ayati
	u/ū	va	vā	*u*dita-	*va*danam	*vā*dayati

[1]The expected *v*, seen, for example, in zero-grade śṛṇ*v*e (versus 1st-grade śṛṇ*av*ai), is often replaced by *uv*, as in zero-grade śuśr*uv*uḥ.

Table 6. Declensional paradigms for nouns/adjectives.

(i) Masculine

[1]	**devaḥ**	devau	devāḥ
	devam	"	devān
	devena	devābhyām	devaiḥ
	devāya	"	devebhyaḥ
	devāt	"	"
	devasya	devayoḥ	devānām
	deve	"	deveṣu
	deva	devau	devāḥ
[2]	**muniḥ**	munī	munayaḥ
	munim	"	munīn
	muninā	munibhyām	munibhiḥ
	munaye	"	munibhyaḥ
	muneḥ	"	"
	"	munyoḥ	munīnām
	munau	"	muniṣu
	mune	munī	munayaḥ
[3]	**paśuḥ**	paśū	paśavaḥ
	paśum	"	paśūn
	paśunā	paśubhyām	paśubhiḥ
	paśave	"	paśubhyaḥ
	paśoḥ	"	"
	"	paśvoḥ	paśūnām
	paśau	"	paśuṣu
	paśo	paśū	paśavaḥ
[4]	**netā**	netārau	netāraḥ
	netāram	"	netṝn
	netrā	netṛbhyām	netṛbhiḥ
	netre	"	netṛbhyaḥ
	netuḥ	"	"
	"	netroḥ	netṝṇām
	netari	"	netṛṣu
	netaḥ	netārau	netāraḥ

[5]	**pitā**	pitarau	pitaraḥ
	pitaram	"	pitṝn
	pitrā	pitṛbhyām	pitṛbhiḥ
	pitre	"	pitṛbhyaḥ
	pituḥ	"	"
	"	pitroḥ	pitṝṇām
	pitari	"	pitṛṣu
	pitaḥ	pitarau	pitaraḥ
[6]	**marut**	marutau	marutaḥ
	marutam	"	"
	marutā	marudbhyām	marudbhiḥ
	marute	"	marudbhyaḥ
	marutaḥ	"	"
	"	marutoḥ	marutām
	maruti	"	marutsu
	marut	marutau	marutaḥ
[7]	**vaṇik**	vaṇijau	vaṇijaḥ
	vaṇijam	"	"
	vaṇijā	vaṇigbhyām	vaṇigbhiḥ
	vaṇije	"	vaṇigbhyaḥ
	vaṇijaḥ	"	"
	"	vaṇijoḥ	vaṇijām
	vaṇiji	"	vaṇikṣu
	vaṇik	vaṇijau	vaṇijaḥ
[8]	**vedhāḥ**	vedhasau	vedhasaḥ
	vedhasam	"	"
	vedhasā	vedhobhyām	vedhobhiḥ
	vedhase	"	vedhobhyaḥ
	vedhasaḥ	"	"
	"	vedhasoḥ	vedhasām
	vedhasi	"	vedhaḥsu
	vedhaḥ	vedhasau	vedhasaḥ

[9]	**ātmā**	ātmānau	ātmānaḥ
	ātmānam	"	ātmanaḥ
	ātmanā	ātmabhyām	ātmabhiḥ
	ātmane	"	ātmabhyaḥ
	ātmanaḥ	"	"
	"	ātmanoḥ	ātmanām
	ātmani	"	ātmasu
	ātman	ātmānau	ātmānaḥ

[10]	**rājā**	rājānau	rājānaḥ
	rājānam	"	rājñaḥ
	rājñā	rājabhyām	rājabhiḥ
	rājñe	"	rājabhyaḥ
	rājñaḥ	"	"
	"	rājñoḥ	rājñām
	rājñi[1]	"	rājasu
	rājan	rājānau	rājānaḥ

[11]	**hastī**	hastinau	hastinaḥ
	hastinam	"	"
	hastinā	hastibhyām	hastibhiḥ
	hastine	"	hastibhyaḥ
	hastinaḥ	"	"
	"	hastinoḥ	hastinām
	hastini	"	hastiṣu
	hastin	hastinau	hastinaḥ

[12]	**nayan**	nayantau	nayantaḥ
	nayantam	"	nayataḥ
	nayatā	nayadbhyām	nayadbhiḥ
	nayate	"	nayadbhyaḥ
	nayataḥ	"	"
	"	nayatoḥ	nayatām
	nayati	"	nayatsu
	nayan	nayantau	nayantaḥ

[1]or rājani

[13]	**dhīmān**	dhīmantau	dhīmantaḥ
	dhīmantam	"	dhīmataḥ
	dhīmatā	dhīmadbhyām	dhīmadbhiḥ
	dhīmate	"	dhīmadbhyaḥ
	dhīmataḥ	"	"
	"	dhīmatoḥ	dhīmatām
	dhīmati	"	dhīmatsu
	dhīman	dhīmantau	dhīmantaḥ
[14]	**śreyān**	śreyāṃsau	śreyāṃsaḥ
	śreyāṃsam	"	śreyasaḥ
	śreyasā	śreyobhyām	śreyobhiḥ
	śreyase	"	śreyobhyaḥ
	śreyasaḥ	"	"
	"	śreyasoḥ	śreyasām
	śreyasi	"	śreyaḥsu
	śreyan	śreyāṃsau	śreyāṃsaḥ
[15]	**tenivān**	tenivāṃsau	tenivāṃsaḥ
	tenivāṃsam	"	tenuṣaḥ
	tenuṣā	tenivadbhyām	tenivadbhiḥ
	tenuṣe	"	tenivadbhyaḥ
	tenuṣaḥ	"	"
	"	tenuṣoḥ	tenuṣām
	tenuṣi	"	tenivatsu
	tenivan	tenivāṃsau	tenivāṃsaḥ
[16]	**cakṛvān**	cakṛvāṃsau	cakṛvāṃsaḥ
	cakṛvāṃsam	"	cakruṣaḥ
	cakruṣā	cakṛvadbhyām	cakṛvadbhiḥ
	cakruṣe	"	cakṛvadbhyaḥ
	cakruṣaḥ	"	"
	"	cakruṣoḥ	cakruṣām
	cakruṣi	"	cakṛvatsu
	cakṛvan	cakṛvāṃsau	cakṛvāṃsaḥ

(ii) Neuter

[17]	**phalam**	phale	phalāni
	"	"	"
	phalena	phalābhyām	phalaiḥ
	phalāya	"	phalebhyaḥ
	phalāt	"	"
	phalasya	phalayoḥ	phalānām
	phale	"	phaleṣu
	phala	phale	phalāni

[18]	**vāri**	vāriṇī	vārīṇi
	"	"	"
	vāriṇā	vāribhyām	vāribhiḥ
	vāriṇe	"	vāribhyaḥ
	vāriṇaḥ	"	"
	"	vāriṇoḥ	vārīṇām
	vāriṇi	"	vāriṣu
	vāri/vāre	vāriṇī	vārīṇi

[19]	**madhu**	madhunī	madhūni
	"	"	"
	madhunā	madhubhyām	madhubhiḥ
	madhune	"	madhubhyaḥ
	madhunaḥ	"	"
	"	madhunoḥ	madhūnām
	madhuni	"	madhuṣu
	madhu/ madho	madhunī	madhūni

[20]	**dhātṛ**	dhātṛṇī	dhātṝṇi
	"	"	"
	dhātṛṇā	dhātṛbhyām	dhātṛbhiḥ
	dhātṛṇe	"	dhātṛbhyaḥ
	dhātṛṇaḥ	"	"
	"	dhātṛṇoḥ	dhātṝṇām
	dhātṛṇi	"	dhātṛṣu
	dhātṛ/ dhātaḥ	dhātṛṇī	dhātṝṇi

[21]	**jagat**	jagatī	jaganti
	"	"	"
	jagatā	jagadbhyām	jagadbhiḥ
	jagate	"	jagadbhyaḥ
	jagataḥ	"	"
	"	jagatoḥ	jagatām
	jagati	"	jagatsu
	jagat	jagatī	jaganti
[22]	**asṛk**	asṛjī	asṛñji
	"	"	"
	asṛjā	asṛgbhyām	asṛgbhiḥ
	asṛje	"	asṛgbhyaḥ
	asṛjaḥ	"	"
	"	asṛjoḥ	asṛjām
	asṛji	"	asṛkṣu
	asṛk	asṛjī	asṛñji
[23]	**manaḥ**	manasī	manāṃsi
	"	"	"
	manasā	manobhyām	manobhiḥ
	manase	"	manobhyaḥ
	manasaḥ	"	"
	"	manasoḥ	manasām
	manasi	"	manaḥsu
	manaḥ	manasī	manāṃsi
[24]	**haviḥ**	haviṣī	havīṃṣi
	"	"	"
	haviṣā	havirbhyām	havirbhiḥ
	haviṣe	"	havirbhyaḥ
	haviṣaḥ	"	"
	"	haviṣoḥ	haviṣām
	haviṣi	"	haviḥṣu
	haviḥ	haviṣī	havīṃṣi

[25]	**āyuḥ**	āyuṣī	āyūṃṣi
	"	"	"
	āyuṣā	āyurbhyām	āyurbhiḥ
	āyuṣe	"	āyurbhyaḥ
	āyuṣaḥ	"	"
	"	āyuṣoḥ	āyuṣām
	āyuṣi	"	āyuḥṣu
	āyuḥ	āyuṣī	āyūṃṣi

[26]	**karma**	karmaṇī	karmāṇi
	"	"	"
	karmaṇā	karmabhyām	karmabhiḥ
	karmaṇe	"	karmabhyaḥ
	karmaṇaḥ	"	"
	"	karmaṇoḥ	karmaṇām
	karmaṇi	"	karmasu
	karma(n)	karmaṇī	karmāṇi

[27]	**nāma**	nām(a)nī	nāmāni
	"	"	"
	nāmnā	nāmabhyām	nāmabhiḥ
	nāmne	"	nāmabhyaḥ
	nāmnaḥ	"	"
	"	nāmnoḥ	nāmnām
	nām(a)ni	"	nāmasu
	nāma(n)	nām(a)nī	nāmāni

[28]	**bali**	balinī	balīni
	"	"	"
	balinā	balibhyām	balibhiḥ
	baline	"	balibhyaḥ
	balinaḥ	"	"
	"	balinoḥ	balinām
	balini	"	baliṣu
	bali(n)	balinī	balīni

[29]	**nayat**	nayantī	nayanti
	"	"	"
	nayatā	nayadbhyām	nayadbhiḥ
	nayate	"	nayadbhyaḥ
	nayataḥ	"	"
	"	nayatoḥ	nayatām
	nayati	"	nayatsu
	nayat	nayantī	nayanti

[30]	**tenivat**	tenuṣī	tenivāṃsi
	"	"	"
	tenuṣā	tenivadbhyām	tenivadbhiḥ
	tenuṣe	"	tenivadbhyaḥ
	tenuṣaḥ	"	"
	"	tenuṣoḥ	tenuṣām
	tenuṣi	"	tenivatsu
	tenivat	tenuṣī	tenivāṃsi

[31]	**cakṛvat**	cakruṣī	cakṛvāṃsi
	"	"	"
	cakruṣā	cakṛvadbhyām	cakṛvadbhiḥ
	cakruṣe	"	cakṛvadbhyaḥ
	cakruṣaḥ	"	"
	"	cakruṣoḥ	cakruṣām
	cakruṣi	"	cakṛvatsu
	cakṛvat	cakruṣī	cakṛvāṃsi

(iii) Feminine

[32]	**kathā**	kathe	kathāḥ
	kathām	"	"
	kathayā	kathābhyām	kathābhiḥ
	kathāyai	"	kathābhyaḥ
	kathāyāḥ	"	"
	"	kathayoḥ	kathānām
	kathāyām	"	kathāsu
	kathe	**kathe**	kathāḥ

[33]	**nadī**	nadyau	nadyaḥ
	nadīm	"	nadīḥ
	nadyā	nadībhyām	nadībhiḥ
	nadyai	"	nadībhyaḥ
	nadyāḥ	"	"
	"	nadyoḥ	nadīnām
	nadyām	"	nadīṣu
	nadi	nadyau	nadyaḥ

[34]	**dhīḥ**	dhiyau	dhiyaḥ
	dhiyam	"	"
	dhiyā	dhībhyām	dhībhiḥ
	dhiyai/-ye	"	dhībhyaḥ
	dhiyā̆ḥ	"	"
	"	dhiyoḥ	dhīnām/dhiyām
	dhiyām/-yi	"	dhīṣu
	dhīḥ	dhiyau	dhiyaḥ

[35]	**matiḥ**	matī	matayaḥ
	matim	"	matīḥ
	matyā	matibhyām	matibhiḥ
	matyai[1]	"	matibhyaḥ
	matyāḥ/-teḥ	"	"
	"	matyoḥ	matīnām
	matyām/-tau	"	matiṣu
	mate	matī	matayaḥ

[36]	**vadhūḥ**	vadhvau	vadhvaḥ
	vadhūm	"	vadhūḥ
	vadhvā	vadhūbhyām	vadhūbhiḥ
	vadhvai	"	vadhūbhyaḥ
	vadhvāḥ	"	"
	"	vadhvoḥ	vadhūnām
	vadhvām	"	vadhūṣu
	vadhu	vadhvau	vadhvaḥ

[1]or mataye

[37]	**bhūḥ**	bhuvau	bhuvaḥ
	bhuvam	"	"
	bhuvā	bhūbhyām	bhūbhiḥ
	bhuvai/-ve	"	bhūbhyaḥ
	bhuvā̆ḥ	"	"
	"	bhuvoḥ	bhūnām/bhuvām
	bhuvām/-vi	"	bhūṣu
	bhūḥ	bhuvau	bhuvaḥ

[38]	**dhenuḥ**	dhenū	dhenavaḥ
	dhenum	"	dhenūḥ
	dhenvā	dhenubhyām	dhenubhiḥ
	dhenvai[1]	"	dhenubhyaḥ
	dhenvāḥ[2]	"	"
	"	dhenvoḥ	dhenūnām
	dhenvām[3]	"	dhenuṣu
	dheno	dhenū	dhenavaḥ

[39]	**nauḥ**	nāvau	nāvaḥ
	nāvam	"	"
	nāvā	naubhyām	naubhiḥ
	nāve	"	naubhyaḥ
	nāvaḥ	"	"
	"	nāvoḥ	nāvām
	nāvi	"	nauṣu
	nauḥ	nāvau	nāvaḥ

[40]	**mātā**	mātarau	mātaraḥ
	mātaram	"	mātṝḥ
	mātrā	mātṛbhyām	mātṛbhiḥ
	mātre	"	mātṛbhyaḥ
	mātuḥ	"	"
	"	mātroḥ	mātṝṇām
	mātari	"	mātṛṣu
	mātaḥ	mātarau	mātaraḥ

[1]or dhenave [2]or dhenoḥ [3]or dhenau

Table 7. Irregular declensions of nouns/adjectives.

(i) Masculine

[41]	**viśvapāḥ**	viśvapau	viśvapāḥ
	viśvapām	"	viśvapaḥ
	viśvapā	viśvapābhyām	viśvapābhiḥ
	viśvape	"	viśvapābhyaḥ
	viśvapaḥ	"	"
	"	viśvapoḥ	viśvapām
	viśvapi	"	viśvapāsu
	viśvapāḥ	viśvapau	viśvapāḥ
[42]	**yavakrīḥ**	yavakriyau	yavakriyaḥ
	yavakriyam	"	"
	yavakriyā	yavakrībhyām	yavakrībhiḥ
	yavakriye	"	yavakrībhyaḥ
	yavakriyaḥ	"	"
	"	yavakriyoḥ	yavakriyām
	yavakriyi	"	yavakrīṣu
	yavakrīḥ	yavakriyau	yavakriyaḥ
[43]	**senānīḥ**	senānyau	senānyaḥ
	senānyam	"	"
	senānyā	senānībhyām	senānībhiḥ
	senānye	"	senānībhyaḥ
	senānyaḥ	"	"
	"	senānyoḥ	senānyām
	senānyām	"	senānīṣu
	senānīḥ	senānyau	senānyaḥ
[44]	**rāḥ**	rāyau	rāyaḥ
	rāyam	"	"
	rāyā	rābhyām	rābhiḥ
	rāye	"	rābhyaḥ
	rāyaḥ	"	"
	"	rāyoḥ	rāyām
	rāyi	"	rāsu
	rāḥ	rāyau	rāyaḥ

[45]	**sakhā**	sakhāyau	sakhāyaḥ
	sakhāyam	"	sakhīn
	sakhyā	sakhibhyām	sakhibhiḥ
	sakhye	"	sakhibhyaḥ
	sakhyuḥ	"	"
	"	sakhyoḥ	sakhīnām
	sakhyau	"	sakhiṣu
	sakhe	sakhāyau	sakhāyaḥ
[46]	**patiḥ**	patī	patayaḥ
	patim	"	patīn
	patyā	patibhyām	patibhiḥ
	patye	"	patibhyaḥ
	patyuḥ	"	"
	"	patyoḥ	patīnām
	patyau	"	patiṣu
	pate	patī	patayaḥ
[47]	**pāt**	pādau	pādaḥ
	pādam	"	padaḥ
	padā	padbhyām	padbhiḥ
	pade	"	padbhyaḥ
	padaḥ	"	"
	"	padoḥ	padām
	padi	"	patsu
	pāt	pādau	pādaḥ
[48]	**dvipāt**	dvipādau	dvipādaḥ
	dvipādam	"	dvipadaḥ
	dvipadā	dvipādbhyām	dvipādbhiḥ
	dvipade	"	dvipādbhyaḥ
	dvipadaḥ	"	"
	"	dvipadoḥ	dvipadām
	dvipadi	"	dvipatsu
	dvipāt	dvipādau	dvipādaḥ

[49]	**anaḍvān**	anaḍvāhau	anaḍvāhaḥ
	anaḍvāham	"	anaḍuhaḥ
	anaḍuhā	anaḍudbhyām	anaḍudbhiḥ
	anaḍuhe	"	anaḍudbhyaḥ
	anaḍuhaḥ	"	"
	"	anaḍuhoḥ	anaḍuhām
	anaḍuhi	"	anaḍutsu
	anaḍvan	anaḍvāhau	anaḍvāhaḥ

[50]	**prāṅ**	prāñcau	prāñcaḥ
	prāñcam	"	prācaḥ
	prācā	prāgbhyām	prāgbhiḥ
	prāce	"	prāgbhyaḥ
	prācaḥ	"	"
	"	prācoḥ	prācām
	prāci	"	prākṣu
	prāṅ	prāñcau	prāñcaḥ

[51]	**pratyaṅ**	pratyañcau	pratyañcaḥ
	pratyañcam	"	pratīcaḥ
	pratīcā	pratyagbhyām	pratyagbhiḥ
	pratīce	"	pratyagbhyaḥ
	pratīcaḥ	"	"
	"	pratīcoḥ	pratīcām
	pratīci	"	pratyakṣu
	pratyaṅ	pratyañcau	pratyañcaḥ

[52]	**udaṅ**	udañcau	udañcaḥ
	udañcam	"	udīcaḥ
	udīcā	udagbhyām	udagbhiḥ
	udīce	"	udagbhyaḥ
	udīcaḥ	"	"
	"	udīcoḥ	udīcām
	udīci	"	udakṣu
	udaṅ	udañcau	udañcaḥ

[53]	**anvaṅ**	anvañcau	anvañcaḥ
	anvañcam	"	anūcaḥ
	anūcā	anvagbhyām	anvagbhiḥ
	anūce	"	anvagbhyaḥ
	anūcaḥ	"	"
	"	anūcoḥ	anūcām
	anūci	"	anvakṣu
	anvaṅ	anvañcau	anvañcaḥ

[54]	**tiryaṅ**	tiryañcau	tiryañcaḥ
	tiryañcam	"	tiraścaḥ
	tiraścā	tiryagbhyām	tiryagbhiḥ
	tiraśce	"	tiryagbhyaḥ
	tiraścaḥ	"	"
	"	tiraścoḥ	tiraścām
	tiraści	"	tiryakṣu
	tiryaṅ	tiryañcau	tiryañcaḥ

[55]	**pumān**	pumāṃsau	pumāṃsaḥ
	pumāṃsam	"	puṃsaḥ
	puṃsā	pumbhyām	pumbhiḥ
	puṃse	"	pumbhyaḥ
	puṃsaḥ	"	"
	"	puṃsoḥ	puṃsām
	puṃsi	"	puṃsu
	puman	pumāṃsau	pumāṃsaḥ

[56]	**panthāḥ**	panthānau	panthānaḥ
	panthānam	"	pathaḥ
	pathā	pathibhyām	pathibhiḥ
	pathe	"	pathibhyaḥ
	pathaḥ	"	"
	"	pathoḥ	pathām
	pathi	"	pathiṣu
	panthāḥ	panthānau	panthānaḥ

[57]	**pūṣā**	pūṣaṇau	pūṣaṇaḥ
	pūṣaṇam	"	pūṣṇaḥ
	pūṣṇā	pūṣabhyām	pūṣabhiḥ
	pūṣṇe	"	pūṣabhyaḥ
	pūṣṇaḥ	"	"
	"	pūṣṇoḥ	pūṣṇām
	pūṣṇi	"	pūṣasu
	pūṣan	pūṣaṇau	pūṣaṇaḥ

[58]	**gohā**	gohanau	gohanaḥ
	gohanam	"	goghnaḥ
	goghnā	gohabhyām	gohabhiḥ
	goghne	"	gohabhyaḥ
	goghnaḥ	"	"
	"	goghnoḥ	goghnām
	goghni[1]	"	gohasu
	gohan	gohanau	gohanaḥ

[59]	**śvā**	śvānau	śvānaḥ
	śvānam	"	śunaḥ
	śunā	śvabhyām	śvabhiḥ
	śune	"	śvabhyaḥ
	śunaḥ	"	"
	"	śunoḥ	śunām
	śuni	"	śvasu
	śvan	śvānau	śvānaḥ

[60]	**yuvā**	yuvānau	yuvānaḥ
	yuvānam	"	yūnaḥ
	yūnā	yuvabhyām	yuvabhiḥ
	yūne	"	yuvabhyaḥ
	yūnaḥ	"	"
	"	yūnoḥ	yūnām
	yūni	"	yuvasu
	yuvan	yuvānau	yuvānaḥ

[1]or gohani

[61]	**maghavā**	maghavānau	maghavānaḥ
	maghavānam	"	maghonaḥ
	maghonā	maghavabhyām	maghavabhiḥ
	maghone	"	maghavabhyaḥ
	maghonaḥ	"	"
	"	maghonoḥ	maghonām
	maghoni	"	maghavasu
	maghavan	maghavānau	maghavānaḥ

[62]	**mahān**	mahāntau	mahāntaḥ
	mahāntam	"	mahataḥ
	mahatā	mahadbhyām	mahadbhiḥ
	mahate	"	mahadbhyaḥ
	mahataḥ	"	"
	"	mahatoḥ	mahatām
	mahati	"	mahatsu
	mahan	mahāntau	mahāntaḥ

(ii) Neuter

[63]	**mahat**	mahatī	mahānti
	"	"	"
	mahatā	mahadbhyām	mahadbhiḥ
	mahate	"	mahadbhyaḥ
	mahataḥ	"	"
	"	mahatoḥ	mahatām
	mahati	"	mahatsu
	mahat	mahatī	mahānti

[64]	**dadhi**	dadhinī	dadhīni
	"	"	"
	dadhnā	dadhibhyām	dadhibhiḥ
	dadhne	"	dadhibhyaḥ
	dadhnaḥ	"	"
	"	dadhnoḥ	dadhnām
	dadh(a)ni	"	dadhiṣu
	dadhe/ dadhi	dadhinī	dadhīni

[65]	**ahaḥ**	ah(a)nī	ahāni
	"	"	"
	ahnā	ahobhyām	ahobhiḥ
	ahne	"	ahobhyaḥ
	ahnaḥ	"	"
	"	ahnoḥ	ahnām
	ah(a)ni	"	ahaḥsu
	ahaḥ	ah(a)nī	ahāni

(iii) Feminine

[66]	**jarā**	jarasau	jarasaḥ
	jarasam	"	"
	jarasā	jarābhyām	jarābhiḥ
	jarase	"	jarābhyaḥ
	jarasaḥ	"	"
	"	jarasoḥ	jarasām
	jarasi	"	jarāsu
	jare	jarasau	jarasaḥ

[67]	**strī**	striyau	striyaḥ
	striyam[1]	"	striyaḥ/strīḥ
	striyā	strībhyām	strībhiḥ
	striyai	"	strībhyaḥ
	striyāḥ	"	"
	"	striyoḥ	strīṇām
	striyām	"	strīṣu
	stri	striyau	striyaḥ

[68]	**lakṣmīḥ**	lakṣmyau	lakṣmyaḥ
	lakṣmīm	"	lakṣmīḥ
	lakṣmyā	lakṣmībhyām	lakṣmībhiḥ
	lakṣmyai	"	lakṣmībhyaḥ
	lakṣmyāḥ	"	"
	"	lakṣmyoḥ	lakṣmīṇām
	lakṣmyām	"	lakṣmīṣu
	lakṣmi	lakṣmyau	lakṣmyaḥ

[1] or strīm

[69]	**dyauḥ**	divau	divaḥ
	divam	"	"
	divā	dyubhyām	dyubhiḥ
	dive	"	dyubhyaḥ
	divaḥ	"	"
	"	divoḥ	divām
	divi	"	dyuṣu
	dyauḥ	divau	divaḥ

[70]	**gauḥ**	gāvau	gāvaḥ
	gām	"	gāḥ
	gavā	gobhyām	gobhiḥ
	gave	"	gobhyaḥ
	goḥ	"	"
	"	gavoḥ	gavām
	gavi	"	goṣu
	gauḥ	gāvau	gāvaḥ

[71]	--	--	**āpaḥ**
	--	--	apaḥ
	--	--	adbhiḥ
	--	--	adbhyaḥ
	--	--	"
	--	--	apām
	--	--	apsu
	--	--	āpaḥ

[72]	**gīḥ**	girau	giraḥ
	giram	"	"
	girā	gīrbhyām	gīrbhiḥ
	gire	"	gīrbhyaḥ
	giraḥ	"	"
	"	giroḥ	girām
	giri	"	gīrṣu
	gīḥ	girau	giraḥ

[73]	**pūḥ**	purau	puraḥ
	puram	"	"
	purā	pūrbhyām	pūrbhiḥ
	pure	"	pūrbhyaḥ
	puraḥ	"	"
	"	puroḥ	purām
	puri	"	pūrṣu
	pūḥ	purau	puraḥ

Table 8. Adjective types in the three genders.

Stem-form	Masculine	Neuter	Feminine
priy*a*-	priyaḥ [1]	priyam [17]	priyā [32]
sundar*a*-	sundaraḥ [1]	sundaram [17]	sundarī [33]
śuc*i*-	śuciḥ [2]	śuci [18]	śuciḥ [35]
sudh*ī*-	sudhīḥ[1]	sudhi [18]	sudhīḥ [34]
tan*u*-	tanuḥ [3]	tanu [19]	tanuḥ [38]/ tanvī [33]
aticam*ū*-	aticamūḥ[2]	aticamu [19]	aticamūḥ [36]
svabh*ū*-	svabhūḥ[3]	svabhu [19]	svabhūḥ [37]
dāt*ṛ*-	dātā [4], ([5])	dātṛ [20]	dātrī [33]
sarvaś*ak*-[4]	sarvaśak [6]	sarvaśak [21]	sarvaśak [6]
priyav*āc*-[5]	priyavāk [7]	priyavāk [22]	priyavāk [7]
suman*as*-	sumanāḥ [8]	sumanaḥ [23]	sumanāḥ [8]
udarc*is*-	udarciḥ [7]	udarciḥ [24]	udarciḥ [7]
dīrghāy*us*-	dīrghāyuḥ [7]	dīrghāyuḥ [25]	dīrghāyuḥ [7]
suparv*an*-	suparvā [9]	suparva [26]	suparvaṇī [33]
sunām*an*-	sunāmā [10]	sunāma [27]	sunāmnī [33]
bal*in*-	balī [11]	bali [28]	balinī [33]
nay*ant*-[6]	nayan [12]	nayat [29]	nayantī [33]
yuñj*ant*-	yuñjan [12]	yuñjat [29]	yuñjatī [33]
dadh*at*-	dadhat [6]	dadhat [21]	dadhatī [33]
dhī*mat*-[7]	dhīmān [13]	dhīmat [21]	dhīmatī [33]
śre*yas*-	śreyān [14]	śreyaḥ [23]	śreyasī [33]
ten*ivas*-	tenivān [15]	tenivat [30]	tenuṣī [33]
vid*vas*-	vidvān [16]	vidvat [31]	viduṣī [33]

[1]See page 25, [34].
[2]See page 25, [36].
[3]See page 25, [37].
[4]This type covers the three consonant finals -k, -t, -p.
[5]This type covers all alternating consonant final pairs such as k—c, t—j; see pages 20-21.
[6]This and the next often cited as nayat-, yuñjat-; but see page 61.
[7]Also covers adjectives in -vat-.

Table 9. Comparison of adjectives by method 1.

Positive	Comparative	Superlative
priya-	priyatara-	priyatama-
śuci-	śucitara-	śucitama-
tanu-	tanutara-	tanutama-
dātṛ-	dātṛtara-	dātṛtama-
priyavāc-	priyavāktara-	priyavāktama-
sumanas-	sumanastara-	sumanastama-
dīrghāyus-	dīrghāyuṣṭara-	dīrghāyuṣṭama-
sunāman-	sunāmatara-	sunāmatama-
balin-	balitara-	balitama-
dadat-	dadattara-	dadattama-
nayant-	nayattara-	nayattama-
dhīmat-	dhīmattara-	dhīmattama-
vidvas-	vidvattara-	vidvattama-

Table 10. Comparison of adjectives by method 2.

Positive	Comparative	Superlative
aṇu-	aṇīyas-	aṇiṣṭha-
antika-	nedīyas-	nediṣṭha-
alpa-	alpīyas-	alpiṣṭha-
alpa-	kanīyas-	kaniṣṭha-
kṣipra-	kṣepīyas-	kṣepiṣṭha-
kṣudra-	kṣodīyas-	kṣodiṣṭha-
guru-	garīyas-	gariṣṭha-
dīrgha-	drāghīyas-	drāghiṣṭha-
dūra-	davīyas-	daviṣṭha-
paṭu-	paṭīyas-	paṭiṣṭha-
priya-	preyas-	preṣṭha-
balin-	balīyas-	baliṣṭha-
bahu-	bhūyas-	bhūyiṣṭha-
bahula-	baṃhīyas-	baṃhiṣṭha-
mahat-	mahīyas-	mahiṣṭha-
mṛdu-	mradīyas-	mradiṣṭha-
yuvan-	yavīyas-	yaviṣṭha-
laghu-	laghīyas-	laghiṣṭha-
vara-	varīyas-	variṣṭha-
vṛddha-	varṣīyas-	varṣiṣṭha-
vṛddha-	jyāyas-	jyeṣṭha-
--	śreyas-	śreṣṭha-
sthira-	stheyas-	stheṣṭha-
hrasva-	hrasīyas-	hrasiṣṭha-

Table 11. The numerals.

	Cardinal	Ordinal
1.	ekaḥ ekam ekā	prathama-
2.	dvau dve dve	dvitīya-
3.	trayaḥ trīṇi tisraḥ	tṛtīya-
4.	catvāraḥ catvāri	tur(ī)ya-
	catasraḥ	caturtha-
5.	pañca	pañcama-
6.	ṣaṭ	ṣaṣṭha-
7.	sapta	saptama-
8.	aṣṭa(u)	aṣṭama-
9.	nava	navama-
10.	daśa	daśama-
11.	ekādaśa	ekādaśa-
12.	dvādaśa	dvādaśa-
13.	trayodaśa	trayodaśa-
14.	caturdaśa	caturdaśa-
15.	pañcadaśa	pañcadaśa-
16.	ṣoḍaśa	ṣoḍaśa-
17.	saptadaśa	saptadaśa-
18.	aṣṭādaśa	aṣṭādaśa-
19.	navadaśa	navadaśa-
	ūnaviṃśatiḥ	ūnaviṃśa-
	ekonaviṃśatiḥ	ekonaviṃśa-
	ekānnaviṃśatiḥ	ekānnaviṃśa-
20.	viṃśatiḥ	viṃśa(titama)-
21.	ekaviṃśatiḥ	ekaviṃśa(titama)-
22.	dvāviṃśatiḥ	dvāviṃśa(titama)-
23.	trayoviṃśatiḥ	trayoviṃśa(titama)-
24.	caturviṃśatiḥ	caturviṃśa(titama)-
25.	pañcaviṃśatiḥ	pañcaviṃśa(titama)-
26.	ṣaḍviṃśatiḥ	ṣaḍviṃśa(titama)-
27.	saptaviṃśatiḥ	saptaviṃśa(titama)-
28.	aṣṭāviṃśatiḥ	aṣṭāviṃśa(titama)-
29.	navaviṃśatiḥ	navaviṃśa(titama)-
30.	triṃśat	triṃśa(ttama)-
31.	ekatriṃśat	ekatriṃśa(ttama)-
32.	dvātriṃśat	dvātriṃśa(ttama)-
33.	trayastriṃśat	trayastriṃśa(ttama)-

34.	catustriṃśat	catustriṃśa(ttama)-
35.	pañcatriṃśat	pañcatriṃśa(ttama)-
36.	ṣaṭtriṃśat	saṭtriṃśa(ttama)-
37.	saptatriṃśat	saptatriṃśa(ttama)-
38.	aṣṭātriṃśat	aṣṭātriṃśa(ttama)-
39.	navatriṃśat	navatriṃśa(ttama)-
40.	catvāriṃśat	catvāriṃśa(ttama)-
41.	ekacatvāriṃśat	ekacatvāriṃśa(ttama)-
42.	dvācatvāriṃśat	dvācatvāriṃśa(ttama)-
	dvicatvāriṃśat	dvicatvāriṃśa(ttama)-
43.	trayaścatvāriṃśat	trayaścatvāriṃśa(ttama)-
	tricatvāriṃśat	tricatvāriṃśa(ttama)-
44.	catuścatvāriṃśat	catuścatvāriṃśa(ttama)-
45.	pañcacatvāriṃśat	pañcacatvāriṃśa(ttama)-
46.	ṣaṭcatvāriṃśat	ṣaṭcatvāriṃśa(ttama)-
47.	saptacatvāriṃsat	saptacatvāriṃśa(ttama)-
48.	aṣṭācatvāriṃśat	aṣṭācatvāriṃśa(ttama)-
49.	navacatvāriṃśat	navacatvāriṃśa(ttama)-
50.	pañcāśat	pañcāśa(ttama)-
51.	ekapañcāśat	ekapañcāśa(ttama)-
52.	dvāpañcāśat	dvāpañcāśa(ttama)-
	dvipañcāśat	dvipañcāśa(ttama)-
53.	trayaḥpañcāśat	trayaḥpañcāśa(ttama)-
	tripañcāśat	tripañcāśa(ttama)-
54.	catuḥpañcāśat	catuḥpañcāśa(ttama)-
55.	pañcapañcāśat	pañcapañcāśa(ttama)-
56.	ṣaṭpañcāśat	ṣaṭpañcāśa(ttama)-
57.	saptapañcāśat	saptapañcāśa(ttama)-
58.	aṣṭāpañcāśat	aṣṭāpañcāśa(ttama)-
59.	navapañcāśat	navapañcāśa(ttama)-
60.	ṣaṣṭiḥ	ṣaṣṭitama-
61.	ekaṣaṣṭiḥ	ekaṣaṣṭ(itam)a-
62.	dvāṣaṣṭiḥ	dvāṣaṣṭ(itam)a-
	dviṣaṣṭiḥ	dviṣaṣṭ(itam)a-
63.	trayaḥṣaṣṭiḥ	trayaḥṣaṣṭ(itam)a-
	triṣaṣṭiḥ	triṣaṣṭ(itam)a-
64.	catuḥṣaṣṭiḥ	catuḥṣaṣṭ(itam)a-
65.	pañcaṣaṣṭiḥ	pañcaṣaṣṭ(itam)a-
66.	ṣaṭṣaṣṭiḥ	ṣaṭṣaṣṭ(itam)a-
67.	saptaṣaṣṭiḥ	saptaṣaṣṭ(itam)a-
68.	aṣṭāṣaṣṭiḥ	aṣṭāṣaṣṭ(itam)a-
69.	navaṣaṣṭiḥ	navaṣaṣṭ(itam)a-

70.	saptatiḥ	saptatitama-
71.	ekasaptatiḥ	ekasaptat(itam)a-
72.	dvāsaptatiḥ	dvāsaptat(itam)a-
	dvisaptatiḥ	dvisaptat(itam)a-
73.	trayaḥsaptatiḥ	trayaḥsaptat(itam)a-
	trisaptatiḥ	trisaptat(itam)a-
74.	catuḥsaptatiḥ	catuḥsaptat(itam)a-
75.	pañcasaptatiḥ	pañcasaptat(itam)a-
76.	ṣaṭsaptatiḥ	ṣaṭsaptat(itam)a-
77.	saptasaptatiḥ	saptasaptat(itam)a-
78.	aṣṭăsaptatiḥ	aṣṭăsaptat(itam)a-
79.	navasaptatiḥ	navasaptat(itam)a-
80.	aśītiḥ	aśītitama-
81.	ekāśītiḥ	ekāśīt(itam)a-
82.	dvyaśītiḥ	dvyaśīt(itam)a-
83.	tryaśītiḥ	tryaśīt(itam)a-
84.	caturaśītiḥ	caturaśīt(itam)a-
85.	pañcāśītiḥ	pañcāśīt(itam)a-
86.	ṣaḍaśītiḥ	ṣaḍaśīt(itam)a-
87.	saptāśītiḥ	saptāśīt(itam)a-
88.	aṣṭāśītiḥ	aṣṭāśīt(itam)a-
89.	navāśītiḥ	navāśīt(itam)a-
90.	navatiḥ	navatitama-
91.	ekanavatiḥ	ekanavat(itam)a-
92.	dvānavatiḥ	dvānavat(itam)a-
	dvinavatiḥ	dvinavat(itam)a-
93.	trayonavatiḥ	trayonavat(itam)a-
	trinavatiḥ	trinavat(itam)a-
94.	caturnavatiḥ	caturnavat(itam)a-
95.	pañcanavatiḥ	pañcanavat(itam)a-
96.	ṣaṇṇavatiḥ	ṣaṇṇavat(itam)a-
97.	saptanavatiḥ	saptanavat(itam)a-
98.	aṣṭănavatiḥ	aṣṭănavat(itam)a-
99.	navanavatiḥ	navanavat(itam)a-
100.	śatam	śatatama-
101.	ekaśatam	ekaśata(tama)-
	ekādhikaśatam	ekādhikaśatatama-
	ekādhikaṃ śatam	ekādhika- śatatama-
102.	dviśatam	dviśata(tama)-
	dvyadhikaśatam	dvyadhikaśatatama-
	dvyadhikaṃ śatam	dvydhika- śatatama-

103.	triśatam	triśata(tama)-
	tryadhikaśatam	*etc.*
	tryadhikaṃ śatam	
112.	dvādaśaśatam	
	dvādaśādhikaśatam	
	dvādaśādhikaṃ śatam	
120.	viṃśatiśatam	
	viṃśatyadhikaśatam	
	viṃśatyadhikaṃ śatam	
130.	triṃśacchatam	
	triṃśadadhikaśatam	
	triṃśadadhikaṃ śatam	
200.	dviśatam	
	dve śate	
300.	triśatam	
	trīṇi śatāni	
345.	pañcacatvāriṃśad-adhikaṃ triśatam	
1000.	sahasram	sahasratama-
1002.	dvisahasram	dvisahasra(tama)-
	dvyadhikasahasram	*etc.*
	dvyadhikaṃ sahasram	
2000.	dvisahasram	
	dve sahasre	
2984.	caturaśītyadhikaṃ navaśatādhikaṃ dvisahasram	
10000.	ayutam	ayutatama-
100000.	lakṣam	lakṣatama-
1000000.	prayutam	prayutatama-
10000000.	koṭiḥ	koṭitama-
100000000.	arbudam	arbudatama-

Table 12. Declension of the numerals 1 to 10.

Masculine:

1	2	3	4	5
ekaḥ	dvau	trayaḥ	catvāraḥ	pañca
ekam	"	trīn	caturaḥ	"
ekena	dvābhyām	tribhiḥ	caturbhiḥ	pañcabhiḥ
ekasmai	"	tribhyaḥ	caturbhyaḥ	pañcabhyaḥ
ekasmāt	"	"	"	"
ekasya	dvayoḥ	trayāṇām	caturṇām	pañcānām
ekasmin	"	triṣu	caturṣu	pañcasu
--	--	--	--	--

Neuter:

ekam	dve	trīṇi	catvāri	pañca
"	"	"	"	"
ekena	dvābhyām	tribhiḥ	caturbhiḥ	pañcabhiḥ
ekasmai	"	tribhyaḥ	caturbhyaḥ	pañcabhyaḥ
ekasmāt	"	"	"	"
ekasya	dvayoḥ	trayāṇām	caturṇām	pañcānām
ekasmin	"	triṣu	caturṣu	pañcasu
--	--	--	--	--

Feminine:

ekā	dve	tisraḥ	catasraḥ	pañca
ekām	"	"	"	"
ekayā	dvābhyām	tisṛbhiḥ	catasṛbhiḥ	pañcabhiḥ
ekasyai	"	tisṛbhyaḥ	catasṛbhyaḥ	pañcabhyaḥ
ekasyāḥ	"	"	"	"
"	dvayoḥ	tisṛṇām	catasṛṇām	paññānām
ekasyām	"	tisṛṣu	catasṛṣu	pañcasu
--	--	--	--	--

6	7	8	9	10
ṣaṭ	sapta	aṣṭa(u)	nava	daśa
"	"	"	"	"
ṣaḍbhiḥ	saptabhiḥ	aṣṭā̆bhiḥ	navabhiḥ	daśabhiḥ
ṣaḍbhyaḥ	saptabhyaḥ	aṣṭā̆bhyaḥ	navabhyaḥ	daśabhyaḥ
"	"	"	"	"
ṣaṇṇām	saptānām	aṣṭānām	navānām	daśānām
ṣaṭsu	saptasu	aṣṭā̆su	navasu	daśasu
--	--	--	--	--

As for masculine

As for masculine

Table 13. Declension of the demonstratives.

'This'

Masculine:

ayam	imau	ime
imam	"	imān
anena	ābhyām	ebhiḥ
asmai	"	ebhyaḥ
asmāt	"	"
asya	anayoḥ	eṣām
asmin	"	eṣu
--	--	--

Neuter:

idam	ime	imāni
"	"	"
anena	ābhyām	ebhiḥ
asmai	"	ebhyaḥ
asmāt	"	"
asya	anayoḥ	eṣām
asmin	"	eṣu
--	--	--

Feminine:

iyam	ime	imāḥ
imām	"	"
anayā	ābhyām	ābhiḥ
asyai	"	ābhyaḥ
asyāḥ	"	"
"	anayoḥ	āsām
asyām	"	āsu
--	--	--

'That'

Masculine:

asau	amū	amī
amum	"	amūn
amunā	amūbhyām	amībhiḥ
amuṣmai	"	amībhyaḥ
amuṣmāt	"	"
amuṣya	amuyoḥ	amīṣām
amuṣmin	"	amīṣu
--	--	--

Neuter:

adaḥ	amū	amūni
"	"	"
amunā	amūbhyām	amībhiḥ
amuṣmai	"	amībhyaḥ
amuṣmāt	"	"
amuṣya	amuyoḥ	amīṣām
amuṣmin	"	amīṣu
--	--	--

Feminine:

asau	amū	amūḥ
amūm	"	"
amuyā	amūbhyām	amūbhiḥ
amuṣyai	"	amūbhyaḥ
amuṣyāḥ	"	"
"	amuyoḥ	amūṣām
amuṣyām	"	amūṣu
--	--	--

Table 14. Declension of the pronouns.

3rd person

Masculine:

saḥ	tau	te
tam	"	tān
tena	tābhyām	taiḥ
tasmai	"	tebhyaḥ
tasmāt	"	"
tasya	tayoḥ	teṣām
tasmin	"	teṣu
--	--	--

Neuter:

tat	te	tāni
"	"	"
tena	tābhyām	taiḥ
tasmai	"	tebhyaḥ
tasmāt	"	"
tasya	tayoḥ	teṣām
tasmin	"	teṣu
--	--	--

Feminine:

sā	te	tāḥ
tām	"	"
tayā	tābhyām	tābhiḥ
tasyai	"	tābhyaḥ
tasyāḥ	"	"
"	tayoḥ	tāsām
tasyām	"	tāsu
--	--	--

2nd person / *2nd person enclitic*

tvam	yuvām	yūyam	--	--	--
tvām	"	yuṣmān	tvā	vām	vaḥ
tvayā	yuvābhyām	yuṣmābhiḥ	--	--	--
tubhyām	"	yuṣmabhyam	te	vām	vaḥ
tvat	"	yuṣmat	--	--	--
tava	yuvayoḥ	yuṣmākam	te	vām	vaḥ
tvayi	"	yuṣmāsu	--	--	--
--	--	--	--	--	--

1st person / *1st person enclitic*

aham	āvām	vayam	--	--	--
mām	"	asmān	mā	nau	naḥ
mayā	āvābhyām	asmābhiḥ	--	--	--
mahyam	"	asmabhyam	me	nau	naḥ
mat	"	asmat	--	--	--
mama	āvayoḥ	asmākam	me	nau	naḥ
mayi	"	asmāsu	--	--	--
--	--	--	--	--	--

3rd person substitute

Masculine:

--	--	--
enam	enau	enān
enena	--	--
--	--	--
--	--	--
--	enayoḥ	--
--	"	--
--	--	--

Neuter:

--	--	--
enat	ene	enāni
enena	--	--
--	--	--
--	--	--
--	enayoḥ	--
--	"	--
--	--	--

Feminine:

--	--	--
enām	ene	enāḥ
enayā	--	--
--	--	--
--	--	--
--	enayoḥ	--
--	"	--
--	--	--

'All'

Masculine:

sarvaḥ	sarvau	sarve
sarvam	"	sarvān
sarveṇa	sarvābhyām	sarvaiḥ
sarvasmai	"	sarvebhyaḥ
sarvasmāt	"	"
sarvasya	sarvayoḥ	sarveṣām
sarvasmin	"	sarveṣu
sarva	sarvau	sarve

Neuter:

sarvam	sarve	sarvāṇi
"	"	"
sarveṇa	sarvābhyām	sarvaiḥ
sarvasmai	"	sarvebhyaḥ
sarvasmāt	"	"
sarvasya	sarvayoḥ	sarveṣām
sarvasmin	"	sarveṣu
sarva	sarve	sarvāṇi

Feminine:

sarvā	sarve	sarvāḥ
sarvām	"	"
sarvayā	sarvābhyām	sarvābhiḥ
sarvasyai	"	sarvābhyaḥ
sarvasyāḥ	"	"
"	sarvayoḥ	sarvāsām
sarvasyām	"	sarvāsu
sarve	sarve	sarvāḥ

Table 15. Conjugations of the verb nayati.

	Active:			Middle:			Passive:		
Present Indic.	**nayati**	nayataḥ	nayanti	nayate	nayete	nayante	nīyate	nīyete	nīyante
	nayasi	nayathaḥ	nayatha	nayase	nayethe	nayadhve	nīyase	nīyethe	nīyadhve
	nayāmi	nayāvaḥ	nayāmaḥ	naye	nayāvahe	nayāmahe	nīye	nīyāvahe	nīyāmahe
Present Optat.	nayet	nayetām	nayeyuḥ	nayeta	nayeyātām	nayeran	nīyeta	nīyeyātām	nīyeran
	nayeḥ	nayetam	nayeta	nayethāḥ	nayeyāthām	nayedhvam	nīyethāḥ	nīyeyāthām	nīyedhvam
	nayeyam	nayeva	nayema	nayeya	nayevahi	nayemahi	nīyeya	nīyevahi	nīyemahi
Present Imperat.	nayatu	nayatām	nayantu	nayatām	nayetām	nayantām	nīyatām	nīyetām	nīyantām
	naya	nayatam	nayata	nayasva	nayethām	nayadhvam	nīyasva	nīyethām	nīyadhvam
	nayāni	nayāva	nayāma	nayai	nayāvahai	nayāmahai	nīyai	nīyāvahai	nīyāmahai
Imperfect Indic.	anayat	anayatām	anayan	anayata	anayetām	anayanta	anīyata	anīyetām	anīyanta
	anayaḥ	anayatam	anayata	anayathāḥ	anayethām	anayadhvam	anīyathāḥ	anīyethām	anīyadhvam
	anayam	anayāva	anayāma	anaye	anayāvahi	anayāmahi	anīye	anīyāvahi	anīyāmahi

Perfect	nināya	ninyatuḥ	ninyuḥ	ninye	ninyāte	ninyire	ninye	ninyāte	ninyire
Indic.	ninetha	ninyathuḥ	ninya	ninyiṣe	ninyāthe	ninyidhve	ninyiṣe	ninyāthe	ninyidhve
	ninā̆ya	ninyiva	ninyima	ninye	ninyivahe	ninyimahe	ninye	ninyivahe	ninyimahe
Aorist	anaiṣīt	anaiṣṭām	anaiṣuḥ	aneṣṭa	aneṣātām	aneṣata	anāyi	anāyiṣātām	anāyiṣata
Indic.	anaiṣīḥ	anaiṣṭam	anaiṣṭa	aneṣṭhāḥ	aneṣāthām	aneḍhvam	anāyiṣṭhāḥ	anāyiṣāthām	anāyiḍhvam
	anaiṣam	anaiṣva	anaiṣma	aneṣi	aneṣvahi	aneṣmahi	anāyiṣi	anāyiṣvahi	anāyiṣmahi
Aorist	nīyāt	nīyāstām	nīyāsuḥ	neṣīṣṭa	neṣīyāstām	neṣīran	nāyiṣīṣṭa	nāyiṣīyāstām	nāyiṣīran
Optat.	nīyāḥ	nīyāstam	nīyāsta	neṣīṣṭhāḥ	neṣīyāsthām	neṣīḍhvam	nāyiṣīṣṭhāḥ	nāyiṣīyāsthām	nāyiṣīḍhvam
	nīyāsam	nīyāsva	nīyāsma	neṣīya	neṣīvahi	neṣīmahi	nāyiṣīya	nāyiṣīvahi	nāyiṣīmahi
Periph.	netā	netārau	netāraḥ	netā	netārau	netāraḥ	nāyitā	nāyitārau	nāyitāraḥ
Future	netāsi	netāsthaḥ	netāstha	netāse	netāsthe	netādhve	nāyitāse	nāyitāsathe	nāyitādhve
Indic.	netāsmi	netāsva	netāsma	netāhe	netāsvahe	netāsmahe	nāyitāhe	nāyitāsvahe	nāyitāsmahe
Simple	neṣyati	neṣyataḥ	neṣyanti	neṣyate	neṣyete	neṣyante	nāyiṣyate	nāyiṣyete	nāyiṣyante
Future	neṣyasi	neṣyathaḥ	neṣyatha	neṣyase	neṣyethe	neṣyadhve	nāyiṣyase	nāyiṣyethe	nāyiṣyadhve
Indic.	neṣyāmi	neṣyāvaḥ	neṣyāmaḥ	neṣye	neṣyāvahe	neṣyāmahe	nāyiṣye	nāyiṣyāvahe	nāyiṣyāmahe
Condit.	aneṣyat	aneṣyatām	aneṣyan	aneṣyata	aneṣyetām	aneṣyanta	anāyiṣyata	anāyiṣyetām	anāyiṣyanta
Indic.	aneṣyaḥ	aneṣyatam	aneṣyata	aneṣyathāḥ	aneṣyethām	aneṣyadhvam	anāyiṣyathāḥ	anāyiṣyethām	anāyiṣyadhvam
	aneṣyam	aneṣyāva	aneṣyāma	aneṣye	aneṣyāvahi	aneṣyāmahi	anāyiṣye	anāyiṣyāvahi	anāyiṣyāmahi

Table 16. Conjugational paradigms for the present and imperfect.

[1]	Active		
Present Indicative	**nayati**	nayataḥ	nayanti
	nayasi	nayathaḥ	nayatha
	nayāmi	nayāvaḥ	nayāmaḥ
Present Optative	nayet	nayetām	nayeyuḥ
	nayeḥ	nayetam	nayeta
	nayeyam	nayeva	nayema
Present Imperative	nayatu	nayatām	nayantu
	naya	nayatam	nayata
	nayāni	nayāva	nayāma
Imperfect Indicative	anayat	anayatām	anayan
	anayaḥ	anayatam	anayata
	anayam	anayāva	anayāma
	Middle		
	nayate	nayete	nayante
	nayase	nayethe	nayadhve
	naye	nayāvahe	nayāmahe
	nayeta	nayeyātām	nayeran
	nayethāḥ	nayeyāthām	nayedhvam
	nayeya	nayevahi	nayemahi
	nayatām	nayetām	nayantām
	nayasva	nayethām	nayadhvam
	nayai	nayāvahai	nayāmahai
	anayata	anayetām	anayanta
	anayathāḥ	anayethām	anayadhvam
	anaye	anayāvahi	anayāmahi

[2] Active

bhāti	bhātaḥ	bhānti
bhāsi	bhāthaḥ	bhātha
bhāmi	bhāvaḥ	bhāmaḥ
bhāyāt	bhāyātām	bhāyuḥ
bhāyāḥ	bhāyātam	bhāyāta
bhāyām	bhāyāva	bhāyāma
bhātu	bhātām	bhāntu
bhāhi	bhātam	bhāta
bhāni	bhāva	bhāma
abhāt	abhātām	abhān[1]
abhāḥ	abhātam	abhāta
abhām	abhāva	abhāma

[3] Active

svapiti	svapitaḥ	svapanti
svapiṣi	svapithaḥ	svapitha
svapimi	svapivaḥ	svapimaḥ
svapyāt	svapyātām	svapyuḥ
svapyāḥ	svapyātam	svapyāta
svapyām	svapyāva	svapyāma
svapitu	svapitām	svapantu
svapihi	svapitam	svapita
svapāni	svapāva	svapāma
asvapat[2]	asvapitām	asvapan
asvapaḥ[3]	asvapitam	asvapita
asvapam	asvapiva	asvapima

[1]or abhuḥ
[2]or asvapīt
[3]or asvapīḥ

[4] Active

stauti[1]	stutaḥ	stuvanti
stauṣi	stuthaḥ	stutha
staumi	stuvaḥ	stumaḥ
stuyāt	stuyātām	stuyuḥ
stuyāḥ	stuyātam	stuyāta
stuyām	stuyāva	stuyāma
stautu	stutām	stuvantu
stuhi	stutam	stuta
stavāni	*stavāva*	*stavāma*
astaut	astutām	astuvan
astauḥ	astutam	astuta
astāvam	astuva	astuma

Middle

stute	stuvāte	stuvate
stuṣe	stuvāthe	studhve
stuve	stuvahe	stumahe
stuvīta	stuvīyātām	stuvīran
stuvīthāḥ	stuvīyāthām	stuvīdhvam
stuvīya	stuvīvahi	stuvīmahi
stutām	stuvātām	stuvatām
stuṣva	stuvāthām	studhvam
stavai	*stavāvahai*	*stavāmahai*
astuta	astuvātām	astuvata
astuthāḥ	astuvāthām	astudhvam
astuvi	astuvahi	astumahi

[1]In the six forms with -au-, this vowel may be replaced by -avī- . In Tables 16 and 17 forms printed in italics have 'strong' stems.

[5] Active

jānāti	jānītaḥ	jānanti
jānāsi	jānīthaḥ	jānītha
jānāmi	jānīvaḥ	jānīmaḥ
jānīyāt	jānīyātām	jānīyuḥ
jānīyāḥ	jānīyātam	jānīyāta
jānīyām	jānīyāva	jānīyāma
jānātu	jānītām	jānantu
jānīhi[1]	jānītam	jānīta
jānāni	*jānāva*	*jānāma*
ajānāt	ajānītām	ajānan
ajānāḥ	ajānītam	ajānīta
ajānām	ajānīva	ajānīma

Middle

jānīte	jānāte	jānate
jānīṣe	jānāthe	jānīdhve
jāne	jānīvahe	jānīmahe
jānīta	jānīyātām	jānīran
jānīthāḥ	jānīyāthām	jānīdhvam
jānīya	jānīvahi	jānīmahi
jānītām	jānātām	jānatām
jānīṣva	jānāthām	jānīdhvam
jānai	*jānāvahai*	*jānāmahai*
ajānīta	ajānātām	ajānata
ajānīthāḥ	ajānāthām	ajānīdhvam
ajāni	ajānīvahi	ajānīmahi

[1]See page 44.

[6] Active

sunoti	sunutaḥ	sunvanti
sunoṣi	sunuthaḥ	sunutha
sunomi	sun(u)vaḥ	sun(u)maḥ
sunuyāt	sunuyātām	sunuyuḥ
sunuyāḥ	sunuyātam	sunuyāta
sunuyām	sunuyāva	sunuyāma
sunotu	sunutām	sunvantu
sunu[1]	sunutam	sunuta
sunavāni	*sunavāva*	*sunavāma*
asunot	asunutām	asunvan
asunoḥ	asunutam	asunuta
asunavam	asun(u)va	asun(u)ma

Middle

sunute	sunvāte	sunvate
sunuṣe	sunvāthe	sunudhve
sunve	sun(u)vahe	sun(u)mahe
sunvīta	sunvīyātām	sunvīran
sunvīthāḥ	sunvīyāthām	sunvīdhvam
sunvīya	sunvīvahi	sunvīmahi
sunutām	sunvātām	sunvatām
sunuṣva	sunvāthām	sunudhvam
sunavai	*sunavāvahai*	*sunavāmahai*
asunuta	asunvātām	asunvata
asunuthāḥ	asunvāthām	asunudhvam
asunvi	asun(u)vahi	asun(u)mahi

[1]See page 44.

[7] Active

juhoti	juhutaḥ	juhvati
juhoṣi	juhuthaḥ	juhutha
juhomi	juhuvaḥ	juhumaḥ
juhuyāt	juhuyātām	juhuyuḥ
juhuyāḥ	juhuyātam	juhuyāta
juhuyām	juhuyāva	juhuyāma
juhotu	juhutām	juhvatu
juhudhi[1]	juhutam	juhuta
juhavāni	*juhavāva*	*juhavāma*
ajuhot	ajuhutām	*ajuhavuḥ*
ajuhoḥ	ajuhutam	ajuhuta
ajuhavam	ajuhuva	ajuhuma

Middle

juhute	juhvāte	juhvate
juhuṣe	juhvāthe	juhudhve
juhve	juhuvahe	juhumahe
juhvīta	juhvīyātām	juhvīran
juhvīthāḥ	juhvīyāthām	juhvīdhvam
juhvīya	juhvīvahi	juhvīmahi
juhutām	juhvātām	juhvatām
juhuṣva	juhvāthām	juhudhvam
juhavai	*juhavāvahai*	*juhavāmahai*
ajuhuta	ajuhvātām	ajuhvata
ajuhuthāḥ	ajuhvāthām	ajuhudhvam
ajuhvi	ajuhuvahi	ajuhumahi

[1]See page 45.

[8] Active

yunakti	yuṅktaḥ	yuñjanti
yunakṣi	yuṅkthaḥ	yuṅktha
yunajmi	yuñjvaḥ	yuñjmaḥ
yuñjyāt	yuñjyātām	yuñjyuḥ
yuñjyāḥ	yuñjyātam	yuñjyāta
yuñjyām	yuñjyāva	yuñjyāma
yunaktu	yuṅktām	yuñjantu
yuṅgdhi	yuṅktam	yuṅkta
yunajāni	*yunajāva*	*yunajāma*
ayunak	ayuṅktām	ayuñjan
ayunak	ayuṅktam	ayuṅkta
ayunajam	ayuñjva	ayuñjma

Middle

yuṅkte	yuñjāte	yuñjate
yuṅkṣe	yuñjāthe	yuṅgdhve
yuñje	yuñjvahe	yuñjmahe
yuñjīta	yuñjīyātām	yuñjīran
yuñjīthāḥ	yuñjīyāthām	yuñjīdhvam
yuñjīya	yuñjīvahi	yuñjīmahi
yuṅktām	yuñjātām	yuñjatām
yuṅkṣva	yuñjāthām	yuṅgdhvam
yunajai	*yunajāvahai*	*yunajāmahai*
ayuṅkta	ayuñjātām	ayuñjata
ayuṅkthāḥ	ayuñjāthām	ayuṅgdhvam
ayuñji	ayuñjvahi	ayuñjmahi

[9] Active

dveṣṭi	dviṣṭaḥ	dviṣanti
dvekṣi	dviṣṭhaḥ	dviṣṭha
dveṣmi	dviṣvaḥ	dviṣmaḥ
dviṣyāt	dviṣyātām	dviṣyuḥ
dviṣyāḥ	dviṣyātam	dviṣyāta
dviṣyām	dviṣyāva	dviṣyāma
dveṣṭu	dviṣṭām	dviṣantu
dviḍḍhi	dviṣṭam	dviṣṭa
dveṣāṇi	*dveṣāva*	*dveṣāma*
adveṭ	adviṣṭām	adviṣan
adveṭ	adviṣṭam	adviṣṭa
adveṣam	adviṣva	adviṣma

Middle

dviṣṭe	dviṣāte	dviṣate
dvikṣe	dviṣāthe	dviḍḍhve
dviṣe	dviṣvahe	dviṣmahe
dviṣīta	dviṣīyātām	dviṣīran
dviṣīthāḥ	dviṣīyāthām	dviṣīdhvam
dviṣīya	dviṣīvahi	dviṣīmahi
dviṣṭām	dviṣātām	dviṣatām
dvikṣva	dviṣāthām	dviḍḍhvam
dveṣai	*dveṣāvahai*	*dveṣāmahai*
adviṣṭa	adviṣātām	adviṣata
adviṣṭhāḥ	adviṣāthām	adviḍḍhvam
adviṣi	adviṣvahi	adviṣmahi

[10] Active

vaṣṭi	uṣṭaḥ	uśanti
vakṣi	uṣṭhaḥ	uṣṭha
vaśmi	uśvaḥ	uśmaḥ
uśyāt	uśyātām	uśyuḥ
uśyāḥ	uśyātam	uśyāta
uśyām	uśyāva	uśyāma
vaṣṭu	uṣṭām	uśantu
uḍḍhi	uṣṭam	uṣṭa
vaśāni	*vaśāva*	*vaśāma*
avaṭ	auṣṭām	auśan
avaṭ	auṣṭam	auṣṭa
avaśam	auśva	auśma

[11] Active

runaddhi	runddhaḥ	rundhanti
ruṇatsi	runddhaḥ	runddha
ruṇadhmi	rundhvaḥ	rundhmaḥ
rundhyāt	rundhyātām	rundhyuḥ
rundhyāḥ	rundhyātam	rundhyāta
rundhyām	rundhyāva	rundhyāma
ruṇaddhu	runddhām	rundhantu
runddhi	runddham	runddha
ruṇadhāni	*ruṇadhāva*	*ruṇadhāma*
aruṇat	arunddhām	arundhan
aruṇat	arunddham	arunddha
aruṇadham	arundhva	arundhma

Middle

runddhe	rundhāte	rundhate
runtse	rundhāthe	runddhve
rundhe	rundhvahe	rundhmahe
rundhīta	rundhīyātām	rundhīran
rundhīthāḥ	rundhīyāthām	rundhīdhvam
rundhīya	rundhīvahi	rundhīmahi
runddhām	rundhātām	rundhatām
runtsva	rundhāthām	runddhvam
ruṇadhai	*ruṇadhāvahai*	*ruṇadhāmahai*
arunddha	arundhātām	arundhata
arunddhāḥ	arundhāthām	arunddhvam
arundhi	arundhvahi	arundhmahi

Table 17. Irregular conjugations in the present and imperfect.

[12] Active

roditi	ruditaḥ	rudanti
rodiṣi	rudithaḥ	ruditha
rodimi	rudivaḥ	rudimaḥ
rudyāt	rudyātām	rudyuḥ
rudyāḥ	rudyātam	rudyāta
rudyām	rudyāva	rudyāma
roditu	ruditām	rudantu
rudihi	ruditam	rudita
rodāni	*rodāva*	*rodāma*
arodat[1]	aruditām	arudan
arodaḥ[2]	aruditam	arudita
arodam	arudiva	arudima

[1]or arodīt
[2]or arodīḥ

[13] Active

bravīti	brūtaḥ	bruvanti
bravīṣi	brūthaḥ	brūtha
bravīmi	brūvaḥ	brūmaḥ
brūyāt	brūyātām	brūyuḥ
brūyāḥ	brūyātam	brūyāta
brūyām	brūyāva	brūyāma
bravītu	brūtām	bruvantu
brūhi	brūtam	brūta
bravāṇi	*bravāva*	*bravāma*
abravīt	abrūtām	abruvan
abravīḥ	abrūtam	abrūta
abravam	abrūva	abrūma

Middle

brūte	bruvāte	bruvate
brūṣe	bruvāthe	brūdhve
bruve	brūvahe	brūmahe
bruvīta	bruvīyātām	bruvīran
bruvīthāḥ	bruvīyāthām	bruvīdhvam
bruvīya	bruvīvahi	bruvīmahi
brūtām	bruvātām	bruvatām
brūṣva	bruvāthām	brūdhvam
bravai	*bravāvahai*	*bravāmahai*
abrūta	abruvātām	abruvata
abrūthāḥ	abruvāthām	abrūdhvam
abruvi	abrūvahi	abrūmahi

[14] Active

eti	itaḥ	yanti
eṣi	ithaḥ	itha
emi	ivaḥ	imaḥ
iyāt	iyātām	iyuḥ
iyāḥ	iyātam	iyāta
iyām	iyāva	iyāma
etu	itām	yantu
ihi	itam	ita
ayāni	*ayāva*	*ayāma*
ait	aitām	āyan
aiḥ	aitam	aita
āyam	aiva	aima

Middle

adhīte[1]	adhīyāte	adhīyate
adhīṣe	adhīyāthe	adhīdhve
adhīye	adhīvahe	adhīmahe
adhīyīta	adhīyīyātām	adhīyīran
adhīyīthāḥ	adhīyīyāthām	adhīyīdhvam
adhīyīya	adhīyīvahi	adhīyīmahi
adhītām	adhīyātām	adhīyatām
adhīṣva	adhīyāthām	adhīdhvam
adhyayai	*adhyayāvahai*	*adhyayāmahai*
adhyaita	adhyaiyātām	adhyaiyata
adhyaithāḥ	adhyaiyāthām	adhyaidhvam
adhyaiyi	adhyaivahi	adhyaimahi

[1]eti has middle forms only with prefix adhi-.

[15] Active

karoti	kurutaḥ	kurvanti
karoṣi	kuruthaḥ	kurutha
karomi	kurvaḥ	kurmaḥ
kuryāt	kuryātām	kuryuḥ
kuryāḥ	kuryātam	kuryāta
kuryām	kuryāva	kuryāma
karotu	kurutām	kurvantu
kuru	kurutam	kuruta
karavāṇi	*karavāva*	*karavāma*
akarot	akurutām	akurvan
akaroḥ	akurutam	akuruta
akaravam	akurva	akurma

Middle

kurute	kurvāte	kurvate
kuruṣe	kurvāthe	kurudhve
kurve	kurvahe	kurmahe
kurvīta	kurvīyātām	kurvīran
kurvīthāḥ	kurvīyāthām	kurvīdhvam
kurvīya	kurvīvahi	kurvīmahi
kurutām	kurvātām	kurvatām
kuruṣva	kurvāthām	kurudhvam
karavai	*karavāvahai*	*karavāmahai*
akuruta	akurvātām	akurvata
akuruthāḥ	akurvāthām	akurudhvam
akurvi	akurvahi	akurmahi

[16] Active

dadhāti	dhattaḥ	dadhati
dadhāsi	dhatthaḥ	dhattha
dadhāmi	dadhvaḥ	dadhmaḥ
dadhyāt	dadhyātām	dadhyuḥ
dadhyāḥ	dadhyātam	dadhyāta
dadhyām	dadhyāva	dadhyāma
dadhātu	dhattām	dadhatu
dhehi	dhattam	dhatta
dadhāni	*dadhāva*	*dadhāma*
adadhāt	adhattām	adadhuḥ
adadhāḥ	adhattam	adhatta
adadhām	adadhva	adadhma

Middle

dhatte	dadhāte	dadhate
dhatse	dadhāthe	dhaddhve
dadhe	dadhvahe	dadhmahe
dadhīta	dadhīyātām	dadhīran
dadhīthāḥ	dadhīyāthām	dadhīdhvam
dadhīya	dadhīvahi	dadhīmahi
dhattām	dadhātām	dadhatām
dhatsva	dadhāthām	dhaddhvam
dadhai	*dadhāvahai*	*dadhāmahai*
adhatta	adadhātām	adadhata
adhatthāḥ	adadhāthām	adhaddhvam
adadhi	adadhvahi	adadhmahi

[17] Active

jahāti	jahī̆taḥ	jahati
jahāsi	jahī̆thaḥ	jahī̆tha
jahāmi	jahī̆vaḥ	jahī̆maḥ
jahyāt	jahyātām	jahyuḥ
jahyāḥ	jahyātam	jahyāta
jahyām	jahyāva	jahyāma
jahātu	jahī̆tām	jahatu
jahī̆hi	jahī̆tam	jahī̆ta
jahāni	*jahāva*	*jahāma*
ajahāt	ajahī̆tām	ajahuḥ
ajahāḥ	ajahī̆tam	ajahī̆ta
ajahām	ajahī̆va	ajahī̆ma

[18] Middle

mimīte	mimāte	mimate
mimīṣe	mimāthe	mimīdhve
mime	mimīvahe	mimīmahe
mimīta	mimīyātām	mimīran
mimīthāḥ	mimīyāthām	mimīdhvam
mimīya	mimīvahi	mimīmahi
mimītām	mimātām	mimatām
mimīṣva	mimāthām	mimīdhvam
mimai	mimāvahai	mimāmahai
amimīta	amimātām	amimata
amimīthāḥ	amimāthām	amimīdhvam
amimi	amimīvahi	amimīmahi

[19] Middle

śete	śayāte	śerate
śeṣe	śayāthe	śedhve
śaye	śevahe	śemahe
śayīta	śayīyātām	śayīran
śayīthāḥ	śayīyāthām	śayīdhvam
śayīya	śayīvahi	śayīmahi
śetām	śayātām	śeratām
śeṣva	śayāthām	śedhvam
śayai	śayāvahai	śayāmahai
aśeta	aśayātām	aśerata
aśethāḥ	aśayāthām	aśedhvam
aśayi	aśevahi	aśemahi

[20] Active

asti	staḥ	santi
asi	sthaḥ	stha
asmi	svaḥ	smaḥ
syāt	syātām	syuḥ
syāḥ	syātam	syāta
syām	syāva	syāma
astu	stām	santu
edhi	stam	sta
asāni	*asāva*	*asāma*
āsīt	āstām	āsan
āsīḥ	āstam	āsta
āsam	āsva	āsma

Middle[1]

ste	sāte	sate
se	sāthe	dhve
he	svahe	smahe

[1]Middle voice forms of asti are rare.

[21] Middle

āste	āsāte	āsate
āsse	āsāthe	ā(d)dhve
āse	āsvahe	āsmahe
āsīta	āsīyātām	āsīran
āsīthāḥ	āsīyāthām	āsīdhvam
āsīya	āsīvahi	āsīmahi
āstām	āsātām	āsatām
āssva	āsāthām	ā(d)dhvam
āsai	āsāvahai	āsāmahai
āsta	āsātām	āsata
āsthāḥ	āsāthām	ā(d)dhvam
āsi	āsvahi	āsmahi

[22] Active

śāsti	śiṣṭaḥ	*śāsati*
śāssi	śiṣṭhaḥ	śiṣṭha
śāsmi	śiṣvaḥ	śiṣmaḥ
śiṣyāt	śiṣyātām	śiṣyuḥ
śiṣyāḥ	śiṣyātam	śiṣyāta
śiṣyām	śiṣyāva	śiṣyāma
śāstu	śiṣṭām	*śāsatu*
śādhi	śiṣṭam	śiṣṭa
śāsāni	*śāsāva*	*śāsāma*
aśāt	aśiṣṭām	*aśāsuḥ*
aśāt/aśāḥ	aśiṣṭam	aśiṣṭa
aśāsam	aśiṣva	aśiṣma

[23] Active

hanti	hataḥ	ghnanti
haṃsi	hathaḥ	hatha
hanmi	hanvaḥ	hanmaḥ
hanyāt	hanyātām	hanyuḥ
hanyāḥ	hanyātam	hanyāta
hanyām	hanyāva	hanyāma
hantu	hatām	ghnantu
jahi	hatam	hata
hanāni	hanāva	hanāma
ahan	ahatām	aghnan
ahan	ahatam	ahata
ahanam	ahanva	ahanma

[24] Active

dogdhi	dugdhaḥ	duhanti
dhokṣi	dugdhaḥ	dugdha
dohmi	duhvaḥ	duhmaḥ
duhyāt	duhyātām	duhyuḥ
duhyāḥ	duhyātam	duhyāta
duhyām	duhyāva	duhyāma
dogdhu	dugdhām	duhantu
dugdhi	dugdham	dugdha
dohāni	*dohāva*	*dohāma*
adhok	adugdhām	aduhan
adhok	adugdham	adugdha
adoham	aduhva	aduhma

Middle

dugdhe	duhāte	duhate
dhukṣe	duhāthe	dhugdhve
duhe	duhvahe	duhmahe
duhīta	duhīyātām	duhīran
duhīthāḥ	duhīyāthām	duhīdhvam
duhīya	duhīvahi	duhīmahi
dugdhām	duhātām	duhatām
dhukṣva	duhāthām	dhugdhvam
dohai	*dohāvahai*	*dohāmahai*
adugdha	aduhātām	aduhata
adugdhāḥ	aduhāthām	adhugdhvam
aduhi	aduhvahi	aduhmahi

[25] Active

leḍhi	līḍhaḥ	lihanti
lekṣi	līḍhaḥ	līḍha
lehmi	lihvaḥ	lihmaḥ
lihyāt	lihyātām	lihyuḥ
lihyāḥ	lihyātam	lihyāta
lihyām	lihyāva	lihyāma
leḍhu	līḍhām	lihantu
līḍhi	līḍham	līḍha
lehāni	*lehāva*	*lehāma*
aleṭ	alīḍhām	alihan
aleṭ	alīḍham	alīḍha
aleham	alihva	alihma

Middle

līḍhe	lihāte	lihate
likṣe	lihāthe	līḍhve
lihe	lihvahe	lihmahe
lihīta	lihīyātām	lihīran
lihīthāḥ	lihīyāthām	lihīdhvam
lihīya	lihīvahi	lihīmahi
līḍhām	lihātām	lihatām
likṣva	lihāthām	līḍhvam
lehai	*lehāvahai*	*lehāmahai*
alīḍha	alihātām	alihata
alīḍhāḥ	alihāthām	alīḍhvam
alihi	alihvahi	alihmahi

Table 18. Conjugational paradigms for the reduplicating perfect.

[1]	**jijīva**	jijīvatuḥ	jijīvuḥ
	jijīvitha	jijīvathuḥ	jijīva
	jijīva	jijīviva	jijīvima
	jijīve	jijīvāte	jijīvire
	jijīviṣe	jijīvāthe	jijīvidhve
	jijīve	jijīvivahe	jijīvimahe
[2]	***viveśa***[1]	viviśatuḥ	viviśuḥ
	viveśitha	viviśathuḥ	viviśa
	viveśa	viviśiva	viviśima
	viviśe	viviśāte	viviśire
	viviśiṣe	viviśāthe	viviśidhve
	viviśe	viviśivahe	viviśimahe
[3]	***iyeṣa***	īṣatuḥ	īṣuḥ
	iyeṣitha	īṣathuḥ	īṣa
	iyeṣa	īṣiva	īṣima
	īṣe	īṣāte	īṣire
	īṣiṣe	īṣāthe	īṣidhve
	īṣe	īṣivahe	īṣimahe
[4]	***nināya****[2]	ninyatuḥ	ninyuḥ
	ninayitha[3]	ninyathuḥ	ninya
	ninăya(*)	ninyiva	ninyima
	ninye	ninyāte	ninyire
	ninyiṣe	ninyāthe	ninyidhve
	ninye	ninyivahe	ninyimahe

[1]Italics = stem vocalic in 1st grade. [2]Italics plus asterisk = stem vocalic in 2nd grade. [3]or ninetha

[5]	***śiśrāya****	śiśriyatuḥ	śiśriyuḥ
	śiśrayitha	śiśriyathuḥ	śiśriya
	śiśrā̆ya[(*)]	śiśriyiva	śiśriyima
	śiśriye	śiśriyāte	śiśriyire
	śiśriyiṣe	śiśriyāthe	śiśriyidhve
	śiśriye	śiśriyivahe	śiśriyimahe
[6]	***uvāca****	ūcatuḥ	ūcuḥ
	uvacitha[1]	ūcathuḥ	ūca
	uvā̆ca[(*)]	ūciva	ūcima
	ūce	ūcāte	ūcire
	ūciṣe	ūcāthe	ūcidhve
	ūce	ūcivahe	ūcimahe
[7]	***tastāra****	*tastaratuḥ*	*tastaruḥ*
	tastaritha	*tastarathuḥ*	*tastara*
	tastā̆ra[(*)]	*tastariva*	*tastarima*
	tastare	*tastarāte*	*tastarire*
	tastariṣe	*tastarāthe*	*tastaridhve*
	tastare	*tastarivahe*	*tastarimahe*
[8]	***cakāra****	cakratuḥ	cakruḥ
	cakartha	cakrathuḥ	cakra
	cakā̆ra[(*)]	cakṛva	cakṛma
	cakre	cakrāte	cakrire
	cakṛṣe	cakrāthe	cakṛdhve
	cakre	cakṛvahe	cakṛmahe

[1]or uvaktha

[9]	***tuṣṭāva****	tuṣṭuvatuḥ	tuṣṭuvuḥ
	tuṣṭotha	tuṣṭuvathuḥ	tuṣṭuva
	tuṣṭăva(*)	tuṣṭuva	tuṣṭuma
	tuṣṭuve	tuṣṭuvāte	tuṣṭuvire
	tuṣṭuṣe	tuṣṭuvāthe	tuṣṭudhve
	tuṣṭuve	tuṣṭuvahe	tuṣṭumahe
[10]	***tatāna****	tenatuḥ	tenuḥ
	tenitha[1]	tenathuḥ	tena
	tatăna(*)	teniva	tenima
	tene	tenāte	tenire
	teniṣe	tenāthe	tenidhve
	tene	tenivahe	tenimahe
[11]	**dadhau**	dadhatuḥ	dadhuḥ
	dadhātha[2]	dadhathuḥ	dadha
	dadhau	dadhiva	dadhima
	dadhe	dadhāte	dadhire
	dadhiṣe	dadhāthe	dadhidhve
	dadhe	dadhivahe	dadhimahe

[1]or tatantha
[2]or dadhita

Table 19. Irregular conjugations in the reduplicating perfect.

[12]	āha	āhatuḥ	āhuḥ
	āttha	āhathuḥ	--
	--	--	--
	--	--	--
	--	--	--
	--	--	--
[13]	*veda*	vidatuḥ	viduḥ
	vettha	vidathuḥ	vida
	veda	vidva	vidma
	--	--	--
	--	--	--
	--	--	--

Table 20. Key to conjugation classes in the reduplicating perfect (active).

I. Final -au; e.g. dadhau, jagau..........[11]
II. Final -a
  A. Initial ā-
    1. āha..........[12]
    2. Other than āha; e.g. āda, ānañja..........[1]
  B. Initial iy- or uv-
    1. Stem vocalic in 1st grade; e.g. iyeṣa, uvoṣa..........[3]
    2. Stem vocalic in 2nd grade; e.g. iyāja, uvāca..........[6]
  C. Initial other than ā-, iy-, or uv-
    1. Stem vocalic in zero grade; e.g. nininda, babhūva..........[1]
    2. Stem vocalic in 1st grade
      a. Stem vocalic -e-, -o-, or -ar-
        (1) veda ....[13]
        (2) cakarta and cakarṣa..........[1]
        (3) Other than the above three verbs; e.g. viveśa, bubodha, sasarja..........[2]
      b. Stem vocalic -a- or -ra-; e.g. caskanda, rarakṣa, papraccha..........[1]
    3. Stem vocalic in 2nd grade
      a. Stem vocalic -āy-
        (1) -āy- preceded by one consonant; e.g. nindruāya, cikāya..........[4]
        (2) -āy-preceded by two consonants; e.g. śiṣrāya, cikrāya..........[5]
      b. Stem vocalic -āv-
        (1) dadhāva..........[1]
        (2) tuṣṭāva, dudrāva, susrāva, and śuśrāva..........[9]
        (3) Other than the above five verbs; e.g. lulāva, juhāva ....[5]
      c. Stem vocalic -ār-
        (1) jajāra..........[7] or [10]
        (2) cacāra and tatāra..........[10]
        (3) cakāra ('do'), babhāra, vavāra, and sasāra..........[8]
        (4) cakāra ('strew')..........[7]

(5) -ār- preceded by one consonant, but excluding the above eight verbs; e.g. dadhāra, mamārja..........[4]

(6) -ār- preceded by two consonants; e.g. tastāra, sasmāra..........[7]

d. Stem vocalic other than -āy-, -āv-, -ār-

(1) babhrāma..........[4] or [10]

(2) paphāla and babhāja..........[10]

(3) cakrāma, cakṣāṇa, cakṣāma, jagāda, jahāsa, tatyāja, dadhvāna, śaśrāma, and sasvāna..........[7]

(4) cakāṅkṣa, cakhāda, vavāñcha, nanātha, yayāca, rarādha, śaśāsa, and sasādha..........[1]

(5) The type $C^1aC^1\bar{a}C^2a$ (where C^1 and C^2 are any two consonants), but excluding those under (4) above (i.e. nanātha to sasādha); e.g. tatāna, papāca, sasāda.........[10]

(6) Other than the above categories (1) to (5); e.g. vivyādha, suṣvāpa, jagrāha, cakhāna..........[4]

Table 21. Conjugational paradigm for the periphrastic perfect.

Active

3rd.:	kalayām āsa/ kalayāṃ cakāra	kalayām āsatuḥ/ kalayāṃ cakratuḥ	kalayām āsuḥ/ kalayāṃ cakruḥ
2nd.:	kalayām āsitha/ kalayāṃ cakartha	kalayām āsathuḥ/ kalayāṃ cakrathuḥ	kalayām āsa/ kalayāṃ cakra
1st.:	kalayām āsa/ kalayāṃ cakăra	kalayām āsiva/ kalayāṃ cakṛva	kalayām āsima/ kalayāṃ cakṛma

Middle

3rd.:	kalayāṃ cakre	kalayāṃ cakrāte	kalayāṃ cakrire
2nd.:	kalayāṃ cakṛṣe	kalayāṃ cakrāthe	kalayāṃ cakṛḍhve
1st.:	kalayāṃ cakre	kalayāṃ cakṛvahe	kalayāṃ cakṛmahe

Table 22. Conjugational paradigms for the aorist.

[1]	**asicat**	asicatām	asican
	asicaḥ	asicatam	asicata
	asicam	asicāva	asicāma
	asicata	asicetām	asicanta
	asicathāḥ	asicethām	asicadhvam
	asice	asicāvahi	asicāmahi
[2]	**adikṣat**	adikṣatām	adikṣan
	adikṣaḥ	adikṣatam	adikṣata
	adikṣam	adikṣāva	adikṣāma
	adikṣata	adikṣātām	adikṣanta
	adikṣathāḥ	adikṣāthām	adikṣadhvam
	adikṣi	adikṣāvahi	adikṣāmahi
[3]	***anaiṣīt**** [1]	*anaiṣṭām**	*anaiṣuḥ**
	*anaiṣīḥ**	*anaiṣṭam**	*anaiṣṭa**
	*anaiṣam**	*anaiṣva**	*anaiṣma**
	aneṣṭa [2]	*aneṣātām*	*aneṣata*
	aneṣṭhāḥ	*aneṣāthām*	*aneḍhvam*
	aneṣi	*aneṣvahi*	*aneṣmahi*
[4]	***akṣaipsīt****	*akṣaiptām**	*akṣaipsuḥ**
	*akṣaipsīḥ**	*akṣaiptam**	*akṣaipta**
	*akṣaipsam**	*akṣaipsva**	*akṣaipsma**
	akṣipta	akṣipsātām	akṣipsata
	akṣipthāḥ	akṣipsāthām	akṣibdhvam
	akṣipsi	akṣipsvahi	akṣipsmahi

[1]Italics with asterisk = stem vocalic in 2nd grade.
[2]Italics without asterisk = stem vocalic in 1st grade.

[5]	***abhāsīt****	*abhāsiṣṭām**	*abhāsiṣuḥ**
	*abhāsīḥ**	*abhāsiṣṭam**	*abhāsiṣṭa**
	*abhāsiṣam**	*abhāsiṣva**	*abhāsiṣma**
	--	--	--
	--	--	--
	--	--	--

[6]	***apāvīt****[1]	*apāviṣṭām**	*apāviṣuḥ**
	*apāvīḥ**	*apāviṣṭam**	*apāviṣṭa**
	*apāviṣam**	*apāviṣva**	*apāviṣma**
	apaviṣṭa	*apaviṣātām*	*apaviṣata*
	apaviṣṭhāḥ	*apaviṣāthām*	*apaviḍhvam*
	apaviṣi	*apaviṣvahi*	*apaviṣmahi*

[7]	***adāt****	*adātām**	*aduḥ**
	*adāḥ**	*adātam**	*adāta**
	*adām**	*adāva**	*adāma**
	adita	adiṣātām	adiṣata
	adithāḥ	adiṣāthām	adiḍhvam
	adiṣi	adiṣvahi	adiṣmahi

[1]Usually in the active of class [6] (-īt class), the stem vocalic is in 1st grade for some verbs and in 2nd grade for others.

Table 23. Irregular conjugations in the aorist.

[8]	***akārṣīt****	*akārṣṭām**	*akārṣuḥ**
	*akārṣīḥ**	*akārṣṭam**	*akārṣṭa**
	*akārṣam**	*akārṣva**	*akārṣma**
	akṛta	akṛṣātām	akṛṣata
	akṛthāḥ	akṛṣāthām	akṛḍhvam
	akṛṣi	akṛṣvahi	akṛṣmahi
[9]	**abhūt**	abhūtām	abhūvan
	abhūḥ	abhūtam	abhūta
	abhūvam	abhūva	abhūma
	--	--	--
	--	--	--
	--	--	--

Table 24. Conjugational paradigm for the precative.

nīyāt	nīyāstām	nīyāsuḥ
nīyāḥ	nīyāstam	nīyāsta
nīyāsam	nīyāsva	nīyāsma
neṣīṣṭa	neṣīyāstām	neṣīran
neṣīṣṭhāḥ	neṣīyāsthām	neṣīḍhvam
neṣīya	neṣīvahi	neṣīmahi

Table 25. Conjugational paradigm for the periphrastic future.

netā	netārau	netāraḥ
netāsi	netāsthaḥ	netāstha
netāsmi	netāsvaḥ	netāsmaḥ
netā	netārau	netāraḥ
netāse	netāsāthe	netādhve
netāhe	netāsvahe	netāsmahe

Table 26. Guide to Table 27 and the paradigms.

Cit: Present indicative active/middle ⇒ Tables 16-17 [1]-[25]
→ Present active participle (pp. 60-61) ⇒ Table 6 [12]/[6] [29]/[21] [33]
→ Present middle participle (p. 61) ⇒ Table 6 [1] [17] [32]

Pas: Present indicative passive ⇒ Table 16 [1] Middle
→ Precative active (-yate → -yāt) ⇒ Table 24 Active
→ Absolutive with prefix (-yate → -ya)

Fut: Simple future ⇒ Table 16 [1] Present Indicative
→ Conditional (---syati/---syate → a---syat/a---syata) ⇒ Table 16 [1] Imperfect
→ Precative middle (-syati/-syate → -sīṣṭa) ⇒ Table 24 Middle
→ Future active participle (-syati → -syant-) ⇒ Table 6 [12] [29]/[21] [33]
→ Future middle participle (-syate → -syamāna-) ⇒ Table 6 [1] [17] [32]

Cau: Causative ⇒ Table 16 [1]
→ Causative passive (-ayati → -yate) ⇒ Table 16 [1] Middle
→ Causative future (-ayati → -ayiṣyati) ⇒ Table 16 [1] Present Indicative Active
→ Causative perfect (-ayati → -ayām āsa) ⇒ Table 21 Active
→ Causative infinitive (-ayati → -ayitum)
→ Causative absolutive without prefix (-ayati → -ayitvā)
→ Causative perfect passive participle (-ayati → -ita-) ⇒ Table 6 [1] [17] [32]
→ Causative future passive participle in -nīya- (-ayati → -anīya-) ⇒ Table 6 [1] [17] [32]
→ Causative future passive participle in -ya- (-ayati → -ya-) ⇒ Table 6 [1] [17] [32]
→ Causative future passive participle in -avya- (-ayati → -ayitavya-) ⇒ Table 6 [1] [17] [32]

Des: Desiderative ⇒ Table 16 [1]
→ Desiderative passive (-sati/-sate → -syate) ⇒ Table 16 [1] Middle
→ Desiderative future (-sati/-sate → -siṣyati/-siṣyate) ⇒ Table 16 [1] Present Indicative
→ Desiderative perfect (-sati/-sate → -sām āsa/-sāṃ cakre) ⇒ Table 21
→ Desiderative aorist (---sati/---sate → a---sīt/a---siṣṭa) ⇒ Table 22 [6]
→ Desiderative infinitive (-sati/-sate → -situm)
→ Desiderative perfect passive participle (-sati/-sate → -sita-) ⇒ Table 6 [1] [17] [32]
fn.: Middle-voice intensive ⇒ Table 16 [1] Middle
→ Intensive passive etc. (p. 59)

Per: Perfect ⇒ Tables 18-19 [1]-[13] & Table 21
→ Perfect active participle in -(i)vas- (pp. 61-62) ⇒ Table 6 [15]/[16] [30]/[31] [33]
→ Perfect middle participle (p. 62) ⇒ Table 6 [1] [17] [32]

Aor: Aorist ⇒ Tables 22-23 [1]-[9]
fn.: Aorist passive in -i ⇒ Table 22 [6] Middle, except 3rd sing.; endings: -i, -iṣātām, etc.
→ Precative passive (a---i → ---iṣīṣṭa) ⇒ Table 24 Middle
→ Periphrastic future passive (a---i → ---itā) ⇒ Table 25 Middle
→ Simple future passive (a---i → ---iṣyate) ⇒ Table 16 [1] Present Indicative Middle
→ Conditional passive (-i → -iṣyata) ⇒ Table 16 [1] Imperfect Middle

CAo: Causative aorist ⇒ Table 22 [1]

Inf: Infinitive
→ Periphrastic future (-um → -ā) ⇒ Table 25
→ Future passive participle in -avya- (-um → -avya-) ⇒ Table 6 [1] [17] [32]

Abs: Absolutive without prefix

PPP: Perfect passive participle ⇒ Table 6 [1] [17] [32]
→ Perfect active participle in -vat- (-a → -avat) ⇒ Table 6 [13] [21] [33]

FPP: Future passive participle in -nīya- ⇒ Table 6 [1] [17] [32]

FPP: Future passive participle in -ya- ⇒ Table 6 [1] [17] [32]

Table 27. Principal parts of verbs.

	1 añc-1 'bend'	2 añj-7 'anoint'	3 aṭ-1 'wander'	4 ad-2 'eat'
Cit:	añcati	anakti[4] M	aṭati M	atti[12]
Pas:	a(ñ)cyate[1]	ajyate	aṭyate	adyate[13]
Fut:	añciṣyati	añjiṣyati[5]	aṭiṣyati	atsyati
Cau:	añcayati	añjayati	āṭayati	ādayati
Des:	añciciṣati	añjijiṣati	aṭiṭiṣati[11]	jighatsati
Per:	ānañca	ānañja M[6]	āṭa	āda
Aor:	āñcīt	āñjīt[7]	āṭīt	aghasat
CAo:		āñjijat	āṭitat	ādidat
Inf:	añcitum	añjitum[8] F	aṭitum	attum F
Abs:	añcitvā[2]	añjitvā[9]	aṭitvā	jagdhvā
PPP:	a(ñ)cita-[3]	akta-	aṭita-	jagdha-
FPP:				adanīya-
FPP:		a(ñ)jya-[10]	aṭya-	adya-

	5 an-2 'breathe'	6 arth-10 'ask for'	7 arh-1 'deserve'	8 av-1 'further'
Cit:	aniti	arthayate	arhati	avati
Pas:	anyate	arthyate	arhyate[15]	avyate
Fut:	aniṣyati	arthayiṣyate	arhiṣyati	aviṣyati
Cau:	ānayati		arhayati	āvayati
Des:	aniniṣati	artithayiṣate	arjihiṣati	aviviṣati
Per:	āna	arthayāṃ c	ānarha	āva
Aor:	ānīt[14]	ārtathata	ārhīt	āvīt[17]
CAo:	āninat		arjihat[16]	āvivat
Inf:	anitum	arthayitum	arhitum	avitum
Abs:	ānitvā	arthayitvā	arhitvā	
PPP:	anita-	arthita-	arhita-	avita-
FPP:		arthanīya-	arhaṇīya-	
FPP:	anīya-			

[1]Abs -acya [2]/aktvā [3]/akta-/akna- [4]Pl añjanti [5]/aṅkṣyati
[6]Mid ānaje [7]Pas āñji [8]/aṅktum [9]/a(ṅ)ktvā [10]/aṅgya-
[11]Int aṭāṭyate [12]Pl adanti [13]Abs -jagdhya [14]Pas āni [15]Abs -arghya
[16]/ārhīt; Pas ārhi [17]Pas āvi

	9 aś-5 'obtain'	10 aś-9 'eat'	11 as-2 'be'	12 as-4 'throw'
Cit:	aśnute [6]	aśnāti	asti [20]	asyati
Pas:	aśyate	aśyate		asyate
Fut:	aśiṣyate[1]	aśiṣyati		asiṣyati
Cau:	āśayati	āśayati		āsayati
Des:	aśiśiṣate	aśiśiṣati		asisiṣati
Per:	ānaśe	āśa	āsa	āsa
Aor:	āṣṭa[2]	āśīt[5]		āsthat[6]
CAo:	āśiśat	āśiśat	*Missing*	āsiṣat
Inf:	aṣṭum[3]	aśitum F	*forms from*	asitum
Abs:	aṣṭvā[4]	aśitvā	*bhū (236)*	as(i)tvā
PPP:	aṣṭa-	aśita-		asta-
FPP:		aśanīya-		asanīya-
FPP:				

	13 ah-1 'say'	14 āp-5 'acquire'	15 ās-2 'sit'	16 ī̆-2/1 'go'
Cit:		āpnoti	āste [21]	eti [14][8]
Pas:		āpyate	āsyate	īyate[9]
Fut:		āpsyati	āsiṣyate	eṣyati
Cau:		āpayati	āsayati	āyayati
Des:		īpsati	āsisiṣate	īyiṣati
Per:	āha [12]	āpa	āsāṃ c	iyāya[10]
Aor:		āpat[7]	āsiṣṭa	aiṣīt
CAo:	*Missing*	āpipat		āyiyat
Inf:	*forms from*	āptum F	āsitum F	etum F
Abs:	*brū (224),*	āptvā	āsitvā	itvā
PPP:	*vac (320),*	āpta-	āsita-	ita-
FPP:	*etc.*	āpanīya-	āsanīya-	
FPP:		āpya-	āsya-	eya-

[1]/akṣyate [2]/āśiṣṭa [3]/aśitum [4]/aśitvā [5]Pas āśi [6]Pas āsi [7]Pas āpi
[8]/ayati. For adhīte (=adhi+i) see p. 206. [9]/Abs -itya [10]/ayām āsa

	17 indh-7 'kindle'	18 iṣ-6 'desire'	19 iṣ-4 'send'	20 īkṣ-1 'see'
Cit:	inddhe	icchati	iṣyati	īkṣate
Pas:	idhyate	iṣyate	iṣyate	īkṣyate
Fut:	indhiṣyate	eṣiṣyati	eṣiṣyati	īkṣiṣyate
Cau:	indhayati	eṣayati	eṣayati	īkṣayati
Des:	indidhiṣate	eṣiṣiṣati	eṣiṣiṣati	īcikṣiṣate
Per:	indhāṃ c	iyeṣa	iyeṣa	īkṣāṃ c
Aor:	aindhiṣṭa	aiṣīt[1]	aiṣīt	aikṣiṣṭa
CAo:		aiṣiṣat		aicikṣat
Inf:	indhitum	eṣitum[2] F	eṣitum[2] F	īkṣitum F
Abs:	indhitvā	iṣṭvā[3]	iṣṭvā[3]	īkṣitvā
PPP:	iddha-	iṣṭa-	iṣita-	īkṣita-
FPP:		eṣaṇīya-		īkṣaṇīya-
FPP:		eṣya-		

	21 īḍ-2 'praise'	22 īr-2 'move'	23 īś-2 'rule'	24 īṣ-1 'flee'
Cit:	īṭṭe	īrte	īṣṭe	īṣate
Pas:	īḍyate	īryate	īśyate	
Fut:	īḍiṣyate	īriṣyate	īśiṣyate	īṣiṣyate
Cau:	īḍayati	īrayati	īśayati	
Des:	īḍiḍiṣate		īśiśiṣate	
Per:	īḍāṃ c	īrāṃ c	īśāṃ c	īṣāṃ c
Aor:	aiḍiṣṭa	airiṣṭa	aiśiṣṭa	aiṣiṣṭa
CAo:	aiḍiḍat	airirat	aiśiśat	
Inf:	īḍitum F	īritum	īśitum F	īṣitum
Abs:	īḍitvā			
PPP:	īḍita-	īrita-[4]	īśita-	īṣita-
FPP:		īraṇīya-		
FPP:	īḍya-	īrya-		

[1]Pas aiṣi [2]/eṣṭum [3]/eṣitvā [4]/īrṇa-

	25 ukṣ-1 'sprinkle'	26 uñch-1/6 'sweep'	27 und-7 'moisten'	28 ubh-9/6 'confine'
Cit:	ukṣati M	uñchati	unatti[2]	ubhnāti[4]
Pas:	ukṣyate	--[1]	udyate	
Fut:	ukṣiṣyati	uñchiṣyati	undiṣyati	u(m)bhiṣyati[5]
Cau:	ukṣayati	uñchayati	undayati	
Des:	ucikṣiṣati	uñcicchiṣati	undidiṣati	
Per:	ukṣām āsa	uñchām āsa	undām āsa	ubobha[6]
Aor:	aukṣīt	auñchīt	aundīt	au(m)bhīt
CAo:		auñcicchat	aundidat	
Inf:	ukṣitum	uñchitum	unditum	u(m)bhitum
Abs:				
PPP:	ukṣita-	uñchita-	utta-[3]	ubdha-[7]
FPP:				
FPP:				

	29 uṣ-1 'burn'	30 ūh-1 'remove'	31 ṛ-1/3/5 'move'	32 ṛc-6 'praise'
Cit:	oṣati	ūhati M	ṛcchati[11]	ṛcati
Pas:	uṣyate	ūhyate	aryate	ṛcyate[13]
Fut:	oṣiṣyati	ūhiṣyate	ariṣyati	arciṣyati
Cau:	oṣayati	ūhayati	arpayati	arcayati
Des:	oṣiṣiṣati		aririṣati	arciciṣati
Per:	uvoṣa[8]	ūhām ā/c	āra	ānarca
Aor:	auṣīt	auhīt[10] M	ārat[12]	ārcīt
CAo:		aujihat	ārpayat	
Inf:	oṣitum	ūhitum F	artum	arcitum
Abs:	oṣitvā	ūhitvā	ṛtvā	arcitvā
PPP:	uṣita-[9]	ūhita-	ṛta-	arcita-
FPP:		ūhaniya-		arcanīya-
FPP:		ūhya-	arya-	arcya-

[1]Abs -uñchya [2]Pl undanti [3]/unna- [4]/u(m)bhati [5]/obhiṣyati
[6]/umbhām āsa [7]/u(m)bhita- [8]/oṣām āsa [9]/uṣṭa-/oṣita-
[10]Pas auhi [11]/iyarti/ṛṇoti [12]/ārṣīt; Pas āri [13]Abs -arcya

	33 ṛj-1 'obtain'	34 ṛdh-5/4 'thrive'	35 ṛṣ-6 'push'	36 edh-1 'thrive'
Cit:	arjati M	ṛdhnoti[2]	ṛṣati	edhate
Pas:	ṛjyate	ṛdhyate		edhyate
Fut:	arjiṣyate	ardhiṣyati	arṣiṣyati	edhiṣyate
Cau:	arjayati	ardhayati	arṣayati	edhayati
Des:	arjijiṣate	ardidhiṣati	arṣiṣiṣati	edidhiṣate
Per:	ānṛje	ānardha	ānarṣa	edhāṃ c
Aor:	ārjiṣṭa	ārdhīt	ārṣīt	aidhiṣṭa
CAo:	ārjijat			aididhat
Inf:	arjitum	ardhitum	arṣitum	edhitum
Abs:		ardhitvā[3]	arṣitvā	edhitvā
PPP:	ṛjita-[1]	ṛddha-	ṛṣṭa-	edhita-
FPP:	arjanīya-			
FPP:		ardhya-		

	37 kath-10 'tell'	38 kamp-1 'tremble'	39 kal-10 'drive'	40 kal-10 'count'
Cit:	kathayati M	kampate A	kālayati M	kalayati M
Pas:	kathyate[4]	kampyate	kālyate	
Fut:	kathayiṣyati	kampiṣyate	kalayiṣyati	kalayiṣyati
Cau:	kāthayati	kampayati		kālayati
Des:	cakathayiṣati	cikampiṣate	cikālayiṣati	cikalayiṣati M
Per:	kathayām ā	cakampe	kālayām āsa	kalayām āsa/c
Aor:	acīkathat	akampiṣṭa	acīkalat[5] M	acakalat M
CAo:		acakampat		
Inf:	kathayitum	kampitum		kalayitum
Abs:	kathayitvā	kampitvā		
PPP:	kathita-	kampita-	kālita-	kalita-
FPP:	kathanīya-	kampanīya-		kalanīya-
FPP:		kampya-		

[1]/arjita- [2]/ṛdhyati [3]/ṛddhvā [4]Abs -kathayya [5]Pas akāli

	41 kas-1 'move'	42 kāṅkṣ-1 'desire'	43 kāś-1/4 'shine'	44 kup-4 'be angry'
Cit:	kasati	kāṅkṣati	kāś(y)ate	kupyati
Pas:	kasyate	kāṅkṣyate	kāśyate	kupyate
Fut:	kasiṣyati	kāṅkṣiṣyati	kāśiṣyate	kopiṣyati
Cau:	kāsayati	kāṅkṣayati	kāśayati	kopayati
Des:	cikasiṣati	cikāṅkṣiṣati	cikāśiṣate	cukopiṣati
Per:	cakāsa	cakāṅkṣa	cakāśe	cukopa
Aor:	akāsīt	akāṅkṣīt	akāśiṣṭa	akupat
CAo:	acīkasat			
Inf:	kasitum	kāṅkṣitum F	kāśitum	kupitum[1]
Abs:		kāṅkṣitvā	kāśitvā	kupitvā
PPP:	kas(i)ta-	kāṅkṣita-	kāśita-	kupita-
FPP:	kāsanīya-	kāṅkṣaṇīya-	kāśanīya-	
FPP:				kopya-

	45 kṛ-8 'do'	46 kṛt-6 'cut'	47 kṛś-4 'grow lean'	48 kṛṣ-1/6 'pull'
Cit:	karoti [15]	kṛntati	kṛśyati	karṣati[9]
Pas:	kriyate[2]	kṛtyate		kṛṣyate
Fut:	kariṣyati[3]	kartiṣyati[5]	karśiṣyati	karkṣyati[10]
Cau:	kārayati	kartayati	karśayati	karṣayati
Des:	cikīrṣati	cikartiṣati		cikṛkṣati
Per:	cakāra [8]	cakarta	cakarśa	cakarṣa
Aor:	akārṣīt[4] [8]	akṛtat[6]	akṛśat	akārkṣīt[11]
CAo:	acīkarat	acakartat		acīkṛṣat
Inf:	kartum	kartitum[7]	karśitum	karṣṭum F[12]
Abs:	kṛtvā	kartitvā	kṛśitvā[8]	kṛṣṭvā
PPP:	kṛta-	kṛtta-	kṛśita-	kṛṣṭa-
FPP:	karaṇīya-			karṣaṇīya-
FPP:	kārya-	kartya-		kṛṣya-

[1]/kopitum [2]Abs -kṛtya [3]Prec Mid kṛṣīṣṭa [4]Pas akāri [5]/kartsyati
[6]/akartīt; Pas akarti [7]FPP karttavya- [8]/karśitvā [9]/kṛṣati 'plough'
[10]/krakṣyati [11]/akrākṣīt/akṛkṣat [12]/krasṭum

	49 kṝ-6 'strew'	50 kḷp-1 'be able'	51 kram-1/4 'step'	52 krī-9 'buy'
Cit:	kirati	kalpate	krām(y)ati[3]	krīṇāti M
Pas:	kīryate		kramyate	krīyate
Fut:	karīṣyati	kalp(i)ṣyate	kramiṣyati[4]	kreṣyati M
Cau:	kārayati	kalpayati	krāmayati	krāpayati
Des:	cikariṣati	cikalpiṣate	cikramiṣati[5]	cikrīṣati M
Per:	cakāra [7]	cakḷpe	cakrāma M	cikrāya M
Aor:	akārīt	akḷpat[1]	akramīt[6]	akraiṣīt[9] M
CAo:		acīkḷpat	acikramat	acikrapat
Inf:	karītum	kalp(i)tum F	kramitum[7] F	kretum F
Abs:	kīrtvā	kḷptvā[2]	krāntvā[8]	krītvā
PPP:	kīrṇa-	kḷpta-	krānta-	krīta-
FPP:		kalpanīya-	kramaṇīya-	krayaṇīya-
FPP:	kīrya-	kalpya-	kramya-	krey(y)a-

	53 krīḍ-1 'play'	54 krudh-4 'be angry'	55 kruś-1 'cry out'	56 kliś-9 'suffer'
Cit:	krīḍati M	krudhyati	krośati	kliśnāti
Pas:	krīḍyate	krudhyate	kruśyate	kliśyate
Fut:	krīḍiṣyati	krotsyati	krokṣyati	kleśiṣyati[12]
Cau:	krīḍayati	krodhayati	krośayati	kleśayati
Des:	cikrīḍiṣati	cukrutsati	cukrukṣati	cikliśiṣati
Per:	cikrīḍa	cukrodha	cukrośa	cikleśa
Aor:	akrīḍīt	akrudhat[10]	akrukṣat[11]	akleśīt[13]
CAo:	acikrīḍat	acukrudhat	acukruśat	
Inf:	krīḍitum	kroddhum	kroṣṭum F	kleśitum[14]
Abs:	krīḍitvā	kruddhvā	kruṣṭvā	kliśitvā[15]
PPP:	krīḍita-	kruddha-	kruṣṭa-	kliśita-[16]
FPP:		krodhanīya-		
FPP:				

[1]Mid akḷpta/akḷpiṣṭa [2]/kalpitvā [3]Mid kramate [4]Mid kraṃsyate
[5]Int caṅkramyate [6]Mid akraṃsta [7]/krāntum [8]/kramitvā
[9]Pas akrāyi [10]Pas akrodhi [11]Pas akrośi [12]/klekṣyati [13]/aklikṣat
[14]/kleṣṭum [15]/kliṣṭvā [16]/kliṣṭa-

	57 kṣaṇ-8 'wound'	58 kṣam-1/4 'endure'	59 kṣar-1 'flow'	60 kṣal-10 'wash'
Cit:	kṣaṇoti M	kṣamati[3] M	kṣarati M	kṣālayati
Pas:	kṣaṇyate	kṣamyate		kṣālyate
Fut:	kṣaṇiṣyati	kṣaṃsyati[4] M	kṣariṣyati	kṣālayiṣyati
Cau:	kṣāṇayati	kṣamayati[5]	kṣārayati	
Des:	cikṣaṇiṣati	cikṣaṃsati M	cikṣariṣati	cikṣālayiṣati
Per:	cakṣāṇa M	cakṣāma M	cakṣāra	kṣālayām āsa
Aor:	akṣaṇīt[1]	akṣamat[6]	akṣārīt	acikṣalat
CAo:		acikṣamat		
Inf:	kṣantum[2]	kṣantum[7] F	kṣaritum	kṣālayitum
Abs:	kṣa(ṇi)tvā	kṣāntvā[8]		kṣālayitvā
PPP:	kṣata-	kṣānta-[9]	kṣarita-	kṣālita-
FPP:		kṣamaṇīya-		
FPP:		kṣāmya-		kṣālya-

	61 kṣi-5/9 'destroy'	62 kṣip-6/4 'throw'	63 kṣud-7 'shatter'	64 kṣudh-4 'hunger'
Cit:	kṣiṇoti[10]	kṣip(y)ati M	kṣuṇatti[14] M	kṣudhyati
Pas:	kṣīyate	kṣipyate	kṣudyate	kṣudhyate
Fut:	kṣeṣyati	kṣepsyati	ksotsyati[15]	kṣotsyati
Cau:	kṣapayati[11]	kṣepayati	kṣodayati	kṣodhayati
Des:	cikṣīṣati	cikṣipsati	cukṣutsati	cukṣutsati
Per:	cikṣāya	cikṣepa M	cukṣoda M	cukṣodha
Aor:	akṣaiṣīt	akṣaipsīt[13] M	akṣudat[16]	akṣudhat[18]
CAo:	acikṣayat	acikṣipat		acukṣudhat
Inf:	kṣetum	kṣeptum F	kṣodum[17]	kṣodhitum[19]
Abs:	kṣitvā	kṣiptvā	kṣutvā	kṣudhitvā[20]
PPP:	kṣita-[12]	kṣipta-	kṣuṇṇa-	kṣudhita-
FPP:				
FPP:	kṣay(y)a-	kṣepya-	kṣodya-	

[1]Mid akṣaṇiṣṭa/akṣata [2]/kṣaṇitum [3]/kṣāmyati [4]/kṣamiṣyati
[5]Mid kṣāmayate [6]Mid akṣamiṣṭa/akṣaṃsta [7]/kṣamitum F
[8]/kṣamitvā [9]/kṣamita- [10]/kṣiṇāti/kṣayati [11]/kṣāyayati [12]/kṣīṇa-
[13]Pas akṣepi [14]Pl kṣundanti [15]Prec Mid kṣutsīṣṭa [16]/akṣautsīt;
Mid akṣutta [17]Peri Fut kṣottā [18]Pas akṣodhi [19]Peri Fut kṣoddhā
[20]/kṣodhitvā

	65 khaṇḍ-10 'break'	66 khan-1 'dig'	67 khād-1 'eat'	68 khid-6/7 'afflict'
Cit:	khaṇḍayati	khanati M	khādati M	khindati[3]
Pas:		khanyate[1]	khādyate	khidyate
Fut:		khaniṣyati	khādiṣyati	khetsyati
Cau:		khānayati	khādayati	khedayati
Des:	cikhaṇḍayiṣati	cikhaniṣati	cikhādiṣati	cikhitsati
Per:		cakhāna M	cakhāda	cikheda M
Aor:	acakhaṇḍat	akhānīt M	akhādīt	akhaitsīt M
CAo:				
Inf:		khanitum	khāditum F	khettum[4]
Abs:		khātvā[2]	khāditvā	khittvā
PPP:	khaṇḍita-	khāta-	khādita-	khinna-
FPP:		khananīya-	khādanīya-	
FPP:		khānya-	khādya-	

	69 khyā-2 'be known'	70 gaṇ-10 'count'	71 gad-1 'speak'	72 gam-1 'go'
Cit:	khyāti	gaṇayati M	gadati	gacchati M
Pas:	khyāyate	gaṇyate[6]	gadyate	gamyate[8]
Fut:	khyāsyati	gaṇayiṣyati	gadiṣyati	gamiṣyati
Cau:	khyāpayati		gādayati	gamayati
Des:	cikhyāsati	jigaṇayiṣati	jigadiṣati	jigamiṣati
Per:	cakhyau M	gaṇayām ā/c	jagāda	jagāma
Aor:	akhyat[5]	ajīgaṇat[7] M	agādīt	agamat[9]
CAo:			ajīgadat	ajīgamat
Inf:	khyātum F	gaṇayitum	gaditum	gantum F
Abs:	khyātvā	gaṇayitvā	gaditvā	gatvā
PPP:	khyāta-	gaṇita-	gadita-	gata-
FPP:		gaṇanīya-		gamanīya-
FPP:	kheya-		gadya-	gamya-

[1]/khāyate [2]/khanitvā [3]Mid khidyate/khintte [4]FPP kheditavya- [5]Pas akhyāyi [6]Abs -gaṇayya [7]/ajagaṇat [8]Abs -gamya/-gatya [9]Pas agāmi

	73 garj-1 'roar'	74 garh-1 'blame'	75 gal-1 'fall'	76 gā-2 'go'
Cit:	garjati	garhate A	galati	gāti[3] M
Pas:	garjyate	garhyate	galyate	gāyate
Fut:	garjiṣyati	garhiṣyate	galiṣyati	gāsyate
Cau:	garjayati	garhayati	gālayati	gāpayati
Des:	jigarjiṣati	jigarhiṣate	jigaliṣati	jigāsati
Per:	jagarja	jagarhe A[1]	jagāla	jage
Aor:	agarjīt	agarhiṣṭa	agālīt[2]	agāt[4]
CAo:		ajagarhat	ajīgalat	ajīgapat
Inf:	garjitum	garhitum F	galitum	gātum
Abs:	garjitvā	garhitvā		
PPP:	garjita-	garhita-	galita-	
FPP:		garhaṇīya-		
FPP:		garhya-		

	77 gāh-1 'plunge'	78 gu-1 'proclaim'	79 gup-1 'guard'	80 guh-1 'conceal'
Cit:	gāhate A	gavate	gopāyati	gūhati M
Pas:	gāhyate		gupyate	guhyate
Fut:	gāhiṣyate[5]	goṣyate	gopiṣyati[10]	gūhiṣyati[12]
Cau:	gāhayati	gāvayati	gopayati	gūhayati
Des:	jigāhiṣate	jugūṣate	jugopiṣati M	jughukṣati
Per:	jagāhe	juguve	jugopa	jugūha[13]
Aor:	agāhiṣṭa[6]	agoṣṭa	agaupsīt	agūhīt[14] M
CAo:	ajīgahat	ajagavat	ajūgupat	ajūguhat
Inf:	gāhitum[7]	gotum	gop(i)tum F	goḍhum F
Abs:	gāhitvā[8]		guptvā[11]	gūḍhvā
PPP:	gāhita-[9]		gup(i)ta-	gūḍha-
FPP:	gāhanīya-		gopanīya-	
FPP:	gāhya-		gopya-	guhya-

[1]Act jagarha [2]Pas agāli [3]/jigāti; Mid gate [4]Mid agāsta; Pas agāyi
[5]/ghākṣyate [6]/agāḍha [7]/gāḍhum [8]/gāḍhvā [9]/gāḍha-
[10]/gopsyati [11]/gopitvā [12]/ghokṣyati M [13]Mid juguhe
[14]/aghukṣat M

	81 gṛdh-4 'covet'	82 gṝ-6 'swallow'	83 gṝ-9 'invoke'	84 gai-1 'sing'
Cit:	gṛdhyati	girati[2] M	gṛṇāti M	gāyati
Pas:		gīryate	--[4]	gīyate[5]
Fut:	gardhiṣyati	garīṣyati	garīṣyati	gāsyati
Cau:	gardhayati	gārayati	gārayati	gāpayati
Des:	jigardhiṣati	jigariṣati	jigarīṣati	jigāsati
Per:	jagardha	jagāra	jagāra	jagau
Aor:	agṛdhat	agārīt[3]	agārīt	agāsīt[6]
CAo:	ajīgardhat		ajīgarat	ajīgapat
Inf:	gardhitum	garītum	garītum	gātum F
Abs:	gardhitvā[1]			gītvā
PPP:	gṛddha-	gīrṇa-	gīrṇa-	gīta-
FPP:				gānīya-
FPP:	gṛdhya-			geya-

	85 gopā-1 'guard'	86 granth-9/1 'compose'	87 gras-1 'swallow'	88 grah-9 'seize'
Cit:	gopāyati	grathnāti[7]	grasati M	gṛhṇāti M
Pas:	gopāyyate	grathyate	grasyate	gṛhyate
Fut:	gopāyiṣyati	granthiṣyati	grasiṣyate	grahīṣyati
Cau:	gopāyayati	granthayati	grāsayati	grāhayati
Des:	jugopāyiṣati	jigranthiṣati	jigrasiṣate	jighṛkṣati
Per:	gopāyām āsa	jagrantha	jagrase	jagrāha M
Aor:	agopāyīt	agranthīt[8]	agrasīt M	agrahīt[10]
CAo:		ajagranthat		ajigrahat
Inf:	gopāyitum	granthitum[9]	grasitum	grahītum
Abs:	gopāyitvā	gra(n)thitvā	gras(i)tvā	gṛhītvā
PPP:	gopāyita-	grathita-	grasta-	gṛhīta-
FPP:	gopanīya-	granthanīya-		grahaṇīya-
FPP:		grathya-	grasya-	grāhya-

[1]/gṛddhvā [2]/gilati, and similarly throughout [3]Pas agāri
[4]Abs -gīrya [5]Abs -gāya; Prec Act geyāt [6]Pas agāyi [7]/granthati
[8]Pas agranthi [9]FPP grathitavya- [10]Mid agrahīṣṭa; Pas agrāhi

	89 ghuṣ-1 'sound'	90 ghṛ-1/3 'sprinkle'	91 ghrā-1 'smell'	92 cakṣ-2 'tell'
Cit:	ghoṣati	gharati[3]	jighrati	caṣṭe[7]
Pas:	ghuṣyate		ghrāyate[4]	cakṣyate
Fut:	ghoṣiṣyati	ghariṣyate	ghrāsyati	--[8]
Cau:	ghoṣayati	ghārayati	ghrāpayati	cakṣayati
Des:	jughoṣiṣati		jighrāsati	
Per:	jughoṣa	jaghāra	jaghrau	cacakṣe[9]
Aor:	aghoṣīt[1]	aghār(ṣ)īt	aghrāt[5]	
CAo:	ajūghuṣat	ajīgharat	ajighrapat	
Inf:	ghoṣitum	ghartum	ghrātum F	caṣṭum
Abs:			jighritvā	
PPP:	ghuṣita-[2]	ghṛta-	ghrāta-[6]	
FPP:	ghoṣaṇīya-			
FPP:	ghuṣya-		ghreya-	cakṣya-

	93 cam-1 'sip'	94 car-1 'go'	95 carv-1 'chew'	96 cal-1 'move'
Cit:	camati[10]	carati	carvati	calati
Pas:	--[11]	caryate	carvyate	calyate
Fut:	camiṣyati	cariṣyati		caliṣyati
Cau:	cāmayati	cārayati	carvayati	cā̆layati
Des:	cicamiṣati	cicar(i)ṣati		cicaliṣati
Per:	cacāma	cacāra	cacarva	cacāla
Aor:	acamīt[12]	acārīt[13]	acarvīt	acālīt
CAo:	acīcamat	acīcarat	acacarvat	acīcalat
Inf:	camitum	car(i)tum F	carvitum	calitum F
Abs:		car(i)tvā		calitvā
PPP:	cānta-	carita-	cūrṇa-	calita-
FPP:		cā̆raṇīya-		
FPP:		cārya-	carvya-	cālya-

[1]/aghuṣat [2]/ghuṣṭa-/ghoṣita- [3]/jigharti [7] [4]Prec Act ghrāyāt/ghreyāt [5]/aghrāsīt; Pas aghrāyi [6]/ghrāṇa- [7]Pl cakṣate [8]This and other missing forms from khyā (69). [9]/cakṣau M [10]All forms only with prefix ā-. [11]Abs -camya [12]Pas acami [13]Pas acāri

	97 ci-5 'gather'	98 cit-1 'consider'	99 cint-10 'think'	100 cud-10 'impel'
Cit:	cinoti M	cetati	cintayati M	codayati M
Pas:	cīyate[1]	cityate	cintyate	codyate
Fut:	ceṣyati M	cetiṣyati	cintayiṣyati	codayiṣyati
Cau:	cāyayati	cetayati		
Des:	cicīṣati M	cicetiṣati		cucodayiṣati
Per:	cikāya[2] M	ciceta	cintayām ā/c	codayām ā/c
Aor:	acaiṣīt[3] M	acetīt	acīcintat[6] M	acūcudat
CAo:		acīcitat		
Inf:	cetum[4]	cetitum	cintayitum F	codayitum F
Abs:	citvā	cetitvā[5]	cintayitvā	
PPP:	cita-	citta-	cintita-	codita-
FPP:	cayanīya-		cintanīya-	codanīya-
FPP:	ceya-	cetya-	cintya-	codya-

	101 cur-10 'steal'	102 cṛt-6 'fasten'	103 ceṣṭ-1 'act'	104 cyu-1 'fall'
Cit:	corayati M	cṛ(n)tati	ceṣṭati M	cyavate A
Pas:	coryate	cṛtyate	ceṣṭyate	
Fut:	corayiṣyati		ceṣṭiṣyate	cyoṣyate
Cau:		cartayati	ceṣṭayati	cyāvayati
Des:	cucorayiṣati	cicartiṣati	ciceṣṭiṣate	cucyūṣate
Per:	corayām ā/c	cacarta	ciceṣṭa M	cucyuve
Aor:	acūcurat[7]	acartīt	aceṣṭīt M	acyoṣṭa
CAo:			aciceṣṭat	
Inf:	corayitum F	cartitum	ceṣṭitum F	cyavitum[8]
Abs:	corayitvā		ceṣṭitvā	
PPP:	corita-	cṛtta-	ceṣṭita-	cyuta-
FPP:	coraṇīya-			
FPP:	corya-			

[1]Abs -cīya/-citya [2]/cicāya M [3]Pas acāyi [4]FPP cayitavya- [5]/cititvā
[6]Pas acinti [7]Pas acori [8]Peri Fut cyotā

	105 chad-10 'cover'	106 chid-7 'cut'	107 jan-4 'be born'	108 jalp-1 'murmur'
Cit:	chādayati M	chinatti[2] M	jāyate	jalpati
Pas:	chādyate	chidyate	janyate	jalpyate
Fut:	chādayiṣyati	chetsyati M	janiṣyate	jalpiṣyati
Cau:		chedayati	janayati	jalpayati
Des:	cicchādayiṣati	cicchitsati M	jijaniṣate	jijalpiṣati
Per:	chādayām ā/c	ciccheda M	jajñe	jajalpa
Aor:	acicchadat M	acchidat[3]	ajaniṣṭa	ajalpīt
CAo:		acicchidat	ajījanat	
Inf:	chādayitum F	chettum F	janitum F	jalpitum
Abs:	chādayitvā	chittvā	janitvā	jalpitvā
PPP:	chādita-[1]	chinna-	jāta-	jalpita-
FPP:		chedanīya-		
FPP:	chādya-	chedya-	janya-	jalpya-

	109 jāgṛ-2 'wake'	110 ji-1 'conquer'	111 jinv-1 'hasten'	112 jīv-1 'live'
Cit:	jāgarti [7]	jayati M	jinvati	jīvati M
Pas:	jāgaryate	jīyate[7]		jīvyate
Fut:	jāgariṣyati	jeṣyati[8] M	jinviṣyati	jīviṣyati M
Cau:	jāgarayati	jāpayati	jinvayati	jīvayati
Des:	jijāgariṣati	jigīṣati[9]		jijīviṣati
Per:	jajāgāra[4]	jigāya	jijinva	jijīva M
Aor:	ajāgarīt[5]	ajaiṣīt M	ajinvīt	ajīvīt
CAo:		ajījapat		ajījivat
Inf:	jāgaritum[6]	jetum F	jinvitum	jīvitum F
Abs:		jitvā		jīvitvā
PPP:	jāgarita-	jita-	jinvita-	jīvita-
FPP:				jīvanīya-
FPP:		jeya-		jīvya-

[1]/channa- [2]Pl chindanti [3]/acchaitsīt M [4]/jāgārām āsa
[5]Pas ajāgāri [6]FPP jāgārtavya- [7]Abs -jitya [8]/jayiṣyati [9]Int jejīyate

	113 juṣ-6 'relish'	114 jṝ-4 'decay'	115 jñā-9 'know'	116 jyā-9 'overpower'
Cit:	juṣate A	jīryati M	jānāti M	jināti
Pas:	juṣyate	jīryate	jñāyate	jīyate[3]
Fut:	joṣiṣyate	jarīṣyati	jñāsyati	jyāsyati
Cau:	joṣayati	jarayati	jñāpayati	jyāpayati
Des:	jujoṣiṣate	jijīrṣati	jijñāsati	jijyāsati
Per:	jujuṣe	jajāra	jajñau M	jijyau
Aor:	ajoṣiṣṭa	ajārīt[1]	ajñāsīt[2]	ajyāsīt[4]
CAo:	ajūjuṣat		ajijñapat	
Inf:	joṣitum	jarītum	jñātum F	jyātum
Abs:		jaritvā	jñātvā	jītvā
PPP:	juṣṭa-	jīrṇa-	jñāta-	jīna-[5]
FPP:				
FPP:	joṣya-		jñeya-	

	117 jval-1 'blaze'	118 ḍhauk-1 'approach'	119 takṣ-1/5 'hew'	120 taḍ-10 'hit'
Cit:	jvalati M	ḍhaukate	takṣati[6] M	tāḍayati M
Pas:	jvalyate	ḍhaukyate	takṣyate	tāḍyate
Fut:	jvaliṣyati	ḍhaukiṣyate	takṣ(iṣ)yati	tāḍayiṣyati
Cau:	jvālayati	ḍhaukayati	takṣayati	
Des:	jijvaliṣati	ḍuḍhaukiṣate	titakṣ(iṣ)ati	
Per:	jajvāla	ḍuḍhauke	tatakṣa	tāḍayām ā/c
Aor:	ajvālīt	aḍhaukiṣṭa	atakṣīt	atītaḍat M
CAo:		aḍuḍhaukat	atatakṣat	
Inf:	jvalitum	ḍhaukitum	takṣitum	tāḍayitum
Abs:			takṣitvā[7]	tāḍayitvā
PPP:	jvalita-	ḍhaukita-	taṣṭa-	tāḍita-
FPP:				tāḍanīya-
FPP:			takṣya-	tāḍya-

[1]/ajarat [2]Mid ajñāsta; Pas ajñāyi [3]Abs -jyāya [4]Pas ajyāyi [5]/jīta-
[6]/takṣṇoti [7]/taṣṭvā

	121 tan-8 'stretch'	122 tap-1 'burn'	123 tam-4 'faint'	124 tark-10 'infer'
Cit:	tanoti M	tapati M	tāmyati	tarkayati
Pas:	tanyate[1]	tapyate		tarkyate
Fut:	taniṣyati[2]	tapsyati[4]	tamiṣyati	tarkayiṣyati
Cau:	tānayati	tāpayati	tamayati	
Des:	titaniṣati	titapsati		
Per:	tatāna M	tatāpa M	tatāma	tarkayām ā/c
Aor:	atānīt[3] M	atāpsīt M	atamat[5]	atatarkat M
CAo:	atītanat	atītapat		
Inf:	tan(i)tum	taptum F	tamitum	tarkayitum
Abs:	ta(ni)tvā	taptvā	tamitvā[6]	tarkayitvā
PPP:	tata-	tap(i)ta-	tānta-	tarkita-
FPP:				tarkaṇīya-
FPP:	tanya-	tapya-		

	125 tij-10 'sharpen'	126 tud-6 'hit'	127 tur-6/3 'hasten'	128 tul-10 'weigh'
Cit:	tejayati	tudati M	turati[9] M	tolayati M
Pas:		tudyate		tolyate
Fut:		totsyate		tolayiṣyati
Cau:		todayati		
Des:		tututsati		
Per:	tejayām āsa	tutoda M		tolayām ā/c
Aor:	atītijat M	atautsīt[7] M	atorīt	atūtulat M
CAo:		atūtudat		
Inf:	tejayitum	toditum[8]	toritum	tolayitum
Abs:		tuttvā		tolayitvā
PPP:	tejita-	tunna-	tūrṇa-	tolita-
FPP:				
FPP:		todya-	turya-	tulya-

[1]/tāyate; Abs -tatya/-tāya [2]Mid taṃsyate [3]Pas atāni [4]/tapiṣyati
[5]Pas atāmi [6]/tantvā [7]Pas atodi [8]Peri Fut tottā [9]/tutorti

	129 tuṣ-4 'be satisfied'	130 tṛd-7 'split'	131 tṛp-4 'be satisfied'	132 tṛṣ-4 'thirst'
Cit:	tuṣyati	tṛṇatti[2] M	tṛpyati	tṛṣyati
Pas:	tuṣyate	tṛdyate	tṛpyate	--[9]
Fut:	tokṣyati	tardiṣyati[3]	tarpiṣyati[6]	tarṣiṣyati
Cau:	toṣayati	tardayati	tarpayati	tarṣayati
Des:	tutukṣati	titardiṣati	titarpiṣati	titarṣiṣati
Per:	tutoṣa	tatarda M	tatarpa	tatarṣa
Aor:	atuṣat[1]	atṛdat[4]	atṛpat[7]	atṛṣat
CAo:	atūtuṣat		atatarpat	atītṛṣat
Inf:	toṣṭum F	tarditum	tarp(i)tum[8]	tarṣitum
Abs:	tuṣṭvā	tarditvā[5]	tṛptvā	tṛṣitvā[10]
PPP:	tuṣṭa-	tṛṇṇa-	tṛpta-	tṛṣṭa-
FPP:	toṣaṇīya-		tarpaṇīya-	
FPP:	toṣya-			

	133 tṝ-1 'cross over'	134 tyaj-1 'leave'	135 tras-1/4 'tremble'	136 trā-2[15] 'rescue'
Cit:	tarati	tyajati	tras(y)ati	trāti[16]
Pas:	tīryate	tyajyate	trasyate	trāyate
Fut:	tarī̆ṣyati	tyakṣyati[12]	trasiṣyati	trāsyate
Cau:	tārayati	tyājayati	trāsayati	trāpayati
Des:	titīrṣati	tityakṣati	titrasiṣati	titrāsate
Per:	tatāra	tatyāja	tatrāsa	tatre
Aor:	atār(ṣ)īt[11]	atyākṣīt[13]	atrā̆sīt[14] [6]	atrāsta[17]
CAo:	atītarat	atityajat	atitrasat	atitrapat
Inf:	tar(ī̆)tum F	tyaktum F	trasitum	trātum F
Abs:	tīrtvā	tyaktvā	trasitvā	trātvā
PPP:	tīrṇa-	tyakta-	trasta-	trāta-[18]
FPP:	tā̆raṇīya-		trasanīya-	
FPP:	tā̆rya-	tyajya-		

[1]Pas atoṣi [2]Pl tṛndanti [3]/tartsyati [4]/atardīt [5]/tṛtvā
[6]/tarpsyati/trapsyati [7]/atarpīt/atrāpsīt/atārpsīt [8]/traptum
[9]Prec Act tṛṣyāt [10]/tarṣitvā [11]Pas atāri [12]/tyajiṣyati [13]Pas atyāji
[14]Pas atrāsi [15]/trai-4 [16]Mid trāyate [17]Pas atrāyi [18]/trāṇa-

	137 tvar-1 'hasten'	138 da(ṃ)ś-1 'bite'	139 dakṣ-1 'be able'	140 daṇḍ-10 'punish'
Cit:	tvarate A	da(ṃ)śati	dakṣati M	daṇḍayati M
Pas:	tvaryate	daśyate		daṇḍyate
Fut:	tvariṣyate	daṅkṣyati	dakṣiṣyate	daṇḍayiṣyati
Cau:	tvărayati	daṃśayati	dakṣayati	
Des:	titvariṣate	dida(ṅ)kṣati		
Per:	tatvare	dadaṃśa	dadakṣe	daṇḍayām ā/c
Aor:	atvariṣṭa	adāṅkṣīt[2] [3]	adakṣiṣṭa	adadaṇḍat M
CAo:	atatvarat		adadakṣat	
Inf:	tvaritum	daṃṣṭum	dakṣitum	daṇḍayitum
Abs:	tvaritvā	da(ṃ)ṣṭvā		daṇḍayitvā
PPP:	tvarita-[1]	daṣṭa-		daṇḍita-
FPP:	tvaraṇīya-			daṇḍanīya-
FPP:				

	141 dam-4 'tame'	142 dambh-1[6] 'deceive'	143 day-1 'pity'	144 das-4 'lack'
Cit:	dāmyati	dabhati[7]	dayate	dasyati
Pas:	damyate	dabhyate		
Fut:	damiṣyati	dambhiṣyati	dayiṣyate	dăsiṣyati
Cau:	damayati	dambhayati		dāsayati
Des:	didamiṣati	didambhiṣati	didayiṣate	
Per:	dadāma	dadambha[8]	dayāṃ c	dadāsa
Aor:	adamīt[3]	adabhat[9]	adayiṣṭa	adasat
CAo:	adīdamat	adadambhat		
Inf:	damitum	dambhitum[10]	dayitum	dăsitum
Abs:	damitvā[4]	dambhitvā[11]		
PPP:	damita-[5]	dabdha-	dayita-	dasta-
FPP:				
FPP:	damya-	dābhya-		dasya-

[1]/tūrṇa- [2]Pas adaṃśi [3]/adamat; Pas adāmi [4]/dāntvā [5]/danta- [6]/-5 [7]/dabhnoti [8]/dadābha [9]/adambhīt [10]/dabdhum [11]/dabdhvā

	145 dah-1 'burn'	146 dā-3 'give'	147 dā-2 'cut'	148 div-4 'play'
Cit:	dahati M	dadāti M [16]	dāti	dīvyati
Pas:	dahyate	dīyate[3]	dīyate[5]	dīvyate
Fut:	dhakṣyati[1]	dāsyati	dāsyati	deviṣyati
Cau:	dāhayati	dāpayati	dāpayati	devayati
Des:	didhakṣati	ditsati	ditsati	dideviṣati
Per:	dadāha	dadau M	dadau M	dideva
Aor:	adhākṣīt [4][2]	adāt[4] M	adāt[6] M	adevīt
CAo:	adīdahat			adīdivat
Inf:	dagdhum F	dātum F	dātum F	devitum F
Abs:	dagdhvā	dattvā	dattvā	dyūtvā[7]
PPP:	dagdha-	datta-	dita-	dyūta-[8]
FPP:		dānīya-	dānīya-	
FPP:	dāhya-	deya-	deya-	

	149 div-1 'lament'	150 diś-6 'show'	151 dih-2 'smear'	152 dīkṣ-1 'consecrate'
Cit:	devati	diśati M	degdhi[10] M	dīkṣate
Pas:		diśyate	dihyate	dīkṣyate
Fut:	deviṣyati	dekṣyati[9]	dhekṣyati	dīkṣiṣyate
Cau:	devayati	deśayati	dehayati	dīkṣayati
Des:		didikṣati	didhikṣati	didīkṣ(iṣ)ate
Per:	dideva	dideśa M	dideha M	didīkṣe
Aor:	adevīt M	adikṣat M	adhikṣat M	adīkṣiṣṭa
CAo:	adīdivat	adīdiśat	adīdihat	adidīkṣat
Inf:	devitum	deṣṭum F	degdhum	dīkṣitum
Abs:		diṣṭvā	digdhvā	dīkṣitvā
PPP:	dyūna-	diṣṭa-	digdha-	dīkṣita-
FPP:				
FPP:		deśya-	dehya-	

[1]/dahiṣyati [2]Mid adagdha [3]Abs -dāya; Prec Act deyāt [4]Pas adāyi
[5]Abs -dāya; Prec Act dāyāt [6]/adāsīt [7]/devitvā [8]/dyūna-
[9]Prec Mid dikṣīṣṭa [10]Pl dihanti, like [24]

	153 dīp-4 'blaze'	154 du-5 'suffer'	155 dul-10 'swing'	156 duṣ-4 'spoil'
Cit:	dīpyate A	dunoti	dolayati	duṣyati
Pas:	dīpyate	dūyate		duṣyate
Fut:	dīpiṣyate	doṣyati		dokṣyati
Cau:	dīpayati	dāvayati		doṣayati
Des:	didīpiṣate	dudūṣati	dudolayiṣati	dudukṣati
Per:	didīpe	dudāva	dolayām āsa	dudoṣa
Aor:	adīpiṣṭa	adoṣīt[1]	adūdulat	adoṣīt[3]
CAo:	adīdipat			adūduṣat
Inf:	dīpitum	dotum	dolayitum	doṣṭum
Abs:	dīptvā			duṣṭvā
PPP:	dīpta-	duta-[2]	dolita-	duṣṭa-
FPP:				
FPP:				dūṣya-

	157 duh-2 'milk'	158 dṛ-6 'heed'	159 dṛp-4 'be proud'	160 dṛś-1 'see'
Cit:	dogdhi [24]	driyate	dṛpyati	paśyati[10]
Pas:	duhyate	driyate[5]	dṛpyate	dṛśyate
Fut:	dhokṣyati	dariṣyate	darpiṣyati[6]	drakṣyati
Cau:	dohayati	dārayati	darpayati	darśayati
Des:	dudhukṣati	didariṣate	didarpiṣati	didṛkṣate[11]
Per:	dudoha M	dadre	dadarpa	dadarśa M
Aor:	adhukṣat[4]	adṛta	adṛpat[7]	adrākṣīt [4][12]
CAo:	adūduhat	adīdarat	adīdṛpat	adīdṛśat
Inf:	dogdhum F	dartum	darp(i)tum[8]	draṣṭum F
Abs:	dugdhvā	dṛtvā	darpitvā[9]	dṛṣṭvā
PPP:	dugdha-	dṛta-	dṛpta-	dṛṣṭa-
FPP:		daraṇīya-		darśanīya-
FPP:	dohya-			dṛśya-

[1]/adauṣīt [2]/dūna- [3]/aduṣat [4]Mid adhukṣata/adugdha
[5]Abs -dṛtya [6]/darpsyati/drapsyati [7]/adarpīt/adārpsīt/adrāpsīt
[8]/draptum [9]/dṛptvā [10]from paś (200) [11]Int darīdṛṣyate
[12]/adarśat; Mid adṛṣṭa

	161 dṛ(ṃ)h-1	162 dṝ-9	163 dyut-1	164 drā-2
	'establish'	'tear'	'gleam'	'run'
Cit:	dṛṃhati M	dṛṇāti	dyotate	drāti
Pas:		dīryate	dyutyate	drāyate
Fut:	dṛṃhiṣyati	darī̆ṣyati	dyotiṣyate	drāsyati
Cau:	dṛṃhayati	dā̆rayati	dyotayati	drāpayati
Des:	didṛṃhiṣati	didarī̆ṣati	didyutiṣate	didrāsati
Per:	dadṛṃha	dadāra	didyute	dadrau
Aor:	adṛṃhīt	adārīt	adyutat[2]	adrāsīt
CAo:		adadarat	adudyutat	adidrapat
Inf:	dṛṃhitum	darī̆tum	dyotitum	drātum
Abs:		dīrtvā	dyutitvā	
PPP:	dṛḍha-[1]	dīrṇa-	dyut(i)ta-	drāṇa-
FPP:		daraṇīya-		
FPP:			dyotya-	

	165 dru-1	166 druh-4	167 dviṣ-2	168 dhā-3
	'run'	'offend'	'hate'	'put'
Cit:	dravati M	druhyati M	dveṣṭi [9]	dadhāti M [16]
Pas:	drūyate[3]	druhyate	dviṣyate	dhīyate[10]
Fut:	droṣyati	drohiṣyati[5]	dvekṣyati	dhāsyati
Cau:	drāvayati	drohayati	dveṣayati	dhāpayati
Des:	dudrūṣati[4]	dudruhiṣati	didvikṣati[9]	dhitsati[11]
Per:	dudrāva	dudroha	didveṣa M	dadhau M
Aor:	adudruvat	adruhat	advikṣat M	adhāt M
CAo:		adudruhat	adidviṣat	adīdhapat
Inf:	drotum	drogdhum[6] F	dveṣṭum	dhātum F
Abs:	drutvā	drugdhvā[7]	dviṣṭvā	(d)hitvā
PPP:	druta-	drugdha-[8]	dviṣṭa-	hita-
FPP:			dveṣaṇīya-	dhānīya-
FPP:		druhya-	dveṣya-	dheya-

[1]/dṛ(ṃ)hita- [2]Mid adyotiṣṭa [3]Abs -drutya [4]Int dodrūyate
[5]/dhrokṣyati [6]/drohitum/droḍhum [7]/druhitvā/drohitvā/druḍhvā
[8]/drūḍha- [9]Int dedviṣyate [10]Abs -dhāya; Prec Act dheyāt
[11]Int dedhīyate

	169 dhāv-1 'rinse'	170 dhu-5 'shake'	171 dhṛ-1 'bear'	172 dhṛṣ-5 'dare'
Cit:	dhāvati M	dhunoti M	dharati M	dhṛṣṇoti
Pas:	dhāvyate	dhūyate	dhriyate[7]	--[9]
Fut:	dhāviṣyati	dhoṣyati[3]	dhariṣyati	dharṣiṣyati
Cau:	dhāvayati	dhāvayati	dhārayati	dharṣayati
Des:	didhāviṣati	dudhūṣati	didhariṣati	didharṣiṣati
Per:	dadhāva M	dudhāva M	dadhāra M	dadharṣa
Aor:	adhāvīt M	adhauṣīt[4] M	adhārṣīt[8]	adhṛṣat[10]
CAo:	adīdhavat		adīdharat	adīdṛṣat
Inf:	dhāvitum	dhavitum[5] F	dhartum	dharṣitum
Abs:	dhāvitvā[1]	dhūtvā	dhṛtvā	
PPP:	dhāvita-[2]	dhū̆ta-[6]	dhṛta-	dhṛṣṭa-[11]
FPP:			dhā̆raṇīya-	dharṣaṇīya-
FPP:			dhārya-	

	173 dhe-1 'suck'	174 dhmā-1 'blow'	175 dhyai-1/2 'ponder'	176 dhraj-1 'advance'
Cit:	dhayati	dhamati	dhyā(ya)ti M	dhra(ñ)jati
Pas:	dhīyate[12]	dhmāyate	dhyāyate	
Fut:	dhāsyati	dhamiṣyati[13]	dhyāsyati	
Cau:	dhāpayati	dhmāpayati	dhyāpayati	
Des:	dhitsati	didhmāsati	didhyāsati[15]	
Per:	dadhau	dadhmau	dadhyau	dadhrāja[16]
Aor:	adhā(sī)t	adhmāsīt	adhyāsīt	adhrā̆jīt[17]
CAo:	adīdhapat	adidhmapat	adidhyapat	
Inf:	dhātum	dhmātum F	dhyātum F	
Abs:	dhītvā		dhyātvā	
PPP:	dhīta-	dhamita-[14]	dhyāta-	
FPP:		dhmānīya-		
FPP:			dhyeya-	

[1]/dhautvā [2]/dhauta- [3]/dhaviṣyati [4]/adhāvīt M [5]/dhotum [6]/dhūna- [7]Abs -dhṛtya [8]Mid adhṛta [9]Abs -dhṛṣya [10]/adharṣīt [11]/dharṣita- [12]Prec Act dheyāt [13]/dhmāsyati [14]/dhmāta- [15]Int dādhyāyate [16]/dadhrañja [17]/adhrāñjīt

	177 dhvaṃs-1 'perish'	178 dhvan-1 'resound'	179 dhvṛ-1 'bend'	180 nakṣ-1 'attain'
Cit:	dhvaṃsati M	dhvanati	dhvarati	nakṣati M
Pas:	dhvasyate	dhvanyate		
Fut:	dhvaṃsiṣyate	dhvaniṣyati	dhvariṣyati	nakṣiṣyati
Cau:	dhvaṃsayati	dhvănayati	dhvārayati	
Des:	didhvaṃsiṣate	didhvaniṣati	dudhūrṣati	
Per:	dadhvaṃsa M	dadhvāna	dadhvāra	nanakṣa M
Aor:	adhvasat M[1]	adhvănīt	adhvārṣīt	anakṣīt
CAo:		adidhvanat		
Inf:	dhvaṃsitum	dhvanitum	dhvartum F	nakṣitum
Abs:	dhvastvā[2]	dhvanitvā		
PPP:	dhvasta-	dhvanita-[3]	dhūrta-	
FPP:				
FPP:		dhvanya-		nakṣya-

	181 nad-1 'roar'	182 nand-1 'rejoice'	183 nabh-1 'burst'	184 namati-1 'bow'
Cit:	nadati	nandati M	nabhate	namati M
Pas:	nadyate	nandyate		namyate
Fut:	nadiṣyati	nandiṣyati		naṃsyati[5]
Cau:	nădayati	nandayati	nabhayati	nămayati
Des:	ninadiṣati	ninandiṣati		ninaṃsati
Per:	nanāda M	nananda	nebhe	nanāma M
Aor:	anădīt	anandīt	anabhat[4]	anaṃsīt[6] [5]
CAo:	anīnadat	ananandat		anīnamat
Inf:	naditum	nanditum		nantum[7]
Abs:	naditvā			natvā
PPP:	nadita-	nandita-		nata-
FPP:		nandanīya-		namanīya-
FPP:		nandya-		nāmya-

[1]Mid adhvaṃsiṣṭa [2]/dhvaṃsitvā [3]/dhvānta- [4]Mid anabhiṣṭa
[5]/namiṣyati [6]Pas anāmi [7]/namitum

	185 naś-4 'perish'	186 nah-4 'bind'	187 nāth-1 'implore'	188 nind-1 'blame'
Cit:	naśyati	nahyati M	nāthati M	nindati
Pas:	naśyate	nahyate	nāthyate	nindyate
Fut:	naśiṣyati[1]	natsyati	nāthiṣyati	nindiṣyati
Cau:	nāśayati	nāhayati		nindayati
Des:	ninaśiṣati	ninatsati[4]		ninindiṣati
Per:	nanāśa	nanāha M	nanātha M	nininda
Aor:	anaśat	anātsīt[5]	anāthīt[6]	anindīt
CAo:	anīnaśat	anīnahat		aninindat
Inf:	naśitum[2]	naddhum F	nāthitum	ninditum
Abs:	naśitvā[3]	naddhvā		ninditvā
PPP:	naṣṭa-	naddha-	nāthita-	nindita-
FPP:				nindanīya-
FPP:	nāśya-	nāhya-		nindya-

	189 nī-1 'lead'	190 nu-2 'praise'	191 nud-6 'push'	192 nṛt-4 'dance'
Cit:	nayati M	nauti	nudati M	nṛtyati M
Pas:	nīyate	nūyate[9]	nudyate	nṛtyate
Fut:	neṣyati	noṣyati[10]	notsyati	nartiṣyati[16]
Cau:	nāyayati	nāvayati	nodayati	nartayati
Des:	ninīṣati[7]	nunūṣati	nunutsati	ninartiṣati
Per:	nināya M	nunāva	nunoda M	nanarta
Aor:	anaiṣīt[8] M	anāvīt[11]	anautsīt[13] M	anartīt
CAo:	anīnayat	anūnavat	anūnudat	anīnṛtat
Inf:	netum F	notum[12]	noditum[14] F	nart(i)tum
Abs:	nītvā	nutvā	nuttvā	nartitvā
PPP:	nīta-	nuta-	nutta-[15]	nṛtta-
FPP:				
FPP:	neya-		nodya-	nṛtya-

[1]/naṅkṣyati [2]/naṃṣṭum [3]/na(ṃ)ṣṭvā [4]Int nānahyate
[5]Mid anaddha; Pas anāhi [6]Mid anāthiṣṭa [7]Int nenīyate [8]Pas anāyi
[9]Abs -nutya [10]/naviṣyati [11]/anauṣīt; Mid anūṣṭa [12]/navitum
[13]Pas anodi [14]Peri Fut nottā [15]/nunna- [16]/nartsyati

	193 pac-1 'cook'	194 paṭ-1 'split'	195 paṭh-1 'read'	196 paṇ-1 'bargain'
Cit:	pacati M	paṭati	paṭhati	paṇate
Pas:	pacyate		paṭhyate	paṇyate
Fut:	pakṣyati	paṭiṣyati	paṭhiṣyati	paṇiṣyate
Cau:	pācayati	pāṭayati	pāṭhayati	pā̆ṇayati
Des:	pipakṣati	pipaṭiṣati	pipaṭhiṣati	pipaṇiṣate
Per:	papāca M	papāṭa	papāṭha	peṇe
Aor:	apākṣīt[1] M	apā̆ṭīt	apāṭhīt[2]	apaṇiṣṭha
CAo:	apīpacat	apīpaṭat	apīpaṭhat	apīpaṇat
Inf:	paktum F	paṭitum	paṭhitum F	paṇitum
Abs:	paktvā		paṭhitvā	paṇitvā
PPP:	pakva-	pāṭa-	paṭhita-	paṇita-
FPP:		paṭanīya-	paṭhanīya-	
FPP:		pāṭya-	pāṭhya-	paṇya-

	197 pat-1 'fall'	198 pad-4 'go'	199 palāy-1 'flee'	200 paś-1 'see'
Cit:	patati M	padyate A	palāyate A	paśyati M
Pas:	patyate	padyate	palāyyate	
Fut:	patiṣyati	patsyate	palāyiṣyate	*Missing*
Cau:	pātayati M	pādayati	palāyayati	*forms from*
Des:	pipatiṣati[3]	pitsate		*dṛś (160)*
Per:	papāta	pede A	palāyāṃ c	
Aor:	apaptat[4]	apatta[5]	apalāyiṣṭa	
CAo:	apīpatat	apīpadat		
Inf:	patitum F	pattum F	palāyitum	
Abs:	patitvā	pattvā		
PPP:	patita-	panna-	palāyita-	
FPP:	patanīya-	pādanīya-		
FPP:	pātya-	pādya-		

[1]Pas apāci [2]Pas apāṭhi [3]Int patipatyate [4]Pas apāti [5]Pas apādi

	201 pā-1 'drink'	202 pā-2 'protect'	203 pinv-1 'swell'	204 piś-6 'adorn'
Cit:	pibati M	pāti	pinvati	pi(ṃ)śati
Pas:	pīyate[1]	pāyate	pinvyate	piśyate
Fut:	pāsyati	pāsyati	pinviṣyate	peśiṣyate
Cau:	pāyayati	pālayati	pinvayati	peśayati
Des:	pipāsati[2]	pipāsati		pipiśiṣati
Per:	papau	papau	pipinva	pipeśa
Aor:	apāt[3]	apāsīt	apinvīt	apeśīt
CAo:	apīpyat	apīpalat		apīpiśat
Inf:	pātum F	pātum F	pinvitum	peśitum
Abs:	pītvā	pālayitvā		piśitvā
PPP:	pīna-[4]	pā(li)ta-	pinvita-	piśita-
FPP:	pānīya-	pālanīya-		
FPP:	peya-			

	205 piṣ-7 'grind'	206 pīḍ-10 'torment'	207 puṣ-9/4/1 'thrive'	208 pū-9/1 'purify'
Cit:	pinaṣṭi[5]	pīḍayati M	puṣṇāti[8]	punāti[13] M
Pas:	piṣyate	pīḍyate	puṣyate	pūyate
Fut:	pekṣyati	pīḍayiṣyati	poṣiṣyati[9]	paviṣyati
Cau:	peṣayati		poṣayati	pāvayati
Des:	pipikṣati	pipīḍayiṣati	pupuṣiṣati	pupūṣati
Per:	pipeṣa	pīḍayām ā/c	pupoṣa	pupāva M
Aor:	apiṣat[6]	apīpiḍat[7] M	apuṣat[10]	apāvīt M
CAo:	apīpiṣat		apūpuṣat	apīpavat
Inf:	peṣṭum	pīḍayitum F	poṣṭum[11]	pavitum
Abs:	piṣṭvā	pīḍayitvā	puṣṭvā	pūtvā
PPP:	piṣṭa-	pīḍita-	puṣṭa-[12]	pūta-
FPP:		pīḍanīya-	poṣaṇīya-	
FPP:	peṣya-		poṣya-	

[1]Prec Act peyāt [2]Int pepīyate [3]Pas apāyi [4]/pīta- [5]Pl piṃṣanti [6]Pas apeṣi [7]/apipīḍat [8]/puṣyati/poṣati [9]/pokṣyati [10]/apoṣīt; Pas apoṣi [11]/poṣitum [12]/poṣita- [13]/pavate

	209 pūj-10 'honour'	210 pṛ[1]-3/9 'fill'	211 pṛ-5/6 'be busy'	212 pṛc-7 'mix'
Cit:	pūjayati M	piparti[2] [7]	pṛṇoti[5]	pṛṇakti[6]
Pas:	pūjyate	pāryate	priyate	pṛcyate
Fut:	pūjayiṣyati	parīṣyati	pariṣyate	parciṣyati
Cau:		pārayati[3]	pārayati	parcayati
Des:	pupūjayiṣati	pupūrṣati	pupūrṣate	piparciṣati
Per:	pūjayām ā/c	papāra	papre	paparca
Aor:	apūpujat M	apār(ṣ)īt	apṛta	aparcīt
CAo:		apīparat	apīparat	
Inf:	pūjayitum F	pūritum	partum	parcitum
Abs:	pūjayitvā	pūrtvā		parcitvā
PPP:	pūjita-	pūrṇa-[4]	pṛta-	pṛkta-
FPP:	pūjanīya-	pūraṇīya-		
FPP:	pūjya-	pūrya-		

	213 pyāy-1 'overflow'	214 prach-6 'ask'	215 prath-1 'proclaim'	216 prī-9 'delight'
Cit:	pyāyate	pṛcchati M	prathate	prīṇāti M
Pas:		pṛcchyate		prīyate
Fut:	pyāyiṣyate	prakṣyati	prathiṣyate	preṣyati
Cau:	pyāyayati	pracchayati	prathayati	prīṇayati
Des:	pipyāyiṣate	pipṛcchiṣati	piprathiṣate	piprīṣati
Per:	pipye	papraccha	paprathe	piprāya M
Aor:	apyāyiṣṭa	aprākṣīt[8]	aprathiṣṭa	apraiṣīt M
CAo:		apapracchat	apaprathat	
Inf:	pyā(yi)tum	praṣṭum F	prathitum	pretum
Abs:	pyāyitvā	pṛṣṭvā		prītvā
PPP:	pyāna-[7]	pṛṣṭa-	prathita-	prīta-
FPP:				
FPP:	pyāyya-	pṛcchya-		priya-

[1]/pṝ [2]/pṛṇāti [3]/pūrayati [4]/pūrta- [5]Mid priyate [6]Pl pṛñcanti
[7]/pīna- [8]Mid apraṣṭa

	217 plu-1 'drench'	218 phal-1 'bear fruit'	219 baṃh-1 'be strong'	220 bandh-9 'bind'
Cit:	plavate	phalati M	baṃhate	badhnāti
Pas:	plūyate[1]			badhyate
Fut:	ploṣyate	phaliṣyati	baṃhiṣyate	bhantsyati[2]
Cau:	plāvayati	phālayati	baṃhayate	bandhayati
Des:	puplūṣate	piphaliṣati		bibhantsati
Per:	pupluve	paphāla		babandha
Aor:	aploṣṭa	aphālīt	abaṃhiṣṭa	abhāntsīt
CAo:	apiplavat	apīphalat		ababandhat
Inf:	plotum	phalitum		ba(n)ddhum[3] F
Abs:	plutvā	phalitvā		ba(d)dhvā
PPP:	pluta-	phalita-	baṃhita-	baddha-
FPP:				bandhanīya-
FPP:	plāvya-			bandhya-

	221 bādh-1 'oppress'	222 budh-1/4 'waken'	223 bṛh-1/6 'be great'	224 brū-2 'say'
Cit:	bādhate A	bodhati M[5]	barhati[12]	bravīti [13]
Pas:	bādhyate	budhyate	bṛhyate	
Fut:	bādhiṣyate	bhotsyate[6]	barhiṣyati[13]	*Missing*
Cau:	bādhayati	bodhayati	barhayati	*forms from*
Des:	bibādhiṣate	bubodhiṣati[7]	bibarhiṣati	*vac (320)*
Per:	babādhe	bubodha M	babarha	
Aor:	abādhiṣṭa[4]	abodhīt[8] M	abarhīt[14]	
CAo:	ababādhat	abūbudhat	ababarhat	
Inf:	bādhitum F	bodhitum[9] F	barhitum	
Abs:	bādhitvā	buddhvā[10]	barhitvā[15]	
PPP:	bādhita-	buddha-[11]	bṛḍha-	
FPP:	bādhanīya-	bodhanīya-		
FPP:	bādhya-	bodhya-		

[1]Abs -plutya [2]/bandhiṣyati [3]/bandhitum [4]Pas abādhi [5]/budhyate [6]/bodhiṣyati [7]M; Int bobudhyate [8]/abudhat; Mid abuddha [9]/boddhum [10]/budhitvā/bodhitvā [11]/budhita- [12]/bṛhati [13]/bharkṣyati [14]/abhṛkṣat [15]/bṛḍhvā

	225 bhakṣ-10 'eat'	226 bhaj-1 'divide'	227 bhañj-7 'break'	228 bhā-2 'shine'
Cit:	bhakṣayati	bhajati M	bhanakti[5]	bhāti
Pas:	bhakṣyate	bhajyate	bhajyate	bhāyate
Fut:	bhakṣayiṣyati	bhakṣyati[2]	bhaṅkṣyati	bhāsyati
Cau:		bhājayati	bhañjayati	bhāpayati
Des:	bibhakṣayiṣati	bibhakṣati	bibhaṅkṣati	bibhāsati
Per:	bhakṣayām ā.	babhāja	babhañja	babhau
Aor:	ababhakṣat	abhākṣīt[3] [4]	abhāṅkṣīt[6]	abhāsīt[7]
CAo:		abībhajat	ababhañjat	abībhapat
Inf:	bhakṣayitum[1]	bhaktum[4] F	bhaṅktum	bhātum
Abs:	bhakṣayitvā	bhaktvā	bha(ṅ)ktvā	bhātvā
PPP:	bhakṣita-	bhakta-	bhagna-	bhāta-
FPP:		bhajanīya-		
FPP:		bhājya-		

	229 bhāṣ-1 'speak'	230 bhās-1 'shine'	231 bhikṣ-1 'beg'	232 bhid-7 'split'
Cit:	bhāṣate	bhāsate	bhikṣate A	bhinatti[9] M
Pas:	bhāṣyate	bhāsyate	bhikṣyate	bhidyate
Fut:	bhāṣiṣyate	bhāsiṣyate	bhikṣiṣyate	bhetsyati
Cau:	bhāṣayati M	bhāsayati	bhikṣayati	bhedayati
Des:	bibhāṣiṣate	bibhāsiṣate		bibhitsati[10]
Per:	babhāṣe	babhāse	bibhikṣe	bibheda M
Aor:	abhāṣiṣṭa[8]	abhāsiṣṭa	abhikṣiṣṭa	abhidat[11] M
CAo:	ababhāṣat	ababhāsat	abibhikṣat	abībhidat
Inf:	bhāṣitum F	bhāsitum	bhikṣitum F	bhettum F
Abs:	bhāṣitvā	bhāsitvā	bhikṣitvā	bhittvā
PPP:	bhāṣita-	bhāsita-	bhikṣita-	bhinna-[12]
FPP:	bhāṣaṇīya-			bhedanīya-
FPP:	bhāṣya-	bhāsya-		bhedya-

[1]F [2]/bhajiṣyati [3]Pas abhāji [4]/bhajitum F [5]Pl bhañjanti
[6]Pas abhañji/abhāji [7]Pas abhāyi [8]/ababhāṣat [9]Pl bhindanti
[10]Int bebhidyate [11]/abhaitsīt M [12]/bhitta-

	233 bhī-3 'fear'	234 bhuj-7 'enjoy'	235 bhuj-6 'bend'	236 bhū-1 'become'
Cit:	bibheti[1]	bhunakti[4] M	bhujati	bhavati
Pas:	bhīyate	bhujyate	bhujyate	bhūyate
Fut:	bheṣyati	bhokṣyati	bhokṣyati	bhaviṣyati
Cau:	bhīṣayati	bhojayati		bhāvayati
Des:	bibhīṣati[2]	bubhukṣati[5]		bubhūṣati[7]
Per:	bibhāya	bubhoja M	bubhoja	babhūva
Aor:	abhaiṣīt[3]	abhaukṣīt[6] M	abhaukṣīt	abhūt[8] [9]
CAo:	abībhiṣat	abūbhujat		abībhavat
Inf:	bhetum F	bhoktum F	bhoktum F	bhavitum F
Abs:	bhītvā	bhu(ṅ)ktvā		bhūtvā
PPP:	bhīta-	bhukta-	bhugna-	bhūta-
FPP:		bhojanīya-		bhavanīya-
FPP:	bheya-	bhojya-		bhāvya-

	237 bhūṣ-1 'adorn'	238 bhṛ-3/1 'bear'	239 bhraṃś-1 'fall'	240 bhram-1/4 'wander'
Cit:	bhūṣati	bibharti[9] M	bhraśyati[13]	bhramati[16] M
Pas:		bhriyate[10]	bhraśyate	bhramyate
Fut:	bhūṣiṣyati	bhariṣyati	bhraṃśiṣyati	bhramiṣyati
Cau:	bhūṣayati	bhārayati	bhraṃśayati	bhrāmayati
Des:	bubhūṣiṣati	bibhariṣati	bibhraṃśiṣati	bibhramiṣati[17]
Per:	bubhūṣa	babhāra[11] M	babhraṃśa M	babhrāma
Aor:	abhūṣīt	abhārṣīt[12]	abhraśat[14]	abhramīt[18]
CAo:	abubhūṣat	abībharat	ababhraṃśat	abibhramat
Inf:	bhūṣitum F	bhartum F	bhraṃśitum	bhrāntum[19]
Abs:		bhṛtvā	bhra(ṃ)śitvā[15]	bhrāntvā[20]
PPP:	bhūṣita-	bhṛta-	bhraṣṭa-	bhrānta-
FPP:	bhūṣaṇīya-	bharaṇīya-		bhramaṇīya-
FPP:	bhūṣya-	bhārya-		

[1]/bibhyati [2]Int bebhīyate [3]Pas abhāyi [4]Pl bhuñjanti
[5]Int bobhujyate [6]Pas abhoji [7]Int bobhūyate [8]Pas abhāvi [9][7]
[10]Abs -bhṛtya [11]/bibharām ā/c [12]Mid abhṛta [13]Mid bhraṃśate
[14]Mid abhraṃṣiṣṭa [15]/bhraṣṭvā [16]/bhrāmyati [17]Int bambhramyate
[18]/abhramat [19]/bhramitum [20]/bhramitvā

	241 bhrasj-6 'roast'	242 bhrāj-1 'shine'	243 maṃh-1 'grow'	244 ma(n)th-9/1 'stir'
Cit:	bhṛjjati M	bhrājate	maṃhate	mathnāti[6] M
Pas:	bhṛjjyate	bhrājyate	maṃhyate	mathyate
Fut:	bhrakṣyati[1]	bhrājiṣyate		ma(n)thiṣyati
Cau:	bhrajjayati[2]	bhrājayati	mahayati	manthayati[7]
Des:	bibhrajjiṣati	bibhrājiṣate	mimaṃhiṣate	mima(n)thiṣati
Per:	babhrajja[3] M	babhrāje	mamaṃhe	mamantha
Aor:	abhrākṣīt[4] M	abhrājiṣṭa	amaṃhiṣṭa	ama(n)thīt
CAo:	ababhrajjat	abibhrajat		amamanthat
Inf:	braṣṭum[5]	bhrājitum	maṃhitum	ma(n)thitum F
Abs:	bhṛṣṭvā	bhrājitvā	mahitvā	ma(n)thitvā
PPP:	bhṛṣṭa-	bhrājita-	maṃhita-	ma(n)thita-
FPP:			maṃhanīya-	manthanīya-
FPP:				ma(n)thya-

	245 mad-4 'rejoice'	246 man 4/8 'think'	247 mand-1 'gladden'	248 masj-6 'sink'
Cit:	mādyati	manyate[8] A	mandate	majjati M
Pas:	madyate	manyate[9]	mandyate	majjyate
Fut:	madiṣyati	maṃsyate[10]	mandiṣyate	maṅkṣyati[12]
Cau:	mădayati	mānayati M	mandayati	majjayati
Des:	mimadiṣati	mimaṃsate		mimaṅkṣati
Per:	mamāda	mene	mamanda M	mamajja
Aor:	amădīt	ama(ṃs)ta[11]	amandīt M	amāṅkṣīt
CAo:	amīmadat	amīmanat		amamajjat
Inf:	maditum F	man(i)tum F	manditum	maṅktum[13]
Abs:	maditvā	ma(ni)tvā		ma(ṅ)ktvā
PPP:	matta-	mata-		magna-
FPP:		mānanīya-		
FPP:	madya-	mănya-		

[1]/bharkṣyati [2]/bharjayati [3]/babharja M [4]/abhārkṣīt; Mid abhraṣṭa/abharṣṭa [5]/bharṣṭum [6]/ma(n)thati [7]/māthayati [8]/manute [9]Abs -manya/-matya [10]/maniṣyate [11]/amaniṣṭa [12]/majjiṣyati [13]/majjitum

	249 mah-1/10	250 mā-2/3/4	251 mith-1	252 mil-6
	'rejoice'	'measure'	'associate'	'meet'
Cit:	mahati M[1]	māti[2]	methati M	milati M
Pas:	mahyate	mīyate[3]		milyate
Fut:	mahiṣyati	māsyati M		meliṣyati
Cau:	mā̆hayati	māpayati		melayati
Des:	mimahiṣati	mitsati M		mimiliṣati
Per:	mamāha M	mamau M	mimetha M	memela M
Aor:	amahīt	amāsīt[4] M	amethīt M	amelīt M
CAo:	amamahat	amīmapat		amīmilat
Inf:	mahitum	mātum F	methitum	melitum
Abs:	mahitvā	mitvā	mithitvā	militvā
PPP:	mahita-	mita-	mithita-	milita-
FPP:				
FPP:		meya-		

	253 miṣ-6	254 mih-1	255 mī-9	256 mīl-1
	'wink'	'urinate'	'lessen'	'wink'
Cit:	miṣati	mehati M	mī̆nāti M	mīlati
Pas:	--[5]		mīyate	mīlyate
Fut:	meṣiṣyati	mekṣyati	meṣyati	mīliṣyati
Cau:		mehayati	māpayati	mīlayati
Des:	mimiṣiṣati	mimikṣati	mitsati	mimīliṣati
Per:	mimeṣa	mimeha	mamau[8]	mimīla
Aor:	ameṣīt[6]	amikṣat	amāsīt[9]	amīlīt
CAo:		amīmihat	amīmapat	amīmilat
Inf:	meṣitum	meḍhum	mātum F	mīlitum
Abs:	miṣitvā[7]	mīḍhvā	mītvā	mīlitvā
PPP:	miṣita-	mīḍha-	mīta-	mīlita-
FPP:		mehanīya-		
FPP:				

[1]/mahayati M [2]Mid mimīte [18]/māyate [3]Abs -maya; Prec Act meyāt [4]Mid amāsta [5]Abs -miṣya [6]/amīmiṣat [7]/meṣitvā [8]Mid mimye [9]Mid amāsta; Pas amāyi

	257 muc-6 'release'	258 mud-1 'rejoice'	259 muṣ-9 'steal'	260 muh-4 'err'
Cit:	muñcati M	modate	muṣṇāti	muhyati
Pas:	mucyate	mudyate	muṣyate	muhyate
Fut:	mokṣyati	modiṣyate	moṣiṣyati	mokṣyati[4]
Cau:	mocayati M	modayati	moṣayati	mohayati
Des:	mumukṣati	mumodiṣate	mumuṣiṣati	mumuhiṣat
Per:	mumoca M	mumude	mumoṣa	mumoha
Aor:	amucat[1]	amodiṣṭa	amoṣīt	amuhat[5]
CAo:	amūmucat	amūmudat	amūmuṣat	amūmuhat
Inf:	moktum F	moditum	moṣitum	mogdhum[6]
Abs:	muktvā	muditvā	muṣitvā	mugdhvā[7]
PPP:	mukta-	mudita-[2]	muṣita-[3]	mugdha-[8]
FPP:	mocanīya-	modanīya-		
FPP:	mocya-		moṣya-	

	261 mūrch-1 'stiffen'	262 mṛ-6 'die'	263 mṛg-10 'hunt'	264 mṛj-2 'rub'
Cit:	mūrcchati	mriyate	mṛgayate	mārṣṭi[9]
Pas:		mriyate	mṛgyate	mṛjyate
Fut:	mūrcchiṣyati	mariṣyati	mṛgayiṣyate	mārjiṣyati[10]
Cau:	mūrcchayati	mārayati		mārjayati
Des:	mumūrcchiṣati	mumūrṣati		mimārjiṣati
Per:	mumūrccha	mamāra	mṛgayām c	mamārja
Aor:	amūrcchīt	amṛta	amamṛgata	amārjīt[11]
CAo:	amumūrcchat	amīmarat		amamārjat
Inf:	mūrcchitum	martum F	mṛgayitum	mārjitum[12] F
Abs:	mūrtvā	mṛtvā		mṛṣṭvā
PPP:	mūr(cchi)ta-	mṛta-		mṛṣṭa-[13]
FPP:				mārjanīya-
FPP:				

[1]Mid amukta [2]/modita- [3]/muṣṭa- [4]/mohiṣyati [5]Pas amohi [6]/mohitum/moḍhum [7]/mohitvā/mūḍhvā [8]mūḍha- [9]Dual mṛṣṭaḥ, Pl mṛjanti/mārjanti [10]/mārkṣyati [11]/amārkṣīt [12]/mārṣṭum [13]/mārjita-

	265 mṛd-9/1 'crush'	266 mṛś-6 'touch'	267 mṛṣ-4 'forget'	268 mnā-1 'recall'
Cit:	mṛdnāti[1]	mṛśati	mṛṣyati M	manati
Pas:	mṛdyate	mṛśyate	mṛṣyate	mnāyate
Fut:	mardiṣyati	markṣyati[2]	marṣiṣyati	mnāsyati
Cau:	mardayati	marśayati	marṣayati	mnāpayati
Des:	mimardiṣati	mimṛkṣati	mimarṣiṣati	mimnāsati
Per:	mamarda	mamarśa	mamarṣa M	mamnau
Aor:	amardīt	amārkṣīt[3]	amarṣīt M [6]	amnāsīt[7]
CAo:	amīmṛdat	amīmṛśat		amimnapat
Inf:	marditum F	marṣṭum[4]	marṣitum	mnātum F
Abs:	mṛditvā	mṛṣṭvā	mṛṣitvā[6]	
PPP:	mṛdita-	mṛṣṭa-[5]	mṛṣita-	mnāta-
FPP:	mardanīya-		marṣaṇīya-	
FPP:		mṛśya-		mnāya-

	269 mluc-1 'go'	270 mlecch-1 'jabber'	271 mlai-1[9] 'wither'	272 yaj-1 'sacrifice'
Cit:	mlocati	mlecchati	mlāyati[10] M	yajati M
Pas:			mlāyate	ijyate
Fut:	mlociṣyati	mlecchiṣyati	mlāsyati	yakṣyati
Cau:		mlecchayati	mlā̆payati	yājayati
Des:		mimlecchiṣati	mimlāsati	yiyakṣati
Per:	mumloca	mimleccha	mamlau	iyāja M
Aor:	amlucat[8]	amlecchīt	amlāsīt[11]	ayākṣīt[12]
CAo:		amimlecchat	amimlapat	ayīyajat
Inf:	mlocitum	mlecchitum	mlātum	yaṣṭum F
Abs:				iṣṭvā
PPP:	mlukta-	mliṣṭa-	mlāna-	iṣṭa-
FPP:				yājanīya-
FPP:				

[1]/mardati M [2]/mrakṣyati [3]/amrākṣīt [4]; Pas amarśi [4]/mraṣṭum [5]/mṛṣita- [6]/marṣitvā [7]Pas amnāyi [8]/amlocīt [9]/mlā-2 [10]/mlāti [11]Pas amlāyi [12]Mid ayaṣṭa; Pas ayāji

	273 yat-1 'strive'	274 yam-1 'give'	275 yā-2 'go'	276 yāc-1 'request'
Cit:	yatate A	yacchati	yāti	yācati M
Pas:	yatyate	yamyate	yāyate	yācyate
Fut:	yatiṣyate	yaṃsyati[2]	yāsyati	yāciṣyati
Cau:	yā̆tayati	yā̆mayati	yāpayati	yācayati
Des:	yiyatiṣate	yiyaṃsati	yiyāsati	yiyāciṣati
Per:	yete	yayāma M	yayau	yayāca M
Aor:	ayatiṣṭa[1]	ayāṃsīt[3]	ayāsīt	ayācīt[5]
CAo:	ayīyatat	ayīyamat	ayīyapat	ayayācat
Inf:	yatitum F	yantum[4] F	yātum F	yācitum F
Abs:	yativā	ya(mi)tvā	yātvā	yācitvā
PPP:	yat(i)ta-	yata-	yāta-	yācita-
FPP:	yatanīya-			yācanīya-
FPP:	yatya-	yamya-		yācya-

	277 yuj-7 'join'	278 yudh-4 'fight'	279 yup-4 'block'	280 raṃh-1 'hasten'
Cit:	yunakti[6] M	yudhyate	yupyati	raṃhati
Pas:	yujyate	yudhyate		
Fut:	yokṣyati	yotsyati M	yopiṣyati	
Cau:	yojayati	yodhayati	yopayati	raṃhayati
Des:	yuyukṣati	yuyutsate		riraṃhiṣati
Per:	yuyoja M	yuyodha M	yuyopa	raraṃha
Aor:	ayujat[7]	ayuddha[9]	ayupat	araṃhīt
CAo:	ayūyujat	ayūyudhat		araraṃhat
Inf:	yoktum F	yoddhum F	yopitum	raṃhitum
Abs:	yuktvā	yuddhvā		
PPP:	yukta-	yuddha-	yupita-	raṃhita-
FPP:	yojanīya-	yodhanīya-		
FPP:	yogya-[8]	yodhya-		

[1]Pas ayāti [2]/yamiṣyati [3]Pas ayāmi [4]/yamitum [5]Mid ayāciṣṭa
[6]Pl yuñjanti [7]/ayaukṣīt M/ayokṣīt [8]/yojya- [9]Pas ayodhi

	281 rakṣ-1 'protect'	282 rac-10 'arrange'	283 rañj-1/4 'be dyed'	284 rabh-1 'grasp'
Cit:	rakṣati	racayati	raj(y)ati M	rabhate
Pas:	rakṣyate	racyate	rajyate	rabhyate
Fut:	rakṣiṣyati	racayiṣyati	raṅkṣyati	rapsyate
Cau:	rakṣayati		rañjayati	rambhayati
Des:	rirakṣiṣati	riracayiṣati	riraṅkṣati	ripsate
Per:	rarakṣa	racayām āsa	rarañja M	rebhe
Aor:	arakṣīt [6]	arīracat[1]	araṅkṣīt[2]	arabdha[3]
CAo:	ararakṣat		ararañjat	ararambhat
Inf:	rakṣitum F	racayitum	raṅktum	rabdhum F
Abs:	rakṣitvā	racayitvā	ra(ṅ)ktvā	rabdhvā
PPP:	rakṣita-	racita-	rakta-	rabdha-
FPP:	rakṣaṇīyā	racanīya-	rañjanīya-	
FPP:	rakṣya-		rañjya-	rabhya-

	285 ram-1 'enjoy'	286 rah-1 'abandon'	287 rā-2 'bestow'	288 rāj-1 'shine'
Cit:	ramate A	rahati	rāti	rājati M
Pas:	ramyate[4]			rājyate
Fut:	raṃsyate	rahiṣyati	rāsyati	rājiṣyati
Cau:	rāmayati	rahayati	rāpayati	rājayati
Des:	riraṃsate	rirahiṣati	rirāsati	rirājiṣati
Per:	reme A	rarāha	rarau M	rarāja
Aor:	araṃsta[5]	arahīt	arāsīt M	arājīt M
CAo:	arīramat	ararahat	arīrapat	ararājat
Inf:	rantum[6] F	rahitum	rātum	rājitum
Abs:	ra(n)tvā			rājitvā
PPP:	rata-	rahita-	rāta-	rājita-
FPP:	ramaṇīya-			
FPP:	ramya-			

[1]/araracat [2]Mid araṅkta [3]Pas arambhi [4]Abs -ramya/-ratya
[5]/araṃsīt [5] [6]/ramitum

	289 rādh-5 'succeed'	290 rī-9/4 'flow'	291 ric-7 'leave'	292 riṣ-1/4 'be hurt'
Cit:	rādhnoti	riṇāti[2] M	riṇakti[3] M	reṣati[5]
Pas:	rādhyate		ricyate	
Fut:	rātsyati	reṣyati	rekṣyati	reṣiṣyati
Cau:	rādhayati	repayati	recayati	reṣayati
Des:	ri(rā)tsati	rirīṣati	ririkṣati	ririṣiṣati
Per:	rarādha	rirāya M	rireca M	rireṣa
Aor:	arātsīt[1]	araiṣīt M	aricat[4]	areṣīt[6]
CAo:	arīradhat	arīripat	arīricat	arīriṣat
Inf:	rāddhum	retum	rektum	reṣitum[7]
Abs:	rāddhvā		riktvā	
PPP:	rāddha-		rikta-	riṣṭa-
FPP:	rādhanīya-		recanīya-	
FPP:	rādhya-		recya-	

	293 ru-2 'cry'	294 ruc-1 'shine'	295 ruj-6 'break'	296 rud-2 'weep'
Cit:	rauti	rocate A	rujati	roditi [12]
Pas:	rūyate	rucyate	rujyate	rudyate
Fut:	raviṣyati	rociṣyate	rokṣyati	rodiṣyati
Cau:	rāvayati	rocayati	rojayati	rodayati
Des:	rurūṣati	ruruciṣate	rurukṣati	rurudiṣati[11]
Per:	rurāva	ruroca M	ruroja	ruroda M
Aor:	arāvīt	arucat[9]	araukṣīt[10]	arudat[12]
CAo:	arūruvat	arūrucat	arūrujat	arūrudat
Inf:	ravitum[8]	rocitum	roktum	roditum
Abs:	rutvā	rucitvā	ruktvā	ruditvā[13]
PPP:	ruta-	rucita-	rugṇa-	rudita-
FPP:				
FPP:				

[1]Pas arādhi [2]/riyati; Mid rīyate [3]Pl riñcanti [4]/araikṣīt M; Pas areci [5]/riṣyati M [6]/ariṣat [7]/reṣṭum [8]/rotum [9]Mid arociṣṭa [10]Dual arauktām [11]Int rorudyate [12]/arodīt; Pas arodi [13]/roditvā

	297 rudh-7	298 ruṣ-1/4	299 ruh-1	300 lag-1
	'obstruct'	'be angry'	'grow'	'adhere'
Cit:	ruṇaddhi[1] M	roṣati[4]	rohati	lagati
Pas:	rudhyate	--[5]	ruhyate	--[11]
Fut:	rotsyati	roṣiṣyati	rokṣyati	lagiṣyati
Cau:	rodhayati	roṣayati	rohayati[9]	lăgayati
Des:	rurutsati	ruruṣiṣati	rurukṣati	lilagiṣati
Per:	rurodha M	ruroṣa	ruroha	lalāga
Aor:	arudhat[2]	aroṣīt[6] [6]	aruhat	alagīt
CAo:	arūrudhat	arūruṣat	arūruhat	
Inf:	roddhum[3]	roṣitum[7]	roḍhum[10] F	lagitum
Abs:	ruddhvā	ruṣitvā[8]	rūḍhvā	lagitvā
PPP:	ruddha-	ruṣita-	rūḍha-	lagna-
FPP:			rohaṇīya-	laganīya-
FPP:	rodhya-		rohya-	

	301 laṅgh-1	302 lajj-6	303 lap-1	304 labh-1
	'jump'	'be ashamed'	'chatter'	'obtain'
Cit:	laṅghati M	lajjate A	lapati M	labhate
Pas:	laṅghyate		lapyate	labhyate
Fut:	laṅghiṣyati	lajjiṣyate	lapiṣyati	lapsyate[13]
Cau:	laṅghayati	lajjayati	lāpayati	lambhayati
Des:	lilaṅghiṣati	lilajjiṣate	lilapiṣati[12]	lipsate
Per:	lalaṅgha M	lalajje	lalāpa	lebhe A
Aor:	alaṅghīt M	alajjiṣṭa	alăpīt	alabdha
CAo:			alīlapat	alalambhat
Inf:	laṅghitum	lajjitum	lap(i)tum F	labdhum F
Abs:	laṅghitvā		lapitvā	labdhvā
PPP:	laṅghita-	lajjita-	lap(i)ta-	labdha-
FPP:	laṅghanīya-		lapanīya-	labhanīya-
FPP:	laṅghya-		lāpya-	labhya-

[1]Pl rundhanti [2]/arautsīt, Dual arauddhām; Mid aruddha, Dual arutsātām; Pas arodhi [3]/rodhitum [4]/ruṣyati [5]Abs -ruṣya [6]/aruṣat [7]/roṣṭum [8]/roṣitvā/ruṣṭvā [9]/ropayati [10]/rohitum [11]Abs -lagya [12]Int lālapyate [13]/labhiṣyate

	305 lamb-1 'hang'	306 lal-1 'play'	307 las-1 'gleam'	308 likh-6 'write'
Cit:	lambhate	lalati	lasati	likhati
Pas:	lambyate		lasyate	likhyate
Fut:	lambiṣyate	laliṣyati	lasiṣyati	lekhiṣyati[1]
Cau:	lambayati	lālayati	lāsayati	lekhayati
Des:	lilambiṣate	lilaliṣati	lilasiṣati	lilikhiṣati
Per:	lalambe		lalāsa	lilekha
Aor:	alambiṣṭa	alalīt	alāsīt	alekhīt
CAo:	alalambat	alīlalat	alīlasat	alīlikhat
Inf:	lambitum F		lasitum	lekhitum[2]
Abs:				lekhitvā[3]
PPP:	lambita-	lalita-	lasita-	likhita-
FPP:		lālanīya-		lekhanīya-
FPP:	lambya-	lālya-	lāsya-	lekhya-

	309 lip-6 'smear'	310 liś-6/4 'tear'	311 lih-2 'lick'	312 lī-9/4 'cling'
Cit:	limpati M	liśati[5]	leḍhi [25]	līnāti M[8]
Pas:	lipyate		lihyate	līyate[9]
Fut:	lepsyati	lekṣyati	lekṣyati M	leṣyati[10] M
Cau:	lepayati	leśayati	lehayati	lāyayati[11]
Des:	lilipsati	lilikṣati	lilikṣati	lilīṣati M
Per:	lilepa M	lileśa M	lileha M	lilāya[12] M
Aor:	alipat[4]	alikṣat[6] M [2]	alikṣat[7]	alaiṣīt[13] M
CAo:	alīlipat	alīliśat	alīlihat	
Inf:	leptum	leṣṭum	leḍhum	letum[14]
Abs:	liptvā		līḍhvā	lītvā
PPP:	lipta-	liṣṭa-	līḍha-	līna-
FPP:				
FPP:	lepya-		lehya-	

[1]/likhiṣyati [2]/likhitum [3]/likhitvā [4]Mid alip(a)ta [5]Mid liśyate
[6]/aliśat [7]Mid alikṣata/alīḍha [8]/līyate [9]Abs -līya/-lāya
[10]/lāsyati [11]/lāpayati [12]/lalau [13]/alāsīt [14]/lātum

	313 luṭ-1/4 'roll'	314 luṇṭh-10 'rob'	315 lup-6 'break'	316 lubh-4/1 'desire'
Cit:	loṭati[1]	luṇṭhayati	lumpati M	lubhyati[5]
Pas:	luṭyate	luṇṭhyate	lupyate	lubhyate
Fut:	loṭiṣyati	luṇṭhayiṣyati	lopsyati	lopsyati[6]
Cau:	loṭayati		lopayati	lobhayati
Des:	luluṭiṣati		lulupsati	lulubhiṣati
Per:	luloṭa	luṇṭhayām ā	lulopa M	lulobha M
Aor:	aloṭīt[2]	aluluṇṭhat	alupat[4]	alubhat[7]
CAo:	aluluṭat		alūlupat	alūlubhat
Inf:	loṭitum	luṇṭhayitum	loptum	lobdhum
Abs:	luṭitvā	luṇṭhayitvā	luptvā	lubdhvā[8]
PPP:	luṭita-[3]	luṇṭhita-	lupta-	lubdha-
FPP:				lobhanīya-
FPP:			lopya-	lobhya-

	317 lū-9 'cut off'	318 lok-1 'look'	319 loc-10 'consider'	320 vac-2 'speak'
Cit:	lunāti M	lokate	locayati M	vakti[11]
Pas:	lūyate	lokyate	locyate	ucyate
Fut:	laviṣyati	lokiṣyate	locayiṣyati	vakṣyati
Cau:	lāvayati	lokayati		vācayati
Des:	lulūṣati	lulokiṣate		vivakṣati
Per:	lulāva M	luloke	locayām ā/c	uvāca M
Aor:	alāvīt[9]	alokiṣṭa	alulocat M	avocat[12]
CAo:	alīlavat	alulokat		avīvacat
Inf:	lavitum	lokitum	locayitum	vaktum F
Abs:	lavitvā[10]			uktvā
PPP:	lūna-	lokita-	locita-	ukta-
FPP:		lokanīya-		vācanīya-
FPP:		lokya-		vācya-

[1]/luṭyati [2]/aluṭat [3]/loṭita- [4]Mid alupta; Pas alopi [5]/lobhati [6]/lobhiṣyati [7]/alobhīt [8]/lubhitvā/lobhitvā [9]Mid alaviṣṭa; Pas alāvi [10]/lūtvā [11]1st Sing vacmi etc. For 3rd Pl use vadanti. [12]Pas avāci/avoci

	321 vañc-1 'stray'	322 vad-1 'speak'	323 vadh-1 'kill'	324 van-8 'love'
Cit:	vañcati	vadati M	hanti[2]	vanoti M
Pas:	vacyate	ūdyate	vadhyate	vanyate
Fut:	vañciṣyati	vadiṣyati	vadhiṣyati	vaniṣyate
Cau:	vañcayati	vādayati	vadhayati	vā̆nayati
Des:	vivañciṣati	vivadiṣati		vivaniṣate
Per:	vavañca	uvāda M		vavāna M
Aor:	avañcīt	avādīt[1] M	avadhīt M	avaniṣṭa[3]
CAo:	avavañcat	avīvadat		
Inf:	vañcitum	vaditum F		vanitum
Abs:	va(ñ)citvā	uditvā		
PPP:	vañcita-	udita-		vanita-
FPP:	vañcanīya-	vādanīya-		vananīya-
FPP:		vadya-	vadhya-	

	325 vand-1 'salute'	326 vap-1 'sow'	327 varṇ-10 'depict'	328 vaś-2 'wish'
Cit:	vandate A	vapati M	varṇayati	vaṣṭi [10]
Pas:	vandyate	upyate	varṇyate	uśyate
Fut:	vandiṣyate	vapsyati[4]		vaśiṣyati
Cau:	vandayati	vāpayati		vāśayati
Des:	vivandiṣate	vivapsati	vivarṇayiṣati	vivaśiṣati
Per:	vavande A	uvāpa M	varṇayām ā	uvāśa
Aor:	avandiṣṭa	avāpsīt[5] M	avavarṇat	avā̆śīt[6]
CAo:	avavandat	avīvapat		avīvaśat
Inf:	vanditum F	vaptum F	varṇ(ay)itum	vaśitum
Abs:	vanditvā	uptvā		uśitvā
PPP:	vandita-	up(i)ta-	varṇita-	uśita-
FPP:	vandanīya-	vapanīya-		
FPP:	vandya-	vāpya-		

[1]Pas avādi [2]This and other missing forms from han (417). [3]/avata
[4]/vapiṣyati [5]Pas avāpi [6]Pas avāśi

	329 vas-1 'dwell'	330 vas-2 'wear'	331 vas-10 'cut'	332 vah-1 'carry'
Cit:	vasati	vaste	vāsayati	vahati M
Pas:	uṣyate	vasyate	vāsyate	uhyate
Fut:	vatsyati[1]	vasiṣyate[5]	vāsayiṣyati	vakṣyati[6]
Cau:	vāsayati	vāsayati		vāhayati
Des:	vivatsati	vivasiṣate		vivakṣati
Per:	uvāsa	vavase		uvāha M
Aor:	avātsīt[2]	avasiṣṭa	avīvasat	avākṣīt[7]
CAo:	avīvasat	avīvasat		avīvahat
Inf:	vas(i)tum[3]	vasitum F	vāsayitum F	voḍhum F
Abs:	uṣitvā[4]	vasitvā		ūḍhvā
PPP:	uṣita-	vasita-	vāsita-	ūḍha-
FPP:	vāsanīya-			vāhanīya-
FPP:	vāsya-			vāhya-

	333 vā-2 'blow'	334 vāñch-1 'wish'	335 vāś-4 'bleat'	336 vic-7 'separate'
Cit:	vāti	vāñchati	vāśyate A	vinakti[9] M
Pas:	vāyate	vāñchyate	vāśyate	vicyate
Fut:	vāsyati	vāñchiṣyati	vāśiṣyate	vekṣyati
Cau:	vāpayati	vāñchayati	vāśayati	vecayati
Des:	vivāsati	vivāñchiṣati	vivāśiṣate	vivikṣati
Per:	vavau	vavāñcha	vavāśe	viveca M
Aor:	avāsīt	avāñchīt[8]	avāśiṣṭa	avicat[10]
CAo:			avavāśat	avīvicat
Inf:	vātum	vāñchitum	vāśitum	vektuṁ
Abs:	vātvā	vāñchitvā	vāśitvā	viktvā
PPP:	vāta-	vāñchita-	vāśita-	vikta-
FPP:		vāñchanīya-		
FPP:			vāśya-	vekya-

[1]/vasiṣyati [2]Dual avāstām [3]FPP vastavya-/uṣitavya- [4]/uṣṭvā
[5]/vatsyate [6]/vahiṣyati [7]Mid avoḍha; Pas avāhi [8]Pas avāñchi
[9]Pl viñcanti [10]/avaikṣīt M

	337 vij-6 'quiver'	338 vid-2 'know'	339 vid-6 'find'	340 viś-6 'enter'
Cit:	vijate	vetti[1]	vindati M	viśati
Pas:	vijyate	vidyate	vidyate	viśyate
Fut:	vijiṣyati	vetsyati[2] M	vetsyati[2]	vekṣyati
Cau:	vejayati	vedayati M	vedayati	veśayati
Des:	vivijiṣati	vividiṣati	vivitsati	vivikṣati
Per:	vivije	viveda[3]	viveda M	viveśa M
Aor:	avijīt M	avedīt	avidat[5]	avikṣat M
CAo:	avīvijat	avīvidat		avīviśat
Inf:	vijitum	veditum[4] F	vettum F	veṣṭum F
Abs:		viditvā	viditvā	viṣṭvā
PPP:	vigna-	vidita-	vidita-[6]	viṣṭa-
FPP:		vedanīya-	vedanīya-	veśanīya-
FPP:		vedya-	vedya-	veśya-

	341 vī-2 'enjoy'	342 vṛ-5/9/1 'cover'	343 vṛj-7/1 'twist'	344 vṛt-1 'turn'
Cit:	veti[7]	vṛṇoti[9] M	vṛṇakti[12]	vartate
Pas:	vīyate	vriyate[10]	vṛjyate	vṛtyate
Fut:	veṣyati	varī̆ṣyati	varjiṣyati[13]	vartiṣyate[14]
Cau:	vāyayati[8]	vā̆rayati	varjayati	vartayati
Des:	vivīṣati	vivarī̆ṣati	vivarjiṣati	vivartiṣate
Per:	vivāya	vavāra M	vavarja M	vavarta M
Aor:	avaiṣīt	avārīt[11] M	avarjīt M	avṛtat[15]
CAo:	avīvayat	avīvarat	avavarjat	avīvṛtat
Inf:	vetum	var(ī)tum	varjitum	vartitum F
Abs:		vṛtvā	varjitvā	vṛttvā[16]
PPP:	vīta-	vṛta-	vṛkta-	vṛtta-
FPP:		vā̆raṇīya-	varjanīya-	vartanīya-
FPP:		vā̆rya-	varjya-	vartya-

[1]Pl vidanti [2]/vediṣyati [3]/veda [13], which however has present reference [4]/vettum [5]Mid avitta/avediṣṭa [6]/vinna-/vitta- [7]like eti [14] [8]/vāpayati [9]/vṛṇāti M/varati M [10]Abs -vṛtya [11]Mid avarī̆ṣṭa/avṛta [12]Pl vṛñjanti, Mid vṛ(ṅ)kte; or Act = varja(ya)ti [13]/varkṣyati [14]/vartsyati [15]Mid avartiṣṭa [16]/vartitvā

	345 vṛdh-1 'grow'	346 vṛṣ-1 'rain'	347 vṛh-6 'tear'	348 ve-1 'weave'
Cit:	vardhate A	varṣati M	vṛhati	vayati M
Pas:	vṛdhyate	vṛṣyate	vṛhyate	ūyate
Fut:	vardhiṣyate[1]	varṣiṣyati	varhiṣyati[4]	vayiṣyati[7]
Cau:	vardhayati	varṣayati	varhayati	vāyayati
Des:	vivardhiṣate	vivarṣiṣati	vivarhiṣati	vivāsati
Per:	vavardha M	vavarṣa M	vavarha	uvāya[8] M
Aor:	avṛdhat[2]	avarṣīt	avṛkṣat	avāsīt M[9]
CAo:	avīvṛdhat	avīvṛṣat		
Inf:	vardhitum	varṣitum	varhitum[5]	vātum[10] F
Abs:	vardhitvā[3]	vṛṣṭvā	varhitvā[6]	utvā
PPP:	vṛddha-	vṛṣṭa-	vṛḍha-	uta-
FPP:	vardhanīya-			
FPP:				

	349 vep-1 'tremble'	350 vyac-6 'embrace'	351 vyath-1 'suffer'	352 vyadh-4 'pierce'
Cit:	vepate A	vicati	vyathate A	vidhyati
Pas:		vicyate	vyathyate	vidhyate
Fut:	vepiṣyate	vyaciṣyati	vyathiṣyate	vyatsyati[11]
Cau:	vepayati	vyācayati	vyathayati	vyādhayati[12]
Des:	vivepiṣate	vivyaciṣati	vivyathiṣate	vivyatsati
Per:	vivepe	vivyāca	vivyathe	vivyādha
Aor:	avepiṣṭa	avyăcīt	avyathiṣṭa	avyātsīt
CAo:		avivyacat		avivyadhat
Inf:	vepitum	vyacitum	vyathitum	veddhum F
Abs:		vicitvā	vyathitvā	viddhvā
PPP:		vicita-	vyathita-	viddha-
FPP:				
FPP:			vyathya-	vedhya-

[1]/vartsyati [2]Mid avardhiṣṭa [3]/vṛddhvā [4]/varkṣyati [5]/varḍhum [6]/vṛḍhvā [7]/vāsyati [8]/vavau M [9]Mid avāsta [10]/otum [11]/vetsyati [12]/vedhayati

	353 vraj-1 'proceed'	354 vraśc-6 'hew'	355 śaṃs-1 'praise'	356 śak-5/4 'be able'
Cit:	vrajati	vṛścati	śaṃsati M	śaknoti[5]
Pas:	vrajyate	vṛścyate	śasyate	śakyate
Fut:	vrajiṣyati	vraściṣyati	śaṃsiṣyati	śak(i)ṣyati M
Cau:	vrājayati	vraścayati	śaṃsayati	śākayati
Des:	vivrajiṣati	vivraściṣati	śiśaṃsiṣati	śikṣati M
Per:	vavrāja	vavraśca	śaśaṃsa M	śaśāka M
Aor:	avrājīt	avrākṣīt[1]	aśaṃsīt M	aśakat[6]
CAo:		avavraścat	aśaśaṃsat	aśīśakat
Inf:	vrajitum	vraścitum[2]	śaṃsitum[3]	śak(i)tum
Abs:	vrajitvā	vṛṣṭvā	śastvā[4]	śaktvā
PPP:	vrajita-	vṛkṇa-	śasta-	śak(i)ta-
FPP:			śaṃsanīya-	
FPP:	vrajya-		śasya-	śakya-

	357 śaṅk-1 'hesitate'	358 śap-1/4 'curse'	359 śam-4/1 'be quiet'	360 śam-10 'observe'
Cit:	śaṅkate	śap(y)ati M	śāmyati[7]	śāmayate
Pas:	śaṅkyate	śapyate	śamyate	śāmyate
Fut:	śaṅkiṣyate	śapsyati	śamiṣyati	
Cau:	śaṅkayati	śāpayati	śamayati	
Des:	śiśaṅkiṣate	śiśapsati	śiśamiṣati	śiśāmayiṣate
Per:	śaśaṅke	śaśāpa M	śaśāma	śāmayāṃ c
Aor:	aśaṅkiṣṭa	aśāpsīt M	aśamat	aśīśamata
CAo:		aśīśapat	aśīśamat	
Inf:	śaṅkitum F	śap(i)tum	śamitum	śāmayitum F
Abs:	śaṅkitvā	śap(i)tva	śamitvā[8]	
PPP:	śaṅkita-	śap(i)ta-	śānta-	
FPP:	śaṅkanīya-		śamanīya-	
FPP:	śaṅkya-		śāmya-	

[1]/avraścīt [2]/vraṣṭum [3]FPP śa(ṃ)stavya- [4]/śaṃsitvā [5]/śakyati
[6]Mid aśakta/aśakiṣṭa [7]/śamati [8]/śāntvā

	361 śās-2 'instruct'	362 śikṣ-1 'learn'	363 śiṣ-7/1 'remain'	364 śī-2 'sleep'
Cit:	śāsti [22]	śikṣate	śinaṣṭi[4]	śete [19]
Pas:	śiṣyate[1]	śikṣyate	śiṣyate	śayyate
Fut:	śāsiṣyati	śikṣiṣyate	śekṣyati M	śayiṣyate[5] A
Cau:	śāsayati	śikṣayati	śeṣayati	śāyayati
Des:	śiśāsiṣati		śiśikṣati	śiśayiṣate
Per:	śaśāsa	śiśikṣe	śiśeṣa M	śiśye
Aor:	aśiṣat	aśikṣiṣṭa	aśiṣat	aśayiṣṭa[6]
CAo:	aśaśāsat	aśiśikṣat	aśīśiṣat	aśīśayat
Inf:	śās(i)tum	śikṣitum	śeṣṭum	śayitum F
Abs:	śiṣṭvā[2]	śikṣitvā	śiṣṭvā	śayitvā
PPP:	śiṣṭa-[3]	śikṣita-	śiṣṭa-	śayita-
FPP:	śāsanīya-	śikṣaṇīya-		śayanīya-
FPP:	śiṣya-		śeṣya-	

	365 śuc-1 'grieve'	366 śudh-4 'be pure'	367 śubh-1/6 'shine'	368 śuṣ-4 'dry up'
Cit:	śocati M	śudhyati	śobhati[11] M	śuṣyati
Pas:	śucyate	śudhyate		śuṣyate
Fut:	śociṣyati	śotsyati	śobhiṣyati[12]	śokṣyati
Cau:	śocayati	śodhayati	śobhayati	śoṣayati
Des:	śuśuciṣati	śuśutsati	śuśobhiṣate	śuśukṣati
Per:		śuśodha	śuśobha[13] M	śuśoṣa
Aor:	aśocīt[7] M	aśudhat[10]	aśubhat[14]	aśuṣat
CAo:	aśūśucat	aśūśudhat	aśūśubhat	aśūśuṣat
Inf:	śocitum[8]	śoddhum	śobhitum[15]	śoṣṭum
Abs:	śocitvā		śobhitvā	
PPP:	śocita-[9]	śuddha-	śobhita-[16]	śuṣka-
FPP:	śocanīya-	śodhanīya-		śoṣaṇīya-
FPP:	śocya-	śodhya-		śoṣya-

[1]/śāsyate [2]/śāsitvā [3]/śāsita- [4]Pl śiṃṣanti [5]/śeṣyate [6]Pas aśāyi
[7]/aśucat [8]/śoktum [9]/śucita- [10]Pas aśodhi [11]/śumbhati M
[12]/śumbhiṣyati [13]/śuśumbha M [14]/aśumbhīt; Mid aśobhiṣṭa
[15]/śumbhitum [16]/śubhita-

	369 śṝ-9 'crush'	370 ścut-1 'drip'	371 śyai-1 'congeal'	372 śrath-1/9 'get loose'
Cit:	śṛṇāti	ścotati	śyāyati M	śrathati[5] M
Pas:	śīryate	ścutyate	śīyate	--[6]
Fut:	śarī̆ṣyati	ścotiṣyati	śyāsyate	śrathiṣyati[7]
Cau:	śārayati	ścotayati	śyāyayati[3]	śrā̆thayati[8]
Des:	śiśarī̆ṣati	cuścotiṣati	śiśyāsate	śiśranthiṣati
Per:	śaśāra	cuścota	śiśye	śaśrātha[9] M
Aor:	aśā̆rīt	aścotīt[1]	aśyāsta	aśrāthīt[10]
CAo:	aśīśarat	acuścutat		aśiśrathat
Inf:	śarī̆tum	ścotitum	śyātum	śrathitum[11]
Abs:				śrathitvā[12]
PPP:	śīrṇa-	ścutita-[2]	śyāna-[4]	śṛthita-[13]
FPP:				
FPP:			śyāya-	

	373 śram-4 'weary'	374 śrambh-1 'err'	375 śrā-2[16] 'cook'	376 śri-1 'take refuge'
Cit:	śrāmyati	śrambhate	śrā(ya)ti	śrayati M
Pas:	śramyate			śrīyate[18]
Fut:	śramiṣyati	śrambhiṣyate	śrāsyati	śrayiṣyati
Cau:	śrā̆mayati	śrambhayati	śrāpayati	śrāyayati[19]
Des:	śiśramiṣati		śiśrāsati	śiśrīṣati
Per:	śaśrāma	śaśrambhe	śaśrau	śiśrāya M
Aor:	aśramīt[14]	aśrambhiṣṭa	aśrāsīt	aśiśriyat[20] M
CAo:	aśiśramat		aśiśrapat	aśiśrayat
Inf:	śramitum	śrambhitum	śṛātum	śrayitum F
Abs:	śrāntvā[15]			śrayitvā
PPP:	śrānta-	śrabdha-	śrāta-[17]	śrita-
FPP:		śrambhaṇīya-		śrayaṇīya-
FPP:				śrāya-

[1]/aścutat [2]/ścotita- [3]/śyāpayati [4]/śīna-/śīta-
[5]/śrathnāti M/śranthati [6]Abs -śrathya [7]/śranthiṣyati [8]/śranthitum
[9]/śaśrantha M [10]/aśranthīt [11]/śranthitum [12]/śranthitvā
[13]/śrathita- [14]/aśramat [15]/śramitvā [16]/śrai-1 [17]/śrāṇa-
[18]Abs -śritya [19]/śrāpayati [20]Pas aśrāyi

	377 śru-5 'hear'	378 ślāgh-1 'confide'	379 śvas-2/1 'breathe'	380 śvi-1 'swell'
Cit:	śṛṇoti M	ślāghate	śvasiti[3]	śvayati
Pas:	śrūyate[1]	ślāghyate	śvasyate	śūyate
Fut:	śroṣyati	ślāghiṣyate	śvasiṣyati	śvayiṣyati
Cau:	śrāvayati	ślāghayati	śvāsayati	śvāyayati
Des:	śuśrūṣate	śiślāghiṣate	śiśvasiṣati	śiśvayiṣati
Per:	śuśrāva	śaślāghe	śaśvāsa	śiśvāya[4]
Aor:	aśrauṣīt[2]	aślāghiṣṭa	aśvasīt	aśva(yī)t
CAo:	aśiśravat	aśaślaghat	aśiśvasat	aśūśavat
Inf:	śrotum F	ślāghitum	śvasitum F	śvayitum
Abs:	śrutvā		śvasitvā	śvayitvā
PPP:	śruta-	ślāghita-	śvas(i)ta-	śūna-
FPP:	śrāvaṇīya-	ślāghanīya-	śvāsanīya-	
FPP:	śrāvya-	ślāghya-	śvāsya-	

	381 sañj-1 'adhere'	382 sad-1 'sit'	383 sah-1 'endure'	384 sādh-5/1 'accomplish'
Cit:	sa(ñ)jati	sīdati M	sahate A	sādhnoti[10]
Pas:	sajyate	sadyate	sahyate	sādhyate
Fut:	saṅkṣyati	satsyati[5]	sahiṣyate[7]	sātsyati
Cau:	sañjayati	sādayati M	sāhayati	sādhayati
Des:	sisaṅkṣati	siṣatsati	sisahiṣate	siṣātsati
Per:	sasañja	sasāda M	sehe A	sasādha
Aor:	asāṅkṣīt	asadat	asahiṣṭa	asātsīt
CAo:	asasañjat	asīṣadat	asīṣahat	asīṣadhat
Inf:	sa(ṅ)ktum F	sattum[6]	soḍhum[8] F	sāddhum[11]
Abs:	saktvā	sattvā	soḍhvā[9]	sāddhvā
PPP:	sakta-	sanna-	soḍha-	saddha-
FPP:	sañjanīya-	sādanīya-	sahanīya-	sādhanīya-
FPP:	sajya-	sādya-	sāhya-	sādhya-

[1]Abs -śrutya [2]Pas aśrāvi [3]/śvasati [4]/śuśāva [5]/sīdiṣyati [6]/sīditum [7]/sakṣyate [8]/sahitum [9]/sahitvā [10]/sādhati M [11]/sādhitum

	385 si-5/9 'bind'	386 sic-6 'sprinkle'	387 sidh-1 'repel'	388 sidh-4 'succeed'
Cit:	sinoti[1] M	siñcati M	sedhati	sidhyati M
Pas:	sīyate	sicyate	sidhyate	sidhyate
Fut:	siṣyati	sekṣyati	setsyati[5]	setsyati
Cau:	sāyayati	secayati[4]	sedhayati	sādhayati[8]
Des:	siṣīṣati	siṣikṣati	sisedhiṣati	siṣitsati
Per:	siṣāya[2] M	siṣeca M	siṣedha M	siṣedha
Aor:	asaiṣīt M	asicat M	asedhīt	asidhat
CAo:	asīṣayat	asīṣicat	asīṣidhat	asīṣidhat
Inf:	setum	sektum F	seddhum[6]	seddhum
Abs:	sitvā	siktvā	sedhitvā[7]	siddhvā[9]
PPP:	sita-[3]	sikta-	siddha-	siddha-
FPP:		secanīya-	sedhanīya-	
FPP:	seya-	secya-	sedhya-	

	389 siv-4 'sew'	390 su-5 'press'	391 sud-1 'achieve'	392 sṛ-1 'flow'
Cit:	sīvyati	sunoti M	sūdate	sarati M
Pas:	sīvyate	sūyate		sriyate[14]
Fut:	seviṣyati	soṣyati[12]	sūdiṣyati	sariṣyati
Cau:	sevayati[10]	sāvayati	sūdayati	sārayati
Des:	siseviṣati	susūṣati M	susūdiṣate	sisīrṣati
Per:	siṣeva	suṣāva M	suṣūde	sasāra M
Aor:	asevīt	asauṣīt[13] M	asūdiṣṭa	asarat[15]
CAo:	asīṣivat	asūṣavat	asūṣudat	
Inf:	sevitum F	sotum	sūditum	sartum F
Abs:	sevitvā[11]	sutvā		sṛtvā
PPP:	syūta-	suta-		sṛta-
FPP:				sāraṇīya-
FPP:	sīvya-			sārya-

[1]/sināti M [2]/sasau [3]/sina- [4]/siñcayati [5]/sedhiṣyati [6]/sedhitum [7]/sidh(it)vā [8]/sedhayati [9]/sedhitvā [10]/sīvayati [11]/syūtvā [12]/saviṣyati [13]/asāvīt M [14]Abs -sṛtya [15]/asārṣīt

	393 sṛj-6/4 'emit'	394 sṛp-1 'creep'	395 sev-1 'serve'	396 skand-1 'dart'
Cit:	sṛjati[1]	sarpati M	sevate	skandati
Pas:	sṛjyate	sṛpyate	sevyate	ska(n)dyate
Fut:	srakṣyati M	sarpsyati[3]	seviṣyate A	skantsyati
Cau:	sarjayati	sarpayati	sevayati	skandayati
Des:	sisṛkṣati M	sisṛpsati	siseviṣate	ciskantsati
Per:	sasarja M	sasarpa	siṣeve	caskanda M
Aor:	asrākṣīt[2]	asṛpat	aseviṣṭa	aska(n)dat[5]
CAo:	asasarjat	asasarpat	asiṣevat	acaskandat
Inf:	sraṣṭum F	sarp(i)tum[4]	sevitum F	skanditum
Abs:	sṛṣṭvā	sṛptvā	sevitvā	skanttvā
PPP:	sṛṣṭa-	sṛpta-	sevita-	skanna-
FPP:			sevanīya-	
FPP:	sarjya-		sevya-	

	397 stambh-9 'uphold'	398 stu-2 'praise'	399 stṛ-5/9 'overthrow'	400 sthā-1 'stand'
Cit:	stabhnāti[6]	stauti M	stṛṇoti[11] M	tiṣṭati M
Pas:	stabhyate	stūyate	staryate[12]	sthīyate[15]
Fut:	stambhiṣyati	stoṣyati	stariṣyati	sthāsyati
Cau:	stambhayati	stāvayati	stārayati	sthāpayati
Des:	tistambhiṣati	tuṣṭūṣati	tistirṣati	tiṣṭhāsati
Per:	tastambha M	tuṣṭāva M	tastāra M	tasthau
Aor:	astambhīt[7] M	astauṣīt[10] M	astār(ṣ)īt M	asthāt M
CAo:	atastambhat	atuṣṭavat	atastarat	atiṣṭhipat
Inf:	stambhitum[8]	stotum	star(ī)tum	sthātum F
Abs:	stambhitvā[9]	stutvā	stṛtvā[13]	sthitvā
PPP:	stabdha-	stuta-	stṛta-[14]	sthita-
FPP:	stambhanīya-	stavanīya-		
FPP:		stavya-		stheya-

[1]Mid sṛjyate [2]Mid asṛṣṭa [3]/srapsyati [4]/srap(i)tum [5]/askāntsīt
[6]/stabhnoti; Mid stambhate [7]/astambhat [8]/stabdhum [9]/stabdhvā
[10]/astāvīt [11]/stṛṇāti M [12]/stīryate/striyate [13]/stīrtvā [14]/stīrṇa-
[15]Abs -sthāya; Prec Act stheyāt

	401 snā-2 'bathe'	402 snih-4 'love'	403 spardh-1 'strive'	404 spṛś-6 'touch'
Cit:	snāti	snihyati	spardhate	spṛśati M
Pas:	snāyate	snihyate	spardhyate[5]	spṛśyate
Fut:	snāsyati M	snehiṣyati[1]	spardhiṣyate	sparkṣyati[7]
Cau:	snāpayati	snehayati	spardhayati	sparśayati
Des:	sisnāsati	sisnikṣati	pispardhiṣate	pispṛkṣati
Per:	sasnau	siṣṇeha	paspardhe[6]	pasparśa M
Aor:	asnāsīt	asnihat	aspardhiṣṭa	asprākṣīt[8]
CAo:		asiṣṇihat		apasparśat
Inf:	snātum F	snegdhum[2]	spardhitum	sparṣṭum[9] F
Abs:	snātvā	snigdhvā[3]	spardhitvā	spṛṣṭvā
PPP:	snāta-	snigdha-[4]	spardhita-	spṛṣṭa-
FPP:			spardhanīya-	sparśanīya-
FPP:	sneya-	snehya-	spardhya-	spṛśya-

	405 spṛh-10 'desire'	406 sphur-6 'dart'	407 smi-1 'smile'	408 smṛ-1 'remember'
Cit:	spṛhayati	sphurati	smayate	smarati
Pas:	spṛhyate		smīyate[11]	smaryate[13]
Fut:	spṛhayiṣyati	sphuriṣyati	smeṣyate	smariṣyati
Cau:		sphorayati	smāyayati	smărayati
Des:	pispṛhayiṣati	pusphuriṣati	sismayiṣate	susmūrṣate
Per:	spṛhayām ā	pusphora M	siṣmiye	sasmāra
Aor:	apispṛhat	asphurīt[10]	asmeṣṭa[12]	asmārṣīt
CAo:		apusphurat		asasmarat
Inf:	spṛhayitum	sphuritum	smetum F	smartum F
Abs:	spṛhayitvā		smitvā	smṛtvā
PPP:	spṛhita-	sphurita-	smita-	smṛta-
FPP:	spṛhaṇīya-		smayanīya-	smaraṇīya-
FPP:			smāya-	smarya-

[1]/snekṣyati [2]/snehitum [3]/snihitvā [4]/snīḍha- [5]Abs -spṛdhya
[6]/paspṛdhe [7]/sprakṣyati [8]/aspārkṣīt/aspṛkṣat [9]/spraṣṭum F
[10]/asphorīt [11]Abs -sm(ay)itya [12]/asmayiṣṭa [13]Abs -smṛtya

	409 syand-1 'flow'	410 sru-1 'flow'	411 svañj-1 'embrace'	412 svad-1 'relish'
Cit:	syandate	sravati	svajate	svădate A
Pas:	syandyate		svajyate	--[7]
Fut:	syandiṣyate[1]	sroṣyati[3]	svaṅkṣyate[4]	
Cau:	syandayati	srăvayati	svañjayati	svădayati
Des:	sisyandiṣate	susrūṣati	sisvaṅkṣate	sisvădiṣate
Per:	sasyande	susrāva M	sasvañje	sasvăde
Aor:	asyandat[2]	asrāvīt	asvaṅkta[5]	asvadiṣṭa
CAo:	asiṣyadat	asusravat	asasvañjat	asiṣvadat
Inf:	syan(di)tum	srotum	sva(ṅ)ktum	svăditum
Abs:	syan(di)tvā		sva(ṅ)ktvā[6]	
PPP:	syanna-	sruta-	svakta-	svadita-
FPP:				svādanīya-
FPP:	syandya-	srāvya-	svajya-	svādya-

	413 svan-1 'resound'	414 svap-2 'sleep'	415 svid-4/1 'sweat'	416 svṛ-1 'sound'
Cit:	svanati	svapiti	svidyati[9]	svarati
Pas:		supyate	svidyate	
Fut:	svaniṣyati	svapsyati	svetsyate[10]	svariṣyati
Cau:	svănayati	svăpayati	svedayati	svărayati
Des:	sisvaniṣate	suṣupsati	sisvidiṣate	sisvariṣati
Per:	sasvāna	suṣvāpa	siṣveda M	sasvāra
Aor:	asvănīt	asvāpsīt[8]	asvidat[11]	asvār(ṣ)īt
CAo:	asiṣvanat	asiṣvapat	asiṣvidat	asiṣvarat
Inf:	svanitum	svaptum F	sveditum[12]	svar(i)tum
Abs:		suptvā	sviditvā	
PPP:	svanita-	supta-	svidita-[13]	
FPP:				
FPP:			svedya-	svārya-

[1]/syantsyate [2]Mid asyan(t)ta/asyandiṣṭa [3]/sraviṣyati [4]/svajiṣyate [5]Pas asvañji [6]/svajitvā [7]Abs -svādya [8]Pas asvāpi [9]Mid svedate [10]/svediṣyate [11]Mid asvediṣṭa [12]/svettum [13]/svedita-/svinna-

	417 han-2 'kill'	418 hary-1 'enjoy'	419 has-1 'laugh'	420 hā-3 'abandon'
Cit:	hanti [23]	haryati M	hasati M	jahāti [17]
Pas:	hanyate[1]		hasyate	hīyate[6]
Fut:	haniṣyati[2]		hasiṣyati	hāsyati
Cau:	ghātayati		hāsayati	hāpayati
Des:	jighāṃsati[3]	jiharyiṣati	jihasiṣati	jihāsati
Per:	jaghāna M	jaharya	jahāsa M	jahau M
Aor:	avadhīt[4] M	aharyīt	ahasīt[5]	ahā(sī)t[7]
CAo:	ajīghanat		ajīhasat	ajīhapat
Inf:	hantum F		hasitum	hātum F
Abs:	hatvā		hasitvā	hitvā
PPP:	hata-		hasita-	hīna-
FPP:			hasanīya-	
FPP:			hāsya-	heya-

	421 hā-3 'go forth'	422 hi-5 'impel'	423 hiṃs-1/7 'injure'	424 hu-3 'sacrifice'
Cit:	jihīte [18]	hinoti M	hiṃsati[8]	juhoti M
Pas:	hāyate	hīyate	hiṃsyate	hūyate
Fut:	hāsyate	heṣyati	hiṃsiṣyati	hoṣyati
Cau:	hāpayati	hāyayati	hiṃsayati	hāvayati
Des:	jihāsate	jihīṣati	jihiṃsiṣati	juhūṣati
Per:	jahe	jighāya M	jihiṃsa	juhāva[9] M
Aor:	ahāsta[7]	ahaiṣīt[7]	ahiṃsīt	ahauṣīt[10]
CAo:	ajīhapat	ajīhayat	ajihiṃsat	ajūhavat
Inf:	hātum F	hetum F	hiṃsitum F	hotum F
Abs:	hātvā		hiṃsitvā	hutvā
PPP:	hāna-	hita-	hiṃsita-	huta-
FPP:			hiṃsanīya-	
FPP:			hiṃsya-	havya-

[1]Abs -hanya/-hatya [2]/haṃsyati [3]Int jaṅghanyate [4]from vadh (323)
[5]Pas ahāsi [6]Abs -haya; Prec Act heyāt [7]Pas ahāyi
[8]/hinasti—hiṃsanti [9]/juhavām āsa [10]Pas ahāvi

	425 hṛ-1 'take'	426 hṛṣ-4 'rejoice'	427 hras-1 'diminish'	428 hrād-1 'rattle'
Cit:	harati M	hṛṣyati M	hrasati M	hrādate
Pas:	hriyate[1]	hṛṣyate		
Fut:	hariṣyati[2]	harṣiṣyati	hrasiṣyati	hrādiṣyate
Cau:	hārayati	harṣayati	hrāsayati	hrādayati
Des:	jihīrṣati	jiharṣiṣati	jihrasiṣati	
Per:	jahāra M	jaharṣa M	jahrāsa	jahrāde
Aor:	ahārṣīt[3]	ahṛṣat[4]	ahrăsīt	ahrādiṣṭa
CAo:	ajīharat	ajīhṛṣat	ajihrasat	
Inf:	hartum F	harṣitum	hrasitum	hrāditum
Abs:	hṛtvā			
PPP:	hṛta-	hṛṣṭa-[5]	hras(i)ta-	hrādita-
FPP:	haraṇīya-		hrāsanīya-	
FPP:	hārya-			

	429 hrī-3 'blush'	430 hlād-1 'refresh'	431 hvṛ-1 'bend'	432 hve-1 'call'
Cit:	jihreti	hlādate	hvarati	hvayati M
Pas:	hrīyate		hvaryate	hūyate
Fut:	hreṣyati	hlādiṣyate	hvariṣyati	hvāsyati[9]
Cau:	hrepayati	hlādayati	hvārayati	hvāyayati
Des:	jihrīṣati	jihlādiṣate	juh(v)ūrṣati	juhūṣati
Per:	jihrāya[6]	jahlāde	jahvāra	juhāva M
Aor:	ahraiṣīt[7]	ahlādiṣṭa	ahvārṣīt	ahvat[10] M
CAo:	ajihripat	ajihladat		ajūhavat
Inf:	hretum	hlāditum	hvartum	hvātum F
Abs:	hrītvā			hūtvā
PPP:	hrīta-[8]	hlanna-	hvṛta-	hūta-
FPP:				
FPP:				havya-

[1]Abs -hṛtya [2]Prec Mid hṛṣīṣṭa [3]Mid ahṛta; Pas ahāri [4]Pas aharṣi [5]/hṛṣita- [6]/jihrayām āsa [7]Pas ahrāyi [8]/hrīṇa- [9]/hvayiṣyati [10]/ahvāsīt; Pas ahvāyi/ahāvi

433, adhi -2
'study'

Cit:	adhīte [14]
Pas:	adhīyate[1]
Fut:	adhyeṣyate
Cau:	adhyāpayati
Des:	adhīyiṣate
Per:	adhīye
Aor:	adhyaiṣṭa
CAo:	adhyāpipat
Inf:	adhyetum F
Abs:	
PPP:	adhīta-
FPP:	
FPP:	adhyeya-

[1]Abs adhītya

Table 28. Index to verb stems.

akamp-	38	Aor	akhit-	68	Aor	acīkal-	39	Aor
akart-	46	Aor	akhid-	68	Aor	acīcint-	99	Aor
akarṣ-	48	Aor	akhait-	68	Aor	acūcud-	100	Aor
akas-	41	Aor	akhy-	69	Aor	acūcur-	101	Aor
akāṅkṣ-	42	Aor	agad-	71	Aor	ace-	97	Aor
akār-	45	Aor	agam-	72	Aor	acet-	98	Aor
akār-	49	Aor	agarj-	73	Aor	aceṣṭ-	103	Aor
akārk-	48	Aor	agarh-	74	Aor	acai-	97	Aor
akāś-	43	Aor	agā-	76	Aor	acchit-	106	Aor
akās-	41	Aor	agā-	84	Aor	acchid-	106	Aor
akup-	44	Aor	agāḍh-	77	Aor	acchait-	106	Aor
akṛ-	45	Aor	agād-	71	Aor	acchaid-	106	Aor
akṛk-	48	Aor	agār-	82	Aor	acy-	1	Pas
akṛt-	46	Aor	agār-	83	Aor	acyo-	104	Aor
akṛś-	47	Aor	agāl-	75	Aor	ajagaṇ-	70	Aor
akḷp-	50	Aor	agāh-	77	Aor	ajan-	107	Aor
akram-	51	Aor	agūh-	80	Aor	ajar-	114	Aor
akram-	51	Aor	agṛdh-	81	Aor	ajalp-	108	Aor
akrāk-	48	Aor	ago-	78	Aor	ajāgar-	109	Aor
akrīḍ-	53	Aor	agopāy-	85	Aor	ajār-	114	Aor
akruk-	55	Aor	agaup-	79	Aor	ajinv-	111	Aor
akrudh-	54	Aor	agranth-	86	Aor	ajīgaṇ-	70	Aor
akruṣ-	55	Aor	agras-	87	Aor	ajīv-	112	Aor
akre-	52	Aor	agrah-	88	Aor	aje-	110	Aor
akrai-	52	Aor	aghas-	4	Aor	ajai-	110	Aor
aklik-	56	Aor	aghār-	90	Aor	ajoṣ-	113	Aor
akleś-	56	Aor	aghuk-	80	Aor	ajñā-	115	Aor
akṣ-	57	Aor	aghuṣ-	89	Aor	ajy-	2	Pas
akṣaṃ-	58	Aor	aghoṣ-	89	Aor	ajyā-	116	Aor
akṣaṇ-	57	Aor	aghrā-	91	Aor	ajvāl-	117	Aor
akṣam-	58	Aor	aghru-	91	Aor	añc-	1	Cit
akṣār-	59	Aor	aṅk-	2	Cit	añcay-	1	Cau
akṣās-	92	Aor	aṅg-	2	Cit	añciṣy-	1	Fut
akṣut-	63	Aor	acakal-	40	Aor	añcy-	1	Pas
akṣud-	63	Aor	acakhaṇḍ-	65	Aor	añj-	2	Cit
akṣudh-	64	Aor	acam-	93	Aor	añjay-	2	Cau
akṣep-	62	Aor	acart-	102	Aor	añjiṣy-	2	Fut
akṣeb-	62	Aor	acarv-	95	Aor	aṭ-	3	Cit
akṣai-	61	Aor	acār-	94	Aor	aṭiṣy-	3	Fut
akṣaip-	62	Aor	acāl-	96	Aor	aṭy-	3	Pas
akṣaut-	63	Aor	acikṣal-	60	Aor	aḍhauk-	118	Aor
akhan-	66	Aor	acicint-	99	Aor	at-	4	Cit
akhād-	67	Aor	acicchad-	105	Aor	atakṣ-	119	Aor
akhān-	66	Aor	acīkath-	37	Aor	atatark-	124	Aor

atap- .... 122 Aor
atam- .... 123 Aor
atard- ... 130 Aor
atarp- ... 131 Aor
atān- .... 121 Aor
atāp- .... 122 Aor
atār- .... 133 Aor
atārp- ... 131 Aor
atītaḍ- ... 120 Aor
atītij- .... 125 Aor
atut- .... 126 Aor
atud- .... 126 Aor
atuṣ- .... 129 Aor
atūtul- ... 128 Aor
atṛd- .... 130 Aor
atṛp- .... 131 Aor
atṛṣ- ..... 132 Aor
ator- .... 127 Aor
ataut- ... 126 Aor
atyāk- ... 134 Aor
atyās- ... 134 Aor
atras- .... 135 Aor
atrā- .... 136 Aor
atrāp- ... 131 Aor
atrās- .... 135 Aor
atvar- ... 137 Aor
atsy- ..... 4 Fut
ad- ...... 4 Cit
adakṣ- ... 139 Aor
adaṅk- ... 138 Aor
adaṅg- ... 138 Aor
adadaṇḍ- . 140 Aor
adabh- ... 142 Aor
adam- ... 141 Aor
adambh- . 142 Aor
aday- .... 143 Aor
adarp- ... 159 Aor
adarś- ... 160 Aor
adas- .... 144 Aor
adā- ..... 146 Aor
adā- ..... 147 Aor
adāg- .... 145 Aor
adāṅk- ... 138 Aor
adār- .... 162 Aor
adārp- ... 159 Aor
adi- ..... 146 Aor
adi- ..... 147 Aor
adikṣ- ... 150 Aor
adīkṣ- ... 152 Aor
adīp- .... 153 Aor
adu- .... 146 Aor
adu- .... 147 Aor
adug- ... 157 Aor
adudruv- . 165 Aor
aduṣ- .... 156 Aor
adūdul- .. 155 Aor
adṛ- ..... 158 Aor
adṛṃh- .. 161 Aor
adṛp- .... 159 Aor
adṛṣ- .... 160 Aor
adev- .... 148 Aor
adev- .... 149 Aor
ado- ..... 154 Aor
adoṣ- .... 156 Aor
adau- .... 154 Aor
ady- ..... 4 Pas
adyut- ... 163 Aor
adyot- ... 163 Aor
adrā- .... 164 Aor
adrāk- ... 160 Aor
adrāp- ... 159 Aor
adrāṣ- ... 160 Aor
adruh- ... 166 Aor
advik- ... 167 Aor
adharṣ- .. 172 Aor
adhav- ... 170 Aor
adhav- ... 169 Aor
adhā- .... 168 Aor
adhā- .... 173 Aor
adhāk- ... 145 Aor
adhār- ... 171 Aor
adhāv- ... 170 Aor
adhāv- ... 169 Aor
adhi- .... 168 Aor
adhikṣ- .. 151 Aor
adhijag- .. 433 Per
adhī- .... 433 Cit
adhīy- ... 433 Pas
adhīy- ... 433 Per
adhu- ... 168 Aor
adhu- ... 173 Aor
adhukṣ- .. 157 Aor
adhṛ- .... 171 Aor
adhṛṣ- ... 172 Aor
adho- .... 170 Aor
adhau- ... 170 Aor
adhmā- .. 174 Aor
adhyay- .. 433 Cit
adhyā- ... 175 Aor
adhyāpay- 433 Cau
adhyeṣy- . 433 Fut
adhyai- .. 433 Cit
adhyai- .. 433 Aor
adhrāj- ... 176 Aor
adhrāj- ... 176 Aor
adhrāñj- .. 176 Aor
adhvaṃs- 177 Aor
adhvan- .. 178 Aor
adhvas- .. 177 Aor
adhvān- .. 178 Aor
adhvār- .. 179 Aor
an- ...... 5 Cit
anaṃ- ... 184 Aor
anak- ..... 2 Cit
anakṣ- ... 180 Aor
anaj- ..... 2 Cit
anad- .... 181 Aor
anad- .... 186 Aor
anand- ... 182 Aor
anabh- ... 183 Aor
anart- ... 192 Aor
anaś- .... 185 Aor
anāt- .... 186 Aor
anāth- ... 187 Aor
anād- .... 181 Aor
anāv- .... 190 Aor
anind- ... 188 Aor
aniṣy- .... 5 Fut
anut- .... 191 Aor
anud- ... 191 Aor
anū- .... 190 Aor
ane- ..... 189 Aor
anai- .... 189 Aor
anau- .... 190 Aor
anaut- ... 191 Aor
any- ...... 5 Pas
apak- .... 193 Aor
apag- .... 193 Aor

apaṭ-	194	Aor
apaṇ-	196	Aor
apat-	198	Aor
apapt- . . .	197	Aor
aparc- . . .	212	Aor
apalāy- . .	199	Aor
apav-	208	Aor
apā-	201	Aor
apā-	202	Aor
apāk-	193	Aor
apāṭ-	194	Aor
apāṭh- . . .	195	Aor
apār-	210	Aor
apāv-	208	Aor
apinv- . . .	203	Aor
apipīḍ- . .	206	Aor
apiṣ-	205	Aor
apispṛh- . .	405	Aor
apīpiḍ- . .	206	Aor
apu-	201	Aor
apuṣ-	207	Aor
apūpuj- . .	209	Aor
apṛ-	211	Aor
apeś-	204	Aor
apoṣ-	207	Aor
apyāy- . . .	213	Aor
aprak- . . .	214	Aor
aprag- . . .	214	Aor
aprath- . .	215	Aor
apraṣ- . . .	214	Aor
aprāk- . . .	214	Aor
aprāṣ- . . .	214	Aor
apre-	216	Aor
aprai- . . .	216	Aor
aplo-	217	Aor
aphāl- . . .	218	Aor
abaṃh- . .	219	Aor
ababhakṣ-	225	Aor
ababhāṣ- .	229	Aor
abarh- . . .	223	Aor
abādh- . . .	221	Aor
abānd- . . .	220	Aor
abudh- . .	222	Aor
abodh- . . .	222	Aor
abharṣ- . .	241	Aor
abhā-	228	Aor
abhāk- . . .	226	Aor
abhāṅk- . .	227	Aor
abhānt- . .	220	Aor
abhār- . . .	238	Aor
abhārk- . .	241	Aor
abhāṣ- . . .	226	Aor
abhāṣ- . . .	229	Aor
abhās- . . .	230	Aor
abhikṣ- . .	231	Aor
abhit- . . .	232	Aor
abhid- . . .	232	Aor
abhuk- . . .	234	Aor
abhug- . . .	234	Aor
abhuṣ- . . .	234	Aor
abhū-	236	Aor
abhūṣ- . . .	237	Aor
abhṛ-	238	Aor
abhṛk- . . .	223	Aor
abhai- . . .	233	Aor
abhauk- . .	234	Aor
abhaukṣ- .	235	Aor
abhait- . . .	232	Aor
abhauṣ- . .	234	Aor
abhauṣ- . .	235	Aor
abhraṃś- .	239	Aor
abhram- . .	240	Aor
abhraś- . .	239	Aor
abhraṣ- . .	241	Aor
abhrāk- . .	241	Aor
abhrāj- . . .	242	Aor
ama-	246	Aor
amaṃ- . . .	246	Aor
amaṃh- . .	243	Aor
amath- . . .	244	Aor
amad- . . .	245	Aor
aman- . . .	246	Aor
amanth- . .	244	Aor
amand- . .	247	Aor
amamṛg- .	263	Aor
amard- . .	265	Aor
amarṣ- . . .	267	Aor
amah- . . .	249	Aor
amā-	250	Aor
amā-	255	Aor
amāṅk- . .	248	Aor
amād- . . .	245	Aor
amārk- . .	264	Aor
amārk- . .	266	Aor
amārj- . . .	264	Aor
amārṣ- . . .	264	Aor
amārṣ- . . .	266	Aor
amik-	254	Aor
amīmiṣ- . .	253	Aor
amīl-	256	Aor
amuk- . . .	257	Aor
amuc- . . .	257	Aor
amuh- . . .	260	Aor
amūrcch- .	261	Aor
amṛ-	262	Aor
ameth- . . .	251	Aor
amel-	252	Aor
ameṣ- . . .	253	Aor
amod- . . .	258	Aor
amoṣ- . . .	259	Aor
amnā- . . .	268	Aor
amrāk- . .	266	Aor
amrāṣ- . . .	266	Aor
amlā-	271	Aor
amluc- . . .	269	Aor
amlecch- .	270	Aor
amloc- . . .	269	Aor
ay-	16	Cit
ayat-	273	Aor
ayaṣ-	272	Aor
ayā-	275	Aor
ayāk-	272	Aor
ayāc-	276	Aor
ayām- . . .	274	Aor
ayāṣ-	272	Aor
ayuk-	277	Aor
ayug-	277	Aor
ayuj-	277	Aor
ayut-	278	Aor
ayud- . . .	278	Aor
ayup- . . .	279	Aor
ayuṣ-	277	Aor
ayauk- . . .	277	Aor
ayauṣ- . . .	277	Aor
araṃ- . . .	285	Aor
araṃṣ- . . .	283	Aor
araṃh- . .	280	Aor
arakṣ- . . .	281	Aor

araṅk-	283	Aor	arṣay-	35	Cau	avart-	344	Aor
araṅg-	283	Aor	arṣiṣy-	35	Fut	avardh-	345	Aor
arap-	284	Aor	arh-	7	Cit	avarṣ-	346	Aor
arab-	284	Aor	arh-	7	Aor	avavarṇ-	327	Aor
ararac-	282	Aor	arhay-	7	Cau	avaś-	328	Aor
arah-	286	Aor	arhiṣy-	7	Fut	avas-	330	Aor
arā-	287	Aor	arhy-	7	Pas	avā-	333	Aor
arāj-	288	Aor	alag-	300	Aor	avā-	348	Aor
arāt-	289	Aor	alaṅgh-	301	Aor	avāk-	332	Aor
arād-	289	Aor	alajj-	302	Aor	avāñch-	334	Aor
arāv-	293	Aor	alap-	303	Aor	avāṭ-	329	Aor
arik-	291	Aor	alap-	304	Aor	avād-	322	Aor
arig-	291	Aor	alab-	304	Aor	avāp-	326	Aor
aric-	291	Aor	alamb-	305	Aor	avār-	342	Aor
ariṣ-	292	Aor	alal-	306	Aor	avāś-	328	Aor
ariṣy-	31	Fut	alas-	307	Aor	avāś-	335	Aor
arīrac-	282	Aor	alā-	312	Aor	avik-	336	Aor
aruc-	294	Aor	alāp-	303	Aor	avik-	340	Aor
arut-	297	Aor	alāv-	317	Aor	avig-	336	Aor
arud-	296	Aor	alās-	307	Aor	avic-	336	Aor
arud-	297	Aor	ạlik-	310	Aor	avij-	337	Aor
arudh-	297	Aor	alik-	311	Aor	avit-	339	Aor
aruṣ-	298	Aor	alip-	309	Aor	avid-	339	Aor
aruh-	299	Aor	aliś-	310	Aor	aviṣy-	8	Fut
are-	290	Aor	alīḍh-	311	Aor	avīvas-	331	Aor
areṣ-	292	Aor	aluṭ-	313	Aor	avṛ-	342	Aor
arai-	290	Aor	alup-	315	Aor	avṛk-	347	Aor
araik-	291	Aor	alubh-	316	Aor	avṛt-	344	Aor
aroc-	294	Aor	aluluṇṭh-	314	Aor	avṛdh-	345	Aor
arod-	296	Aor	aluloc-	319	Aor	aved-	338	Aor
aroṣ-	298	Aor	ale-	312	Aor	aved-	339	Aor
arauk-	295	Aor	alekh-	308	Aor	avep-	349	Aor
araut-	297	Aor	alai-	312	Aor	avai-	341	Aor
araud-	297	Aor	alok-	318	Aor	avaik-	336	Aor
arcay-	32	Cau	aloṭ-	313	Aor	avo-	332	Aor
arciṣy-	32	Fut	alobh-	316	Aor	avoc-	320	Aor
arj-	33	Cit	av-	8	Cit	avy-	8	Pas
arjay-	33	Cau	av-	324	Aor	avyac-	350	Aor
arjiṣy-	33	Fut	avañc-	321	Aor	avyath-	351	Aor
arthay-	6	Cit	avad-	322	Aor	avyāc-	350	Aor
arthayiṣy-	6	Fut	avadh-	323	Aor	avyāt-	352	Aor
arthy-	6	Pas	avan-	324	Aor	avyād-	352	Aor
ardhay-	34	Cau	avand-	325	Aor	avraśc-	354	Aor
ardhiṣy-	34	Fut	avap-	326	Aor	avrāk-	354	Aor
arpay-	31	Cau	avar-	342	Aor	avrāj-	353	Aor
ary-	31	Pas	avarj-	343	Aor	avrās-	354	Aor

aśaṃs-	355	Aor
aśak-	356	Aor
aśaṅk-	357	Aor
aśap-	358	Aor
aśam-	359	Aor
aśay-	364	Aor
aśar-	369	Aor
aśāp-	358	Aor
aśār-	369	Aor
aśikṣ-	362	Aor
aśiśriy-	376	Aor
aśiṣ-	361	Aor
aśiṣ-	363	Aor
aśiṣy-	9	Fut
aśiṣy-	10	Fut
aśīśam-	360	Aor
aśuc-	365	Aor
aśudh-	366	Aor
aśubh-	367	Aor
aśumbh-	367	Aor
aśuṣ-	368	Aor
aśoc-	365	Aor
aśobh-	367	Aor
aścut-	370	Aor
aścot-	370	Aor
aśn-	9	Cit
aśn-	10	Cit
aśy-	9	Paś
aśy-	10	Paś
aśyā-	371	Aor
aśranth-	372	Aor
aśram-	373	Aor
aśrambh-	374	Aor
aśrā-	375	Aor
aśrāth-	372	Aor
aśrau-	377	Aor
aślāgh-	378	Aor
aśv-	380	Aor
aśvay-	380	Aor
aśvaś-	379	Aor
as-	11	Cit
asaṅk-	381	Aor
asad-	382	Aor
asar-	392	Aor
asav-	390	Aor
asah-	383	Aor
asāt-	384	Aor
asād-	384	Aor
asār-	392	Aor
asāv-	390	Aor
asic-	386	Aor
asidh-	388	Aor
asiṣy-	12	Fut
asud-	391	Aor
asṛp-	394	Aor
asṛṣ-	393	Aor
ase-	385	Aor
asedh-	387	Aor
asev-	389	Aor
asev-	395	Aor
asai-	385	Aor
aso-	390	Aor
asau-	390	Aor
askad-	396	Aor
askand-	396	Aor
askant-	396	Aor
astambh-	397	Aor
astar-	399	Aor
astav-	398	Aor
astār-	399	Aor
astāv-	398	Aor
asto-	398	Aor
astau-	398	Aor
asthā-	400	Aor
asthi-	400	Aor
asthu-	400	Aor
asna-	401	Aor
asnih-	402	Aor
aspardh-	403	Aor
aspārk-	404	Aor
aspārṣ-	404	Aor
aspṛk-	404	Aor
asprāk-	404	Aor
asprāṣ-	404	Aor
asphur-	406	Aor
asphor-	406	Aor
asmār-	408	Aor
asme-	407	Aor
asy-	12	Cit
asy-	12	Pas
asyan-	409	Aor
asyant-	409	Aor
asyand-	409	Aor
asrāk-	393	Aor
asrāv-	410	Aor
asrāṣ-	393	Aor
asvaṅk-	411	Aor
asvaṅg-	411	Aor
asvad-	412	Aor
asvan-	413	Aor
asvān-	413	Aor
asvāp-	414	Aor
asvār-	416	Aor
asvid-	415	Aor
asved-	415	Aor
ahary-	418	Aor
ahas-	419	Aor
ahā-	420	Aor
ahā-	421	Aor
ahār-	425	Aor
ahiṃs-	423	Aor
ahu-	420	Aor
ahṛ-	425	Aor
ahṛṣ-	426	Aor
ahai-	422	Aor
ahau-	424	Aor
ahras-	427	Aor
ahrād-	428	Aor
ahrās-	427	Aor
ahrai-	429	Aor
ahlād-	430	Aor
ahv-	432	Aor
ahvār-	431	Aor
ā-	15	Cit
āñc-	1	Aor
āñj-	2	Aor
āṭ-	3	Per
āṭ-	3	Aor
āṭay-	3	Cau
āt-	13	Per
ād-	4	Per
ād-	15	Cit
āday-	4	Cau
ān-	5	Per
ān-	5	Aor
ānak-	9	Per
ānaṅk-	2	Per
ānaj-	2	Per

ānañc-	1	Per
ānañj-	2	Per
ānay-	5	Cau
ānarc-	32	Per
ānardh-	34	Per
ānarṣ-	35	Per
ānarh-	7	Per
ānaś-	9	Per
ānṛj-	33	Per
āp-	14	Per
āp-	14	Aor
āpay-	14	Cau
āpn-	14	Cit
āpy-	14	Pas
āpsy-	14	Fut
āyay-	16	Cau
ār-	31	Per
ār-	31	Aor
ārc-	32	Aor
ārj-	33	Aor
ārtath-	6	Aor
ārdh-	34	Aor
ārṣ-	35	Aor
āv-	8	Aor
āva-	8	Per
āvay-	8	Cau
āś-	9	Aor
āś-	10	Per
āś-	10	Aor
āśay-	9	Cau
āśay-	10	Cau
āṣ-	9	Aor
ās-	11	Per
ās-	12	Per
ās-	15	Cit
ās-	15	Aor
āsay-	12	Cau
āsay-	15	Cau
āsiṣy-	15	Fut
āsth-	12	Aor
āsy-	15	Pas
āh-	13	Per
i-	16	Cit
icch-	18	Cit
ijy-	272	Pas
idhy-	17	Pas
inadh-	17	Cit
int-	17	Cit
ind-	17	Cit
indh-	17	Cit
indhay-	17	Cau
indhiṣy-	17	Fut
iyaj-	272	Per
iyay-	16	Per
iyar-	31	Cit
iyaṣ-	272	Per
iyāj-	272	Per
iyāy-	16	Per
iye-	16	Per
iyeṣ-	18	Per
iyeṣ-	19	Per
iṣy-	18	Pas
iṣy-	19	Cit
iṣy-	19	Pas
īkṣ-	20	Cit
īkṣay-	20	Cau
īkṣiṣy-	20	Fut
īkṣy-	20	Pas
īj-	272	Per
īṭ-	21	Cit
īḍ-	21	Cit
īḍay-	21	Cau
īṣiṣy-	21	Fut
īḍy-	21	Pas
īy-	16	Pas
īy-	16	Per
īr-	22	Cit
īray-	22	Cau
īriṣy-	22	Fut
īry-	22	Pas
īś-	23	Cit
īśay-	23	Cau
īśiṣy-	23	Fut
īśy-	23	Pas
īṣ-	18	Per
īṣ-	19	Per
īṣ-	23	Cit
īṣ-	24	Cit
īṣiṣy-	24	Fut
ukṣ-	25	Cit
ukṣay-	25	Cau
ukṣiṣy-	25	Fut
ukṣy-	25	Pas
ucy-	320	Pas
uñch-	26	Cit
uñchay-	26	Cau
uñchiṣy-	26	Fut
uḍ-	328	Cit
udy-	27	Pas
udy-	322	Pas
unat-	27	Cit
unad-	27	Cit
unt-	27	Cit
und-	27	Cit
unday-	27	Cau
undiṣy-	27	Fut
upy-	326	Pas
ububh-	28	Per
ubobh-	28	Per
ubhiṣy-	28	Fut
ubhn-	28	Cit
umbh-	28	Cit
umbhiṣy-	28	Fut
uvak-	320	Per
uvac-	320	Per
uvad-	322	Per
uvap-	326	Per
uvay-	348	Per
uvaś-	328	Per
uvas-	329	Per
uvah-	332	Per
uvāc-	320	Per
uvād-	322	Per
uvāp-	326	Per
uvāy-	348	Per
uvāś-	328	Per
uvās-	329	Per
uvāh-	332	Per
uvo-	332	Per
uvoṣ-	29	Per
uś-	328	Cit
uśy-	328	Pas
uṣ-	328	Cit
uṣy-	29	Pas
uṣy-	329	Pas
uhy-	332	Pas
ūc-	320	Per
ūd-	322	Per

ūp-	326	Per
ūy-	348	Pas
ūy-	348	Per
ūś-	328	Per
ūṣ-	29	Per
ūṣ-	329	Per
ūh	30	Cit
ūh-	332	Per
ūhay-	30	Cau
ūhiṣy-	30	Fut
ūhy-	30	Pas
ṛ-	31	Cit
ṛc-	32	Cit
ṛcch-	31	Cit
ṛcy-	32	Pas
ṛjy-	33	Pas
ṛdhn-	34	Cit
ṛdhy-	34	Cit
ṛdhy-	34	Pas
ṛṣ-	35	Cit
e-	11	Cit
e-	16	Cit
edh-	36	Cit
edhay-	36	Cau
edhiṣy-	36	Fut
edhy-	36	Pas
eṣay-	18	Cau
eṣay-	19	Cau
eṣiṣy-	18	Fut
eṣiṣy-	19	Fut
eṣy-	16	Fut
ai-	16	Aor
aikṣ-	20	Aor
aid-	21	Aor
aidh-	36	Aor
aindh-	17	Aor
air-	22	Aor
aiś-	23	Aor
aiṣ-	18	Aor
aiṣ-	19	Aor
aiṣ-	24	Aor
obhiṣy-	28	Fut
oṣ-	29	Cit
oṣay-	29	Cau
oṣiṣy-	29	Fut
aukṣ-	25	Aor
auñch-	26	Aor
aund-	27	Aor
aubh-	28	Aor
aumbh-	28	Aor
auṣ-	29	Aor
auh-	30	Aor
kathay-	37	Cit
kathayiṣy-	37	Fut
kathy-	37	Pas
kamp-	38	Cit
kampay-	38	Cau
kampiṣy-	38	Fut
kampy-	38	Pas
karav-	45	Cit
kariṣy-	45	Fut
kariṣy-	49	Fut
karīṣy-	49	Fut
karo-	45	Cit
karkṣy-	48	Fut
kartay-	46	Cau
kartiṣy-	46	Fut
karśay-	47	Cau
karśiṣy-	47	Fut
karṣ-	48	Cit
karṣay-	48	Cau
kalay-	40	Cit
kalayiṣy-	39	Fut
kalayiṣy-	40	Fut
kalp-	50	Cit
kalpay-	50	Cau
kalpiṣy-	50	Fut
kalpsy-	50	Fut
kaly-	40	Pas
kas-	41	Cit
kasiṣy-	41	Fut
kasy-	41	Pas
kāṅkṣ-	42	Cit
kāṅkṣay-	42	Cau
kāṅkṣiṣy-	42	Fut
kāṅkṣy-	42	Pas
kāthay-	37	Cau
kāray-	45	Cau
kāray-	49	Cau
kālay-	39	Cit
kālay-	40	Cau
kāly-	39	Pas
kāś-	43	Cit
kāśay-	43	Cau
kāśiṣy-	43	Fut
kāśy-	43	Cit
kāśy-	43	Pas
kāsay-	41	Cau
kir-	49	Cit
kiry-	49	Pas
kupy-	44	Cit
kupy-	44	Pas
kur-	45	Cit
kuru-	45	Cit
kurv-	45	Cit
kṛty-	46	Pas
kṛnt-	46	Cit
kṛśy-	47	Cit
kṛṣy-	48	Pas
kopay-	44	Cau
kopiṣy-	44	Fut
kramay-	51	Cau
kramiṣy-	51	Fut
kramy-	51	Pas
krāpay-	52	Cau
krām-	51	Cit
krāmay-	51	Cau
krāmy-	51	Cit
kriy-	45	Pas
krīḍ-	53	Cit
krīḍay-	53	Cau
krīḍiṣy-	53	Fut
krīḍy-	53	Pas
krīṇ-	52	Cit
krīy-	52	Pas
krudhy-	54	Cit
krudhy-	54	Pas
kruśy-	55	Pas
kreṣy-	52	Fut
krokṣy-	55	Fut
krotsy-	54	Fut
krodhay-	54	Cau
kroś-	55	Cit
krośay-	55	Cau
kliśn-	56	Cit
kliśy-	56	Pas
kleśay-	56	Cau
kleśiṣy-	56	Fut

kṣaṃsy- . .	58	Fut
kṣaṇ-	57	Cit
kṣaṇay- . .	57	Cau
kṣaṇiṣy- . .	57	Fut
kṣaṇy- . . .	57	Pas
kṣapay- . .	61	Cau
kṣam- . . .	58	Cit
kṣamay- .	58	Cau
kṣamiṣy- .	58	Fut
kṣamy- . .	58	Pas
kṣay-	61	Cit
kṣayay- . .	61	Cau
kṣar-	59	Cit
kṣariṣy- . .	59	Fut
kṣāṇay- . .	57	Cau
kṣāmy- . .	58	Cit
kṣāyay- . .	61	Cau
kṣāray- . .	59	Cau
kṣālay- . . .	60	Cit
kṣālayiṣy .	60	Fut
kṣāly- . . .	60	Pas
kṣiṇ-	61	Cit
kṣip-	62	Cit
kṣipy- . . .	62	Pas
kṣipy- . . .	62	Cit
kṣīy-	61	Pas
kṣuṇat- . .	63	Cit
kṣuṇad- . .	63	Cit
kṣudy- . . .	63	Pas
kṣudhy- . .	64	Cit
kṣudhy- . .	64	Pas
kṣunt- . . .	63	Cit
kṣund- . . .	63	Cit
kṣepay- . .	62	Cau
kṣepsy- . .	62	Fut
kṣeṣy- . . .	61	Fut
kṣotsy- . .	63	Fut
kṣotsy- . .	64	Fut
kṣoday- . .	63	Cau
kṣodhay- .	64	Cau
khaṇḍay- .	65	Cit
khan-	66	Cit
khaniṣy- .	66	Fut
khany- . . .	66	Pas
khād- . . .	67	Cit
khāday- . .	67	Cau
khādiṣy- .	67	Fut
khādy- . . .	67	Pas
khānay- . .	66	Cau
khidy- . . .	68	Cit
khidy- . . .	68	Pas
khint- . . .	68	Cit
khind- . . .	68	Cit
khetsy- . .	68	Fut
kheday- . .	68	Cau
khyā-	69	Cit
khyāpay- .	69	Cau
khyāy- . . .	69	Pas
khyāsy- . .	69	Fut
ga-	76	Cit
gacch- . . .	72	Cit
gaṇay- . . .	70	Cit
gaṇayiṣy- .	70	Fut
gaṇy-	70	Pas
gad-	71	Cit
gadiṣy- . .	71	Fut
gady-	71	Pas
gamay- . .	72	Cau
gamiṣy- . .	72	Fut
gamy- . . .	72	Pas
gariṣy- . . .	82	Fut
gariṣy- . . .	83	Fut
garīṣy- . . .	83	Fut
garīṣy- . . .	82	Fut
garj-	73	Cit
garjay- . . .	73	Cau
garjiṣy- . .	73	Fut
garjy-	73	Pas
gardhay- .	81	Cau
gardhiṣy- .	81	Fut
garh-	74	Cit
garhay- . .	74	Cau
garhiṣy- . .	74	Fut
garhy- . . .	74	Pas
gal-	75	Cit
galiṣy- . . .	75	Fut
galy-	75	Pas
gav-	78	Cit
gā-	76	Cit
gāday- . . .	71	Cau
gāpay- . . .	76	Cau
gāpay- . . .	84	Cau
gāy-	76	Pas
gāy-	84	Cit
gāray- . . .	82	Cau
gāray- . . .	83	Cau
gālay- . . .	75	Cau
gāvay- . . .	78	Cau
gāsy-	76	Fut
gāsy-	84	Fut
gāh-	77	Cit
gāhay- . . .	77	Cau
gāhiṣy- . .	77	Fut
gāhy-	77	Pas
gir-	82	Cit
gīy-	84	Pas
gīry-	82	Pas
gupy- . . .	79	Pas
guhy- . . .	80	Pas
gūh-	80	Cit
gūhay- . . .	80	Cau
gūhiṣy- . .	80	Fut
gṛṇ-	83	Cit
gṛdhy- . . .	81	Cit
gṛhṇ-	88	Cit
gṛhy-	88	Pas
gopay- . . .	79	Cau
gopāy- . . .	79	Cit
gopāy- . . .	85	Cit
gopāyay- .	85	Cau
gopāyiṣy-	85	Fut
gopāyy- . .	85	Pas
gopiṣy- . .	79	Fut
gopsy- . . .	79	Fut
goṣy-	78	Fut
grathn- . .	86	Cit
grathy- . .	86	Pas
granth- . .	86	Cit
granthay-	86	Cau
granthiṣy-	86	Fut
gras-	87	Cit
grasiṣy- . .	87	Fut
grasy- . . .	87	Pas
grahīṣy- . .	88	Fut
grāsay- . .	87	Cau
grāhay- . .	88	Cau
greth- . . .	86	Per
ghar-	90	Cit

ghariṣy-	90	Fut
ghātay-	417	Cau
ghāray-	90	Cau
ghuṣy-	89	Pas
ghoṣ-	89	Cit
ghoṣay-	89	Cau
ghoṣiṣy-	89	Fut
ghna-	417	Cit
ghrāpay-	91	Cau
ghrāy-	91	Pas
ghrāsy-	91	Fut
cakamp-	38	Per
cakar-	45	Per
cakar-	49	Per
cakart-	46	Per
cakarś-	47	Per
cakarṣ-	48	Per
cakas-	41	Per
cakāṅks-	42	Per
cakār-	45	Per
cakār-	49	Per
cakāś-	43	Per
cakās-	41	Per
cakṛ-	45	Per
cakṛś-	47	Per
cakḷp-	50	Per
cakr-	45	Per
cakr-	49	Per
cakram-	51	Per
cakrām-	51	Per
cakṣ-	41	Per
cakṣ-	92	Cit
cakṣ-	92	Per
cakṣaṇ-	57	Per
cakṣan-	58	Per
cakṣam-	58	Per
cakṣay-	92	Cau
cakṣar-	59	Per
cakṣāṇ-	57	Per
cakṣām-	58	Per
cakṣār-	59	Per
cakṣy-	92	Pas
cakhan-	66	Per
cakhād-	67	Per
cakhān-	66	Per
cakhn-	66	Per
cakhy-	69	Per
cacakṣ-	92	Per
cacam-	93	Per
cacar-	94	Per
cacart-	102	Per
cacarv-	95	Per
cacal-	96	Per
cacām-	93	Per
cacār-	94	Per
cacāl-	96	Per
cacṛt-	102	Per
cacṛv-	95	Per
caḍ-	92	Cit
cam-	93	Cit
camiṣy-	93	Fut
cayay-	97	Cau
car-	94	Cit
cariṣy-	94	Fut
cartay-	102	Cau
cary-	94	Pas
carv-	95	Cit
carvay-	95	Cau
carvy-	95	Pas
cal-	96	Cit
calay-	96	Cau
caliṣy-	96	Fut
caly-	96	Pas
caṣ-	92	Cit
caskand-	396	Per
cāmay-	93	Cau
cāyay-	97	Cau
cāray-	94	Cau
cālay-	96	Cau
cikay-	97	Per
cikāy-	97	Per
cike-	97	Per
ciky-	97	Per
cikray-	52	Per
cikrāy-	52	Per
cikriy-	52	Per
cikrīḍ-	53	Per
cikliś-	56	Per
cikleś-	56	Per
cikleṣ-	56	Per
cikṣay-	61	Per
cikṣāy-	61	Per
cikṣip-	62	Per
cikṣiy-	61	Per
cikṣep-	62	Per
cikhid-	68	Per
cikheḍ-	68	Per
cicay-	97	Per
cicāy-	97	Per
cicit-	98	Per
ciciṣṭ-	103	Per
cice-	97	Per
cicet-	98	Per
ciceṣṭ-	103	Per
cicchid-	106	Per
cicched-	106	Per
cicy-	97	Per
city-	98	Pas
cin-	97	Cit
cintay-	99	Cit
cintayiṣy-	99	Fut
cinty-	99	Pas
cīy-	97	Pas
cukup-	44	Per
cukop-	44	Per
cukrudh-	54	Per
cukruś-	55	Per
cukrodh-	54	Per
cukroś-	55	Per
cukṣud-	63	Per
cukṣudh-	64	Per
cukṣod-	63	Per
cukṣodh-	64	Per
cucyuv-	104	Per
cuścut-	370	Per
cuścot-	370	Per
cṛt-	102	Cit
cṛty-	102	Pas
cṛnt-	102	Cit
cet-	98	Cit
cetay-	98	Cau
cetiṣy-	98	Fut
cem-	93	Per
cer-	94	Per
cel-	96	Per
ceṣṭ-	103	Cit
ceṣṭay-	103	Cau
ceṣṭiṣy-	103	Fut

ceṣṭy- . . . . 103 Pas
ceṣy- . . . . 97 Fut
coday- . . . 100 Cit
codayiṣy- . 100 Fut
cody- . . . . 100 Pas
coray- . . . 101 Cit
corayiṣy- . 101 Fut
cory- . . . . 101 Pas
cyav- . . . . 104 Cit
cyāvay- . . 104 Cau
cyosy- . . . 104 Fut
chāday- . . 105 Cit
chādayiṣy- 105 Fut
chādy- . . . 105 Pas
chidy- . . . 106 Pas
chinat- . . . 106 Cit
chinad- . . 106 Cit
chint- . . . . 106 Cit
chind- . . . 106 Cit
chetsy- . . . 106 Fut
cheday- . . 106 Cau
ja- . . . . . . 417 Cit
jag- . . . . . 76 Per
jag- . . . . . 84 Per
jagad- . . . 71 Per
jagan- . . . 72 Per
jagam- . . . 72 Per
jagar- . . . . 83 Per
jagar- . . . . 82 Per
jagarj- . . . 73 Per
jagardh- . . 81 Per
jagarh- . . . 74 Per
jagal- . . . . 75 Per
jagād- . . . 71 Per
jagām- . . . 72 Per
jagār- . . . . 82 Per
jagār- . . . . 83 Per
jagāl- . . . . 75 Per
jagāh- . . . 77 Per
jagṛj- . . . . 73 Per
jagṛdh- . . 81 Per
jagṛh- . . . 88 Per
jagm- . . . . 72 Per
jagr- . . . . 82 Per
jagr- . . . . 83 Per
jagranth- . 86 Per
jagras- . . . 87 Per
jagrah- . . . 88 Per
jagrāh- . . . 88 Per
jagl- . . . . . 75 Per
jaghan- . . 417 Per
jaghar- . . . 90 Per
jaghā- . . . 77 Per
jaghāk- . . 77 Per
jaghān- . . 417 Per
jaghār- . . . 90 Per
jaghn- . . . 417 Per
jaghr- . . . 90 Per
jaghr- . . . 91 Per
jajar- . . . . 114 Per
jajalp- . . . 108 Per
jajāgar- . . 109 Per
jajāgār- . . 109 Per
jajāgr- . . . 109 Per
jajār- . . . . 114 Per
jajñ- . . . . . 107 Per
jajñ- . . . . . 115 Per
jajr- . . . . . 114 Per
jajval- . . . 117 Per
jajvāl- . . . 117 Per
janay- . . . 107 Cau
janiṣy- . . . 107 Fut
jany- . . . . 107 Pas
jay- . . . . . 110 Cit
jayiṣy- . . . 110 Fut
jaray- . . . . 114 Cau
jariṣy- . . . 114 Fut
jarīṣy- . . . 114 Fut
jalp- . . . . . 108 Cit
jalpay- . . . 108 Cau
jalpiṣy- . . 108 Fut
jalpy- . . . . 108 Pas
jah- . . . . . 420 Cit
jah- . . . . . 420 Per
jah- . . . . . 421 Per
jahar- . . . . 425 Per
jahary- . . . 418 Per
jaharṣ- . . . 426 Per
jahas- . . . . 419 Per
jahār- . . . . 425 Per
jahās- . . . . 419 Per
jahṛy- . . . 418 Per
jahṛṣ- . . . . 426 Per
jahr- . . . . 425 Per
jahras- . . . 427 Per
jahrād- . . . 428 Per
jahrās- . . . 427 Per
jahlād- . . . 430 Per
jahvar- . . . 431 Per
jahvār- . . . 431 Per
jagar- . . . . 109 Cit
jagaray- . . 109 Cau
jagariṣy- . 109 Fut
jagary- . . . 109 Pas
jagṛ- . . . . 109 Cit
jagr- . . . . 109 Cit
jān- . . . . . 115 Cit
jāpay- . . . 110 Cau
jāy- . . . . . 107 Cit
jigay- . . . . 110 Per
jigā- . . . . . 76 Cit
jigāy- . . . . 110 Per
jige- . . . . . 110 Per
jigy- . . . . . 110 Per
jighay- . . . 422 Per
jighar- . . . 90 Cit
jighāy- . . . 422 Per
jighṛ- . . . . 90 Cit
jighe- . . . . 422 Per
jighy- . . . . 422 Per
jighr- . . . . 91 Cit
jijinv- . . . . 111 Per
jijīv- . . . . . 112 Per
jijy- . . . . . 116 Per
jin- . . . . . 116 Cit
jinv- . . . . 111 Cit
jinvay- . . . 111 Cau
jinviṣy- . . 111 Fut
jih- . . . . . 421 Cit
jihiṃs- . . . 423 Per
jihray- . . . 429 Cit
jihray- . . . 429 Per
jihrāy- . . . 429 Per
jihri- . . . . 429 Cit
jihre- . . . . 429 Cit
jīy- . . . . . 110 Pas
jīy- . . . . . 116 Pas
jīry- . . . . . 114 Cit

jīry-	114	Pas	ḍhauky-	118	Pas	tarday-	130	Cau
jīv-	112	Cit	taṃsy-	121	Fut	tardiṣy-	130	Fut
jīvay-	112	Cau	takṣ-	119	Cit	tarpay-	131	Cau
jīviṣy-	112	Fut	takṣay-	119	Cau	tarpiṣy-	131	Fut
jīvy-	112	Pas	takṣiṣy-	119	Fut	tarpsy-	131	Fut
jugup-	79	Per	takṣy-	119	Pas	tarṣay-	132	Cau
juguv-	78	Per	takṣy-	119	Fut	tarṣiṣy-	132	Fut
juguh-	80	Per	tatakṣ-	119	Per	tastambh-	397	Per
jugū-	80	Per	tatan-	121	Per	tastar-	399	Per
jugūh-	80	Per	tatap-	122	Per	tastār-	399	Per
jugo-	80	Per	tatam-	123	Per	tasth-	400	Per
jugop-	79	Per	tatar-	133	Per	tāḍay-	120	Cit
jughuṣ-	89	Per	tatard-	130	Per	tāḍayiṣy-	120	Fut
jughoṣ-	89	Per	tatarp-	131	Per	tāḍy-	120	Pas
jujuṣ-	113	Per	tatarṣ-	132	Per	tānay-	121	Cau
juṣ-	113	Cit	tatān-	121	Per	tāpay-	122	Cau
juṣy-	113	Pas	tatāp-	122	Per	tāmy-	123	Cit
juhav-	424	Cit	tatām-	123	Per	tāy-	121	Pas
juhav-	424	Per	tatār-	133	Per	tāray-	133	Cau
juhav-	432	Per	tatṛd-	130	Per	tiṣṭh-	400	Cit
juhāv-	424	Per	tatṛp-	131	Per	tīry-	133	Pas
juhāv-	432	Per	tatṛṣ-	132	Per	tutud-	126	Per
juhu-	424	Cit	tatṛṣ-	135	Per	tutur-	127	Cit
juhuv-	424	Per	tatyak-	134	Per	tutuṣ-	129	Per
juhuv-	432	Per	tatyaj-	134	Per	tutod-	126	Per
juho-	424	Cit	tatyāj-	134	Per	tutor-	127	Cit
juho-	424	Per	tatr-	136	Per	tutoṣ-	129	Per
juhv-	424	Cit	tatrap-	131	Per	tud-	126	Cit
jer-	114	Per	tatras-	135	Per	tudy-	126	Pas
jeṣy-	110	Fut	tatrās-	135	Per	tur-	127	Cit
joṣay-	113	Cau	tatvar-	137	Per	tuṣṭav-	398	Per
joṣiṣy-	113	Fut	tan-	121	Cit	tuṣṭāv-	398	Per
jñāpay-	115	Cau	taniṣy-	121	Fut	tuṣṭu-	398	Per
jñāy-	115	Pas	tany-	121	Pas	tuṣṭuv-	398	Per
jñāsy-	115	Fut	tap-	122	Cit	tuṣṭo-	398	Per
jyapay-	116	Cau	tapiṣy-	122	Fut	tuṣy-	129	Cit
jyasy-	116	Fut	tapy-	122	Pas	tuṣy-	129	Pas
jval-	117	Cit	tapsy-	122	Fut	tṛṇat-	130	Cit
jvalay-	117	Cau	tamay-	123	Cau	tṛṇad-	130	Cit
jvaliṣy-	117	Fut	tamiṣy-	123	Fut	tṛdy-	130	Pas
jvaly-	117	Pas	tar-	133	Cit	tṛnt-	130	Cit
jvālay-	117	Cau	tariṣy-	133	Fut	tṛnd-	130	Cit
ḍuḍhauk-	118	Per	tarīṣy-	133	Fut	tṛpy-	131	Cit
ḍhauk-	118	Cit	tarkay-	124	Cit	tṛpy-	131	Pas
ḍhaukay-	118	Cau	tarkayiṣy-	124	Fut	tṛṣy-	132	Cit
ḍhaukiṣy-	118	Fut	tarky-	124	Pas	tejay-	125	Cit

ten- ..... 121 Per
tep- ..... 122 Per
tem- .... 123 Per
ter- ..... 133 Per
tokṣy- ... 129 Fut
totsy- .... 126 Fut
today- ... 126 Cau
tolay- .... 128 Cit
tolayiṣy- . 128 Fut
toly- .... 128 Pas
toṣay- ... 129 Cau
tyakṣy- .. 134 Fut
tyaj- ..... 134 Cit
tyajiṣy- .. 134 Fut
tyajy- .... 134 Pas
tyājay- ... 134 Cau
trapsy- ... 131 Fut
tras- ..... 135 Cit
trasiṣy- .. 135 Fut
trasy- .... 135 Cit
trasy- .... 135 Pas
trā- ..... 136 Cit
trāpay- .. 136 Cau
trāy- .... 136 Cit
trāy- .... 136 Pas
trāsay- ... 135 Cau
trāsy- .... 136 Fut
tvar- .... 137 Cit
tvaray- .. 137 Cau
tvariṣy- .. 137 Fut
tvary- ... 137 Pas
tvāray- .. 137 Cau
daṃś- ... 138 Cit
daṃśay- . 138 Cau
dakṣ- .... 139 Cit
dakṣay- .. 139 Cau
dakṣiṣy- .. 139 Fut
daṅkṣy- .. 138 Fut
daṇḍay- .. 140 Cit
daṇḍayiṣy- 140 Fut
daṇḍy- .. 140 Pas
dat- ..... 146 Cit
dad- .... 146 Cit
dad- .... 146 Per
dad- .... 147 Per
dadaṃś- . 138 Per
dadakṣ- .. 139 Per
dadag- ... 145 Per
dadabh- .. 142 Per
dadam- .. 141 Per
dadambh- 142 Per
dadar- ... 162 Per
dadarp- .. 159 Per
dadarś- .. 160 Per
dadas- ... 144 Per
dadah- ... 145 Per
dadābh- .. 142 Per
dadām- .. 141 Per
dadār- ... 162 Per
dadās- ... 144 Per
dadāh- ... 145 Per
dadṛṃh- . 161 Per
dadṛp- ... 159 Per
dadṛś- ... 160 Per
dadr- .... 158 Per
dadr- .... 162 Per
dadr- .... 164 Per
dadrap- .. 159 Per
dadraṣ- .. 160 Per
dadh- ... 168 Cit
dadh- ... 168 Per
dadh- ... 173 Per
dadhar- .. 171 Per
dadharṣ- . 172 Per
dadhār- .. 171 Per
dadhāv- .. 169 Per
dadhṛṣ- .. 172 Per
dadhm- .. 174 Per
dadhy- .. 175 Per
dadhr- ... 171 Per
dadhraj- . 176 Per
dadhrañj- 176 Per
dadhrāj- . 176 Per
dadhvaṃs- 177 Per
dadhvan- . 178 Per
dadhvar- . 179 Per
dadhvān- . 178 Per
dadhvār- . 179 Per
dabh- .... 142 Cit
dabhy- ... 142 Pas
damay- .. 141 Cau
damiṣy- .. 141 Fut
dambhay- 142 Cau
dambhiṣy- 142 Fut
damy- ... 141 Pas
day- .... 143 Cit
dayiṣy- .. 143 Fut
daray- ... 162 Cau
dariṣy- ... 158 Fut
dariṣy- ... 162 Fut
darīṣy- ... 162 Fut
darpay- .. 159 Cau
darpiṣy- .. 159 Fut
darpsy- .. 159 Fut
darṣay- .. 160 Cau
daś- ..... 138 Cit
daśy- .... 138 Pas
dasiṣy- ... 144 Fut
dasy- .... 144 Cit
dah- .... 145 Cit
dahiṣy- .. 145 Fut
dahy- ... 145 Pas
dā- ..... 147 Cit
dāpay- ... 146 Cau
dāpay- ... 147 Cau
dāmy- ... 141 Cit
dāray- ... 158 Cau
dāray- ... 162 Cau
dāvay- ... 154 Cau
dāsay- ... 144 Cau
dāsiṣy- ... 144 Fut
dāsy- .... 146 Fut
dāsy- .... 147 Fut
dāhay- ... 145 Cau
dig- ..... 151 Cit
didiv- ... 148 Per
didiv- ... 149 Per
didiś- .... 150 Per
didih- ... 151 Per
didīkṣ- ... 152 Per
didīp- ... 153 Per
didev- ... 148 Per
didev- ... 149 Per
dideś- ... 150 Per
dideh- ... 151 Per
didyut- .. 163 Per
didviṣ- ... 167 Per
didveṣ- .. 167 Per

diś-	150	Cit
diśy-	150	Pas
dih-	151	Cit
dihy-	151	Pas
dīkṣ-	152	Cit
dīkṣay-	152	Cau
dīkṣiṣy-	152	Fut
dīkṣy-	152	Pas
dīpay-	153	Cau
dīpiṣy-	153	Fut
dīpy-	153	Cit
dīpy-	153	Pas
dīy-	146	Pas
dīy-	147	Pas
dīry-	162	Pas
dīvy-	148	Cit
dīvy-	148	Pas
dug-	157	Cit
dudav-	154	Per
dudāv-	154	Per
duduv-	154	Per
duduṣ-	156	Per
duduh-	157	Per
dudoṣ-	156	Per
dudoh-	157	Per
dudrav-	165	Per
dudrāv-	165	Per
dudru-	165	Per
dudruv-	165	Per
dudruh-	166	Per
dudro-	165	Per
dudro-	166	Per
dudrog-	166	Per
dudroh-	166	Per
dudhav-	170	Per
dudhāv-	170	Per
dudhuv-	170	Per
dun-	154	Cit
duṣy-	156	Cit
duṣy-	156	Pas
duh-	157	Cit
duhy-	157	Pas
dūy-	154	Pas
dṛṃh-	161	Cit
dṛṃhay-	161	Cau
dṛṃhiṣy-	161	Fut
dṛṇ-	162	Cit
dṛpy-	159	Cit
dṛpy-	159	Pas
dṛṣy-	160	Pas
de-	146	Cit
dekṣy-	150	Fut
deg-	151	Cit
debh-	142	Per
dem-	141	Per
dev-	149	Cit
devay-	148	Cau
devay-	149	Cau
deviṣy-	148	Fut
deviṣy-	149	Fut
deśay-	150	Cau
deṣ-	144	Per
deh-	145	Per
deh-	151	Cit
dehay-	151	Cau
dokṣy-	156	Fut
dog-	157	Cit
dolay-	155	Cit
doṣay-	156	Cau
doṣy-	154	Fut
doh-	157	Cit
dohay-	157	Cau
dyut-	163	Pas
dyot-	163	Cit
dyotay-	163	Cau
dyotiṣy-	163	Fut
drakṣy-	160	Fut
drapsy-	159	Fut
drav-	165	Cit
drā-	164	Cit
drāpay-	164	Cau
drāy-	164	Pas
drāvay-	165	Cau
drāsy-	164	Fut
driy-	158	Cit
driy-	158	Pas
druhiṣy-	166	Fut
druhy-	166	Cit
druhy-	166	Pas
drūy-	165	Pas
drokṣy-	166	Fut
droṣy-	165	Fut
drohay-	166	Cau
dvik-	167	Cit
dviḍ-	167	Cit
dviṣ-	167	Cit
dviṣy-	167	Pas
dve-	167	Cit
dvek-	167	Cit
dvekṣy-	167	Fut
dveṣ-	167	Cit
dveṣay-	167	Cau
dhakṣy-	145	Fut
dhat-	168	Cit
dhad-	168	Cit
dham-	174	Cit
dhamiṣy-	174	Fut
dhay-	173	Cit
dhar-	171	Cit
dhariṣy-	171	Fut
dharṣiṣy-	172	Fut
dhāpay-	168	Cau
dhāpay-	173	Cau
dhāray-	171	Cau
dhārṣay-	172	Cau
dhāv-	169	Cit
dhāvay-	169	Cau
dhāvay-	170	Cau
dhāviṣy-	169	Fut
dhāvy-	169	Pas
dhāsy-	168	Fut
dhāsy-	173	Fut
dhik-	151	Cit
dhig-	151	Cit
dhīy-	168	Pas
dhīy-	173	Pas
dhuk-	157	Cit
dhug-	157	Cit
dhun-	170	Cit
dhūy-	170	Pas
dhṛṣṇ-	172	Cit
dhe-	168	Cit
dhek-	151	Cit
dhekṣy-	151	Fut
dhok-	157	Cit
dhokṣy-	157	Fut
dhoṣy-	170	Fut
dhmāpay-	174	Cau

dhmāy-	174	Pas
dhmāsy-	174	Fut
dhyā-	175	Cit
dhyāpay-	175	Cau
dhyāy-	175	Cit
dhyāy-	175	Pas
dhyāsy-	175	Fut
dhraj-	176	Cit
dhrañj-	176	Cit
dhriy-	171	Pas
dhvaṃs-	177	Cit
dhvaṃsay-	177	Cau
dhvaṃsiṣy-	177	Fut
dhvan-	178	Cit
dhvanay-	178	Cau
dhvaniṣy-	178	Fut
dhvany-	178	Pas
dhvar-	179	Cit
dhvariṣy-	179	Fut
dhvasy-	177	Pas
dhvānay-	178	Cau
dhvāray-	179	Cau
naṃsy-	184	Fut
nakṣ-	180	Cit
nakṣiṣy-	180	Fut
naṅkṣy-	185	Fut
natsy-	186	Fut
nad-	181	Cit
naday-	181	Cau
nadiṣy-	181	Fut
nady-	181	Pas
nanaṃṣ-	185	Per
nanakṣ-	180	Per
nanad-	181	Per
nanad-	186	Per
nanan-	184	Per
nanand-	182	Per
nanam-	184	Per
nanart-	192	Per
nanaś-	185	Per
nanah-	186	Per
nanāth-	187	Per
nanād-	181	Per
nanām-	184	Per
nanāś-	185	Per
nanāh-	186	Per
nanṛt-	192	Per
nand-	182	Cit
nanday-	182	Cau
nandiṣy-	182	Fut
nandy-	182	Pas
nabh-	183	Cit
nabhay-	183	Cau
nam-	184	Cit
namay-	184	Cau
namiṣy-	184	Fut
namy-	184	Pas
nay-	189	Cit
nartay-	192	Cau
nartiṣy-	192	Fut
nartsy-	192	Fut
nav-	190	Cit
naviṣy-	190	Fut
naśiṣy-	185	Fut
naśy-	185	Cit
naśy-	185	Pas
nahy-	186	Cit
nahy-	186	Pas
nāth-	187	Cit
nāthiṣy-	187	Fut
nāthy-	187	Pas
nāday-	181	Cau
nāmay-	184	Cau
nāyay-	189	Cau
nāvay-	190	Cau
nāśay-	185	Cau
nāhay-	186	Cau
ninay-	189	Per
nināy-	189	Per
ninind-	188	Per
nine-	189	Per
nind-	188	Cit
ninday-	188	Cau
nindiṣy-	188	Fut
nindy-	188	Pas
niny-	189	Per
nīy-	189	Pas
nu-	190	Cit
nud-	191	Cit
nudy-	191	Pas
nunav-	190	Per
nunāv-	190	Per
nunud-	191	Per
nunuv-	190	Per
nuno-	190	Per
nunod-	191	Per
nūy-	190	Pas
nṛty-	192	Cit
nṛty-	192	Pas
ned-	181	Per
nebh-	183	Per
nem-	184	Per
neś-	185	Per
neśy-	189	Fut
neh-	186	Per
notsy-	191	Fut
noday-	191	Cau
noṣy-	190	Fut
nau-	190	Cit
pakṣy-	193	Fut
pac-	193	Cit
pacy-	193	Pas
paṭ-	194	Cit
paṭiṣy-	194	Fut
paṭh-	195	Cit
paṭhiṣy-	195	Fut
paṭhy-	195	Pas
paṇ-	196	Cit
paṇay-	196	Cau
paṇiṣy-	196	Fut
paṇy-	196	Pas
pat-	197	Cit
patiṣy-	197	Fut
paty-	197	Pas
patsy-	198	Fut
pady-	198	Cit
pady-	198	Pas
pap-	201	Per
pap-	202	Per
papak-	193	Per
papac-	193	Per
papaṭ-	194	Per
papaṭh-	195	Per
papat-	197	Per
papar-	210	Per
paparc-	212	Per
papāc-	193	Per
papāṭ-	194	Per

papāṭh-	195	Per
papāt-	197	Per
papār-	210	Per
papṛc-	212	Per
papr-	210	Per
papr-	211	Per
papracch-	214	Per
paprath-	215	Per
paphal-	218	Per
paphāl-	218	Per
pariṣy-	210	Fut
pariṣy-	211	Fut
parīṣy-	210	Fut
parcay-	212	Cau
parciṣy-	212	Fut
palāy-	199	Cit
palāyay-	199	Cau
palāyiṣy-	199	Fut
palāyy-	199	Pas
pav-	208	Cit
paviṣy-	208	Fut
paśy-	200	Cit
paspardh-	403	Per
pasparś-	404	Per
paspṛdh-	403	Per
paspṛś-	404	Per
pā-	202	Cit
pācay-	193	Cau
pāṭay-	194	Cau
pāṭhay-	195	Cau
pāṇay-	196	Cau
pātay-	197	Cau
pāday-	198	Cau
pāy-	202	Pās
pāyay-	201	Cau
pāray-	210	Cau
pāray-	211	Cau
pāry-	210	Pās
pālay-	202	Cau
pāvay-	208	Cau
pāsy-	201	Fut
pāsy-	202	Fut
piṃś-	204	Cit
piṃṣ-	205	Cit
piṇḍ-	205	Cit
pinak-	205	Cit
pinaṣ-	205	Cit
pinv-	203	Cit
pinvay-	203	Cau
pinviṣy-	203	Fut
pinvy-	203	Pas
pipar-	210	Cit
pipinv-	203	Per
pipiś-	204	Per
pipiṣ-	205	Per
pipṛ-	210	Cit
pipeś-	204	Per
pipeṣ-	205	Per
pipy-	213	Per
pipr-	210	Cit
pipr-	216	Per
pipray-	216	Per
piprāy-	216	Per
pipre-	216	Per
pib-	201	Cit
piś-	204	Cit
piśy-	204	Pas
piṣy-	205	Pas
pīḍay-	206	Cit
pīḍayiṣy-	206	Fut
pīḍy-	206	Pas
pīy-	201	Pas
pun-	208	Cit
pupav-	208	Per
pupāv-	208	Per
pupuv-	208	Per
pupuṣ-	207	Per
pupo-	208	Per
pupoṣ-	207	Per
pupluv-	217	Per
puṣṇ-	207	Cit
puṣy-	207	Pas
pusphur-	406	Per
pusphor-	406	Per
pūjay-	209	Cit
pūjayiṣy-	209	Fut
pūjy-	209	Pas
pūy-	208	Pas
pūray-	210	Cau
pṛṅk-	212	Cit
pṛcch-	214	Cit
pṛcchy-	214	Pas
pṛcy-	212	Pas
pṛñc-	212	Cit
pṛṇ-	210	Cit
pṝṇ-	211	Cit
pṛṇak-	212	Cit
pṛṇac-	212	Cit
pekṣy-	205	Fut
pec-	193	Per
peṭ-	194	Per
peṭh-	195	Per
peṇ-	196	Per
pet-	197	Per
ped-	198	Per
peśay-	204	Cau
peśiṣy-	204	Fut
peṣay-	205	Cau
poṣ-	207	Cit
poṣay-	207	Cau
poṣiṣy-	207	Fut
pyāy-	213	Cit
pyāyay-	213	Cau
pyāyiṣy-	213	Fut
prakṣy-	214	Fut
pracchay-	214	Cau
prath-	215	Cit
prathay-	215	Cau
prathiṣy-	215	Fut
priy-	211	Cit
priy-	211	Pas
prīṇ-	216	Cit
prīṇay-	216	Cau
prīy-	216	Pas
preṣy-	216	Fut
plav-	217	Cit
plāvay-	217	Cau
plūy-	217	Pas
ploṣy-	217	Fut
phal-	218	Cit
phaliṣy-	218	Fut
phālay-	218	Cau
phel-	218	Per
baṃh-	219	Cit
baṃhay-	219	Cau
baṃhiṣy-	219	Fut
badhn-	220	Cit
badhy-	220	Pas

bandhay-	220	Cau
bandhiṣy-	220	Fut
baband-	220	Per
babandh-	220	Per
babarh-	223	Per
babādh-	221	Per
babṛh-	223	Per
babh-	228	Per
babhaṅk-	227	Per
babhaj-	226	Per
babhañj-	227	Per
babhar-	238	Per
babharj-	241	Per
babharṣ-	241	Per
babhāj-	226	Per
babhār-	238	Per
babhās-	229	Per
babhās-	230	Per
babhūv-	236	Per
babhṛ-	238	Per
babhr-	238	Per
babhraṃś-	239	Per
babhrajj-	241	Per
babhram-	240	Per
babhraṣ-	241	Per
babhrāj-	242	Per
babhrām-	240	Per
barh-	223	Cit
barhay-	223	Cau
barhiṣy-	223	Fut
bādh-	221	Cit
bādhay-	221	Cau
bādhiṣy-	221	Fut
bādhy-	221	Pas
bibhah-	238	Cit
bibhay-	233	Cit
bibhay-	233	Per
bibhar-	238	Cit
bibhāy-	233	Per
bibhi-	233	Cit
bibhikṣ-	231	Per
bibhid-	232	Per
bibhṛ-	238	Cit
bibhe-	233	Cit
bibhe-	233	Per
bibhed-	232	Per
bibhy-	233	Cit
bibhy-	233	Per
bibhr-	238	Cit
budhy-	222	Pas
budhy-	222	Cit
bubudh-	222	Per
bubodh-	222	Per
bubhuj-	234	Per
bubhuj-	235	Per
bubhuṣ-	237	Per
bubhoj-	234	Per
bubhoj-	235	Per
bṛh-	223	Cit
bṛhy-	223	Pas
bodh-	222	Cit
bodhay-	222	Cau
bodhiṣy-	222	Fut
brav-	224	Cit
bravī-	224	Cit
bruv-	224	Cit
brū-	224	Cit
bhakṣay-	225	Cit
bhakṣayiṣy-	225	Fut
bhakṣy-	225	Pas
bhakṣy-	226	Fut
bhaṅk-	227	Cit
bhaṅkṣy-	227	Fut
bhaṅg-	227	Cit
bhaj-	226	Cit
bhajiṣy-	226	Fut
bhajy-	226	Pas
bhajy-	227	Pas
bhañj-	227	Cit
bhañjay-	227	Cau
bhanak-	227	Cit
bhantsy-	220	Fut
bhariṣy-	238	Fut
bharkṣy-	223	Fut
bharkṣy-	241	Fut
bharjay-	241	Cau
bhav-	236	Cit
bhaviṣy-	236	Fut
bhā-	228	Cit
bhājay-	226	Cau
bhāpay-	228	Cau
bhāy-	228	Pas
bhāray-	238	Cau
bhāvay-	236	Cau
bhāṣ-	229	Cit
bhāṣay-	229	Cau
bhāṣiṣy-	229	Fut
bhāṣy-	229	Pas
bhās-	230	Cit
bhāsay-	230	Cau
bhāsiṣy-	230	Fut
bhāsy-	228	Fut
bhāsy-	230	Pas
bhikṣ-	231	Cit
bhikṣay-	231	Cau
bhikṣiṣy-	231	Fut
bhikṣy-	231	Pas
bhid-	232	Cit
bhidy-	232	Pas
bhinat-	232	Cit
bhinad-	232	Cit
bhint-	232	Cit
bhind-	232	Cit
bhīy-	233	Pas
bhīṣay-	233	Cau
bhuṅk-	234	Cit
bhuṅg-	234	Cit
bhuj-	235	Cit
bhujy-	234	Pas
bhujy-	235	Pas
bhuñj-	234	Cit
bhunak-	234	Cit
bhunaj-	234	Cit
bhūy-	236	Pas
bhūṣ-	237	Cit
bhūṣay-	237	Cau
bhūṣiṣy-	237	Fut
bhṛjj-	241	Cit
bhṛjjy-	241	Pas
bhej-	226	Per
bhetsy-	232	Fut
bheday-	232	Cau
bheṣy-	233	Fut
bhokṣy-	234	Fut
bhokṣy-	235	Fut
bhojay-	234	Cau
bhotsy-	222	Fut
bhraṃś-	239	Cit

bhraṃśay-	239	Cau	mam- . . .	255	Per	mārkṣy- . .	264	Fut
bhraṃśiṣy-	239	Fut	mamaṃh-	243	Per	mārj-	264	Cit
bhrakṣy- .	241	Fut	mamajj- . .	248	Per	mārjay- . .	264	Cau
bhrajjay- .	241	Cau	mamad- . .	245	Per	mārjiṣy- . .	264	Fut
bhram- . .	240	Cit	mamanth-	244	Per	mārḍ- . . .	264	Cit
bhramay- .	240	Cau	mamand- .	247	Per	mārṣ-	264	Cit
bhramiṣy-	240	Fut	mamar- . .	262	Per	māsy- . . .	250	Fut
bhramy- .	240	Cit	mamard- .	265	Per	māhay- . .	249	Cau
bhramy- .	240	Pas	mamarś- .	266	Per	min-	255	Cit
bhraśy- . .	239	Cit	mamarṣ- .	267	Per	mim-	250	Cit
bhraśy- . .	239	Pas	mamah- . .	249	Per	mimith- . .	251	Per
bhrāj- . . .	242	Cit	mamād- . .	245	Per	mimil- . . .	252	Per
bhrājay- . .	242	Cau	mamār- . .	262	Per	mimiṣ- . . .	253	Per
bhrājiṣy- .	242	Fut	mamārj- . .	264	Per	mimih- . .	254	Per
bhrājy- . . .	242	Pas	mamārṣ- .	264	Per	mimīl- . . .	256	Per
bhrāmay- .	240	Cau	mamāh- . .	249	Per	mimeth- .	251	Per
bhrāmy- .	240	Cit	mamṛj- . .	264	Per	mimel- . . .	252	Per
bhrīy- . . .	238	Pas	mamṛd- . .	265	Per	mimeṣ- . .	253	Per
bhrem- . .	240	Per	mamṛś- . .	266	Per	mimeh- . .	254	Per
maṃsy- . .	246	Fut	mamṛṣ- . .	267	Per	mimy- . . .	255	Per
maṃh- . .	243	Cit	mamn- . .	268	Per	mimlecch-	270	Per
maṃhy- . .	243	Pas	mamr- . . .	262	Per	mil-	252	Cit
maṅkṣy- .	248	Fut	maml- . . .	271	Per	mily-	252	Pas
majj-	248	Cit	mariṣy- . .	262	Fut	miṣ-	253	Cit
majjay- . .	248	Cau	markṣy- . .	266	Fut	mīn-	255	Cit
majjiṣy- . .	248	Fut	mard- . . .	265	Cit	mīy-	250	Pas
majjy- . . .	248	Pas	marday- .	265	Cau	mīy-	255	Pas
mathiṣy- .	244	Fut	mardiṣy- .	265	Fut	mīl-	256	Cit
mathn- . .	244	Cit	marśay- . .	266	Cau	mīlay- . . .	256	Cau
mathy- . .	244	Pas	marṣay- . .	267	Cau	mīliṣy- . . .	256	Fut
maday- . .	245	Cau	marṣiṣy- .	267	Fut	mīly-	256	Pas
madiṣy- . .	245	Fut	mah-	249	Cit	mucy- . . .	257	Pas
mady- . . .	245	Pas	mahay- . .	243	Cau	muñc- . . .	257	Cit
man-	246	Cit	mahay- . .	249	Cau	mudy- . . .	258	Pas
man-	268	Cit	mahiṣy- . .	249	Fut	mumuc- .	257	Per
maniṣy- . .	246	Fut	mahy- . . .	249	Pas	mumud- .	258	Per
manthay- .	244	Cau	mā-	250	Cit	mumuṣ- . .	259	Per
manthiṣy-	244	Fut	māthay- . .	244	Cau	mumuh- .	260	Per
manthn- .	244	Cit	māday- . .	245	Cau	mumūrcch-	261	Per
mand- . . .	247	Cit	mādy- . . .	245	Cit	mumo- . .	260	Per
manday- .	247	Cau	mānay- . .	246	Cau	mumog- .	260	Per
mandiṣy- .	247	Fut	māpay- . .	250	Cau	mumoc- . .	257	Per
mandy- . .	247	Pas	māpay- . .	255	Cau	mumoṣ- . .	259	Per
many- . . .	246	Cit	māy-	250	Cit	mumoh- .	260	Per
many- . . .	246	Pas	māray- . .	262	Cau	mumluc- .	269	Per
mam- . . .	250	Per	mārk- . . .	264	Cit	mumloc- .	269	Per

muṣṇ- . . . 259 Cit
muṣy- . . . 259 Pas
muhy- . . . 260 Cit
muhy- . . . 260 Pas
mūrcch- . . 261 Cit
mūrcchay- 261 Cau
mūrcchiṣy- 261 Fut
mṛgay- . . 263 Cit
mṛgayiṣy- 263 Fut
mṛgy- . . . 263 Pas
mṛj- . . . . . 264 Cit
mṛjy- . . . . 264 Pas
mṛdn- . . . 265 Cit
mṛdy- . . . 265 Pas
mṛś- . . . . 266 Cit
mṛśy- . . . 266 Pas
mṛṣ- . . . . 264 Cit
mṛṣy- . . . 267 Cit
mṛṣy- . . . 267 Pas
mekṣy- . . 254 Fut
meth- . . . 251 Cit
med- . . . . 245 Per
men- . . . . 246 Per
melay- . . . 252 Cau
meliṣy- . . 252 Fut
meṣiṣy- . . 253 Fut
meṣy- . . . 255 Fut
meh- . . . . 249 Per
meh- . . . . 254 Cit
mehay- . . 254 Cau
mokṣy- . . 257 Fut
mokṣy- . . 260 Fut
mocay- . . 257 Cau
mod- . . . . 258 Cit
moday- . . 258 Cau
modiṣy- . . 258 Fut
moṣay- . . 259 Cau
moṣiṣy- . . 259 Fut
mohay- . . 260 Cau
mohiṣy- . . 260 Fut
mnāpay- . 268 Cau
mnāy- . . . 268 Pas
mnāsy- . . 268 Fut
mrakṣy- . . 266 Fut
mriy- . . . . 262 Cit
mriy- . . . . 262 Pas
mlapay- . . 271 Cau
mlā- . . . . 271 Cit
mlāpay- . . 271 Cau
mlāy- . . . . 271 Cit
mlāy- . . . . 271 Pas
mlāsy- . . . 271 Fut
mlecch- . . 270 Cit
mlecchay- 270 Cau
mlecchiṣy- 270 Fut
mloc- . . . . 269 Cit
mlociṣy- . 269 Fut
yaṃsy- . . 274 Fut
yakṣy- . . . 272 Fut
yacch- . . . 274 Cit
yaj- . . . . . 272 Cit
yat- . . . . . 273 Cit
yatay- . . . 273 Cau
yatiṣy- . . . 273 Fut
yaty- . . . . 273 Pas
yamay- . . 274 Cau
yamiṣy- . . 274 Fut
yamy- . . . 274 Pas
yay- . . . . . 275 Per
yayam- . . 274 Per
yayāc- . . . 276 Per
yayām- . . 274 Per
yā- . . . . . . 275 Cit
yāc- . . . . . 276 Cit
yācay- . . . 276 Cau
yāciṣy- . . . 276 Fut
yācy- . . . . 276 Pas
yājay- . . . 272 Cau
yātay- . . . 273 Cau
yāpay- . . . 275 Cau
yāmay- . . 274 Cau
yāy- . . . . . 275 Pas
yāsy- . . . . 275 Fut
yuṅk- . . . 277 Cit
yuṅg- . . . 277 Cit
yujy- . . . . 277 Pas
yuñj- . . . . 277 Cit
yudhy- . . 278 Cit
yudhy- . . 278 Pas
yunak- . . . 277 Cit
yunaj- . . . 277 Cit
yupy- . . . 279 Cit
yuyuj- . . . 277 Per
yuyudh- . 278 Per
yuyup- . . 279 Per
yuyoj- . . . 277 Per
yuyodh- . 278 Per
yuyop- . . 279 Per
yet- . . . . . 273 Per
yem- . . . . 274 Per
yokṣy- . . . 277 Fut
yojay- . . . 277 Cau
yotsy- . . . 278 Fut
yodhay- . . 278 Cau
yopay- . . . 279 Cau
yopiṣy- . . 279 Fut
raṃsy- . . . 285 Fut
raṃh- . . . 280 Cit
raṃhay- . 280 Cau
rakṣ- . . . . 281 Cit
rakṣay- . . 281 Cau
rakṣiṣy- . . 281 Fut
rakṣy- . . . 281 Pas
raṅkṣy- . . 283 Fut
racay- . . . 282 Cit
racayiṣy- . 282 Fut
racy- . . . . 282 Pas
raj- . . . . . 283 Cit
rajy- . . . . 283 Cit
rajy- . . . . 283 Pas
rañjay- . . . 283 Cau
rapsy- . . . 284 Fut
rabh- . . . . 284 Cit
rabhy- . . . 284 Pas
ram- . . . . 285 Cit
ramay- . . 285 Cau
rambhay- . 284 Cau
ramy- . . . 285 Pas
rar- . . . . . 287 Per
raraṃh- . . 280 Per
rarakṣ- . . . 281 Per
rarañj- . . . 283 Per
rarah- . . . 286 Per
rarāj- . . . . 288 Per
rarādh- . . 289 Per
rarāh- . . . 286 Per
rav- . . . . . 293 Cit
raviṣy- . . . 293 Fut

rah-	286	Cit
rahay-	286	Cau
rahiṣy-	286	Fut
rā-	287	Cit
rāj-	288	Cit
rājay-	288	Cau
rājiṣy-	288	Fut
rājy-	288	Pas
rātsy-	289	Fut
rādhay-	289	Cau
rādhn-	289	Cit
rādhy-	289	Pas
rāpay-	287	Cau
rāmay-	285	Cau
rāvay-	293	Cau
rāsy-	287	Fut
riṅg-	291	Cit
ricy-	291	Pas
riñc-	291	Cit
riṇ-	290	Cit
riṇak-	291	Cit
riṇac-	291	Cit
riy-	290	Cit
riray-	290	Per
rirāy-	290	Per
riric-	291	Per
ririṣ-	292	Per
rire-	290	Per
rirec-	291	Per
rireṣ-	292	Per
riry-	290	Per
riṣy-	292	Cit
rīy-	290	Cit
ru-	293	Cit
rucy-	294	Pas
ruj-	295	Cit
rujy-	295	Pas
ruṇat-	297	Cit
ruṇadh-	297	Cit
rud-	296	Cit
rudy-	296	Pas
rudhy-	297	Pas
runt-	297	Cit
rund-	297	Cit
rundh-	297	Cit
rurav-	293	Per
rurāv-	293	Per
ruruc-	294	Per
ruruj-	295	Per
rurud-	296	Per
rurudh-	297	Per
ruruv-	293	Per
ruruṣ-	298	Per
ruruh-	299	Per
ruroc-	294	Per
ruroj-	295	Per
rurod-	296	Per
rurodh-	297	Per
ruroṣ-	298	Per
ruroh-	299	Per
ruṣy-	298	Cit
ruhy-	299	Pas
rūy-	293	Pas
rekṣy-	291	Fut
recay-	291	Cau
rej-	288	Per
repay-	290	Cau
rebh-	284	Per
rem-	285	Per
reṣ-	292	Cit
reṣay-	292	Cau
reṣiṣy-	292	Fut
resy-	290	Fut
reh-	286	Per
rokṣy-	295	Fut
rokṣy-	299	Fut
roc-	294	Cit
rocay-	294	Cau
rociṣy-	294	Fut
rojay-	295	Cau
rotsy-	297	Fut
rod-	296	Cit
roday-	296	Cau
rodiṣy-	296	Fut
rodhay-	297	Cau
ropay-	299	Cau
roṣ-	298	Cit
roṣay-	298	Cau
roṣiṣy-	298	Fut
roh-	299	Cit
rohay-	299	Cau
rau-	293	Cit
lag-	300	Cit
lagay-	300	Cau
lagiṣy-	300	Fut
laṅgh-	301	Cit
laṅghay-	301	Cau
laṅghiṣy-	301	Fut
laṅghy-	301	Pas
lajj-	302	Cit
lajjay-	302	Cau
lajjiṣy-	302	Fut
lap-	303	Cit
lapiṣy-	303	Fut
lapy-	303	Pas
lapsy-	304	Fut
labh-	304	Cit
labhiṣy-	304	Fut
labhy-	304	Pas
lamb-	305	Cit
lambay-	305	Cau
lambiṣy-	305	Fut
lamby-	305	Pas
lambhay-	304	Cau
lal-	306	Cit
lalag-	300	Per
lalaṅgh-	301	Per
lalajj-	302	Per
lalap-	303	Per
lalamb-	305	Per
lalay-	306	Cau
lalas-	307	Per
lalāg-	300	Per
lalāp-	303	Per
lalās-	307	Per
laliṣy-	306	Fut
laviṣy-	317	Fut
las-	307	Cit
lasiṣy-	307	Fut
lasy-	307	Pas
lāgay-	300	Cau
lāpay-	303	Cau
lāpay-	312	Cau
lāyay-	312	Cau
lālay-	306	Cau
lāvay-	317	Cau
lāsay-	307	Cau
lāsy-	312	Fut

likh- .... 308 Cit
likhiṣy- .. 308 Fut
likhy- ... 308 Pas
lin- .... 312 Cit
lipy- .... 309 Pas
limp- .... 309 Cit
lil- ...... 312 Per
lilay- .... 312 Per
lilāy- .... 312 Per
lilikh- ... 308 Per
lilip- .... 309 Per
liliś- ..... 310 Per
lilih- .... 311 Per
lile- ..... 312 Per
lilekh- ... 308 Per
lilep- .... 309 Per
lileś- .... 310 Per
lileh- .... 311 Per
lily- ..... 312 Per
liś- ...... 310 Cit
liśy- ..... 310 Cit
lih- ..... 311 Cit
lihy- .... 311 Pas
līḍh- .... 311 Cit
līn- ..... 312 Cit
līy- ..... 312 Cit
līy- ..... 312 Pas
luṭy- .... 313 Pas
luṇṭhay- . 314 Cit
luṇṭhayiṣy- 314 Fut
luṇṭhy- .. 314 Pas
lun- ..... 317 Cit
lupy- .... 315 Pas
lubhy- ... 316 Cit
lubhy- ... 316 Pas
lump- ... 315 Cit
lulav- ... 317 Per
lulāv- ... 317 Per
lulut- .... 313 Per
lulup- ... 315 Per
lulubh- .. 316 Per
luluv- ... 317 Per
lulok- ... 318 Per
lulot- .... 313 Per
lulop- ... 315 Per
lulobh- .. 316 Per
lūy- ..... 317 Pas
lek- ..... 311 Cit
lekṣy- ... 310 Fut
lekṣy- ... 311 Fut
lekhay- .. 308 Cau
lekhiṣy- .. 308 Fut
leg- ..... 300 Per
leḍh- .... 311 Cit
lep- ..... 303 Per
lepay- ... 309 Cau
lepsy- ... 309 Fut
lebh- .... 304 Per
leśay- ... 310 Cau
leṣ- ..... 307 Per
leṣy- .... 312 Fut
leh- ..... 311 Cit
lehay- ... 311 Cau
lok- ..... 318 Cit
lokay- ... 318 Cau
lokiṣy- ... 318 Fut
loky- .... 318 Pas
locay- ... 319 Cit
locayiṣy- . 319 Fut
locy- .... 319 Pas
loṭ- ..... 313 Cit
loṭay- .... 313 Cau
loṭiṣy- ... 313 Fut
lopay- ... 315 Cau
lopsy- ... 315 Fut
lopsy- ... 316 Fut
lobh- .... 316 Cit
lobhay- .. 316 Cau
lobhiṣy- .. 316 Fut
vak- ..... 320 Cit
vak- ..... 328 Cit
vak- ..... 330 Cit
vakṣy- ... 320 Fut
vakṣy- ... 332 Fut
vac- ..... 320 Cit
vacy- .... 321 Pas
vañc- .... 321 Cit
vañcay- .. 321 Cau
vañciṣy- .. 321 Fut
vaṭ- ..... 328 Cit
vatsy- ... 329 Fut
vatsy- ... 330 Fut
vad- .... 322 Cit
vad- .... 330 Cit
vadiṣy- .. 322 Fut
vadhay- .. 323 Cau
vadhiṣy- . 323 Fut
vadhy- ... 323 Pas
van- ..... 324 Cit
vanay- ... 324 Cau
vaniṣy- .. 324 Fut
vand- ... 325 Cit
vanday- .. 325 Cau
vandiṣy- . 325 Fut
vandy- ... 325 Pas
vany- .... 324 Pas
vap- .... 326 Cit
vapsy- ... 326 Fut
vay- ..... 341 Cit
vay- ..... 348 Cit
vayiṣy- .. 348 Fut
var- ..... 342 Cit
variṣy- ... 342 Fut
varīṣy- ... 342 Fut
varkṣy- .. 347 Fut
varj- .... 343 Cit
varjay- ... 343 Cau
varjiṣy- .. 343 Fut
varṇay- .. 327 Cit
varṇy- ... 327 Pas
vart- .... 344 Cit
vartay- .. 344 Cau
vartiṣy- .. 344 Fut
vartsy- ... 344 Fut
vardh- ... 345 Cit
vardhay- . 345 Cau
vardhiṣy- . 345 Fut
varṣ- .... 346 Cit
varṣay- .. 346 Cau
varṣiṣy- .. 346 Fut
varhay- .. 347 Cau
varhiṣy- .. 347 Fut
vav- ..... 333 Per
vavañc- .. 321 Per
vavan- ... 324 Per
vavand- .. 325 Per
vavar- ... 342 Per
vavarj- ... 343 Per

vavart-	344	Per	vāśay-	328	Cau	vivy-	341	Per
vavardh-	345	Per	vāśay-	335	Cau	vivyac-	350	Per
vavarṣ-	346	Per	vāśiṣy-	335	Fut	vivyat-	352	Per
vavarh-	347	Per	vāśy-	335	Cit	vivyath-	351	Per
vavas-	330	Per	vāśy-	335	Pas	vivyadh-	352	Per
vavāñch-	334	Per	vāsay-	329	Cau	vivyāc-	350	Per
vavān-	324	Per	vāsay-	330	Cau	vivyādh-	352	Per
vavār-	342	Per	vāsay-	331	Cit	viś-	340	Cit
vavās-	335	Per	vāsayiṣy-	331	Fut	viśy-	340	Pas
vavṛ-	342	Per	vāsy-	331	Pas	vīy-	341	Pas
vavṛ-	347	Per	vāsy-	333	Fut	vṛṅk-	343	Cit
vavṛj-	343	Per	vāhay-	332	Cau	vṛṅg-	343	Cit
vavṛt-	344	Per	vi-	341	Cit	vṛjy-	343	Pas
vavṛdh-	345	Per	viṅk-	336	Cit	vṛñj-	343	Cit
vavṛṣ-	346	Per	viṅg-	336	Cit	vṛṇ-	342	Cit
vavṛh-	347	Per	vic-	350	Cit	vṛṇak-	343	Cit
vavr-	342	Per	vicy-	336	Pas	vṛṇaj-	343	Cit
vavrak-	353	Per	vicy-	350	Pas	vṛty-	344	Pas
vavraj-	353	Per	vij-	337	Cit	vṛdhy-	345	Pas
vavraśc-	354	Per	vijiṣy-	337	Fut	vṛn-	342	Cit
vavrāj-	353	Per	vijy-	337	Pas	vṛśc-	354	Cit
vaś-	328	Cit	viñc-	336	Cit	vṛścy-	354	Pas
vaśiṣy-	328	Fut	vit-	338	Cit	vṛṣy-	346	Pas
vaṣ-	328	Cit	vid-	338	Cit	vṛh-	347	Cit
vas-	329	Cit	vid-	338	Per	vṛhy-	347	Pas
vas-	330	Cit	vidy-	338	Pas	ve-	341	Cit
vasiṣy-	329	Fut	vidy-	339	Pas	vekṣy-	336	Fut
vasiṣy-	330	Fut	vidhy-	352	Cit	vekṣy-	340	Fut
vasy-	330	Pas	vidhy-	352	Pas	vecay-	336	Cau
vah-	332	Cit	vinak-	336	Cit	vejay-	337	Cau
vahiṣy-	332	Fut	vinac-	336	Cit	vet-	338	Cit
vā-	333	Cit	vind-	339	Cit	vet-	338	Per
vācay-	320	Cau	vivay-	341	Per	vetsy-	338	Fut
vāñch-	334	Cit	vivāy-	341	Per	vetsy-	339	Fut
vāñchay-	334	Cau	vivic-	336	Per	vetsy-	352	Fut
vāñchiṣy-	334	Fut	vivic-	350	Per	ved-	338	Cit
vānchy-	334	Pas	vivij-	337	Per	ved-	338	Per
vāday-	322	Cau	vivid-	338	Per	veday-	338	Cau
vānay-	324	Cau	vivid-	339	Per	veday-	339	Cau
vāpay-	326	Cau	viviś-	340	Per	vediṣy-	339	Fut
vāpay-	333	Cau	vive-	341	Per	vedhay-	352	Cau
vāpay-	341	Cau	vivec-	336	Per	ven-	324	Per
vāy-	333	Pas	vived-	338	Per	vep-	349	Cit
vāyay-	341	Cau	vived-	339	Per	vepay-	349	Cau
vāyay-	348	Cau	vivep-	349	Per	vepiṣy-	349	Fut
vāray-	342	Cau	viveś-	340	Per	veśay-	340	Cau

Form	Page	Type
veṣy-	341	Fut
vyaciṣy-	350	Fut
vyatsy-	352	Fut
vyath-	351	Cit
vyathay-	351	Cau
vyathiṣy-	351	Fut
vyathy-	351	Pas
vyadhay-	352	Cau
vyācay-	350	Cau
vyādhay-	352	Cau
vraj-	353	Cit
vrajiṣy-	353	Fut
vrajy-	353	Pas
vraścay-	354	Cau
vraściṣy-	354	Fut
vrājay-	353	Cau
vriy-	342	Pas
śaṃs-	355	Cit
śaṃsay-	355	Cau
śaṃsiṣy-	355	Fut
śakiṣy-	356	Fut
śakn-	356	Cit
śaky-	356	Cit
śaky-	356	Pas
śakṣy-	356	Fut
śaṅk-	357	Cit
śaṅkay-	357	Cau
śaṅkiṣy-	357	Fut
śaṅky-	357	Pas
śap-	358	Cit
śapy-	358	Cit
śapy-	358	Pas
śapsy-	358	Fut
śam-	359	Cit
śamay-	359	Cau
śamay-	360	Cit
śamiṣy-	359	Fut
śamy-	359	Pas
śay-	364	Cit
śayiṣy-	364	Fut
śayy-	364	Pas
śariṣy-	369	Fut
śarīṣy-	369	Fut
śaśaṃs-	355	Per
śaśak-	356	Per
śaśaṅk-	357	Per
śaśap-	358	Per
śaśam-	359	Per
śaśar-	369	Per
śaśāk-	356	Per
śaśāp-	358	Per
śaśām-	359	Per
śaśār-	369	Per
śaśās-	361	Per
śaśr-	369	Per
śaśr-	375	Per
śaśrath-	372	Per
śaśranth-	372	Per
śaśram-	373	Per
śaśrambh-	374	Per
śaśrāth-	372	Per
śaśrām-	373	Per
śaślāgh-	378	Per
śaśvas-	379	Per
śaśvās-	379	Per
śasy-	355	Pas
śā-	361	Cit
śākay-	356	Cau
śāpay-	358	Cau
śāmay-	360	Cit
śāmy-	359	Cit
śāmy-	360	Pas
śāyay-	364	Cau
śāray-	369	Cau
śās-	361	Cit
śāsay-	361	Cau
śāsiṣy-	361	Fut
śiṃḍ-	363	Cit
śiṃṣ-	363	Cit
śikṣ-	362	Cit
śikṣay-	362	Cau
śikṣiṣy-	362	Fut
śikṣy-	362	Pas
śiṅk-	363	Cit
śinak-	363	Cit
śinaṭ-	363	Cit
śinaḍ-	363	Cit
śinaṣ-	363	Cit
śiśikṣ-	362	Per
śiśiṣ-	363	Per
śiśeṣ-	363	Per
śiśy-	364	Per
śiśy-	371	Per
śiśray-	376	Per
śiśrāy-	376	Per
śiśriy-	376	Per
śiśvay-	380	Per
śiśvāy-	380	Per
śiśviy-	380	Per
śiṣ-	361	Cit
śiṣy-	361	Pas
śiṣy-	363	Pas
śīy-	371	Pas
śīry-	369	Pas
śucy-	365	Pas
śudhy-	366	Cit
śudhy-	366	Pas
śumbh-	367	Cit
śumbhiṣy-	367	Fut
śuśudh-	366	Per
śuśubh-	367	Per
śuśumbh-	367	Per
śuśuṣ-	368	Per
śuśodh-	366	Per
śuśobh-	367	Per
śuśoṣ-	368	Per
śuśrav-	377	Per
śuśrāv-	377	Per
śuśru-	377	Per
śuśruv-	377	Per
śuśro-	377	Per
śuṣy-	368	Cit
śuṣy-	368	Pas
śūy-	380	Pas
śṛṇ-	369	Cit
śṛṇ-	377	Cit
śṛn-	377	Cit
śe-	364	Cit
śek-	356	Per
śekṣy-	363	Fut
śep-	358	Per
śem-	359	Per
śer-	364	Cit
śeṣay-	363	Cau
śeṣy-	364	Fut
śokṣy-	368	Fut
śoc-	365	Cit
śocay-	365	Cau

śociṣy-	365	Fut	ślāghy-	378	Pas	sasvād-	412	Per
śotsy-	366	Fut	śvay-	380	Cit	sasvān-	413	Per
śodhay-	366	Cau	śvayiṣy-	380	Fut	sasvār-	416	Per
śobh-	367	Cit	śvas-	379	Cit	sah-	383	Cit
śobhay-	367	Cau	śvasiṣy-	379	Fut	sahiṣy-	383	Fut
śobhiṣy-	367	Fut	śvasy-	379	Pas	sahy-	383	Pas
śoṣay-	368	Cau	śvāyay-	380	Cau	sātsy-	384	Fut
ścuty-	370	Pas	śvāsay-	379	Cau	sāday-	382	Cau
ścot-	370	Cit	s-	11	Cit	sādh-	384	Cit
ścotay-	370	Cau	sakṣy-	383	Fut	sādhay-	384	Cau
ścotiṣy-	370	Fut	saṅkṣy-	381	Fut	sādhay-	388	Cau
śyāpay-	371	Cau	saj-	381	Cit	sādhn-	384	Cit
śyāy-	371	Cit	sajy-	381	Pas	sādhy-	384	Pas
śyāyay-	371	Cau	sañj-	381	Cit	sāyay-	385	Cau
śyāsy-	371	Fut	sañjay-	381	Cau	sāray-	392	Cau
śrath-	372	Cit	satsy-	382	Fut	sāvay-	390	Cau
śrathay-	372	Cau	sady-	382	Pas	sāhay-	383	Cau
śrathiṣy-	372	Fut	sar-	392	Cit	sicy-	386	Pas
śrathn-	372	Cit	sariṣy-	392	Fut	siñc-	386	Cit
śrathy-	372	Pas	sarjay-	393	Cau	siñcay-	386	Cau
śranthay-	372	Cau	sarp-	394	Cit	sidhy-	387	Pas
śranthiṣy-	372	Fut	sarpay-	394	Cau	sidhy-	388	Cit
śramay-	373	Cau	sarpsy-	394	Fut	sidhy-	388	Pas
śramiṣy-	373	Fut	saviṣy-	390	Fut	sin-	385	Cit
śrambh-	374	Cit	sasañj-	381	Per	siṣay-	385	Per
śrambhay-	374	Cau	sasad-	382	Per	siṣāy-	385	Per
śrambhiṣy-	374	Fut	sasar-	392	Per	siṣic-	386	Per
śramy-	373	Pas	sasarj-	393	Per	siṣidh-	387	Per
śray-	376	Cit	sasarp-	394	Per	siṣidh-	388	Per
śrayiṣy-	376	Fut	sasād-	382	Per	siṣiv-	389	Per
śrā-	375	Cit	sasādh-	384	Per	siṣiv-	395	Per
śrāthay-	372	Cau	sasār-	392	Per	siṣe-	385	Per
śrāpay-	375	Cau	sasṛ-	392	Per	siṣec-	386	Per
śrāpay-	376	Cau	sasṛj-	393	Per	siṣed-	387	Per
śrāmay-	373	Cau	sasṛp-	394	Per	siṣedh-	387	Per
śrāmy-	373	Cit	sasn-	401	Per	siṣedh-	388	Per
śrāy-	375	Cit	sasmar-	408	Per	siṣev-	389	Per
śrāyay-	376	Cau	sasmār-	408	Per	siṣev-	395	Per
śrāvay-	377	Cau	sasyand-	409	Per	siṣṇih-	402	Per
śrāsy-	375	Fut	sasr-	392	Per	siṣṇe-	402	Per
śrīy-	376	Pas	sasras-	393	Per	siṣṇeg-	402	Per
śrūy-	377	Pas	sasvaj-	411	Per	siṣṇeh-	402	Per
śroṣy-	377	Fut	sasvañj-	411	Per	siṣmiy-	407	Per
ślāgh-	378	Cit	sasvad-	412	Per	siṣy-	385	Fut
ślāghay-	378	Cau	sasvan-	413	Per	siṣy-	385	Per
ślāghiṣy-	378	Fut	sasvar-	416	Per	siṣvid-	415	Per

siṣved- . . . 415 Per
sīd- . . . . . 382 Cit
sīdiṣy- . . . 382 Fut
sīy- . . . . . 385 Pas
sīvay- . . . 389 Cau
sīvy- . . . . 389 Cit
sīvy- . . . . 389 Pas
sun- . . . . . 390 Cit
supy- . . . . 414 Pas
suṣav- . . . 390 Per
suṣāv- . . . 390 Per
suṣup- . . . 414 Per
suṣuv- . . . 390 Per
suṣūd- . . . 391 Per
suṣvap- . . 414 Per
suṣvāp- . . 414 Per
susrav- . . 410 Per
susrāv- . . 410 Per
susru- . . . 410 Per
susruv- . . 410 Per
susro- . . . 410 Per
sūd- . . . . . 391 Cit
sūday- . . . 391 Cau
sūdiṣy- . . 391 Fut
sūy- . . . . . 390 Pas
sṛj- . . . . . . 393 Cit
sṛjy- . . . . . 393 Cit
sṛjy- . . . . . 393 Pas
sṛpy- . . . . 394 Pas
sekṣy- . . . 386 Fut
secay- . . . 386 Cau
setsy- . . . . 387 Fut
setsy- . . . . 388 Fut
sed- . . . . . 382 Per
sedh- . . . . 387 Cit
sedhay- . . 387 Cau
sedhay- . . 388 Cau
sedhiṣy- . . 387 Fut
sev- . . . . . 395 Cit
sevay- . . . 389 Cau
sevay- . . . 395 Cau
seviṣy- . . . 389 Fut
seviṣy- . . . 395 Fut
sevy- . . . . 395 Pas
seh- . . . . . 383 Per
soṣy- . . . . 390 Fut
skady- . . . 396 Pas
skantsy- . . 396 Fut
skand- . . . 396 Cit
skanday- . 396 Cau
skandy- . . 396 Pas
stabhn- . . 397 Cit
stabhy- . . 397 Pas
stambh- . . 397 Cit
stambhay- 397 Cau
stambhiṣy- 397 Fut
stariṣy- . . 399 Fut
stary- . . . . 399 Pas
stav- . . . . 398 Cit
stāray- . . . 399 Cau
stāvay- . . 398 Cau
stīry- . . . . 399 Pas
stu- . . . . . 398 Cit
stūy- . . . . 398 Pas
stṛṇ- . . . . 399 Cit
stṛn- . . . . 399 Cit
stoṣy- . . . . 398 Fut
stau- . . . . 398 Cit
striy- . . . . 399 Pas
sthāpay- . 400 Cau
sthāsy- . . . 400 Fut
sthīy- . . . . 400 Pas
snā- . . . . . 401 Cit
snāpay- . . 401 Cau
snāy- . . . . 401 Pas
snāsy- . . . 401 Fut
snihy- . . . 402 Cit
snihy- . . . 402 Pas
snekṣy- . . 402 Fut
snehay- . . 402 Cau
snehiṣy- . . 402 Fut
sparkṣy- . 404 Fut
spardh- . . 403 Cit
spardhay- 403 Cau
spardhiṣy- 403 Fut
spardhy- . 403 Pas
sparśay- . . 404 Cau
spṛś- . . . . 404 Cit
spṛśy- . . . 404 Pas
spṛhay- . . 405 Cit
spṛhayiṣy- 405 Fut
spṛhy- . . . 405 Pas
sprakṣy- . 404 Fut
sphur- . . . 406 Cit
sphuriṣy- . 406 Fut
sphoray- . 406 Cau
smay- . . . 407 Cit
smar- . . . . 408 Cit
smaray- . . 408 Cau
smariṣy- . 408 Fut
smary- . . . 408 Pas
smāyay- . 407 Cau
smāray- . . 408 Cau
smīy- . . . . 407 Pas
smeṣy- . . . 407 Fut
syantsy- . . 409 Fut
syand- . . . 409 Cit
syanday- . 409 Cau
syandiṣy- . 409 Fut
syandy- . . 409 Pas
srakṣy- . . 393 Fut
srapsy- . . 394 Fut
srav- . . . . 410 Cit
sravay- . . 410 Cau
srāvay- . . 410 Cau
sriy- . . . . 392 Pas
sroṣy- . . . 410 Fut
svankṣy- . 411 Fut
svaj- . . . . 411 Cit
svajiṣy- . . 411 Fut
svajy- . . . 411 Pas
svañjay- . . 411 Cau
svad- . . . . 412 Cit
svaday- . . 412 Cau
svan- . . . . 413 Cit
svanay- . . 413 Cau
svaniṣy- . . 413 Fut
svap- . . . . 414 Cit
svapay- . . 414 Cau
svapsy- . . 414 Fut
svar- . . . . 416 Cit
svaray- . . 416 Cau
svariṣy- . . 416 Fut
svād- . . . . 412 Cit
svāday- . . 412 Cau
svānay- . . 413 Cau
svāpay- . . 414 Cau
svāray- . . 416 Cau

svidy-	415	Cit
svidy-	415	Pas
svetsy-	415	Fut
sved-	415	Cit
sveday-	415	Cau
ha-	417	Cit
haṃ-	417	Cit
haṃsy-	417	Fut
han-	417	Cit
haniṣy-	417	Fut
hany-	417	Pas
har-	425	Cit
hariṣy-	425	Fut
hary-	418	Cit
harṣay-	426	Cau
harṣiṣy-	426	Fut
has-	419	Cit
hasiṣy-	419	Fut
hasy-	419	Pas
hāpay-	420	Cau
hāpay-	421	Cau
hāy-	421	Pas
hāyay-	422	Cau
hāray-	425	Cau
hāvay-	424	Cau
hāsay-	419	Cau
hāsy-	420	Fut
hāsy-	421	Fut
hiṃs-	423	Cit
hiṃsay-	423	Cau
hiṃsiṣy-	423	Fut
hiṃsy-	423	Pas
hin-	422	Cit
hin-	423	Cit
hinas-	423	Cit
hīy-	420	Pas
hīy-	422	Pas
hūy-	424	Pas
hūy-	432	Pas
hṛṣy-	426	Cit
hṛṣy-	426	Pas
heṣy-	422	Fut
hoṣy-	424	Fut
hras-	427	Cit
hrasiṣy-	427	Fut
hrād-	428	Cit
hrāday-	428	Cau
hrādiṣy-	428	Fut
hrāsay-	427	Cau
hriy-	425	Pas
hrīy-	429	Pas
hrepay-	429	Cau
hreṣy-	429	Fut
hlād-	430	Cit
hlāday-	430	Cau
hlādiṣy-	430	Fut
hvay-	432	Cit
hvayiṣy-	432	Fut
hvar-	431	Cit
hvariṣy-	431	Fut
hvary-	431	Pas
hvāyay-	432	Cau
hvāray-	431	Cau
hvāsy-	432	Fut

Table 29. Index to verb endings.

-	16	[8]	Imf	Act	3	sg
-	16	[9]	Imf	Act	3	sg
-	16	[10]	Imf	Act	3	sg
-	16	[8]	Imf	Act	2	sg
-	16	[9]	Imf	Act	2	sg
-	16	[10]	Imf	Act	2	sg
-	16	[11]	Imf	Act	3	sg
-	16	[11]	Imf	Act	2	sg
-a	16	[1]	Imv	Act	2	sg
-a	19	[1]	Per	Act	3	sg
-a	19	[1]	Per	Act	2	pl
-a	19	[1]	Per	Act	1	sg
-a	19	[8]	Per	Act	3	sg
-a	19	[8]	Per	Act	2	pl
-a	19	[8]	Per	Act	1	sg
-a	19	[11]	Per	Act	2	pl
-aḥ	16	[1]	Imf	Act	2	sg
-aḥ	16	[3]	Imf	Act	2	sg
-aḥ	22	[1]	Aor	Act	2	sg
-at	16	[1]	Imf	Act	3	sg
-at	16	[3]	Imf	Act	3	sg
-at	22	[1]	Aor	Act	3	sg
-ata	16	[1]	Imv	Act	2	pl
-ata	16	[1]	Imf	Act	2	pl
-ata	16	[1]	Imf	Mid	3	sg
-ata	16	[5]	Imf	Mid	3	pl
-ata	16	[8]	Imf	Mid	3	pl
-ata	16	[9]	Imf	Mid	3	pl
-ata	16	[11]	Imf	Mid	3	pl
-ata	22	[1]	Aor	Act	2	pl
-ata	22	[1]	Aor	Mid	3	sg
-ataḥ	16	[1]	Ind	Act	3	du
-atam	16	[1]	Imv	Act	2	du
-atam	16	[1]	Imf	Act	2	du
-atam	22	[1]	Aor	Act	2	du
-atām	16	[1]	Imv	Act	3	du
-atām	16	[1]	Imf	Act	3	du
-atām	16	[1]	Imv	Mid	3	sg
-atām	16	[5]	Imv	Mid	3	pl
-atām	16	[8]	Imv	Mid	3	pl
-atām	16	[9]	Imv	Mid	3	pl
-atām	16	[11]	Imv	Mid	3	pl
-atām	22	[1]	Aor	Act	3	du
-ati	16	[1]	Ind	Act	3	sg
-atu	16	[1]	Imv	Act	3	sg
-atuḥ	19	[1]	Per	Act	3	du
-atuḥ	19	[11]	Per	Act	3	du
-atuḥ	19	[8]	Per	Act	3	du
-ate	16	[1]	Ind	Mid	3	sg
-ate	16	[5]	Ind	Mid	3	pl
-ate	16	[8]	Ind	Mid	3	pl
-ate	16	[9]	Ind	Mid	3	pl
-ate	16	[11]	Ind	Mid	3	pl
-ate	19	[11]	Per	Mid	3	du
-atha	16	[1]	Ind	Act	2	pl
-athaḥ	16	[1]	Ind	Act	2	du
-athaḥ	16	[1]	Imf	Mid	2	sg
-athaḥ	22	[1]	Aor	Mid	2	sg
-athuḥ	19	[1]	Per	Act	2	du
-athuḥ	19	[8]	Per	Act	2	du
-athuḥ	19	[11]	Per	Act	2	du
-adhvam	16	[1]	Imv	Mid	2	pl
-adhvam	16	[1]	Imf	Mid	2	pl
-adhvam	22	[1]	Aor	Mid	2	pl
-adhve	16	[1]	Ind	Mid	2	pl
-an	16	[1]	Imf	Act	3	pl
-an	16	[3]	Imf	Act	3	pl
-an	16	[5]	Imf	Act	3	pl
-an	16	[8]	Imf	Act	3	pl
-an	16	[9]	Imf	Act	3	pl
-an	16	[10]	Imf	Act	3	pl
-an	16	[11]	Imf	Act	3	pl
-an	22	[1]	Aor	Act	3	pl
-anta	16	[1]	Imf	Mid	3	pl
-anta	22	[1]	Aor	Mid	3	pl
-antām	16	[1]	Imv	Mid	3	pl
-anti	16	[1]	Ind	Act	3	pl
-anti	16	[3]	Ind	Act	3	pl
-anti	16	[5]	Ind	Act	3	pl
-anti	16	[8]	Ind	Act	3	pl
-anti	16	[9]	Ind	Act	3	pl
-anti	16	[10]	Ind	Act	3	pl
-anti	16	[11]	Ind	Act	3	pl
-antu	16	[1]	Imv	Act	3	pl
-antu	16	[3]	Imv	Act	3	pl
-antu	16	[5]	Imv	Act	3	pl
-antu	16	[8]	Imv	Act	3	pl
-antu	16	[9]	Imv	Act	3	pl

-antu . . .	16	[10]	Imv	Act	3 pl
-antu . . .	16	[11]	Imv	Act	3 pl
-ante . . .	16	[1]	Ind	Mid	3 pl
-am	16	[1]	Imf	Act	1 sg
-am	16	[3]	Imf	Act	1 sg
-am	16	[8]	Imf	Act	1 sg
-am	16	[9]	Imf	Act	1 sg
-am	16	[10]	Imf	Act	1 sg
-am	16	[11]	Imf	Act	1 sg
-am	22	[1]	Aor	Act	1 sg
-avam . .	16	[6]	Imf	Act	1 sg
-avam . .	16	[7]	Imf	Act	1 sg
-avāni . .	16	[4]	Imv	Act	1 sg
-avāni . .	16	[6]	Imv	Act	1 sg
-avāni . .	16	[7]	Imv	Act	1 sg
-avāma .	16	[4]	Imv	Act	1 pl
-avāma .	16	[6]	Imv	Act	1 pl
-avāma .	16	[7]	Imv	Act	1 pl
-avāmahai	16	[4]	Imv	Mid	1 pl
-avāmahai	16	[6]	Imv	Mid	1 pl
-avāmahai	16	[7]	Imv	Mid	1 pl
-avāva . .	16	[4]	Imv	Act	1 du
-avāva . .	16	[6]	Imv	Act	1 du
-avāva . .	16	[7]	Imv	Act	1 du
-avāvahai	16	[4]	Imv	Mid	1 du
-avāvahai	16	[6]	Imv	Mid	1 du
-avāvahai	16	[7]	Imv	Mid	1 du
-avīḥ . . .	16	[4]	Imf	Act	2 sg
-avīt . . .	16	[4]	Imf	Act	3 sg
-avīti . . .	16	[4]	Ind	Act	3 sg
-avītu . .	16	[4]	Imv	Act	3 sg
-avīmi . .	16	[4]	Ind	Act	1 sg
-avīṣi . . .	16	[4]	Ind	Act	2 sg
-avuḥ . .	16	[7]	Imf	Act	3 pl
-avai . . .	16	[4]	Imv	Mid	1 sg
-avai . . .	16	[6]	Imv	Mid	1 sg
-avai . . .	16	[7]	Imv	Mid	1 sg
-asi	16	[1]	Ind	Act	2 sg
-ase	16	[1]	Ind	Mid	2 sg
-asva . . .	16	[1]	Imv	Mid	2 sg
-āḥ	16	[2]	Imf	Act	2 sg
-āḥ	16	[5]	Imf	Act	2 sg
-āḥ	22	[7]	Aor	Act	2 sg
-āṇi	16	[9]	Imv	Act	1 sg
-āt	16	[2]	Imf	Act	3 sg
-āt	16	[5]	Imf	Act	3 sg
-āt	22	[7]	Aor	Act	3 sg
-āta	16	[2]	Imv	Act	2 pl
-āta	16	[2]	Imf	Act	2 pl
-āta	22	[7]	Aor	Act	2 pl
-ātaḥ . . .	16	[2]	Ind	Act	3 du
-ātam . . .	16	[2]	Imv	Act	2 du
-ātam . . .	16	[2]	Imf	Act	2 du
-ātam . . .	22	[7]	Aor	Act	2 du
-ātām . . .	16	[2]	Imv	Act	3 du
-ātām . . .	16	[2]	Imf	Act	3 du
-ātām . . .	16	[5]	Imv	Mid	3 du
-ātām . . .	16	[5]	Imf	Mid	3 du
-ātām . . .	16	[8]	Imv	Mid	3 du
-ātām . . .	16	[9]	Imv	Mid	3 du
-ātām . . .	16	[8]	Imf	Mid	3 du
-ātām . . .	16	[9]	Imf	Mid	3 du
-ātām . . .	16	[11]	Imv	Mid	3 du
-ātām . . .	16	[11]	Imf	Mid	3 du
-ātām . . .	22	[7]	Aor	Act	3 du
-āti	16	[2]	Ind	Act	3 sg
-āti	16	[5]	Ind	Act	3 sg
-ātu	16	[2]	Imv	Act	3 sg
-ātu	16	[5]	Imv	Act	3 sg
-āte	16	[5]	Ind	Mid	3 du
-āte	16	[8]	Ind	Mid	3 du
-āte	16	[9]	Ind	Mid	3 du
-āte	16	[11]	Ind	Mid	3 du
-āte	19	[1]	Per	Mid	3 du
-āte	19	[8]	Per	Mid	3 du
-ātha . . .	16	[2]	Ind	Act	2 pl
-ātha . . .	19	[11]	Per	Act	2 sg
-āthaḥ . .	16	[2]	Ind	Act	2 du
-āthām . .	16	[5]	Imv	Mid	2 du
-āthām . .	16	[5]	Imf	Mid	2 du
-āthām . .	16	[8]	Imv	Mid	2 du
-āthām . .	16	[9]	Imv	Mid	2 du
-āthām . .	16	[8]	Imf	Mid	2 du
-āthām . .	16	[9]	Imf	Mid	2 du
-āthām . .	16	[11]	Imv	Mid	2 du
-āthām . .	16	[11]	Imf	Mid	2 du
-āthe . . .	16	[5]	Ind	Mid	2 du
-āthe . . .	16	[8]	Ind	Mid	2 du
-āthe . . .	16	[9]	Ind	Mid	2 du
-āthe . . .	16	[11]	Ind	Mid	2 du
-āthe . . .	19	[1]	Per	Mid	2 du
-āthe . . .	19	[8]	Per	Mid	2 du

-āthe	19	[11]	Per	Mid	2du
-ān	16	[2]	Imf	Act	3 pl
-āna	16	[5]	Imv	Act	2 sg
-āni	16	[1]	Imv	Act	1 sg
-āni	16	[2]	Imv	Act	1 sg
-āni	16	[3]	Imv	Act	1 sg
-āni	16	[5]	Imv	Act	1 sg
-āni	16	[8]	Imv	Act	1 sg
-āni	16	[10]	Imv	Act	1 sg
-āni	16	[11]	Imv	Act	1 sg
-ānti	16	[2]	Ind	Act	3 pl
-āntu	16	[2]	Imv	Act	3 pl
-ām	16	[2]	Imf	Act	1 sg
-ām	16	[5]	Imf	Act	1 sg
-ām	22	[7]	Aor	Act	1 sg
-āma	16	[1]	Imv	Act	1 pl
-āma	16	[1]	Imf	Act	1 pl
-āma	16	[2]	Imv	Act	1 pl
-āma	16	[2]	Imf	Act	1 pl
-āma	16	[3]	Imv	Act	1 pl
-āma	16	[5]	Imv	Act	1 pl
-āma	16	[8]	Imv	Act	1 pl
-āma	16	[9]	Imv	Act	1 pl
-āma	16	[10]	Imv	Act	1 pl
-āma	16	[11]	Imv	Act	1 pl
-āma	22	[1]	Aor	Act	1 pl
-āma	22	[7]	Aor	Act	1 pl
-āmaḥ	16	[1]	Ind	Act	1 pl
-āmaḥ	16	[2]	Ind	Act	1 pl
-āmahi	16	[1]	Imf	Mid	1 pl
-āmahi	22	[1]	Aor	Mid	1 pl
-āmahe	16	[1]	Ind	Mid	1 pl
-āmahai	16	[1]	Imv	Mid	1 pl
-āmahai	16	[5]	Imv	Mid	1 pl
-āmahai	16	[9]	Imv	Mid	1 pl
-āmahai	16	[8]	Imv	Mid	1 pl
-āmahai	16	[11]	Imv	Mid	1 pl
-āmi	16	[1]	Ind	Act	1 sg
-āmi	16	[2]	Ind	Act	1 sg
-āmi	16	[5]	Ind	Act	1 sg
-āyāḥ	16	[2]	Opt	Act	2 sg
-āyāt	16	[2]	Opt	Act	3 sg
-āyāta	16	[2]	Opt	Act	2 pl
-āyātam	16	[2]	Opt	Act	2du
-āyātām	16	[2]	Opt	Act	3du
-āyām	16	[2]	Opt	Act	1 sg
-āyāma	16	[2]	Opt	Act	1 pl
-āyāva	16	[2]	Opt	Act	1du
-āyuḥ	16	[2]	Opt	Act	3 pl
-āva	16	[1]	Imv	Act	1du
-āva	16	[1]	Imf	Act	1du
-āva	16	[2]	Imv	Act	1du
-āva	16	[2]	Imf	Act	1du
-āva	16	[3]	Imv	Act	1du
-āva	16	[5]	Imv	Act	1du
-āva	16	[8]	Imv	Act	1du
-āva	16	[9]	Imv	Act	1du
-āva	16	[10]	Imv	Act	1du
-āva	16	[11]	Imv	Act	1du
-āva	22	[1]	Aor	Act	1du
-āva	22	[7]	Aor	Act	1du
-āvaḥ	16	[1]	Ind	Act	1du
-āvaḥ	16	[2]	Ind	Act	1du
-āvam	16	[4]	Imf	Act	1 sg
-āvahi	16	[1]	Imf	Mid	1du
-āvahi	22	[1]	Aor	Mid	1du
-āvahe	16	[1]	Ind	Mid	1du
-āvahai	16	[1]	Imv	Mid	1du
-āvahai	16	[5]	Imv	Mid	1du
-āvahai	16	[8]	Imv	Mid	1du
-āvahai	16	[9]	Imv	Mid	1du
-āvahai	16	[11]	Imv	Mid	1du
-āsi	16	[2]	Ind	Act	2 sg
-āsi	16	[5]	Ind	Act	2 sg
-āhi	16	[2]	Imv	Act	2 sg
-i	16	[5]	Imf	Mid	1 sg
-i	16	[8]	Imf	Mid	1 sg
-i	16	[9]	Imf	Mid	1 sg
-i	16	[11]	Imf	Mid	1 sg
-iḍhvam	22	[6]	Aor	Mid	2 pl
-iḍhvam	22	[7]	Aor	Mid	2 pl
-ita	16	[3]	Imv	Act	2 pl
-ita	16	[3]	Imf	Act	2 pl
-ita	22	[7]	Aor	Mid	3 sg
-itaḥ	16	[3]	Ind	Act	3du
-itam	16	[3]	Imv	Act	2du
-itam	16	[3]	Imf	Act	2du
-itām	16	[3]	Imv	Act	3du
-itām	16	[3]	Imf	Act	3du
-iti	16	[3]	Ind	Act	3 sg
-itu	16	[3]	Imv	Act	3 sg
-itha	16	[3]	Ind	Act	2 pl

-itha . . .	19	[1]	Per	Act	2 sg
-itha . . .	19	[11]	Per	Act	2 sg
-ithaḥ . .	16	[3]	Ind	Act	2du
-ithāḥ . .	22	[7]	Aor	Mid	2 sg
-idhve . .	19	[1]	Per	Mid	2 pl
-idhve . .	19	[11]	Per	Mid	2 pl
-ima . . .	16	[3]	Imf	Act	1 pl
-ima . . .	19	[1]	Per	Act	1 pl
-ima . . .	19	[11]	Per	Act	1 pl
-imaḥ . .	16	[3]	Ind	Act	1 pl
-imahe . .	19	[1]	Per	Mid	1 pl
-imahe . .	19	[11]	Per	Mid	1 pl
-imi	16	[3]	Ind	Act	1 sg
-ire	19	[1]	Per	Mid	3 pl
-ire	19	[8]	Per	Mid	3 pl
-ire	19	[11]	Per	Mid	3 pl
-iva	16	[3]	Imf	Act	1du
-iva	19	[1]	Per	Act	1du
-iva	19	[11]	Per	Act	1du
-ivaḥ . . .	16	[3]	Ind	Act	1du
-ivahe . .	19	[1]	Per	Mid	1du
-ivahe . .	19	[11]	Per	Mid	1du
-iṣata . . .	22	[6]	Aor	Mid	3 pl
-iṣata . . .	22	[7]	Aor	Mid	3 pl
-iṣam . . .	22	[5]	Aor	Act	1 sg
-iṣam . . .	22	[6]	Aor	Act	1 sg
-iṣātām .	22	[6]	Aor	Mid	3du
-iṣātām .	22	[7]	Aor	Mid	3du
-iṣāthām	22	[6]	Aor	Mid	2du
-iṣāthām	22	[7]	Aor	Mid	2du
-iṣi	16	[3]	Ind	Act	2 sg
-iṣi	22	[6]	Aor	Mid	1 sg
-iṣi	22	[7]	Aor	Mid	1 sg
-iṣuḥ . . .	22	[5]	Aor	Act	3 pl
-iṣuḥ . . .	22	[6]	Aor	Act	3 pl
-iṣe	19	[1]	Per	Mid	2 sg
-iṣe	19	[11]	Per	Mid	2 sg
-iṣṭa	22	[5]	Aor	Act	2 pl
-iṣṭa	22	[6]	Aor	Act	2 pl
-iṣṭa	22	[6]	Aor	Mid	3 sg
-iṣṭam . .	22	[5]	Aor	Act	2du
-iṣṭam . .	22	[6]	Aor	Act	2du
-iṣṭām . .	22	[5]	Aor	Act	3du
-iṣṭām . .	22	[6]	Aor	Act	3du
-iṣṭhāḥ . .	22	[6]	Aor	Mid	2 sg
-iṣma . . .	22	[5]	Aor	Act	1 pl
-iṣma . . .	22	[6]	Aor	Act	1 pl
-iṣmahi .	22	[6]	Aor	Mid	1 pl
-iṣmahi .	22	[7]	Aor	Mid	1 pl
-iṣva . . .	22	[5]	Aor	Act	1du
-iṣva . . .	22	[6]	Aor	Act	1du
-iṣvahi . .	22	[6]	Aor	Mid	1du
-iṣvahi . .	22	[7]	Aor	Mid	1du
-ihi	16	[3]	Imv	Act	2 sg
-īḥ	16	[3]	Imf	Act	2 sg
-īḥ	22	[5]	Aor	Act	2 sg
-īḥ	22	[6]	Aor	Act	2 sg
-īt	16	[3]	Imf	Act	3 sg
-īt	22	[5]	Aor	Act	3 sg
-īt	22	[6]	Aor	Act	3 sg
-īta	16	[5]	Imv	Act	2 pl
-īta	16	[5]	Imf	Act	2 pl
-īta	16	[5]	Opt	Mid	3 sg
-īta	16	[5]	Imf	Mid	3 sg
-īta	16	[8]	Opt	Mid	3 sg
-īta	16	[9]	Opt	Mid	3 sg
-īta	16	[11]	Opt	Mid	3 sg
-ītaḥ . . .	16	[5]	Ind	Act	3du
-ītam . . .	16	[5]	Imv	Act	2du
-ītam . . .	16	[5]	Imf	Act	2du
-ītām . . .	16	[5]	Imv	Act	3du
-ītām . . .	16	[5]	Imf	Act	3du
-ītām . . .	16	[5]	Imv	Mid	3 sg
-īte	16	[5]	Ind	Mid	3 sg
-ītha . . .	16	[5]	Ind	Act	2 pl
-īthaḥ . .	16	[5]	Ind	Act	2du
-īthāḥ . .	16	[5]	Opt	Mid	2 sg
-īthāḥ . .	16	[5]	Imf	Mid	2 sg
-īthāḥ . .	16	[9]	Opt	Mid	2 sg
-īthāḥ . .	16	[8]	Opt	Mid	2 sg
-īthāḥ . .	16	[11]	Opt	Mid	2 sg
-īdhvam	16	[5]	Opt	Mid	2 pl
-īdhvam	16	[5]	Imv	Mid	2 pl
-īdhvam	16	[5]	Imf	Mid	2 pl
-īdhvam	16	[9]	Opt	Mid	2 pl
-īdhvam	16	[8]	Opt	Mid	2 pl
-īdhvam	16	[11]	Opt	Mid	2 pl
-īdhve . .	16	[5]	Ind	Mid	2 pl
-īma . . .	16	[5]	Imf	Act	1 pl
-īmaḥ . .	16	[5]	Ind	Act	1 pl
-īmahi . .	16	[5]	Opt	Mid	1 pl
-īmahi . .	16	[5]	Imf	Mid	1 pl

-īmahi	16	[9]	Opt	Mid	1 pl
-īmahi	16	[8]	Opt	Mid	1 pl
-īmahi	16	[11]	Opt	Mid	1 pl
-īmahe	16	[5]	Ind	Mid	1 pl
-īya	16	[5]	Opt	Mid	1 sg
-īya	16	[8]	Opt	Mid	1 sg
-īya	16	[9]	Opt	Mid	1 sg
-īya	16	[11]	Opt	Mid	1 sg
-īyāḥ	16	[5]	Opt	Act	2 sg
-īyāt	16	[5]	Opt	Act	3 sg
-īyāta	16	[5]	Opt	Act	2 pl
-īyātam	16	[5]	Opt	Act	2du
-īyātām	16	[5]	Opt	Act	3du
-īyātām	16	[5]	Opt	Mid	3du
-īyātām	16	[8]	Opt	Mid	3du
-īyātām	16	[9]	Opt	Mid	3du
-īyātām	16	[11]	Opt	Mid	3du
-īyāthām	16	[5]	Opt	Mid	2du
-īyāthām	16	[8]	Opt	Mid	2du
-īyāthām	16	[9]	Opt	Mid	2du
-īyāthām	16	[11]	Opt	Mid	2du
-īyām	16	[5]	Opt	Act	1 sg
-īyāma	16	[5]	Opt	Act	1 pl
-īyāva	16	[5]	Opt	Act	1du
-īyuḥ	16	[5]	Opt	Act	3 pl
-īran	16	[5]	Opt	Mid	3 pl
-īran	16	[8]	Opt	Mid	3 pl
-īran	16	[9]	Opt	Mid	3 pl
-īran	16	[11]	Opt	Mid	3 pl
-īva	16	[5]	Imf	Act	1du
-īvaḥ	16	[5]	Ind	Act	1du
-īvahi	16	[5]	Opt	Mid	1du
-īvahi	16	[5]	Imf	Mid	1du
-īvahi	16	[8]	Opt	Mid	1du
-īvahi	16	[9]	Opt	Mid	1du
-īvahi	16	[11]	Opt	Mid	1du
-īvahe	16	[5]	Ind	Mid	1du
-īṣe	16	[5]	Ind	Mid	2 sg
-īṣva	16	[5]	Imv	Mid	2 sg
-īhi	16	[5]	Imv	Act	2 sg
-u	16	[6]	Imv	Act	2 sg
-uḥ	16	[2]	Imf	Act	3 pl
-uḥ	19	[1]	Per	Act	3 pl
-uḥ	19	[8]	Per	Act	3 pl
-uḥ	19	[11]	Per	Act	3 pl
-uḥ	22	[7]	Aor	Act	3 pl
-uta	16	[4]	Imv	Act	2 pl
-uta	16	[4]	Imf	Act	2 pl
-uta	16	[4]	Imf	Mid	3 sg
-uta	16	[6]	Imv	Act	2 pl
-uta	16	[6]	Imf	Act	2 pl
-uta	16	[6]	Imf	Mid	3 sg
-uta	16	[7]	Imv	Act	2 pl
-uta	16	[7]	Imf	Act	2 pl
-uta	16	[7]	Imf	Mid	3 sg
-utaḥ	16	[4]	Ind	Act	3du
-utaḥ	16	[6]	Ind	Act	3du
-utaḥ	16	[7]	Ind	Act	3du
-utam	16	[4]	Imv	Act	2du
-utam	16	[4]	Imf	Act	2du
-utam	16	[6]	Imv	Act	2du
-utam	16	[6]	Imf	Act	2du
-utam	16	[7]	Imv	Act	2du
-utam	16	[7]	Imf	Act	2du
-utām	16	[4]	Imv	Act	3du
-utām	16	[4]	Imf	Act	3du
-utām	16	[4]	Imv	Mid	3 sg
-utām	16	[6]	Imv	Act	3du
-utām	16	[6]	Imf	Act	3du
-utām	16	[6]	Imv	Mid	3 sg
-utām	16	[7]	Imv	Act	3du
-utām	16	[7]	Imf	Act	3du
-utām	16	[7]	Imv	Mid	3 sg
-ute	16	[4]	Ind	Mid	3 sg
-ute	16	[6]	Ind	Mid	3 sg
-ute	16	[7]	Ind	Mid	3 sg
-utha	16	[4]	Ind	Act	2 pl
-utha	16	[6]	Ind	Act	2 pl
-utha	16	[7]	Ind	Act	2 pl
-uthaḥ	16	[4]	Ind	Act	2du
-uthaḥ	16	[6]	Ind	Act	2du
-uthaḥ	16	[7]	Ind	Act	2du
-uthāḥ	16	[4]	Imf	Mid	2 sg
-uthāḥ	16	[6]	Imf	Mid	2 sg
-uthāḥ	16	[7]	Imf	Mid	2 sg
-udhi	16	[7]	Imv	Act	2 sg
-udhvam	16	[4]	Imv	Mid	2 pl
-udhvam	16	[4]	Imf	Mid	2 pl
-udhvam	16	[6]	Imv	Mid	2 pl
-udhvam	16	[6]	Imf	Mid	2 pl
-udhvam	16	[7]	Imv	Mid	2 pl
-udhvam	16	[7]	Imf	Mid	2 pl

-udhve .	16	[4]	Ind	Mid	2 pl	-uvaḥ . .	16	[4]	Ind	Act	1 du
-udhve .	16	[6]	Ind	Mid	2 pl	-uvaḥ . .	16	[6]	Ind	Act	1 du
-udhve .	16	[7]	Ind	Mid	2 pl	-uvaḥ . .	16	[7]	Ind	Act	1 du
-unoḥ . .	16	[6]	Imf	Act	2 sg	-uvata . .	16	[4]	Imf	Mid	3 pl
-uma . . .	16	[4]	Imf	Act	1 pl	-uvatām .	16	[4]	Imv	Mid	3 pl
-uma . . .	16	[6]	Imf	Act	1 pl	-uvate . .	16	[4]	Ind	Mid	3 pl
-uma . . .	16	[7]	Imf	Act	1 pl	-uvan . .	16	[4]	Imf	Act	3 pl
-umaḥ . .	16	[4]	Ind	Act	1 pl	-uvanti .	16	[4]	Ind	Act	3 pl
-umaḥ . .	16	[6]	Ind	Act	1 pl	-uvantu .	16	[4]	Imv	Act	3 pl
-umaḥ . .	16	[7]	Ind	Act	1 pl	-uvahi . .	16	[4]	Imf	Mid	1 du
-umahi .	16	[4]	Imf	Mid	1 pl	-uvahi . .	16	[6]	Imf	Mid	1 du
-umahi .	16	[6]	Imf	Mid	1 pl	-uvahi . .	16	[7]	Imf	Mid	1 du
-umahi .	16	[7]	Imf	Mid	1 pl	-uvahe . .	16	[4]	Ind	Mid	1 du
-umahe .	16	[4]	Ind	Mid	1 pl	-uvahe . .	16	[6]	Ind	Mid	1 du
-umahe .	16	[6]	Ind	Mid	1 pl	-uvahe . .	16	[7]	Ind	Mid	1 du
-umahe .	16	[7]	Ind	Mid	1 pl	-uvātām .	16	[4]	Imv	Mid	3 du
-uyāḥ . . .	16	[4]	Opt	Act	2 sg	-uvātām .	16	[4]	Imf	Mid	3 du
-uyāḥ . . .	16	[6]	Opt	Act	2 sg	-uvāte . .	16	[4]	Ind	Mid	3 du
-uyāḥ . . .	16	[7]	Opt	Act	2 sg	-uvāthām	16	[4]	Imv	Mid	2 du
-uyāt . . .	16	[4]	Opt	Act	3 sg	-uvāthām	16	[4]	Imf	Mid	2 du
-uyāt . . .	16	[6]	Opt	Act	3 sg	-uvāthe .	16	[4]	Ind	Mid	2 du
-uyāt . . .	16	[7]	Opt	Act	3 sg	-uvi	16	[4]	Imf	Mid	1 sg
-uyāta . .	16	[4]	Opt	Act	2 pl	-uvīta . .	16	[4]	Opt	Mid	3 sg
-uyāta . .	16	[6]	Opt	Act	2 pl	-uvīthāḥ	16	[4]	Opt	Mid	2 sg
-uyāta . .	16	[7]	Opt	Act	2 pl	-uvīdhvam	16	[4]	Opt	Mid	2 pl
-uyātam .	16	[4]	Opt	Act	2 du	-uvīmahi	16	[4]	Opt	Mid	1 pl
-uyātam .	16	[6]	Opt	Act	2 du	-uvīya . .	16	[4]	Opt	Mid	1 sg
-uyātam .	16	[7]	Opt	Act	2 du	-uvīyātām	16	[4]	Opt	Mid	3 du
-uyātām .	16	[4]	Opt	Act	3 du	-uvīyāthām	16	[4]	Opt	Mid	2 du
-uyātām .	16	[6]	Opt	Act	3 du	-uvīran .	16	[4]	Opt	Mid	3 pl
-uyātām .	16	[7]	Opt	Act	3 du	-uvīvahi	16	[4]	Opt	Mid	1 du
-uyām . .	16	[4]	Opt	Act	1 sg	-uve	16	[4]	Ind	Mid	1 sg
-uyām . .	16	[6]	Opt	Act	1 sg	-uṣe	16	[4]	Ind	Mid	2 sg
-uyām . .	16	[7]	Opt	Act	1 sg	-uṣe	16	[6]	Ind	Mid	2 sg
-uyāma .	16	[4]	Opt	Act	1 pl	-uṣe	16	[7]	Ind	Mid	2 sg
-uyāma .	16	[6]	Opt	Act	1 pl	-uṣva . . .	16	[4]	Imv	Mid	2 sg
-uyāma .	16	[7]	Opt	Act	1 pl	-uṣva . . .	16	[6]	Imv	Mid	2 sg
-uyāva . .	16	[4]	Opt	Act	1 du	-uṣva . . .	16	[7]	Imv	Mid	2 sg
-uyāva . .	16	[6]	Opt	Act	1 du	-uhi	16	[4]	Imv	Act	2 sg
-uyāva . .	16	[7]	Opt	Act	1 du	-uhi	16	[6]	Imv	Act	2 sg
-uyuḥ . .	16	[4]	Opt	Act	3 pl	-e	16	[1]	Ind	Mid	1 sg
-uyuḥ . .	16	[6]	Opt	Act	3 pl	-e	16	[1]	Imf	Mid	1 sg
-uyuḥ . .	16	[7]	Opt	Act	3 pl	-e	16	[5]	Ind	Mid	1 sg
-uva . . .	16	[4]	Imf	Act	1 du	-e	16	[8]	Ind	Mid	1 sg
-uva . . .	16	[6]	Imf	Act	1 du	-e	16	[9]	Ind	Mid	1 sg
-uva . . .	16	[7]	Imf	Act	1 du	-e	16	[11]	Ind	Mid	1 sg

-e	19	[1]	Per	Mid	3 sg
-e	19	[1]	Per	Mid	1 sg
-e	19	[8]	Per	Mid	3 sg
-e	19	[8]	Per	Mid	1 sg
-e	19	[11]	Per	Mid	3 sg
-e	19	[11]	Per	Mid	1 sg
-e	22	[1]	Aor	Mid	1 sg
-eḥ	16	[1]	Opt	Act	2 sg
-et	16	[1]	Opt	Act	3 sg
-eta	16	[1]	Opt	Act	2 pl
-eta	16	[1]	Opt	Mid	3 sg
-etam . . .	16	[1]	Opt	Act	2du
-etām . . .	16	[1]	Opt	Act	3du
-etām . . .	16	[1]	Imv	Mid	3du
-etām . . .	16	[1]	Imf	Mid	3du
-etām . . .	22	[1]	Aor	Mid	3du
-ete	16	[1]	Ind	Mid	3du
-etham . .	16	[1]	Imv	Mid	2du
-ethāḥ . .	16	[1]	Opt	Mid	2 sg
-ethām . .	16	[1]	Imf	Mid	2du
-ethām . .	22	[1]	Aor	Mid	2du
-ethe . . .	16	[1]	Ind	Mid	2du
-edhvam	16	[1]	Opt	Mid	2 pl
-ema . . .	16	[1]	Opt	Act	1 pl
-emahi . .	16	[1]	Opt	Mid	1 pl
-eya	16	[1]	Opt	Mid	1 sg
-eyam . .	16	[1]	Opt	Act	1 sg
-eyātām .	16	[1]	Opt	Mid	3du
-eyāthām	16	[1]	Opt	Mid	2du
-eyuḥ . . .	16	[1]	Opt	Act	3 pl
-eran . . .	16	[1]	Opt	Mid	3 pl
-eva	16	[1]	Opt	Act	1du
-evahi . .	16	[1]	Opt	Mid	1du
-ai	16	[1]	Imv	Mid	1 sg
-ai	16	[5]	Imv	Mid	1 sg
-ai	16	[8]	Imv	Mid	1 sg
-ai	16	[9]	Imv	Mid	1 sg
-ai	16	[11]	Imv	Mid	1 sg
-oḥ	16	[7]	Imf	Act	2 sg
-ot	16	[6]	Imf	Act	3 sg
-ot	16	[7]	Imf	Act	3 sg
-oti	16	[6]	Ind	Act	3 sg
-oti	16	[7]	Ind	Act	3 sg
-otu	16	[6]	Imv	Act	3 sg
-otu	16	[7]	Imv	Act	3 sg
-omi . . .	16	[6]	Ind	Act	1 sg
-omi . . .	16	[7]	Ind	Act	1 sg
-osi	16	[6]	Ind	Act	2 sg
-oṣi	16	[7]	Ind	Act	2 sg
-au	19	[11]	Per	Act	3 sg
-au	19	[11]	Per	Act	1 sg
-auḥ . . .	16	[4]	Imf	Act	2 sg
-aut	16	[4]	Imf	Act	3 sg
-auti . . .	16	[4]	Ind	Act	3 sg
-autu . . .	16	[4]	Imv	Act	3 sg
-aumi . .	16	[4]	Ind	Act	1 sg
-auṣi . . .	16	[4]	Ind	Act	2 sg
-ṭa	16	[9]	Imv	Act	2 pl
-ṭa	16	[10]	Imv	Act	2 pl
-ṭa	16	[9]	Imf	Act	2 pl
-ṭa	16	[10]	Imf	Act	2 pl
-ṭa	16	[9]	Imf	Mid	3 sg
-ṭaḥ	16	[9]	Ind	Act	3du
-ṭaḥ	16	[10]	Ind	Act	3du
-ṭam . . .	16	[9]	Imv	Act	2du
-ṭam . . .	16	[10]	Imv	Act	2du
-ṭam . . .	16	[9]	Imf	Act	2du
-ṭam . . .	16	[10]	Imf	Act	2du
-ṭām . . .	16	[9]	Imv	Act	3du
-ṭām . . .	16	[10]	Imv	Act	3du
-ṭām . . .	16	[9]	Imf	Act	3du
-ṭām . . .	16	[10]	Imf	Act	3du
-ṭām . . .	16	[9]	Imv	Mid	3 sg
-ṭi	16	[9]	Ind	Act	3 sg
-ṭi	16	[10]	Ind	Act	3 sg
-ṭu	16	[9]	Imv	Act	3 sg
-ṭu	16	[10]	Imv	Act	3 sg
-ṭe	16	[9]	Ind	Mid	3 sg
-ṭha	16	[9]	Ind	Act	2 pl
-ṭha	16	[10]	Ind	Act	2 pl
-ṭhaḥ . . .	16	[9]	Ind	Act	2du
-ṭhaḥ . . .	16	[10]	Ind	Act	2du
-ṭhāḥ . . .	16	[9]	Imf	Mid	2 sg
-ḍhi	16	[9]	Imv	Act	2 sg
-ḍhi	16	[10]	Imv	Act	2 sg
-ḍhvam .	16	[9]	Imv	Mid	2 pl
-ḍhvam .	16	[9]	Imf	Mid	2 pl
-ḍhvam .	22	[3]	Aor	Mid	2 pl
-ḍhve . . .	16	[9]	Ind	Mid	2 pl
-ḍhve . . .	19	[8]	Per	Mid	2 pl
-ta	16	[8]	Imv	Act	2 pl
-ta	16	[8]	Imf	Act	2 pl

-ta	16	[8]	Imf	Mid	3 sg
-ta	22	[4]	Aor	Act	2 pl
-ta	22	[4]	Aor	Mid	3 sg
-taḥ	16	[8]	Ind	Act	3du
-tam	16	[8]	Imv	Act	2du
-tam	16	[8]	Imf	Act	2du
-tam	22	[4]	Aor	Act	2du
-tām	16	[8]	Imv	Act	3du
-tām	16	[8]	Imf	Act	3du
-tām	16	[8]	Imv	Mid	3 sg
-tām	22	[4]	Aor	Act	3du
-ti	16	[8]	Ind	Act	3 sg
-tu	16	[8]	Imv	Act	3 sg
-te	16	[8]	Ind	Mid	3 sg
-tha	16	[8]	Ind	Act	2 pl
-tha	19	[8]	Per	Act	2 sg
-thaḥ	16	[8]	Ind	Act	2du
-thāḥ	16	[8]	Imf	Mid	2 sg
-thāḥ	22	[4]	Aor	Mid	2 sg
-dha	16	[11]	Ind	Act	2 pl
-dha	16	[11]	Imv	Act	2 pl
-dha	16	[11]	Imf	Act	2 pl
-dha	16	[11]	Imf	Mid	3 sg
-dhaḥ	16	[11]	Ind	Act	3du
-dhaḥ	16	[11]	Ind	Act	2du
-dham	16	[11]	Imv	Act	2du
-dham	16	[11]	Imf	Act	2du
-dhāḥ	16	[11]	Imf	Mid	2 sg
-dhām	16	[11]	Imv	Act	3du
-dhām	16	[11]	Imf	Act	3du
-dhām	16	[11]	Imv	Mid	3 sg
-dhi	16	[8]	Imv	Act	2 sg
-dhi	16	[11]	Ind	Act	3 sg
-dhi	16	[11]	Imv	Act	2 sg
-dhu	16	[11]	Imv	Act	3 sg
-dhe	16	[11]	Ind	Mid	3 sg
-dhvam	16	[8]	Imv	Mid	2 pl
-dhvam	16	[8]	Imf	Mid	2 pl
-dhvam	16	[11]	Imv	Mid	2 pl
-dhvam	16	[11]	Imf	Mid	2 pl
-dhvam	22	[4]	Aor	Mid	2 pl
-dhve	16	[8]	Ind	Mid	2 pl
-dhve	16	[11]	Ind	Mid	2 pl
-ma	16	[6]	Imf	Act	1 pl
-ma	16	[8]	Imf	Act	1 pl
-ma	16	[9]	Imf	Act	1 pl
-ma	16	[10]	Imf	Act	1 pl
-ma	16	[11]	Imf	Act	1 pl
-ma	19	[8]	Per	Act	1 pl
-maḥ	16	[6]	Ind	Act	1 pl
-maḥ	16	[8]	Ind	Act	1 pl
-maḥ	16	[9]	Ind	Act	1 pl
-maḥ	16	[10]	Ind	Act	1 pl
-maḥ	16	[11]	Ind	Act	1 pl
-mahi	16	[6]	Imf	Mid	1 pl
-mahi	16	[9]	Imf	Mid	1 pl
-mahi	16	[8]	Imf	Mid	1 pl
-mahi	16	[11]	Imf	Mid	1 pl
-mahe	16	[6]	Ind	Mid	1 pl
-mahe	16	[8]	Ind	Mid	1 pl
-mahe	16	[9]	Ind	Mid	1 pl
-mahe	16	[11]	Ind	Mid	1 pl
-mahe	19	[8]	Per	Mid	1 pl
-mi	16	[8]	Ind	Act	1 sg
-mi	16	[9]	Ind	Act	1 sg
-mi	16	[10]	Ind	Act	1 sg
-mi	16	[11]	Ind	Act	1 sg
-yāḥ	16	[3]	Opt	Act	2 sg
-yāḥ	16	[8]	Opt	Act	2 sg
-yāḥ	16	[9]	Opt	Act	2 sg
-yāḥ	16	[10]	Opt	Act	2 sg
-yāḥ	16	[11]	Opt	Act	2 sg
-yāt	16	[3]	Opt	Act	3 sg
-yāt	16	[8]	Opt	Act	3 sg
-yāt	16	[9]	Opt	Act	3 sg
-yāt	16	[10]	Opt	Act	3 sg
-yāt	16	[11]	Opt	Act	3 sg
-yāta	16	[3]	Opt	Act	2 pl
-yāta	16	[8]	Opt	Act	2 pl
-yāta	16	[9]	Opt	Act	2 pl
-yāta	16	[10]	Opt	Act	2 pl
-yāta	16	[11]	Opt	Act	2 pl
-yātam	16	[3]	Opt	Act	2du
-yātam	16	[8]	Opt	Act	2du
-yātam	16	[9]	Opt	Act	2du
-yātam	16	[10]	Opt	Act	2du
-yātam	16	[11]	Opt	Act	2du
-yātām	16	[3]	Opt	Act	3du
-yātām	16	[8]	Opt	Act	3du
-yātām	16	[9]	Opt	Act	3du
-yātām	16	[10]	Opt	Act	3du
-yātām	16	[11]	Opt	Act	3du

-yām	16	[3]	Opt	Act	1 sg
-yām	16	[8]	Opt	Act	1 sg
-yām	16	[9]	Opt	Act	1 sg
-yām	16	[10]	Opt	Act	1 sg
-yām	16	[11]	Opt	Act	1 sg
-yāma	16	[3]	Opt	Act	1 pl
-yāma	16	[8]	Opt	Act	1 pl
-yāma	16	[9]	Opt	Act	1 pl
-yāma	16	[10]	Opt	Act	1 pl
-yāma	16	[11]	Opt	Act	1 pl
-yāva	16	[3]	Opt	Act	1du
-yāva	16	[8]	Opt	Act	1du
-yāva	16	[9]	Opt	Act	1du
-yāva	16	[10]	Opt	Act	1du
-yāva	16	[11]	Opt	Act	1du
-yuḥ	16	[3]	Opt	Act	3 pl
-yuḥ	16	[8]	Opt	Act	3 pl
-yuḥ	16	[9]	Opt	Act	3 pl
-yuḥ	16	[10]	Opt	Act	3 pl
-yuḥ	16	[11]	Opt	Act	3 pl
-va	16	[6]	Imf	Act	1du
-va	16	[8]	Imf	Act	1du
-va	16	[9]	Imf	Act	1du
-va	16	[10]	Imf	Act	1du
-va	16	[11]	Imf	Act	1du
-va	19	[8]	Per	Act	1du
-vaḥ	16	[6]	Ind	Act	1du
-vaḥ	16	[8]	Ind	Act	1du
-vaḥ	16	[9]	Ind	Act	1du
-vaḥ	16	[10]	Ind	Act	1du
-vaḥ	16	[11]	Ind	Act	1du
-vata	16	[6]	Imf	Mid	3 pl
-vata	16	[7]	Imf	Mid	3 pl
-vatām	16	[6]	Imv	Mid	3 pl
-vatām	16	[7]	Imv	Mid	3 pl
-vati	16	[7]	Ind	Act	3 pl
-vatu	16	[7]	Imv	Act	3 pl
-vate	16	[6]	Ind	Mid	3 pl
-vate	16	[7]	Ind	Mid	3 pl
-van	16	[6]	Imf	Act	3 pl
-vanti	16	[6]	Ind	Act	3 pl
-vantu	16	[6]	Imv	Act	3 pl
-vahi	16	[6]	Imf	Mid	1du
-vahi	16	[8]	Imf	Mid	1du
-vahi	16	[9]	Imf	Mid	1du
-vahi	16	[11]	Imf	Mid	1du
-vahe	16	[6]	Ind	Mid	1du
-vahe	16	[8]	Ind	Mid	1du
-vahe	16	[9]	Ind	Mid	1du
-vahe	16	[11]	Ind	Mid	1du
-vahe	19	[8]	Per	Mid	1du
-vātām	16	[6]	Imv	Mid	3du
-vātām	16	[6]	Imf	Mid	3du
-vātām	16	[7]	Imv	Mid	3du
-vātām	16	[7]	Imf	Mid	3du
-vāte	16	[6]	Ind	Mid	3du
-vāte	16	[7]	Ind	Mid	3du
-vāthām	16	[6]	Imv	Mid	2du
-vāthām	16	[6]	Imf	Mid	2du
-vāthām	16	[7]	Imv	Mid	2du
-vāthām	16	[7]	Imf	Mid	2du
-vāthe	16	[6]	Ind	Mid	2du
-vāthe	16	[7]	Ind	Mid	2du
-vi	16	[6]	Imf	Mid	1 sg
-vi	16	[7]	Imf	Mid	1 sg
-vīta	16	[6]	Opt	Mid	3 sg
-vīta	16	[7]	Opt	Mid	3 sg
-vīthāḥ	16	[6]	Opt	Mid	2 sg
-vīthāḥ	16	[7]	Opt	Mid	2 sg
-vīdhvam	16	[6]	Opt	Mid	2 pl
-vīdhvam	16	[7]	Opt	Mid	2 pl
-vīmahi	16	[6]	Opt	Mid	1 pl
-vīmahi	16	[7]	Opt	Mid	1 pl
-vīya	16	[6]	Opt	Mid	1 sg
-vīya	16	[7]	Opt	Mid	1 sg
-vīyātām	16	[6]	Opt	Mid	3du
-vīyātām	16	[7]	Opt	Mid	3du
-vīyāthām	16	[6]	Opt	Mid	2du
-vīyāthām	16	[7]	Opt	Mid	2du
-vīran	16	[6]	Opt	Mid	3 pl
-vīran	16	[7]	Opt	Mid	3 pl
-vīvahi	16	[6]	Opt	Mid	1du
-vīvahi	16	[7]	Opt	Mid	1du
-ve	16	[6]	Ind	Mid	1 sg
-ve	16	[7]	Ind	Mid	1 sg
-ṣaḥ	22	[2]	Aor	Act	2 sg
-ṣat	22	[2]	Aor	Act	3 sg
-ṣata	22	[2]	Aor	Act	2 pl
-ṣata	22	[3]	Aor	Mid	3 pl
-ṣatam	22	[2]	Aor	Act	2du
-ṣatām	22	[2]	Aor	Act	3du
-ṣathāḥ	22	[2]	Aor	Mid	2 sg

-ṣadhvam	22 [2]	Aor	Mid	2	pl
-ṣan	22 [2]	Aor	Act	3	pl
-ṣanta	22 [2]	Aor	Mid	3	pl
-ṣam	22 [2]	Aor	Act	1	sg
-ṣam	22 [3]	Aor	Act	1	sg
-ṣāta	22 [2]	Aor	Mid	3	sg
-ṣātām	22 [2]	Aor	Mid	3	du
-ṣātām	22 [3]	Aor	Mid	3	du
-ṣāthām	22 [2]	Aor	Mid	2	du
-ṣāthām	22 [3]	Aor	Mid	2	du
-ṣāma	22 [2]	Aor	Act	1	pl
-ṣāmahi	22 [2]	Aor	Mid	1	pl
-ṣāva	22 [2]	Aor	Act	1	du
-ṣāvahi	22 [2]	Aor	Mid	1	du
-ṣi	16 [8]	Ind	Act	2	sg
-ṣi	16 [9]	Ind	Act	2	sg
-ṣi	16 [10]	Ind	Act	2	sg
-ṣi	22 [2]	Aor	Mid	1	sg
-ṣi	22 [3]	Aor	Mid	1	sg
-ṣīḥ	22 [3]	Aor	Act	2	sg
-ṣīt	22 [3]	Aor	Act	3	sg
-ṣuḥ	22 [3]	Aor	Act	3	pl
-ṣe	16 [8]	Ind	Mid	2	sg
-ṣe	16 [9]	Ind	Mid	2	sg
-ṣe	19 [8]	Per	Mid	2	sg
-ṣṭa	22 [3]	Aor	Act	2	pl
-ṣṭa	22 [3]	Aor	Mid	3	sg
-ṣṭam	22 [3]	Aor	Act	2	du
-ṣṭām	22 [3]	Aor	Act	3	du
-ṣṭhāḥ	22 [3]	Aor	Mid	2	sg
-ṣma	22 [3]	Aor	Act	1	pl
-ṣmahi	22 [3]	Aor	Mid	1	pl
-ṣva	16 [8]	Imv	Mid	2	sg
-ṣva	16 [9]	Imv	Mid	2	sg
-ṣva	22 [3]	Aor	Act	1	du
-ṣvahi	22 [3]	Aor	Mid	1	du
-sata	22 [4]	Aor	Mid	3	pl
-sam	22 [4]	Aor	Act	1	sg
-sātām	22 [4]	Aor	Mid	3	du
-sāthām	22 [4]	Aor	Mid	2	du
-si	16 [11]	Ind	Act	2	sg
-si	22 [4]	Aor	Mid	1	sg
-sīḥ	22 [4]	Aor	Act	2	sg
-sīt	22 [4]	Aor	Act	3	sg
-suḥ	22 [4]	Aor	Act	3	pl
-se	16 [11]	Ind	Mid	2	sg
-sma	22 [4]	Aor	Act	1	pl
-smahi	22 [4]	Aor	Mid	1	pl
-sva	16 [11]	Imv	Mid	2	sg
-sva	22 [4]	Aor	Act	1	du
-svahi	22 [4]	Aor	Mid	1	du

Table 30. Index to noun/adjective endings.

-	6	[6]	Nom	sg
-	6	[6]	Voc	sg
-	6	[7]	Nom	sg
-	6	[7]	Voc	sg
-	6	[21]	Nom	sg
-	6	[21]	Acc	sg
-	6	[21]	Voc	sg
-	6	[22]	Nom	sg
-	6	[22]	Acc	sg
-	6	[22]	Voc	sg
-a	6	[1]	Voc	sg
-a	6	[17]	Voc	sg
-a	6	[26]	Nom	sg
-a	6	[26]	Acc	sg
-a	6	[26]	Voc	sg
-a	6	[27]	Nom	sg
-a	6	[27]	Acc	sg
-a	6	[27]	Voc	sg
-aḥ	6	[1]	Nom	sg
-aḥ	6	[4]	Voc	sg
-aḥ	6	[5]	Voc	sg
-aḥ	6	[6]	Nom	pl
-aḥ	6	[6]	Acc	pl
-aḥ	6	[6]	Voc	pl
-aḥ	6	[6]	Abl	sg
-aḥ	6	[6]	Gen	sg
-aḥ	6	[7]	Nom	pl
-aḥ	6	[7]	Acc	pl
-aḥ	6	[7]	Voc	pl
-aḥ	6	[7]	Abl	sg
-aḥ	6	[7]	Gen	sg
-aḥ	6	[8]	Voc	sg
-aḥ	6	[20]	Voc	sg
-aḥ	6	[21]	Abl	sg
-aḥ	6	[21]	Gen	sg
-aḥ	6	[22]	Abl	sg
-aḥ	6	[22]	Gen	sg
-aḥ	6	[23]	Nom	sg
-aḥ	6	[23]	Acc	sg
-aḥ	6	[23]	Voc	sg
-aḥ	6	[40]	Voc	sg
-aḥsu	6	[8]	Loc	pl
-aḥsu	6	[14]	Loc	pl
-aḥsu	6	[23]	Loc	pl
-aṇaḥ	6	[26]	Abl	sg
-aṇaḥ	6	[26]	Gen	sg
-aṇā	6	[26]	Ins	sg
-aṇām	6	[26]	Gen	pl
-aṇi	6	[26]	Loc	sg
-aṇī	6	[26]	Nom	du
-aṇī	6	[26]	Acc	du
-aṇī	6	[26]	Voc	du
-aṇe	6	[26]	Dat	sg
-aṇoḥ	6	[26]	Gen	du
-aṇoḥ	6	[26]	Loc	du
-at	6	[29]	Nom	sg
-at	6	[29]	Acc	sg
-at	6	[29]	Voc	sg
-ataḥ	6	[12]	Acc	pl
-ataḥ	6	[12]	Abl	sg
-ataḥ	6	[12]	Gen	sg
-ataḥ	6	[13]	Acc	pl
-ataḥ	6	[13]	Abl	sg
-ataḥ	6	[13]	Gen	sg
-ataḥ	6	[29]	Abl	sg
-ataḥ	6	[29]	Gen	sg
-atā	6	[12]	Ins	sg
-atā	6	[13]	Ins	sg
-atā	6	[29]	Ins	sg
-atām	6	[12]	Gen	pl
-atām	6	[13]	Gen	pl
-atām	6	[29]	Gen	pl
-ati	6	[12]	Loc	sg
-ati	6	[13]	Loc	sg
-ati	6	[29]	Loc	sg
-ate	6	[12]	Dat	sg
-ate	6	[13]	Dat	sg
-ate	6	[29]	Dat	sg
-atoḥ	6	[12]	Gen	du
-atoḥ	6	[12]	Loc	du
-atoḥ	6	[13]	Gen	du
-atoḥ	6	[13]	Loc	du
-atoḥ	6	[29]	Gen	du
-atoḥ	6	[29]	Loc	du
-atsu	6	[12]	Loc	pl
-atsu	6	[13]	Loc	pl
-atsu	6	[29]	Loc	pl
-adbhiḥ	6	[12]	Ins	pl

-adbhiḥ	6	[13]	Ins	pl
-adbhiḥ	6	[29]	Ins	pl
-adbhyaḥ	6	[12]	Dat	pl
-adbhyaḥ	6	[12]	Abl	pl
-adbhyaḥ	6	[13]	Dat	pl
-adbhyaḥ	6	[13]	Abl	pl
-adbhyaḥ	6	[29]	Dat	pl
-adbhyaḥ	6	[29]	Abl	pl
-adbhyām	6	[12]	Ins	du
-adbhyām	6	[12]	Dat	du
-adbhyām	6	[12]	Abl	du
-adbhyām	6	[13]	Ins	du
-adbhyām	6	[13]	Dat	du
-adbhyām	6	[13]	Abl	du
-adbhyām	6	[29]	Ins	du
-adbhyām	6	[29]	Dat	du
-adbhyām	6	[29]	Abl	du
-an	6	[9]	Voc	sg
-an	6	[10]	Voc	sg
-an	6	[12]	Nom	sg
-an	6	[12]	Voc	sg
-an	6	[13]	Voc	sg
-an	6	[14]	Voc	sg
-an	6	[26]	Voc	sg
-an	6	[27]	Voc	sg
-anaḥ	6	[9]	Acc	pl
-anaḥ	6	[9]	Abl	sg
-anaḥ	6	[9]	Gen	sg
-anā	6	[9]	Ins	sg
-anām	6	[9]	Gen	pl
-ani	6	[9]	Loc	sg
-ani	6	[10]	Loc	sg
-ani	6	[27]	Loc	sg
-anī	6	[27]	Nom	du
-anī	6	[27]	Acc	du
-anī	6	[27]	Voc	du
-ane	6	[9]	Dat	sg
-anoḥ	6	[9]	Gen	du
-anoḥ	6	[9]	Loc	du
-antaḥ	6	[12]	Nom	pl
-antaḥ	6	[12]	Voc	pl
-antaḥ	6	[13]	Nom	pl
-antaḥ	6	[13]	Voc	pl
-antam	6	[12]	Acc	sg
-antam	6	[13]	Acc	sg
-anti	6	[29]	Nom	pl
-anti	6	[29]	Acc	pl
-anti	6	[29]	Voc	pl
-antī	6	[29]	Nom	du
-antī	6	[29]	Acc	du
-antī	6	[29]	Voc	du
-antau	6	[12]	Nom	du
-antau	6	[12]	Acc	du
-antau	6	[12]	Voc	du
-antau	6	[13]	Nom	du
-antau	6	[13]	Acc	du
-antau	6	[13]	Voc	du
-abhiḥ	6	[9]	Ins	pl
-abhiḥ	6	[10]	Ins	pl
-abhiḥ	6	[26]	Ins	pl
-abhiḥ	6	[27]	Ins	pl
-abhyaḥ	6	[9]	Dat	pl
-abhyaḥ	6	[9]	Abl	pl
-abhyaḥ	6	[10]	Dat	pl
-abhyaḥ	6	[10]	Abl	pl
-abhyaḥ	6	[26]	Dat	pl
-abhyaḥ	6	[26]	Abl	pl
-abhyaḥ	6	[27]	Dat	pl
-abhyaḥ	6	[27]	Abl	pl
-abhyām	6	[9]	Ins	du
-abhyām	6	[9]	Dat	du
-abhyām	6	[9]	Abl	du
-abhyām	6	[10]	Ins	du
-abhyām	6	[10]	Dat	du
-abhyām	6	[10]	Abl	du
-abhyām	6	[26]	Ins	du
-abhyām	6	[26]	Dat	du
-abhyām	6	[26]	Abl	du
-abhyām	6	[27]	Ins	du
-abhyām	6	[27]	Dat	du
-abhyām	6	[27]	Abl	du
-am	6	[1]	Acc	sg
-am	6	[6]	Acc	sg
-am	6	[7]	Acc	sg
-am	6	[17]	Nom	sg
-am	6	[17]	Acc	sg
-ayaḥ	6	[2]	Nom	pl
-ayaḥ	6	[2]	Voc	pl
-ayaḥ	6	[35]	Nom	pl
-ayaḥ	6	[35]	Voc	pl
-ayā	6	[32]	Ins	sg
-aye	6	[2]	Dat	sg

-aye .... 6 [35] Dat sg
-ayoḥ .... 6 [1] Gen du
-ayoḥ .... 6 [1] Loc du
-ayoḥ .... 6 [17] Gen du
-ayoḥ .... 6 [17] Loc du
-ayoḥ .... 6 [32] Gen du
-ayoḥ .... 6 [32] Loc du
-araḥ .... 6 [5] Nom pl
-araḥ .... 6 [5] Voc pl
-araḥ .... 6 [40] Nom pl
-araḥ .... 6 [40] Voc pl
-aram ...... 6 [5] Acc sg
-aram ...... 6 [40] Acc sg
-ari .... 6 [4] Loc sg
-ari .... 6 [5] Loc sg
-ari .... 6 [40] Loc sg
-arau .... 6 [5] Nom du
-arau .... 6 [5] Acc du
-arau .... 6 [5] Voc du
-arau .... 6 [40] Nom du
-arau .... 6 [40] Acc du
-arau .... 6 [40] Voc du
-avaḥ .... 6 [3] Nom pl
-avaḥ .... 6 [3] Voc pl
-avaḥ .... 6 [38] Nom pl
-avaḥ .... 6 [38] Voc pl
-ave .... 6 [3] Dat sg
-ave .... 6 [38] Dat sg
-asaḥ .... 6 [8] Nom pl
-asaḥ .... 6 [8] Acc pl
-asaḥ .... 6 [8] Voc pl
-asaḥ .... 6 [8] Abl sg
-asaḥ .... 6 [8] Gen sg
-asaḥ .... 6 [14] Acc pl
-asaḥ .... 6 [14] Abl sg
-asaḥ .... 6 [14] Gen sg
-asaḥ .... 6 [23] Abl sg
-asaḥ .... 6 [23] Gen sg
-asam ...... 6 [8] Acc sg
-asā .... 6 [8] Ins sg
-asā .... 6 [14] Ins sg
-asā .... 6 [23] Ins sg
-asām ...... 6 [8] Gen pl
-asām ...... 6 [14] Gen pl
-asām ...... 6 [23] Gen pl
-asi .... 6 [8] Loc sg
-asi .... 6 [14] Loc sg
-asi .... 6 [23] Loc sg
-asī .... 6 [23] Nom du
-asī .... 6 [23] Acc du
-asī .... 6 [23] Voc du
-asu .... 6 [9] Loc pl
-asu .... 6 [10] Loc pl
-asu .... 6 [26] Loc pl
-asu .... 6 [27] Loc pl
-ase .... 6 [8] Dat sg
-ase .... 6 [14] Dat sg
-ase .... 6 [23] Dat sg
-asoḥ .... 6 [8] Gen du
-asoḥ .... 6 [8] Loc du
-asoḥ .... 6 [14] Gen du
-asoḥ .... 6 [14] Loc du
-asoḥ .... 6 [23] Gen du
-asoḥ .... 6 [23] Loc du
-asau .... 6 [8] Nom du
-asau .... 6 [8] Acc du
-asau .... 6 [8] Voc du
-asya .... 6 [1] Gen sg
-asya .... 6 [17] Gen sg
-ā .... 6 [4] Nom sg
-ā .... 6 [5] Nom sg
-ā .... 6 [6] Ins sg
-ā .... 6 [7] Ins sg
-ā .... 6 [9] Nom sg
-ā .... 6 [10] Nom sg
-ā .... 6 [21] Ins sg
-ā .... 6 [22] Ins sg
-ā .... 6 [32] Nom sg
-ā .... 6 [40] Nom sg
-āṃsaḥ ..... 6 [14] Nom pl
-āṃsaḥ ..... 6 [14] Voc pl
-āṃsam ..... 6 [14] Acc sg
-āṃsi .... 6 [23] Nom pl
-āṃsi .... 6 [23] Acc pl
-āṃsi .... 6 [23] Voc pl
-āṃsau ..... 6 [14] Nom du
-āṃsau ..... 6 [14] Acc du
-āṃsau ..... 6 [14] Voc du
-āḥ .... 6 [1] Nom pl
-āḥ .... 6 [1] Voc pl
-āḥ .... 6 [8] Nom sg
-āḥ .... 6 [32] Nom pl

-āḥ	6	[32]	Acc	pl
-āḥ	6	[32]	Voc	pl
-āṇi	6	[26]	Nom	pl
-āṇi	6	[26]	Acc	pl
-āṇi	6	[26]	Voc	pl
-āt	6	[1]	Abl	sg
-āt	6	[17]	Abl	sg
-ān	6	[1]	Acc	pl
-ān	6	[13]	Nom	sg
-ān	6	[14]	Nom	sg
-ānaḥ	6	[9]	Nom	pl
-ānaḥ	6	[9]	Voc	pl
-ānaḥ	6	[10]	Nom	pl
-ānaḥ	6	[10]	Voc	pl
-ānam	6	[9]	Acc	sg
-ānam	6	[10]	Acc	sg
-ānām	6	[1]	Gen	pl
-ānām	6	[17]	Gen	pl
-ānām	6	[32]	Gen	pl
-āni	6	[17]	Nom	pl
-āni	6	[17]	Acc	pl
-āni	6	[17]	Voc	pl
-āni	6	[27]	Nom	pl
-āni	6	[27]	Acc	pl
-āni	6	[27]	Voc	pl
-ānau	6	[9]	Nom	du
-ānau	6	[9]	Acc	du
-ānau	6	[9]	Voc	du
-ānau	6	[10]	Nom	du
-ānau	6	[10]	Acc	du
-ānau	6	[10]	Voc	du
-ābhiḥ	6	[32]	Ins	pl
-ābhyaḥ	6	[32]	Dat	pl
-ābhyaḥ	6	[32]	Abl	pl
-ābhyām	6	[1]	Ins	du
-ābhyām	6	[1]	Dat	du
-ābhyām	6	[1]	Abl	du
-ābhyām	6	[17]	Ins	du
-ābhyām	6	[17]	Dat	du
-ābhyām	6	[17]	Abl	du
-ābhyām	6	[32]	Ins	du
-ābhyām	6	[32]	Dat	du
-ābhyām	6	[32]	Abl	du
-ām	6	[6]	Gen	pl
-ām	6	[7]	Gen	pl
-ām	6	[21]	Gen	pl
-ām	6	[22]	Gen	pl
-ām	6	[32]	Acc	sg
-āya	6	[1]	Dat	sg
-āya	6	[17]	Dat	sg
-āyāḥ	6	[32]	Abl	sg
-āyāḥ	6	[32]	Gen	sg
-āyām	6	[32]	Loc	sg
-āyai	6	[32]	Dat	sg
-āraḥ	6	[4]	Nom	pl
-āraḥ	6	[4]	Voc	pl
-āram	6	[4]	Acc	sg
-ārau	6	[4]	Nom	du
-ārau	6	[4]	Acc	du
-ārau	6	[4]	Voc	du
-āvaḥ	6	[39]	Nom	pl
-āvaḥ	6	[39]	Acc	pl
-āvaḥ	6	[39]	Voc	pl
-āvaḥ	6	[39]	Abl	sg
-āvaḥ	6	[39]	Gen	sg
-āvam	6	[39]	Acc	sg
-āvā	6	[39]	Ins	sg
-āvām	6	[39]	Gen	pl
-āvi	6	[39]	Loc	sg
-āve	6	[39]	Dat	sg
-āvoḥ	6	[39]	Gen	du
-āvoḥ	6	[39]	Loc	du
-āvau	6	[39]	Nom	du
-āvau	6	[39]	Acc	du
-āvau	6	[39]	Voc	du
-āsu	6	[32]	Loc	pl
-i	6	[6]	Loc	sg
-i	6	[7]	Loc	sg
-i	6	[18]	Nom	sg
-i	6	[18]	Acc	sg
-i	6	[18]	Voc	sg
-i	6	[21]	Nom	pl
-i	6	[21]	Acc	pl
-i	6	[21]	Voc	pl
-i	6	[21]	Loc	sg
-i	6	[22]	Nom	pl
-i	6	[22]	Acc	pl
-i	6	[22]	Voc	pl
-i	6	[22]	Loc	sg
-i	6	[28]	Nom	sg
-i	6	[28]	Acc	sg
-i	6	[28]	Voc	sg

-i	6 [33]	Voc	sg
-iḥ	6 [2]	Nom	sg
-iḥ	6 [24]	Nom	sg
-iḥ	6 [24]	Acc	sg
-iḥ	6 [24]	Voc	sg
-iḥ	6 [35]	Nom	sg
-iḥṣu	6 [24]	Loc	pl
-iṇaḥ	6 [18]	Abl	sg
-iṇaḥ	6 [18]	Gen	sg
-iṇā	6 [18]	Ins	sg
-iṇi	6 [18]	Loc	sg
-iṇī	6 [18]	Nom	du
-iṇī	6 [18]	Acc	du
-iṇī	6 [18]	Voc	du
-iṇe	6 [18]	Dat	sg
-iṇoḥ	6 [18]	Gen	du
-iṇoḥ	6 [18]	Loc	du
-in	6 [11]	Voc	sg
-in	6 [28]	Voc	sg
-inaḥ	6 [11]	Nom	pl
-inaḥ	6 [11]	Acc	pl
-inaḥ	6 [11]	Voc	pl
-inaḥ	6 [11]	Abl	sg
-inaḥ	6 [11]	Gen	sg
-inaḥ	6 [28]	Abl	sg
-inaḥ	6 [28]	Gen	sg
-inam	6 [11]	Acc	sg
-inā	6 [2]	Ins	sg
-inā	6 [11]	Ins	sg
-inā	6 [28]	Ins	sg
-inām	6 [11]	Gen	pl
-inām	6 [28]	Gen	pl
-ini	6 [11]	Loc	sg
-ini	6 [28]	Loc	sg
-inī	6 [28]	Nom	du
-inī	6 [28]	Acc	du
-inī	6 [28]	Voc	du
-ine	6 [11]	Dat	sg
-ine	6 [28]	Dat	sg
-inoḥ	6 [11]	Gen	du
-inoḥ	6 [11]	Loc	du
-inoḥ	6 [28]	Gen	du
-inoḥ	6 [28]	Loc	du
-inau	6 [11]	Nom	du
-inau	6 [11]	Acc	du
-inau	6 [11]	Voc	du

-ibhiḥ	6 [2]	Ins	pl
-ibhiḥ	6 [11]	Ins	pl
-ibhiḥ	6 [18]	Ins	pl
-ibhiḥ	6 [28]	Ins	pl
-ibhiḥ	6 [35]	Ins	pl
-ibhyaḥ	6 [2]	Dat	pl
-ibhyaḥ	6 [2]	Abl	pl
-ibhyaḥ	6 [11]	Dat	pl
-ibhyaḥ	6 [11]	Abl	pl
-ibhyaḥ	6 [18]	Dat	pl
-ibhyaḥ	6 [18]	Abl	pl
-ibhyaḥ	6 [28]	Dat	pl
-ibhyaḥ	6 [28]	Abl	pl
-ibhyaḥ	6 [35]	Dat	pl
-ibhyaḥ	6 [35]	Abl	pl
-ibhyām	6 [2]	Ins	du
-ibhyām	6 [2]	Dat	du
-ibhyām	6 [2]	Abl	du
-ibhyām	6 [11]	Ins	du
-ibhyām	6 [11]	Dat	du
-ibhyām	6 [11]	Abl	du
-ibhyām	6 [18]	Ins	du
-ibhyām	6 [18]	Dat	du
-ibhyām	6 [18]	Abl	du
-ibhyām	6 [28]	Ins	du
-ibhyām	6 [28]	Dat	du
-ibhyām	6 [28]	Abl	du
-ibhyām	6 [35]	Ins	du
-ibhyām	6 [35]	Dat	du
-ibhyām	6 [35]	Abl	du
-im	6 [2]	Acc	sg
-im	6 [35]	Acc	sg
-iyaḥ	6 [34]	Nom	pl
-iyaḥ	6 [34]	Acc	pl
-iyaḥ	6 [34]	Voc	pl
-iyaḥ	6 [34]	Abl	sg
-iyaḥ	6 [34]	Gen	sg
-iyā	6 [34]	Ins	sg
-iyāḥ	6 [34]	Abl	sg
-iyāḥ	6 [34]	Gen	sg
-iyām	6 [34]	Gen	pl
-iyām	6 [34]	Loc	sg
-iyi	6 [34]	Loc	sg
-iye	6 [34]	Dat	sg
-iyai	6 [34]	Dat	sg
-iyoḥ	6 [34]	Gen	du

-iyoḥ	6 [34]	Loc	du
-iyau	6 [34]	Nom	du
-iyau	6 [34]	Acc	du
-iyau	6 [34]	Voc	du
-irbhiḥ	6 [24]	Ins	pl
-irbhyaḥ	6 [24]	Dat	pl
-irbhyaḥ	6 [24]	Abl	pl
-irbhyām	6 [24]	Ins	du
-irbhyām	6 [24]	Dat	du
-irbhyām	6 [24]	Abl	du
-ivat	6 [30]	Nom	sg
-ivat	6 [30]	Acc	sg
-ivat	6 [30]	Voc	sg
-ivatsu	6 [15]	Loc	pl
-ivatsu	6 [30]	Loc	pl
-ivadbhiḥ	6 [15]	Ins	pl
-ivadbhiḥ	6 [30]	Ins	pl
-ivadbhyaḥ	6 [15]	Dat	pl
-ivadbhyaḥ	6 [15]	Abl	pl
-ivadbhyaḥ	6 [30]	Dat	pl
-ivadbhyaḥ	6 [30]	Abl	pl
-ivadbhyām	6 [15]	Ins	du
-ivadbhyām	6 [15]	Dat	du
-ivadbhyām	6 [15]	Abl	du
-ivadbhyām	6 [30]	Ins	du
-ivadbhyām	6 [30]	Dat	du
-ivadbhyām	6 [30]	Abl	du
-ivan	6 [15]	Voc	sg
-ivāṃsaḥ	6 [15]	Nom	pl
-ivāṃsaḥ	6 [15]	Voc	pl
-ivāṃsam	6 [15]	Acc	sg
-ivāṃsi	6 [30]	Nom	pl
-ivāṃsi	6 [30]	Acc	pl
-ivāṃsi	6 [30]	Voc	pl
-ivāṃsau	6 [15]	Nom	du
-ivāṃsau	6 [15]	Acc	du
-ivāṃsau	6 [15]	Voc	du
-ivān	6 [15]	Nom	sg
-iṣaḥ	6 [24]	Abl	sg
-iṣaḥ	6 [24]	Gen	sg
-iṣā	6 [24]	Ins	sg
-iṣām	6 [24]	Gen	pl
-iṣi	6 [24]	Loc	sg
-iṣī	6 [24]	Nom	du
-iṣī	6 [24]	Acc	du
-iṣī	6 [24]	Voc	du
-iṣu	6 [2]	Loc	pl
-iṣu	6 [11]	Loc	pl
-iṣu	6 [18]	Loc	pl
-iṣu	6 [28]	Loc	pl
-iṣu	6 [35]	Loc	pl
-iṣe	6 [24]	Dat	sg
-iṣoḥ	6 [24]	Gen	du
-iṣoḥ	6 [24]	Loc	du
-ī	6 [2]	Nom	du
-ī	6 [2]	Acc	du
-ī	6 [2]	Voc	du
-ī	6 [11]	Nom	sg
-ī	6 [21]	Nom	du
-ī	6 [21]	Acc	du
-ī	6 [21]	Voc	du
-ī	6 [22]	Nom	du
-ī	6 [22]	Acc	du
-ī	6 [22]	Voc	du
-ī	6 [33]	Nom	sg
-ī	6 [35]	Nom	du
-ī	6 [35]	Acc	du
-ī	6 [35]	Voc	du
-īṃṣi	6 [24]	Nom	pl
-īṃṣi	6 [24]	Acc	pl
-īṃṣi	6 [24]	Voc	pl
-īḥ	6 [33]	Acc	pl
-īḥ	6 [34]	Nom	sg
-īḥ	6 [34]	Voc	sg
-īḥ	6 [35]	Acc	pl
-īṇām	6 [18]	Gen	pl
-īṇi	6 [18]	Nom	pl
-īṇi	6 [18]	Acc	pl
-īṇi	6 [18]	Voc	pl
-īn	6 [2]	Acc	pl
-īnām	6 [2]	Gen	pl
-īnām	6 [33]	Gen	pl
-īnām	6 [34]	Gen	pl
-īnām	6 [35]	Gen	pl
-īni	6 [28]	Nom	pl
-īni	6 [28]	Acc	pl
-īni	6 [28]	Voc	pl
-ībhiḥ	6 [33]	Ins	pl
-ībhiḥ	6 [34]	Ins	pl
-ībhyaḥ	6 [33]	Dat	du
-ībhyaḥ	6 [33]	Abl	du
-ībhyaḥ	6 [34]	Dat	du

-ībhyaḥ	6	[34]	Abl	du
-ībhyām	6	[33]	Ins	du
-ībhyām	6	[33]	Dat	du
-ībhyām	6	[33]	Abl	du
-ībhyām	6	[34]	Ins	du
-ībhyām	6	[34]	Dat	du
-ībhyām	6	[34]	Abl	du
-īm	6	[33]	Acc	sg
-īṣu	6	[33]	Loc	pl
-īṣu	6	[34]	Loc	pl
-u	6	[19]	Nom	sg
-u	6	[19]	Acc	sg
-u	6	[19]	Voc	sg
-u	6	[36]	Voc	sg
-uḥ	6	[3]	Nom	sg
-uḥ	6	[4]	Abl	sg
-uḥ	6	[4]	Gen	sg
-uḥ	6	[5]	Abl	sg
-uḥ	6	[5]	Gen	sg
-uḥ	6	[25]	Nom	sg
-uḥ	6	[25]	Acc	sg
-uḥ	6	[25]	Voc	sg
-uḥ	6	[38]	Nom	sg
-uḥ	6	[40]	Abl	sg
-uḥ	6	[40]	Gen	sg
-uḥṣu	6	[25]	Loc	pl
-unaḥ	6	[19]	Abl	sg
-unaḥ	6	[19]	Gen	sg
-unā	6	[3]	Ins	sg
-unā	6	[19]	Ins	sg
-uni	6	[19]	Loc	sg
-unī	6	[19]	Nom	du
-unī	6	[19]	Acc	du
-unī	6	[19]	Voc	du
-une	6	[19]	Dat	sg
-unoḥ	6	[19]	Gen	du
-unoḥ	6	[19]	Loc	du
-ubhiḥ	6	[3]	Ins	pl
-ubhiḥ	6	[19]	Ins	pl
-ubhiḥ	6	[36]	Ins	pl
-ubhiḥ	6	[38]	Ins	pl
-ubhyaḥ	6	[3]	Dat	pl
-ubhyaḥ	6	[3]	Abl	pl
-ubhyaḥ	6	[19]	Dat	pl
-ubhyaḥ	6	[19]	Abl	pl
-ubhyaḥ	6	[38]	Dat	pl
-ubhyaḥ	6	[38]	Abl	pl
-ubhyām	6	[3]	Ins	du
-ubhyām	6	[3]	Dat	du
-ubhyām	6	[3]	Abl	du
-ubhyām	6	[19]	Ins	du
-ubhyām	6	[19]	Dat	du
-ubhyām	6	[19]	Abl	du
-ubhyām	6	[38]	Ins	du
-ubhyām	6	[38]	Dat	du
-ubhyām	6	[38]	Abl	du
-um	6	[3]	Acc	sg
-um	6	[38]	Acc	sg
-urbhiḥ	6	[25]	Ins	pl
-urbhyaḥ	6	[25]	Dat	pl
-urbhyaḥ	6	[25]	Abl	pl
-urbhyām	6	[25]	Ins	du
-urbhyām	6	[25]	Dat	du
-urbhyām	6	[25]	Abl	du
-uvaḥ	6	[37]	Nom	pl
-uvaḥ	6	[37]	Acc	pl
-uvaḥ	6	[37]	Voc	pl
-uvaḥ	6	[37]	Abl	sg
-uvaḥ	6	[37]	Gen	sg
-uvam	6	[37]	Acc	sg
-uvā	6	[37]	Ins	sg
-uvāḥ	6	[37]	Abl	sg
-uvāḥ	6	[37]	Gen	sg
-uvām	6	[37]	Gen	pl
-uvām	6	[37]	Loc	sg
-uvi	6	[37]	Loc	sg
-uve	6	[37]	Dat	sg
-uvai	6	[37]	Dat	sg
-uvoḥ	6	[37]	Gen	du
-uvoḥ	6	[37]	Loc	du
-uvau	6	[37]	Nom	du
-uvau	6	[37]	Acc	du
-uvau	6	[37]	Voc	du
-uṣaḥ	6	[15]	Abl	sg
-uṣaḥ	6	[15]	Gen	sg
-uṣaḥ	6	[15]	Acc	pl
-uṣaḥ	6	[25]	Abl	sg
-uṣaḥ	6	[25]	Gen	sg
-uṣaḥ	6	[30]	Abl	sg
-uṣaḥ	6	[30]	Gen	sg
-uṣā	6	[15]	Ins	sg
-uṣā	6	[25]	Ins	sg

-uṣā	6	[30]	Ins	sg
-uṣām	6	[15]	Gen	pl
-uṣām	6	[25]	Gen	pl
-uṣām	6	[30]	Gen	pl
-uṣi	6	[15]	Loc	sg
-uṣi	6	[25]	Loc	sg
-uṣi	6	[30]	Loc	sg
-uṣī	6	[25]	Nom	du
-uṣī	6	[25]	Acc	du
-uṣī	6	[25]	Voc	du
-uṣī	6	[30]	Nom	du
-uṣī	6	[30]	Acc	du
-uṣī	6	[30]	Voc	du
-uṣu	6	[3]	Loc	pl
-uṣu	6	[19]	Loc	pl
-uṣu	6	[38]	Loc	pl
-uṣe	6	[15]	Dat	sg
-uṣe	6	[25]	Dat	sg
-uṣe	6	[30]	Dat	sg
-uṣoḥ	6	[15]	Gen	du
-uṣoḥ	6	[15]	Loc	du
-uṣoḥ	6	[25]	Gen	du
-uṣoḥ	6	[25]	Loc	du
-uṣoḥ	6	[30]	Gen	du
-uṣoḥ	6	[30]	Loc	du
-ū	6	[3]	Nom	du
-ū	6	[3]	Acc	du
-ū	6	[3]	Voc	du
-ū	6	[38]	Nom	du
-ū	6	[38]	Acc	du
-ū	6	[38]	Voc	du
-ūṃṣi	6	[25]	Nom	pl
-ūṃṣi	6	[25]	Acc	pl
-ūṃṣi	6	[25]	Voc	pl
-ūḥ	6	[36]	Nom	sg
-ūḥ	6	[36]	Acc	pl
-ūḥ	6	[37]	Nom	sg
-ūḥ	6	[37]	Voc	sg
-ūḥ	6	[38]	Acc	pl
-ūn	6	[3]	Acc	pl
-ūnām	6	[3]	Gen	pl
-ūnām	6	[19]	Gen	pl
-ūnām	6	[36]	Gen	pl
-ūnām	6	[37]	Gen	pl
-ūnām	6	[38]	Gen	pl
-ūni	6	[19]	Nom	pl
-ūni	6	[19]	Acc	pl
-ūni	6	[19]	Voc	pl
-ūbhiḥ	6	[37]	Ins	pl
-ūbhyaḥ	6	[36]	Dat	pl
-ūbhyaḥ	6	[36]	Abl	pl
-ūbhyaḥ	6	[37]	Dat	pl
-ūbhyaḥ	6	[37]	Abl	pl
-ūbhyām	6	[36]	Ins	du
-ūbhyām	6	[36]	Dat	du
-ūbhyām	6	[36]	Abl	du
-ūbhyām	6	[37]	Ins	du
-ūbhyām	6	[37]	Dat	du
-ūbhyām	6	[37]	Abl	du
-ūm	6	[36]	Acc	sg
-ūṣu	6	[36]	Loc	pl
-ūṣu	6	[37]	Loc	pl
-ṛ	6	[20]	Nom	sg
-ṛ	6	[20]	Acc	sg
-ṛ	6	[20]	Voc	sg
-ṛṇaḥ	6	[20]	Abl	sg
-ṛṇaḥ	6	[20]	Gen	sg
-ṛṇā	6	[20]	Ins	sg
-ṛṇi	6	[20]	Loc	sg
-ṛṇī	6	[20]	Nom	du
-ṛṇī	6	[20]	Acc	du
-ṛṇī	6	[20]	Voc	du
-ṛṇe	6	[20]	Dat	sg
-ṛṇoḥ	6	[20]	Gen	du
-ṛṇoḥ	6	[20]	Loc	du
-ṛbhiḥ	6	[4]	Ins	pl
-ṛbhiḥ	6	[5]	Ins	pl
-ṛbhiḥ	6	[20]	Ins	pl
-ṛbhiḥ	6	[40]	Ins	pl
-ṛbhyaḥ	6	[4]	Dat	pl
-ṛbhyaḥ	6	[4]	Abl	pl
-ṛbhyaḥ	6	[5]	Dat	pl
-ṛbhyaḥ	6	[5]	Abl	pl
-ṛbhyaḥ	6	[20]	Dat	pl
-ṛbhyaḥ	6	[20]	Abl	pl
-ṛbhyaḥ	6	[40]	Dat	pl
-ṛbhyaḥ	6	[40]	Abl	pl
-ṛbhyām	6	[4]	Ins	du
-ṛbhyām	6	[4]	Dat	du
-ṛbhyām	6	[4]	Abl	du
-ṛbhyām	6	[5]	Ins	du
-ṛbhyām	6	[5]	Dat	du

-ṛbhyām	6	[5]	Abl	du
-ṛbhyām	6	[20]	Ins	du
-ṛbhyām	6	[20]	Dat	du
-ṛbhyām	6	[20]	Abl	du
-ṛbhyām	6	[40]	Ins	du
-ṛbhyām	6	[40]	Dat	du
-ṛbhyām	6	[40]	Abl	du
-ṛvat	6	[31]	Nom	sg
-ṛvat	6	[31]	Acc	sg
-ṛvat	6	[31]	Voc	sg
-ṛvatsu	6	[16]	Loc	pl
-ṛvatsu	6	[31]	Loc	pl
-ṛvadbhiḥ	6	[16]	Ins	pl
-ṛvadbhiḥ	6	[31]	Ins	pl
-ṛvadbhyaḥ	6	[16]	Dat	pl
-ṛvadbhyaḥ	6	[16]	Abl	pl
-ṛvadbhyaḥ	6	[31]	Dat	pl
-ṛvadbhyaḥ	6	[31]	Abl	pl
-ṛvadbhyām	6	[16]	Ins	du
-ṛvadbhyām	6	[16]	Dat	du
-ṛvadbhyām	6	[16]	Abl	du
-ṛvadbhyām	6	[31]	Ins	du
-ṛvadbhyām	6	[31]	Dat	du
-ṛvadbhyām	6	[31]	Abl	du
-ṛvan	6	[16]	Voc	sg
-ṛvāṃsaḥ	6	[16]	Nom	pl
-ṛvāṃsaḥ	6	[16]	Voc	pl
-ṛvāṃsam	6	[16]	Acc	sg
-ṛvāṃsi	6	[31]	Nom	pl
-ṛvāṃsi	6	[31]	Acc	pl
-ṛvāṃsi	6	[31]	Voc	pl
-ṛvāṃsau	6	[16]	Nom	du
-ṛvāṃsau	6	[16]	Acc	du
-ṛvāṃsau	6	[16]	Voc	du
-ṛvān	6	[16]	Nom	sg
-ṛṣu	6	[4]	Loc	pl
-ṛṣu	6	[5]	Loc	pl
-ṛṣu	6	[20]	Loc	pl
-ṛṣu	6	[40]	Loc	pl
-ṝḥ	6	[40]	Acc	pl
-ṝṇām	6	[4]	Gen	pl
-ṝṇām	6	[5]	Gen	pl
-ṝṇām	6	[20]	Gen	pl
-ṝṇām	6	[40]	Gen	pl
-ṝṇi	6	[20]	Nom	pl
-ṝṇi	6	[20]	Acc	pl
-ṝṇi	6	[20]	Voc	pl
-ṝn	6	[4]	Acc	pl
-ṝn	6	[5]	Acc	pl
-e	6	[1]	Loc	sg
-e	6	[2]	Voc	sg
-e	6	[6]	Dat	sg
-e	6	[7]	Dat	sg
-e	6	[17]	Nom	du
-e	6	[17]	Acc	du
-e	6	[17]	Voc	du
-e	6	[17]	Loc	sg
-e	6	[18]	Voc	sg
-e	6	[21]	Dat	sg
-e	6	[22]	Dat	sg
-e	6	[32]	Nom	du
-e	6	[32]	Acc	du
-e	6	[32]	Voc	du
-e	6	[32]	Voc	sg
-e	6	[35]	Voc	sg
-eḥ	6	[2]	Abl	sg
-eḥ	6	[2]	Gen	sg
-eḥ	6	[35]	Abl	sg
-eḥ	6	[35]	Gen	sg
-ena	6	[1]	Ins	sg
-ena	6	[17]	Ins	sg
-ebhyaḥ	6	[1]	Dat	pl
-ebhyaḥ	6	[1]	Abl	pl
-ebhyaḥ	6	[17]	Dat	pl
-ebhyaḥ	6	[17]	Abl	pl
-eṣu	6	[1]	Loc	pl
-eṣu	6	[17]	Loc	pl
-aiḥ	6	[1]	Ins	pl
-aiḥ	6	[17]	Ins	pl
-o	6	[3]	Voc	sg
-o	6	[19]	Voc	sg
-o	6	[38]	Voc	sg
-oḥ	6	[3]	Abl	sg
-oḥ	6	[3]	Gen	sg
-oḥ	6	[6]	Gen	du
-oḥ	6	[6]	Loc	du
-oḥ	6	[7]	Gen	du
-oḥ	6	[7]	Loc	du
-oḥ	6	[21]	Gen	du
-oḥ	6	[21]	Loc	du
-oḥ	6	[22]	Gen	du
-oḥ	6	[22]	Loc	du

-oḥ	6	[38]	Abl	sg
-oḥ	6	[38]	Gen	sg
-obhiḥ	6	[8]	Ins	pl
-obhiḥ	6	[14]	Ins	pl
-obhiḥ	6	[23]	Ins	pl
-obhyaḥ	6	[8]	Dat	pl
-obhyaḥ	6	[8]	Abl	pl
-obhyaḥ	6	[14]	Dat	pl
-obhyaḥ	6	[14]	Abl	pl
-obhyaḥ	6	[23]	Dat	pl
-obhyaḥ	6	[23]	Abl	pl
-obhyām	6	[8]	Ins	du
-obhyām	6	[8]	Dat	du
-obhyām	6	[8]	Abl	du
-obhyām	6	[14]	Ins	du
-obhyām	6	[14]	Dat	du
-obhyām	6	[14]	Abl	du
-obhyām	6	[23]	Ins	du
-obhyām	6	[23]	Dat	du
-obhyām	6	[23]	Abl	du
-au	6	[1]	Nom	du
-au	6	[1]	Acc	du
-au	6	[1]	Voc	du
-au	6	[2]	Loc	sg
-au	6	[3]	Loc	sg
-au	6	[6]	Nom	du
-au	6	[6]	Acc	du
-au	6	[6]	Voc	du
-au	6	[7]	Nom	du
-au	6	[7]	Acc	du
-au	6	[7]	Voc	du
-au	6	[35]	Loc	sg
-au	6	[38]	Loc	sg
-auḥ	6	[39]	Nom	sg
-auḥ	6	[39]	Voc	sg
-aubhiḥ	6	[39]	Ins	pl
-aubhyaḥ	6	[39]	Dat	pl
-aubhyaḥ	6	[39]	Abl	pl
-aubhyām	6	[39]	Ins	du
-aubhyām	6	[39]	Dat	du
-aubhyām	6	[39]	Abl	du
-auṣu	6	[39]	Loc	pl
-ñaḥ	6	[10]	Acc	pl
-ñaḥ	6	[10]	Abl	sg
-ñaḥ	6	[10]	Gen	sg
-ñā	6	[10]	Ins	sg
-ñām	6	[10]	Gen	pl
-ñi	6	[10]	Loc	sg
-ñe	6	[10]	Dat	sg
-ñoḥ	6	[10]	Gen	du
-ñoḥ	6	[10]	Loc	du
-naḥ	6	[27]	Abl	sg
-naḥ	6	[27]	Gen	sg
-nā	6	[27]	Ins	sg
-nām	6	[27]	Gen	pl
-ni	6	[27]	Loc	sg
-nī	6	[27]	Nom	du
-nī	6	[27]	Acc	du
-nī	6	[27]	Voc	du
-ne	6	[27]	Dat	sg
-noḥ	6	[27]	Gen	du
-noḥ	6	[27]	Loc	du
-bhiḥ	6	[6]	Ins	pl
-bhiḥ	6	[7]	Ins	pl
-bhiḥ	6	[21]	Ins	pl
-bhiḥ	6	[22]	Ins	pl
-bhyaḥ	6	[6]	Dat	pl
-bhyaḥ	6	[6]	Abl	pl
-bhyaḥ	6	[7]	Dat	pl
-bhyaḥ	6	[7]	Abl	pl
-bhyaḥ	6	[21]	Dat	pl
-bhyaḥ	6	[21]	Abl	pl
-bhyaḥ	6	[22]	Dat	pl
-bhyaḥ	6	[22]	Abl	pl
-bhyām	6	[6]	Ins	du
-bhyām	6	[6]	Dat	du
-bhyām	6	[6]	Abl	du
-bhyām	6	[7]	Ins	du
-bhyām	6	[7]	Dat	du
-bhyām	6	[7]	Abl	du
-bhyām	6	[21]	Ins	du
-bhyām	6	[21]	Dat	du
-bhyām	6	[21]	Abl	du
-bhyām	6	[22]	Ins	du
-bhyām	6	[22]	Dat	du
-bhyām	6	[22]	Abl	du
-yaḥ	6	[33]	Nom	pl
-yaḥ	6	[33]	Voc	pl
-yam	6	[34]	Acc	sg
-yā	6	[33]	Ins	sg
-yā	6	[35]	Ins	sg
-yāḥ	6	[33]	Abl	sg

-yāḥ	6 [33]	Gen	sg
-yāḥ	6 [35]	Abl	sg
-yāḥ	6 [35]	Gen	sg
-yām	6 [33]	Loc	sg
-yām	6 [35]	Loc	sg
-yai	6 [33]	Dat	sg
-yai	6 [35]	Dat	sg
-yoḥ	6 [2]	Gen	du
-yoḥ	6 [2]	Loc	du
-yoḥ	6 [33]	Gen	du
-yoḥ	6 [33]	Loc	du
-yoḥ	6 [35]	Gen	du
-yoḥ	6 [35]	Loc	du
-yau	6 [33]	Nom	du
-yau	6 [33]	Acc	du
-yau	6 [33]	Voc	du
-rā	6 [4]	Ins	sg
-rā	6 [5]	Ins	sg
-rā	6 [40]	Ins	sg
-ruṣaḥ	6 [16]	Acc	pl
-ruṣaḥ	6 [16]	Abl	sg
-ruṣaḥ	6 [16]	Gen	sg
-ruṣaḥ	6 [31]	Abl	sg
-ruṣaḥ	6 [31]	Gen	sg
-ruṣā	6 [16]	Ins	sg
-ruṣā	6 [31]	Ins	sg
-ruṣām	6 [16]	Gen	pl
-ruṣām	6 [31]	Gen	pl
-ruṣi	6 [16]	Loc	sg
-ruṣi	6 [31]	Loc	sg
-ruṣī	6 [31]	Nom	du
-ruṣī	6 [31]	Acc	du
-ruṣī	6 [31]	Voc	du
-ruṣe	6 [16]	Dat	sg
-ruṣe	6 [31]	Dat	sg
-ruṣoḥ	6 [16]	Gen	du
-ruṣoḥ	6 [16]	Loc	du
-ruṣoḥ	6 [31]	Gen	du
-ruṣoḥ	6 [31]	Loc	du
-re	6 [4]	Dat	sg
-re	6 [5]	Dat	sg
-re	6 [40]	Dat	sg
-roḥ	6 [4]	Gen	du
-roḥ	6 [4]	Loc	du
-roḥ	6 [5]	Gen	du
-roḥ	6 [5]	Loc	du
-roḥ	6 [40]	Gen	du
-roḥ	6 [40]	Loc	du
-vaḥ	6 [36]	Nom	pl
-vaḥ	6 [36]	Voc	pl
-vā	6 [36]	Ins	sg
-vā	6 [38]	Ins	sg
-vāḥ	6 [36]	Abl	sg
-vāḥ	6 [36]	Gen	sg
-vāḥ	6 [38]	Abl	sg
-vāḥ	6 [38]	Gen	sg
-vām	6 [36]	Loc	sg
-vām	6 [38]	Loc	sg
-vai	6 [36]	Dat	sg
-vai	6 [38]	Dat	sg
-voḥ	6 [3]	Gen	du
-voḥ	6 [3]	Loc	du
-voḥ	6 [36]	Gen	du
-voḥ	6 [36]	Loc	du
-voḥ	6 [38]	Gen	du
-voḥ	6 [38]	Loc	du
-vau	6 [36]	Nom	du
-vau	6 [36]	Acc	du
-vau	6 [36]	Voc	du
-ṣu	6 [7]	Loc	pl
-ṣu	6 [22]	Loc	pl
-su	6 [6]	Loc	pl
-su	6 [21]	Loc	pl

ABBREVIATIONS

A, Act	active voice
ā	āsa (in citing periphrastic perfect active)
ă	a or ā
Abl	ablative case
Abs	absolutive (written with a hyphen if with prefix)
ā/c	āsa or cakre (in citing periphrastic perfect active/middle)
Acc	accusative case
Aor	aorist tense
C	consonant
c	cakre (in citing periphrastic perfect middle)
CAo	causative aorist
Cit	citation form of verb, i.e. 3rd singular of the present indicative active/middle
Condit	conditional tense
Dat	dative case
Des	desiderative
du	dual number
F	future passive participle in -avya-
Fem	feminine gender
fn	footnote
FPP	future passive participle
Fut	simple future tense
Gen	genitive case
ĭ	i or ī
Imf	imperfect tense
Imperat	imperative mood
Imv	imperative mood
Ind	present indicative (Table 29)
Indic	indicative mood
Inf	infinitive
Ins	instrumental case
Int	intensive
Loc	locative case
M, Mid	middle voice
Masc	masculine gender
Neut	neuter gender

Nom	nominative case
Opt, Optat	optative mood
Pas	passive voice
Per	perfect tense
Peri fut	periphrastic future tense
Periph	periphrastic
Pl, Plur	plural number
PPP	perfect passive participle
Prec	precative
Pres	present tense
S Fut	simple future tense
Sg, Sing	singular number
ŭ	u or ū
V	vowel
Voc	vocative case
-Vti	-eti, -oti, -arti, or -āti
ø	zero, a non-sound, as in the open gradation series ø a ā.
1	first person
2	second person
3	third person
( )	optional; e.g. nām(a)ni = nāmni or nāmani
/	or; e.g. bhuvai/-ve = bhuvai or bhuve
*	stem vocalic in 2nd grade (Tables 18, 22)
→	'may be transformed into'
⇒	'is fed into' (Table 26)
"	identical with the form immediately above
--	lacking the expected form

BIBLIOGRAPHY

APTE, Vaman S. *The Practical Sanskrit-English Dictionary.* 3rd ed. Delhi: Motilal Banarsidass, 1965.

COULSON, Michael. *Sanskrit: An Introduction to the Classical Language.* Teach Yourself Books. Sevenoaks, Kent: Hodder & Stoughton, 1976.

KALE, Moreshwar R. *A Higher Sanskrit Grammar.* 1884; repr. Delhi: Motilal Banarsidass, 1977.

LANMAN, Charles R. *A Sanskrit Reader.* 1884; repr. Cambridge, Mass.: Harvard University Press, 1963.

MACDONELL, Arthur A. *A Sanskrit Grammar for Students.* 3rd ed. 1927; repr. Oxford: Oxford University Press, 1962.

MAYRHOFER, Manfred. *A Sanskrit Grammar.* transl. by G. B. Ford. Alabama: University of Alabama Press, 1972.

MONIER-WILLIAMS, Monier. *Sanskrit Manual.* 1868; repr. Delhi: Ajanta Books, 1976.

MONIER-WILLIAMS, Monier. *A Sanskrit-English Dictionary.* new ed. 1899; repr. Delhi: Motilal Banarsidass, 1979.

ŚĀSTRĪ, K. L. V. *Śabda-Mañjarī.* rev. 12th ed. Kalpathi: R. S. Vadhyar & Sons, 1970.

THUMB, Albert. *Handbuch des Sanskrit. 1. Teil: Grammatik.* Heidelberg: Carl Winter's, 1905.

WHITNEY, William D. *Sanskrit Grammar.* 2nd ed. 1889; repr. Delhi: Motilal Banarsidass, 1969.

WHITNEY, William D. *The Roots, Verb-forms and Primary Derivatives of the Sanskrit Language.* 1885; repr. Delhi: Motilal Banarsidass, 1979.